Hollywood in China

Soft Power with Chinese Characteristics: China's Campaign for Hearts and Minds

Two Billion Eyes: The Story of China Central Television

Art, Politics, and Commerce in Chinese Cinema

TV China

TV Drama in China

Television in Post-Reform China: Serial Dramas, Confucian Leadership and the Global Television Market

Chinese Cinema During the Era of Reform: The Ingenuity of the System

Hollywood in China

Behind the Scenes of the
World's Largest Movie Market

Ying Zhu

THE
NEW
PRESS

NEW YORK
LONDON

Requests for permission to reproduce selections from this book should be made through our
website: https://thenewpress.com/contact.

Published in the United States by The New Press, New York, 2022
Distributed by Two Rivers Distribution

ISBN 978-1-62097-218-2 (hc)
ISBN 978-1-62097-219-9 (ebook)
CIP data is available

The New Press publishes books that promote and enrich public discussion and understanding
of the issues vital to our democracy and to a more equitable world. These books are made
possible by the enthusiasm of our readers; the support of a committed group of donors, large
and small; the collaboration of our many partners in the independent media and the not-for-
profit sector; booksellers, who often hand-sell New Press books; librarians; and above all by
our authors.

www.thenewpress.com

Composition by Westchester Publishing Services
This book was set in Adobe Caslon Pro

Printed in the United States of America

2 4 6 8 10 9 7 5 3 1

For my mother and my daughter

Contents

Hollywood in China

From Paris Theater to Huaihai Cinema: As the Cinematic Universe Turns

In March 1922, Mingxing (Star/Bright Star), a newly established Chinese film studio, set up its corporate headquarters at No. 380 Avenue Joffre, in Shanghai's French Concession. Named after Joseph Joffre, the French general best known for defeating the German invasion during the First World War, Avenue Joffre was a tree-flanked residential street in suburban style—lined with row houses and dotted with churches, cemeteries, schools, parks, coffeehouses, cafés, and cinemas instead of businesses and factories. On Avenue Joffre, as one local jazz aficionado observed at the time, "there are no skyscrapers, no especially large structures," but "every night there are the intoxicating sounds of jazz music coming from the cafés and bars that line both sides."[1] With a headquarters situated in such a trendy location, it is no surprise that Star would soon become one of the dominant players in Shanghai's flourishing movie industry in the 1920s and 1930s.

I spent part of my childhood a short walk from Star's headquarters, in a courtyard complex, Joffre Arcade, built in 1934 by the St. Petersburg–born Russian architect and builder Boris Krivoss, who left Russia for China in 1921.[2] The complex had flats lining up on two sides of an open courtyard with a circular fountain in the middle, which became a frequent playground for me and the neighboring kids.

Also on Avenue Joffre, a few doors up from my childhood home, at No. 550, was the Paris Theater, a legendary movie house that was the setting of a well-known 1931 short story by Shi Zhecun, a pioneer of Chinese modernist literature. "At the Paris Theater" depicts a night out on a movie date between a married man and his mistress, capturing the jitters of a titillating extramarital affair.[3] The Paris Theater, in Shi's story, serves as a social space for romantic and sexual exploits in addition to film viewing. The film on the date night in question was a German picture made by UFA, the renowned German production company during the silent era. The sentiment felt by

The author in front of her childhood home next to the Paris Theater. Courtesy of Frances Hisgen.

the male character, an urbane Shanghainese, was that German films were "better than anything that comes out of Hollywood."[4] Never mind that the Paris Theater was actually contracted to screen Hollywood films, which by the late 1910s had swept the Chinese market. So popular was Hollywood in China that when the Chinese film industry took its initial shape in the 1910s through the 1920s, it simply followed the Hollywood-style production practice including the studio model. While mesmerizing local audiences and theater owners, Hollywood also encountered resistance from local cultural elites who fretted about vulgar entertainment from time to time.

Built in 1926 by a Shanghai merchant, Ding Runyang, the Paris Theater began life as the Palais Oriental Theater at its debut in May. In January 1927, the Palais Oriental signed a contract with Peacock Motion Picture Corporation (Peacock), the earliest and largest Sino-U.S. joint venture at the time, to screen films distributed by Peacock.[5] Registered in the United States in November 1922 and officially opening its shop in Shanghai in January 1923, Peacock's establishment was facilitated by the Columbia University–educated Zhou Zhiqi, a prominent Chinese educator and politician in the late Qing dynasty and early Republican period who served in multiple ministry positions and was briefly an acting president of

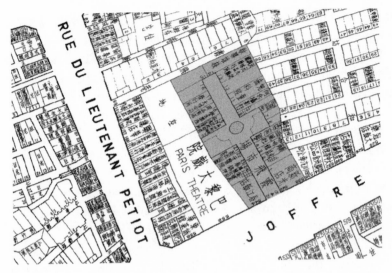

Map of Joffre Arcade. Source: *Shanghai Commercial Atlas* (1939). Shading by Katya Knyazeva.

the Republic and an acting premier in 1922. Zhou also had a stint as a Chinese embassy counselor in the United States under the Qing government and studied film while in the United States. With the encouragement of the U.S.–educated Chinese film pioneer Shureng (S.J.) Benjamin Cheng (*Peacock Flies Southeast*, 1926), Peacock was at the forefront of introducing quality (predominantly American) foreign films of "educational, industrial, moral and entertaining values" to China such as *Hearts Aflame* (Reginald Barker, 1923), *Parted Curtains* (Bertram Bracken, 1920), *Rich Men's Wives* (Louis J. Gasnier, 1922), and *Trifling Women* (Rex Ingram, 1922).[6]

With the translation of the Hollywood film *The Toll of the Sea* (Chester Franklin, 1922), Peacock initiated the trend of adding Chinese subtitles to imports. During its peak between 1926 and 1931, Peacock signed exclusive rights with major U.S. studios and was instrumental in importing a number of quality Hollywood titles.[7] It was during this period that the Palais Oriental Theater signed with Peacock to screen European and Hollywood films imported by Peacock. The Palais Oriental was promptly renamed Peacock Oriental Theater upon the signing of the contract in January 1927. The Peacock Oriental Theater was renamed Paris Theater in January 1930, as Peacock's distribution power gradually declined. While continuing to show Hollywood films, the Paris Theater made a "left" turn in the mid-1940s, staging several CCP-influenced theater performances and by the late 1940s screening Soviet films including *Lenin in 1918* (Mikhail Romm, 1939).[8]

The Paris Theater would change its name again in 1951, to Huaihai Cinema, following the renaming of Avenue Joffre to Huaihai Road the same year, striking out the colonial imprint on the city and instead commemorating the Huaihai Campaign, or Battle of Hsupeng, a decisive Communist victory in the Chinese Civil War.

Whatever the banner it was under, the theater became my madeleine of early cinema going. I had my share of movie dates there, though the young dates of my adolescence were far more innocent than the lascivious man leering at his mistress in Shi's fictionalized universe. And I had no discerning taste when it came to foreign films, which were few and far between. When there was a foreign screening, it was mostly revolutionary pictures from the USSR and the affiliated Eastern Bloc, including India, North Korea, and Vietnam. UFA and Hollywood pictures were long gone by the time I came of age during the Cultural Revolution (1966–76).

The post-1949 transition from Hollywood entertainment to Soviet revolutionary pictures took time. The Communist government aggressively promoted Soviet films, but the Hollywood-addicted Shanghai audiences did not take well to the pictures from the USSR. To maintain social stability, the new municipal government tolerated a few Hollywood films still in circulation to provide comfort and much needed distractions to the jittery middle class unsure of its future under the CCP. Hollywood served briefly as "opiate of the masses," to quote Marx, albeit under Shanghai's Communist leadership.

The outbreak of the Korean War would cast a decisive end to Hollywood's early sojourn in China, leading to a wholesale ban on all things American including Hollywood pictures. The party swiftly moved to rid Chinese screens of all remnants of Hollywood films. A massive campaign was launched to discredit Hollywood films, equating watching American films with unpatriotic and counterrevolutionary activity. The Paris Theater severed its ties with Hollywood with a bang on November 10, 1950, when patriotic employees draped a big banner of "Resisting American Films" over its building. The day after the Paris Theater's grand gesture, the Shanghai Movie Theater Association called for an emergency meeting to hash out a plan to halt the screening of American films. By November 14, all theaters in Shanghai had stopped screening American films, and the Chinese film industry

Parade along Middle Huaihai Road in the 1950s. Source: Collection of Shengkai Li.

itself would soon enter a period of radical transformation. Run entirely as a private and commercial entertainment business during the Republic era, the industry had to adopt a centralized Soviet model under the CCP, which treated film as an instrument for carrying a political torch for the party.

The ban on Hollywood would last throughout the Mao era (1949–76), during which domestic socialist films and revolutionary films from the Communist Bloc were the staple screeners for Huaihai Cinema. Yet there was no shortage of Hollywood films and films from Western Europe, which were all lavishly dubbed in Chinese. But these Western films were reserved as "internal reference films," open for viewing only to the party's top echelon under the direct control of Madame Mao (the wife of Chairman Mao), the local party *nomenklatura* including the party's cultural establishment, and occasionally relations of the rarefied coteries. While the masses were called to watch revolutionary socialist films to purify their thoughts, the leaders audaciously exposed themselves to the decadent capitalist entertainment. The restricted Hollywood-led Western classics did become available to the masses after the end of the Cultural Revolution, and these films became my earliest exposure to Hollywood and some of the European classics.

New Hollywood films were permitted to officially reenter China by the late 1970s when the country reopened its doors to the outside. In 1979, the year China officially established its diplomatic relationship with the United States, it also established the China Film Coproduction Corporation (CFCC), a government agency overseeing production efforts with foreign companies. Sporadic and inexpensive U.S. TV and films entered China on a flat-fee basis throughout the 1980s. Both the flat-fee-based small-scale importation on a budget and the establishment of CFCC would open a floodgate to new imports, creating a viewing frenzy among the deprived Chinese audiences eager for Hollywood-led Western films, and eventually ushering in the contemporary era of expensive, revenue-sharing, Hollywood blockbuster film.

Though film screenings continued, the Huaihai Cinema had been left largely uncared for throughout the years, and the building's condition deteriorated. In 1993, with the demand for imports, especially popular Hollywood fare, on the rise, a Sino-U.S. joint venture company injected fresh cash to give the run-down Huaihai Cinema a face-lift. Hollywood films, together with Hollywood investment, revived the dilapidated theater. The renovation was completed in 1994, the year China allowed the first revenue-sharing Hollywood film, *The Fugitive* (Andrew Davis, 1993), to enter the country amidst declining cinema attendance, with the Chinese film industry struggling to reconnect with the market.

The post-Mao China saw a reversal of the Soviet model, and the centralized and state-subsidized film industry was forced to earn a commercial living. Production budgets dwindled and film outputs were reduced during the transition, leading to the massive shedding of audiences. The return of Hollywood brought audiences back to the movie theaters, benefiting the refurbished Huaihai Cinema, which, by March 1997, would be certified as one of the three four-star cinemas in Shanghai, together with the Yongle Palace, a theater used to screen restrictive internal reference films,[9] and the historic Grand Cinema, built in 1933 and designed by László Hudec, the Hungarian–Slovak architect active in Shanghai during the Republican era who was responsible for some of the city's most iconic landmark constructions, including the art deco–style Park Hotel. The newly renovated Huaihai Cinema immediately attracted a large number of audiences, with attendance breaking national records that year. But even a new Hollywood boom time couldn't save the Huaihai Cinema, and it was demolished in August 2003 to make way for the construction of a luxury shopping complex, the Times Square in Shanghai.[10] The old courtyard

Joffre Apartment heritage sign. Source: Facebook page "Shanghai Architecture Wandering," https://www.facebook.com/jodie.tang.0204/posts/864088227347286.

apartment complex a few doors up has stood largely unchanged and is now listed as a "Heritage Architecture" by the Shanghai municipal government. I would visit my childhood dwelling, the area surrounded by Shanghai's cinematic history, whenever I came to Shanghai. But I never stepped a foot into the shopping complex that once housed my favorite theater.

A decade after the demolition of the Huaihai Cinema, Chinese domestic production surged, challenging Hollywood's stronghold at the Chinese domestic box office. China's film market grew to be the world's largest in 2020, partly as the result of prolonged theater shutdowns in the United States amidst the COVID-19 crisis.

The metamorphosis of the movie house from Palais Oriental Theater in 1926 to Peacock Oriental Theater in 1927, Paris Theater in 1930, and finally Huaihai Cinema in 1951 is emblematic of the transformation of Chinese cinema and its relationship to Hollywood against the backdrop of the shifting Sino-U.S. relationship. The shifting banner and popularity of my neighborhood theater corresponds to three major phases in the Sino-Hollywood saga: the overwhelming presence of Hollywood in China during the Republic era; the wholesale erasure of Hollywood during Mao's era; and the triumphant return of Hollywood since the mid-1990s. My childhood movie house was long gone by the time the Chinese market grew into the world's largest, ready to redefine Sino-Hollywood relations.

As the cinematic universe turns, *Hollywood in China* takes us down the memory lane of the Sino-Hollywood relationship. Hollywood has become less American over the past decades, and more a clearinghouse for global financial and creative forces gathered under the corporate rubric of the "Hollywood Way." China during the post-Mao era has reverted its film industry to the Hollywood Way but has redeployed the Way "with Chinese characteristics" to compete with Hollywood for domestic box-office share while co-opting Hollywood into the service of burnishing China's image abroad. China has in recent years succeeded in reclaiming its domestic market and curbing Hollywood's China expansion. What might be the ramifications to the American film and media industry of the world's largest market becoming less reliant on Hollywood? What might be the ramifications to the global political and cultural hierarchy of a Hollywood that is beholden to China's interest?

To make a play on two Hollywood titles, *The Great Dictator* (Hollywood film directed by Charlie Chaplin) and "The Great Communicator/Storyteller" (nickname of Hollywood actor and American president Ronald Reagan), Hollywood has been the Great Communicator or Storyteller of our time. Might China use its huge domestic box office as a cudgel to bend Hollywood to its will, and become "The Great Dictator" of the global cinematic universe?

One of the most consequential stories of our time is shaping up to be the Sino-U.S. conflict, which threatens to shatter the existing world order, with China challenging U.S. dominance. As China doubles down on its power projection, Sino-Hollywood relations have become a crucial arena in the political, economic, and ideological contestation between the United States and China. *Hollywood in China* charts the ups and downs as well as the ins and outs of the world's great storyteller in the now world's largest yet most opaque film market. Against the backdrop of the shifting Sino-U.S. relationship, the book maps out multiple power dynamics and charts a century-long trajectory. In doing so, it teases out how competing political, economic, and cultural values have been played out in the art and artifice of filmmaking on a global scale and with global ramifications.

1

Global Expansion and Local Protection: American and Chinese Film Industries from Inception Through the Early 1930s

> The [U.S.] State Department was involved to the hilt, then, as always,
> it was the servant of the film industry.
> —Charles Higham in *Merchant of Dreams:*
> *Louis B. Mayer, MGM, and the Secret Hollywood*[1]

The first feature film was shown in China on August 11, 1896, as part of the attractions in a variety show at a Shanghai tea house called Xu Gardens. It was less than eight months following the first projection of motion pictures at the Grand Café in Paris on December 28, 1895, when the Lumière Brothers screened their short actuality films to eager patrons. Film exhibition in China became extremely popular in the late Qing period, and the Imperial Palace held regular screenings to entertain the royal family and high-ranking officials. The novelty of motion pictures opened the door to a new form of amusement for both royalty and the public.

Domestic exhibitors in China did not emerge until 1903, and the first domestic production did not appear until 1905, the year when local motion picture operators gradually transitioned to a more production-focused phase, making filmed recordings of "opera films" wherein famed Peking opera performers acted out scenes from well-known operas, mostly stage adaptations of popular Chinese classics such as *Romance of the Three Kingdoms*. Lack of domestic capital investment kept China's nascent film business under foreign control, since much of the finance stemmed from foreign banks. Short of production capital, early domestic films were mostly co-productions dependent upon foreign investment and technology, limiting domestic productions to the treaty ports, especially Shanghai, where foreign resources were most easily accessible. Treaty ports and expanding transport linkages in late Qing created economic and commercial contact zones including Manchuria to the northeast, Shanghai and the Yangtze River on the east coast, and Hong Kong and Canton to the south. Matthew Johnson noted that from 1907 to 1922 there was no single unified Chinese film industry to speak of, but only a few parallel circuits of exhibition, each with its own regional characteristics.[2] Film production and consumption eventually coalesced along the three major geopolitical centers. The first real cinema in China, the Arcade Theater (Ping'an), was built in Beijing in 1907 by foreign merchants and catered exclusively to foreign patrons.

Chinese Film Pioneers and Their American Counterparts

Film pioneers in China came from an eclectic background, mostly amateur film lovers and playwrights. Zhang Shichuan (1890–1954), the co-founder in 1922 of the formidable Chinese studio Star, worked at an American-owned import-export company in Shanghai where his maternal uncle was the general manager and a well-connected comprador.[3] Zhang came from a wealthy merchant family in Ningbo, a port city close to Shanghai known as the birthplace of a number of shipping tycoons in Shanghai and Hong Kong as well as Sir Runrun Shaw, another trailblazer of the early Chinese film industry. Zhang left home for Shanghai at the age of sixteen to work for his uncle as a bookkeeper during the day while taking English lessons in the evening. He managed to speak decent enough pidgin English to directly converse with the Americans and was soon promoted to the bank's marketing division. In 1912, his theater-loving uncle started a drama troupe and entrusted him with the responsibility of managing it. While putting together plays for the troupe, Zhang met a fellow theater lover turned playwright, Zheng Zhengqiu (1888–1935), the Shanghai-born progressive intellectual from a wealthy Cantonese merchant family who was active in China's theater scene. Zhang and Zheng would form a long-lasting collaborative relationship that shaped the early trajectory of Chinese filmmaking.

At the time when Zhang and Zheng experimented with their theater business, a Ukrainian American businessman turned film entrepreneur, Benjamin Brodsky (1877–1960; *A Trip Through China*, 1917), founded China's first film company, the Asia Film Company, in 1909 to produce local films utilizing Chinese talent and traditional Chinese folklore. Brodsky had traveled around the world as a film projectionist before coming to China in 1909 to start his film equipment trading related business. Anticipating a blossoming motion picture business in China, he purchased new films from the United States while also making films in China.[4] He befriended young Chinese intellectuals and devotees of Western drama and cinema including Zhang and Zheng.[5] The fall of the Qing dynasty in 1912 led to the founding of the Republic of China. Concerned about the political instability in China, Brodsky transferred ownership of the Asia Film Company to Yashell and Suffert, two managers of the Shanghai offices of an American insurance company, before leaving for Hong Kong the same year. Brodsky eventually returned to the United States, settling in San Francisco. Yashell and Suffert outsourced the company's production business to Zhang and Zheng, who founded the short-lived Xinmin Company, a director unit–style production company in 1913, to make films for distribution by Asia Film. Neither Zhang nor Zheng knew much about filmmaking, but they managed to make a four-reel short film, *The Difficult Couple* (1913), which became the first Chinese feature film.

Many founders of small and short-lived Chinese production companies were cinema lovers but lacked real experience in the entertainment business, unlike those cinema owners turned production moguls in Hollywood. In the United States, the founders of the major studios were mostly former retailers who engaged marketing professionals to run their film exhibition business. Universal's Carl Laemmle, for instance, opened nickelodeon theaters in 1906 after a retail career in clothing. He then moved on to build a film exchange in 1907 and a film studio in 1909. The senior marketing staff were all former advertising agency executives at Universal, MGM, and Columbia.[6] When the major U.S. studios emerged in the 1910s and 1920s, the professionals ran marketing operations known as exploitation departments that included specialized units to handle studios' advertising, publicity, and promotion. This basic structure would remain intact until the studio era ended in the late 1940s.

The only two Chinese studio founders who had their roots in movie theater operation were Luo Mingyou, who founded Lianhua[7] in 1930, and the Shaw brothers, who founded Tianyi[8] in 1925. Lianhua and Tianyi, together with Star, would carve out their respective niches to form China's first film oligopoly in the 1930s, just as the big five (RKO, Warner Brothers, MGM, Paramount, and Fox) and the little three (Universal, Columbia, and United Artists) of the U.S. studios took their initial shape in Hollywood.

The outbreak of World War I soon cut off all supplies of film stock in China, shutting down Xinmin and a few other Chinese production companies for good. The war nonetheless created an opportunity for a nascent Chinese indigenous film industry to develop, as European powers temporarily reduced their business activities in China. Some wealthy Chinese merchants began to invest in film production, though the shortage of film stock impeded the process. The supply chain restarted after the war just as the postwar economic recovery freed up more domestic capital for film production, leading to several waves of speculative film financing in China, all of which struggled under the shadow of imports, particularly imports from the United States, where the absence of European productions created an opportunity for the American film industry to thrive and expand globally. Early film markets in the United States and elsewhere were dominated by European, chiefly French, productions. In the early 1900s, European companies supplied at least half of the films shown in the United States. World War I made it impossible for European film companies to secure capital for lavish production expenditures just as demand for feature films mandated bigger budgets. The European film industry started to decline and its domestic and global market share diminished substantially. By the 1920s, most large European companies had given up film production altogether. Pathé and Gaumont sold their U.S. and international business and left filmmaking to focus exclusively on distribution in France. By late 1924, American films were shown everywhere, ushering in the era of Hollywood dominance that has lasted to this day.

Unlike Hollywood's more sophisticated business strategy, the nascent film industry in China operated on a short-term strategy of "small investment, fast production turnout, and marketable products,"[9] which hampered Chinese cinema's early development. The postwar era witnessed the founding of a few production companies that would later become the pillars of Chinese film industry. Zhang Shichuan and Zheng Zhengqiu, the two owners of the defunct Xinmin, went on to form a new production company, Star, in 1922, initially focusing on producing narrative shorts. As Hollywood-style feature-length film was becoming the global prototype for narrative films, Star began to experiment with making narrative features in an attempt to compete with Hollywood for a share of the domestic feature market. Star would become one of the leading film companies in China during the Republican era.

Meanwhile in the United States, from the 1910s and 1920s, with theater owners as founding members, Hollywood majors focused on expanding their theater chains by acquiring existing regional circuits that served diverse and distinct market segments. Paramount's Publix chain targeted adult middle-class audiences in the large American cities with strategically located and opulent movie palaces that supplied high-end products.[10] Loews-MGM targeted female audiences. Fox Film operated on a low-cost budget and segmented its movies and cinemas accordingly.[11] RKO produced high-quality movies supplemented by B movies on double features to appeal to East Coast–based elite audiences.[12] Universal targeted its movies to theaters in the Midwest.[13] Warner Brothers produced films that appealed to the working class.[14] And Disney, a small studio at the time, used a niche strategy to focus on animated movies for family entertainment. U.S. domestic movie production, buttressed by the demand of the professionally operated theater chains, paved the way for the global expansion of the U.S. film industry.

Before Sunny Hollywood in California,
There Was Fort Lee in New Jersey

Though sunny Hollywood on the West Coast has come to symbolize American cinema, the U.S. film industry actually had its kick-start on the East Coast, where Thomas Edison's invention of the motion picture camera in the Garden State of New Jersey made it possible for amateur techies to record and replay images. Edison patented his new inventions in the late 1890s and effectively monopolized film production and distribution in the United States, leaving his domestic rivals with little recourse other than to turn to importing foreign films, mainly from France and Britain.

The late nineteenth and early twentieth centuries were a time of cartel formation in many industries in the United States.[15] In the film industry, the first attempt to form a cartel took place early in 1908 with the Edison company, Vitagraph, and others combining into the Film Service Association (FSA). To limit foreign competition, FSA members, aside from Pathé and Méliès, two major French companies, stopped importing foreign pictures. As per Vitagraph, this move helped the industry as it "shut out the importation of foreign stuff that was not suitable or good enough for the American market."[16]

FSA merged with the Biograph Association of Licensees in 1908 to form the Motion Picture Patents Company (MPPC), commonly referred to as "the Trust." The Trust comprised all the major U.S. film companies as well as foreign firms active in the United States, including Star Film Paris and American Pathé. The Trust also included the leading film distributor George Kleine, and the biggest supplier of raw film stock, Eastman Kodak. The Trust had a legal monopoly within the U.S. market and used legal and other means to prohibit renegade filmmakers and theater operators from using MPPC equipment. A group of small studios and nickelodeon owners led by Carl Laemmle, the future Universal founder, remained independent. The independents imported foreign equipment, traded films amongst each other, and eventually took the MPPC to court for antitrust violation. The Trust threatened constant lawsuits against independent filmmakers who refused to abide by its rules. Most of these fights occurred when the American film industry was still located on the East Coast, where Fort Lee, New Jersey, was the center of the cinematic universe at the time.

Fort Lee was the center of American film production when Hollywood was still mostly orange groves. D.W. Griffith made many one-reelers there for Biograph, the first motion picture company in the United States devoted entirely to film production and exhibition.[17] In 1907, the year when China's capital city Beijing saw the unveiling of its first movie house, the Arcade Theater[18] on East Chang'an Road, Thomas Edison used the cliffs of the Palisades in Fort Lee as the exterior for the Edwin S. Porter and J. Searle Dawley film *Rescued from an Eagle's Nest*, which featured D.W. Griffith in his acting debut. A year later, Griffith shot *The Curtain Pole* (1908), an early example of the "slapstick" comedy, on the streets of Fort Lee. In the "Far East" in 1918, the Shanghai-based Commercial Press created the Department of Motion Pictures, China's first domestically funded and operated production company. In Shanghai in March of the same year, the Italian expat A.E. Loulos shot several short actuality films including *The Operation of Shanghai's First Electric Bus*,[19] *Snapshots of Various Shanghai Foreign Concessions*, and *Forced Cutting of Pigtails*.[20] The year 1908 also saw the arrival of Shanghai's first movie theater, Hongkou daxiyuan (Hongkew Theater), built by a Spanish merchant, Antonio Ramos, who went on to build more cinemas in China.

The year after Loulos shot his Shanghai actuality films, Griffith directed Mary Pickford in *The Lonely Villa* (1909) in Fort Lee, deploying his now trademark "crosscutting" technique. Contemporaneously, China in 1909 saw the founding of Benjamin Brodsky's Asia Film Company while German-born Carl Laemmle founded Independent Moving Pictures Company (IMP), with offices set up in both New York City and Fort Lee. IMP shot its first film, *Hiawatha* (1909), on location in the Coytesville neighborhood of Fort Lee. The remote Coytesville area became the site for the founding in 1909 of the first permanent film studio, Champion Film Company, which was launched by the Austro-Hungarian American film producer Mark M. Dintenfass (1872–1933). Champion would become part of the Universal Film Manufacturing Company spearheaded by Carl Laemmle in competition against Edison's monopoly in 1912. Laemmle would go on to become Universal's inaugural president.

Fort Lee is where Universal started its operation. Carl Laemmle immigrated to the United States in 1884 and ventured into the film business by buying nickelodeons in Chicago in 1906, the year when Shanghai started to operate open-air cinemas. Laemmle eventually established a film distribution business, the Laemmle Film Service, which expanded his operation into Canada.

Laemmle's production company, IMP, made a number of multireel films while Edison's agents did their best to shut him down. Edison's Trust filed incessant claims of patent infringement on independent companies like IMP. Between 1908 and 1912, the Trust dictated U.S. film output and format by setting limits on film length and film rental prices.[21]

Films were initially limited to one reel in length, which ran roughly from thirteen to seventeen minutes. Competition from independent and foreign producers by 1912 led to the introduction of two-reelers, and, by 1913, three- and four-reelers, which represented the early stage of feature films that emerged when cinema owners discovered that films with longer duration combined with better quality could command higher ticket prices and attract more spectators, thus bringing in higher profits. The transition from short films to longer feature films in American cinema occurred gradually between 1911 and 1914, under the shadow of the Trust. Despite the rise in popularity of feature films from independent producers and foreign imports in 1912–13, the Trust resisted change as it would necessitate changes in its production-distribution-exhibition chain.

During the first three years of IMP, Laemmle fought, with gusto, a total of 289 legal actions brought about by the Trust and ultimately prevailed. Emerging as a leader against Edison's monopolistic practice, Laemmle led several other studios to form the Universal Film Manufacturing Company in 1912, with the studio's headquarters based initially in Fort Lee.[22] The same year, the Department of Justice filed an antitrust lawsuit against the monopolistic practice of the Trust, leading to the end of patent royalties to the Trust in September 1913. By then, many of the independent filmmakers, including future film moguls Adolph Zukor and Jesse L. Lasky, the co-founders of Paramount Pictures, had left for California as a way out of the patent litigation fights while staking out on their own in the Wild West. Laemmle eventually made his way to the West, building two California studios in 1912–14, one in Hollywood and the other in the San Fernando Valley. In 1914, Laemmle acquired the Taylor Ranch on the north side of the Hollywood Hills to build Universal City, which opened in 1915, the same year the U.S. courts ordered the Trust to dissolve under antitrust laws. The Trust officially terminated in 1918. Its demise led to a race for quality feature production, which had been artificially restricted by the Trust's refusal to expand film length and raise film rental prices. The rise of quality feature production coincided with the First World War that left European production companies strapped for cash, paving the way for the ascendance of Hollywood. Universal went on to become the largest and most prolific studio in the world—until 1925, when MGM overtook Universal in size and scale. Though West Coast focused now, Universal maintained two East Coast offices.[23]

Aside from Universal, several other legendary U.S. production companies and personalities, including Fox Film by William Fox in 1917, set their foot in Fort Lee, though most of the productions actually took place on the West Coast, where branches were set up to take advantage of a more hospitable climate and cost-effective environment. In 1918, *Les Misérables*, a Fox studio production, featured the largest outdoor set ever built in Fort Lee.[24] Though the initial impetus for the independents to move their operations to Hollywood was to create distance from Edison's home base in New Jersey, and thus away from MPPC's control, the choice of Hollywood in Southern California as a destination was not random. For one thing, the Ninth Circuit Court of Appeals headquartered in San Francisco was averse to enforcing patent claims. Equally important, Southern California's topography, with semi-arid climate, widespread irrigation, and the resulting lush landscape, offered ample opportunities for scenes set in deserts, jungles, and mountains. Hollywood would soon come to symbolize the American film industry.

After venturing westward to Hollywood, Universal produced a number of popular films, including *The Hunchback of Notre Dame* (Wallace Worlsey, 1923) and *The Phantom of the Opera* (Rupert Julian, 1925), both casting Lon Chaney before the actor was lured away to MGM, and both popular in China. At the same time in Shanghai, the Chinese production company Star, which targeted urban audiences, released a long narrative feature, *Orphan Saves Grandpa* (Zhang Shichuan, 1923), to record-breaking audience attendance, creating a wave of domestic picture fever, though Hollywood continued to dominate China's upscale film market. But back in the United States, Universal did not occupy the upscale market. The studio lacked urban theater chains and thus targeted independent rural theatrical houses by offering affordable packages to exhibitors that allowed them to change bills numerous times a week. Meanwhile in China, from 1928 to 1931, Star was busy producing and releasing the popular martial arts ghost film series *The Burning of the Red Lotus Temple* (*BRLT*), with nineteen installments in total. The series was among the longest films ever produced and the longest major release, running twenty-seven hours in total until it was banned by the Chinese government in 1931 during a campaign to root out superstitious elements in Chinese cinema.

Poster for *Burning of the Red Lotus Temple*.

Chinese studios actively competed with Hollywood for China's domestic market, especially when sound emerged. Sound productions became the norm by 1929. Universal responded by increasing the number of quality productions with sound, scoring its first Academy Award for Best Picture with *All Quiet on the Western Front* (Lewis Milestone, 1930), a film that met resistance in China during the Sino-Japanese war for its antiwar sentiment. The director's 1936 Paramount film *The General Died at Dawn*, featuring the offensive General Yang, "a monstrous, megalomaniacal warlord," would also be banned in China.[25]

Universal became famous for popularizing the monster craze, beginning with *Dracula* (Tod Browning and Karl Freund, 1931), which was also banned in China for superstition just as China's film industry was handed a ban on its domestic martial arts ghost films led by *Burning of the Red Lotus Temple.*[26] The banning of *Dracula* was compounded further by the censure of *East Is West* (Monta Bell, 1930),[27] a Universal film perceived as insulting to the Chinese. The film followed the fashionable trope of white men caught in the exotic world of the Orient as they clashed with backwater local cultures and customs, which in this case was the underbelly of San Francisco's Chinatown. Chinese diplomats in Chicago alerted Chinese censors of the film's objectionable elements before it was shipped to China. Chinese censors subsequently barred the film from being shown in China until Universal agreed to delete scenes and dialogue that the censors deemed derogatory. Despite the hiccups, Universal's films, especially horror pictures, were enormously popular in China, never mind the resistance from Chinese policy makers and cultural gatekeepers.

Hollywood's Washington Lobby

In a strategic attempt to solidify government support for the American movie business, Carl Laemmle began courting President Woodrow Wilson's administration in 1915, the year when he opened Universal City in Hollywood and when the U.S. courts ordered the dissolution of Edison's Trust. Laemmle suggested that the president address the American people on film via the movie theaters, arguing that movies could serve as an efficient tool to disseminate American goods and ideals. Wilson was presented with Griffith's *The Birth of a Nation* (1915), and allegedly remarked after the viewing that "it is like writing history in lightning."[28] Wilson publicly commended film's role in exporting America's cultural values, declaring the motion picture business an essential industry in America's war effort. This guaranteed studios the continuation of essential supplies despite material shortages during the war, something that other governments were neither willing nor able to do.[29] The same year in China, film production came to a halt as the war cut off supply chains for film stock. Incidentally, that same year, Yuan Shikai, a Chinese Qing dynasty military and government official turned inaugural president of the Republic of China, attempted to restore the monarchy by declaring himself emperor of China, leading to prolonged domestic warfare, which further distracted the government from supporting the country's nascent industrial development, including that of the film industry.

In the United States, 1916 saw the formation of the National Association of the Motion Picture Industry (NAMPI). Woodrow Wilson asked NAMPI's president William A. Brady to devise the means to distribute U.S. and Allied movies in France, Italy, and Russia. Wilson remarked that "the film has come to rank as the very highest medium for the dissemination of public intelligence, and since it speaks a universal language, it lends itself importantly to the presentation [of] America's plans and purposes."[30] In 1917, the Congress created the Committee on Public Information (known as the Creel Committee after chairman George Creel) to influence public opinion on the government's war effort. Hollywood films, books, English language classes, and advertisements were all leveraged to serve the war effort.[31] NAMPI's War Cooperation Committee subsequently set up the American Cinema Commission to distribute films in Europe. The commission worked with the Division of Films under the Creel Committee to decide which films to promote abroad. All films going overseas were required to obtain a War Trade Board license endorsed by Creel. Creel in turn helped to expedite film shipments by cutting through the red tape and securing shipping space. Hollywood agreed to include 20 percent education material in all export shipments, to rent films only to exhibitors who agreed to screen Creel-sponsored product, and to not screen U.S. films at cinemas that showcased German films. The Division of Film under Creel helped firmly implant American films abroad.

From 1914 to 1922, pictures grew longer and more costly to make and theaters became more expensive to build. Block booking and blind booking were established and imposed around the globe. Blind booking was the practice of forcing an exhibitor to take an existing film without the benefit of a preview screening, while block booking compelled a cinema to take yet unmade series of films for a designated period. These practices severely limited the ability of newcomers to enter the market, particularly impacting countries with limited financial resources, which led to anti-Hollywood backlashes around the world during and after World War I.[32]

Film Regulation and Censorship in China

The relationship between government and the film industry in China was more of control and censorship than that of service and advocacy as in the United States. Chinese governments since the early days offered little financial assistance to the industry in the form of marketing research and tax levies but exercised restrictions initially on film exhibition and later film content through regulation and censorship, which curtailed Chinese filmmakers' financial resources and choice of story and style.[33] Government intervention influenced how films were produced and exhibited as well as what types of films could be made. Film in China was expected to toe "the party line," be it Qing, KMT, or the CCP, though control during both late Qing and the KMT eras was far more relaxed than during the Mao and now the Xi eras under the CCP.

In 1907, the Beijing police department issued "Eleven Rules Governing the Showing of Motion Pictures in the Evenings," which became the Chinese government's first regulation concerning film exhibition. Six of the eleven rules dealt with theater and management-related issues including registration, safety provisions, observation of seating capacity and showtime limits, and audience behavior–related rules stipulating the segregation of the sexes and prohibition of gambling and carrying firearms. One clause in the document banned "racy" pictures.[34] Before the age of electricity, theatrical performances were commonly staged during the day and the Qing government prohibited theaters from staging shows after sunset for safety reasons. Women were not allowed to enter theaters out of the same concern for safety. Until enough movie theaters were built, most film screenings had to take place in the evenings in venues where traditional operas were staged during the day, which inevitably violated the existing prohibition against theaters staging shows after sunset. The Qing government eventually relented, making exceptions for motion pictures to be screened in the evenings and for admitting female movie audiences.

But the officials were uneasy about the unsupervised audiences sitting in dark auditoriums. In early 1906, a conservative official named Bi Shou proposed banning film exhibition in Beijing, arguing precisely that film screenings violated the two existing rules governing theatrical activities: the prohibition against theaters operating after dark and the ban on admitting women. Bi further accused the police department of taking bribes from theater owners to promote cinema viewing.[35] Shen Zhaojian, an official representing the police department, submitted a rebuttal, arguing that film was a useful educational tool and would contribute to China's modernization effort, and that the formation of a modern police force in China offered adequate official supervision of audience behavior in the theaters and thus rendered the ban on theatrical performances in the evenings outdated. Despite the righteous rhetoric, the police department did benefit from film screenings by collecting monthly taxes and fees for police protection and for processing monthly exhibition permit renewals.

Shen further linked film screenings to patriotism, arguing that the government should promote the growth of established local exhibition venues of domestic ownership so that film would not be dominated completely by foreign interests.[36] It is curious that the police department would make a case for cinema's pedagogical and nation-building function and to argue for protectionist policy. Nonetheless, the protectionist instinct formed the basis for another strand of government regulation in China. One of the eleven rules explicitly prohibits Chinese theater owners from renting films and projection equipment from foreigners, though the purpose of the rule had less to do with promoting domestic exhibition than with preventing foreigners and foreign films from stirring up antigovernment sentiment.[37]

A group of traveling exhibitors from Austria, Greece, Italy, and Russia went to northeastern China in 1906 and screened films without permission. The Qing officials in Jilin Province shut down the shows. The foreign exhibitors appealed to the Russian authorities to pressure the Chinese authority to return their confiscated equipment and money. The Russians told the Chinese that the exhibitors had received an endorsement from the Russian government to screen films in China. The Qing government did not budge and asserted, in a series of diplomatic exchanges, its jurisdiction in the region, refusing to return the confiscated equipment. The foreign showmen were denied permission to continue their exhibition activities in the region.[38]

Government control over film exhibition gradually moved into content regulation, with sexual transgression being its main target. The notion of "injury to social mores"[39] featured prominently in censors' decisions. By and large, though, the enforcement of film regulations in the final years of the Qing remained sporadic, fragmented, and inconsistent. The early Republican regime stepped up the censorship effort by establishing institutions responsible for supervising film production and exhibition, though there was initial confusion as to which agency should be responsible for supervising the production, distribution, and exhibition of motion pictures. Approval of business licenses fell on the Bureau of Industry, while the Office of Tax collected fees and the Department of Public Safety ensured sanitation and fire safety. In 1918, a businessman, Cheng Che, applied to the Beiyang government in Beijing for a permit to set up a film studio in Shanghai.[40] In his application, Cheng declared that he was to make documentaries rather than feature films in order "to enlighten the public and transmit knowledge." Cheng submitted his application to the Ministry of Education, but the ministry rejected his application on the grounds that the production and distribution of films were economic and commercial issues and should thus fall under the jurisdiction of the Ministries of Agriculture and Commerce. The Ministry of Education stated nevertheless that although the business license should be issued by the Ministries of Agriculture and Commerce, the finished film should be reviewed by the Ministry of Education prior to its distribution.[41]

Without an adequate institutional framework to regulate movies, early censorship efforts were inconsistently applied across Chinese regions. In Beijing, content monitoring seemed to have fallen on the police department, which acted as the chief enforcer of censorship rules and targeted sexually suggestive scenes such as men and women swimming together or long passionate kisses between lovers.[42] In the east province of Jiangsu, the Jiangsu Board of Film Censors, the first government agency in China established in 1923 to regulate films, placed film censorship squarely in the hands of the educators. The board's official policy was to limit intervention by focusing on recommending good films with educational value and positive social function and banning only "extremely bad films," i.e., morally compromised films harmful to social mores.[43] While leaving the majority of films untouched, the Jiangsu board recommended a number of films that exemplified "the best of Chinese ethics" and inspired "righteous behavior among the audience" for official awards.[44] It banned two controversial crime films involving murder, *Yan*

Ruisheng (Ren Pengnian, 1921) and *Zhang Xinsheng* (Zhang Shichua, 1922), both based on real-life murder cases.[45]

The Hays Code and Film Censorship in Hollywood

Hollywood too had to deal with censorship and public opinion. While expanding its international market share, Hollywood was under siege domestically from the growing public outcry against the film industry's perceived immorality both in its films and in people who made these films. In the United States, the movie industry has always been seen as morally dubious to certain religious, civic, and political organizations. The U.S. Supreme Court decided unanimously in 1915, in Mutual Film Corporation *v.* Industrial Commission of Ohio, that free speech did not extend to motion pictures. Several risqué films and off-screen scandals involving Hollywood stars in 1922, the same year the sensational Chinese real-life crime movie *Zhang Xinsheng* debuted, brought the industry widespread condemnation, and led to the introduction later that year in thirty-seven states of almost one hundred movie censorship bills.

To fend off the prospect of having to cope with hundreds and potentially thousands of inconsistent and changeable decency laws, the Motion Picture Producers and Distributors Association of America (MPPDA), which was established in 1922 to replace NAMPI as the official trade organization for the industry, launched a domestic PR campaign led by its inaugural president Will Hays—former chairman of the Republican National Committee who in 1920 helped elect Warren Harding to succeed Woodrow Wilson as U.S. president—to ease societal hostilities and to eventually rehabilitate Hollywood's tarnished image. In 1927, the year after China issued its official eleven censorship regulations, Hays suggested that the studios form a public relations committee to discuss film censorship, which led to a list of "Don'ts" and "Be Carefuls" based on collective items compiled by local censor boards. This list consisted of eleven subjects best to be avoided and twenty-six to be handled very carefully. The list was approved by the Federal Trade Commission (FTC). Hays further created the Studio Relations Committee (SRC) to oversee the implementation of the list and to demonstrate to the public the film industry's willingness to set itself on an ethical path. All MPPDA members appointed representatives to the Studio Relations Committee, though the committee did not enforce real censorship. Instead, each studio's representative was put in charge of looking over scripts to preempt scenes that might be objectionable both domestically and internationally. The representative was also expected to visit production locations to make sure that directors did not deviate from the approved script.

Yet as public pressure mounted, MPPDA changed the Studio Relations Committee to a Production Code Administration in 1930, and appointed Joseph Breen, a journalist and Philadelphia native influential in the Catholic community, as the head of the administration. The Production Code Administration formalized the guideline and turned it into the Production Code to ensure that Hollywood movies pandered to conservative values by restricting provocative themes, indecent language, and sexual content. The code stipulated that a script must be vetted from outline to treatment to shooting script, and the finished film would also be inspected. Only an acceptable motion picture could receive a seal of approval from the MPPDA. Without one, there was little likelihood of a film getting exhibited.[46]

Building a Patriotic and Profitable Chinese Cinema in the 1920s–30s

Patriotic film practitioners in China considered film production an important cultural investment and were thus skeptical of competition regulated solely by a free market, since the market would discourage socially conscious films with less entertainment value. Building a profitable film industry at the service of the national interest by battling foreign aggression and oppression was coupled with an enlightenment mission to transform the masses into an informed public. The competing interest between enlightenment and entertainment would pose a persistent challenge throughout the history of Chinese cinema. Chinese cinema's early entanglement with political parties was voluntary. But the legacy would incur repercussions for the film industry in later years, with political patronage during the Republic era and political cohesion during the People's Republic of China (PRC) era.

Despite the lack of direct assistance from the government during the period, the Chinese film industry marched forward with much gusto. The economic recovery after the war freed up domestic capital for film production; thus the early 1920s saw several waves of speculative film financing in China, and Chinese domestic production took off in terms of investment, commercial success, and decreased dependence on foreign expertise. The theatrical exhibition business also began to attract greater numbers of Chinese investors during the 1920s.

To compete more successfully with Hollywood imports, Chinese filmmakers tried in the early to mid-1920s to consolidate capital and human resources. Between 1919 and 1922, a few noteworthy local companies gained traction, including the Commercial Press Motion Picture Department (*Shangwu yinshuguan huodong yingxi bu*) of Shanghai Commercial Press (SCP), a major Chinese publisher of books and magazines on current affairs, education, and literature founded in 1897. SCP established the Motion Picture Department in 1917 to produce films including current event newsreels, education reform programs, scenes of historic sites, and opera performances. The company also made feature films of "civilized play," a hybrid dramatic form combining elements of modern Western drama and Chinese traditional opera. In an April 1919 petition to the government, SCP equated filmmaking with nation building, and pointed out that the image of China in foreign imports was frequently "flippant and mendacious, extremely harmful to customs and popular sentiment, frequently satirical concerning inferior conditions in our society, thus material for derision."[47] The company urged the boycott of imported films that were harmful to decency. It stated that "we hope to aid popular education, in part by exporting and selling our films overseas, glorifying our national culture, and mitigating foreigners' spiteful feelings, while simultaneously mobilizing the affections of overseas Chinese toward their homeland."[48]

SCP's 1919 statement on producing domestic films with positive China images echoed the prevailing nationalistic sentiment at the time. The same year in the United States, Hollywood films *The Red Lantern* (Albert Capellani, 1919) and *Broken Blossoms* (D.W. Griffith, 1919) provoked an outcry among Chinese Americans for perceived racist depiction of China and Chinese. In response, the U.S. Film Censorship Board told the

Chinese protesters that they should produce their own films as counter discourse. James B. Leong, a Los Angeles–based film industry veteran, in turn established his own production company in 1920 to make films that would showcase "the real China on the screen, thereby correcting the general impression that Chinese life, as it may be seen through the camera's eye, is chiefly concerned with tong wars, opium smoking, and strange methods of gambling."[49]

SCP argued that its lofty goal needed support from the government and submitted in April 1919 a "Petition for Approval of Tax Exemption for Self-Produced Motion Pictures." The petition laid down its ambitions to create a national distribution network that would reach "every province in China." Though touting patriotism in fending off Hollywood, SCP's Motion Picture Department collaborated with Universal Pictures on *The Dragon's Net* (Henry MacRae, 1920), a 1920 action film serial adapted from J. Allan Dunn's *The Petals of Lao-Tze*. Many scenes of the film were shot in the Far East and Hawaii, where SCP's filmmakers underwent training by the Universal studio.[50] SCP further loaned out its studio to produce several feature films by other companies, including the notorious crime films *Yan Ruisheng* and *The Women Skeletons* (Guan Haifeng, 1922). Both films premiered at the Embassy, a first-run Shanghai theater primarily for foreign films. From 1922 until the closure of its Motion Picture Department in 1926, the SCP's production focused on the lucrative feature and opera films.

The Great Wall Picture Company and Beyond

Another company founded as the result of the 1919 outcry against *The Red Lantern* and *Broken Blossoms* was the Great Wall Picture Company (*Changcheng zhizhao huapian gongsi*), which was formed in May 1921 by a group of Brooklyn-based Chinese American film students in New York with the aim to produce patriotic films. The Great Wall Picture Company became the first professional Chinese American production company. Among Great Wall's earliest productions were *Martial Arts of China* (*Zhongguo de wushu*, 1922) and *Clothing of China* (*Zhongguo de fuzhuang*, 1922). Struggling to find its footing in New York, the company relocated to the French Concession in Shanghai around 1923–24[51] and eventually dissolved in 1930 due to financial difficulties.[52]

Amidst the fervor of nation building, several major figures in Chinese cinema came of age during the 1920s. Some had close ties with the Republic government. Li Minwei (Lai Man-Wai, 1893–1953), the personal cinematographer to Dr. Sun Yat-sen, joined Dr. Sun's Revolutionary Alliance in 1911 and made anti-warlord movies.[53] Li directed Hong Kong's first feature film, *Zhuangzi Tests His Wife*, in 1913 and founded the China Sun Motion Picture Company in Hong Kong ten years later in 1923. He moved the company to Shanghai in 1926 to produce films that would "educate the masses" (*jiaoyu qunzhong*) and "change habits and customs" (*yi feng yi su*). In 1930, he co-founded Lianhua, one of the "Big Three" studios of the 1930s in China.

Political and cultural elites in China were keen to harness the popularity of cinema for nation building from early on. Patriotic film practitioners such as Hong Shen wrote screenplays and advocated the use of film as a "vehicle" for enlightenment and for educating Chinese in the idea of citizenship. One cultural critic asked a rhetorical question: "Can we find any better tool than film to educate our people?"[54] The critic said further that "in order to develop the intelligence of our fellow countrymen, we must first develop our domestic film production. . . . Once our domestic films become popular, our countrymen's knowledge will be enriched correspondingly . . . we can transform China from a weak country into a strong one."

Early Chinese films catered mostly to less affluent patrons consisting largely of students, shopkeepers, office clerks, and other petty bourgeoisie, since well-off and better-educated Chinese elites frequented upscale theaters dominated by Hollywood films. To counter the trend, policy makers, patriotic film commentators, and filmmakers urged elite patrons to go to see Chinese films, and watching domestic pictures was equated with carrying out one's patriotic duty. Popular domestic films during the period were *The King of Comedy Visits China* (Zhang Shichuan, 1922), a Charlie Chaplin–style slapstick comedy featuring an imaginative Chaplin and his China visit; *Laborer's Love* (Zhang Shichuan, 1922), a romantic comedy; and *Zhang Xinsheng* (1922), a crime movie. Star was the studio that produced these popular films. The company would go on to become one of China's most successful studios in the 1920s and 1930s.

Hollywood Reigned

Despite the effort made by the Chinese film industry, Hollywood continued to dominate the Chinese market. During the period, the popularity of Hollywood films forced Chinese exhibitors to accept high exhibition fees and low ticket prices. Demand for Hollywood imports was the force that drove the rapid theater expansion in China in the 1920s and 1930s. It is worth noting that the growth in the motion picture business in China, particularly in Shanghai in the early 1920s, owed much to the United Artists Corporation's attempt to establish a distribution system to ensure its copyrights, rights of exhibition, and profit under extraterritoriality in the foreign settlements in Shanghai.[55] The early 1920s marked UA's initiative in opening foreign markets in the Far East. As Jessica Ka Yee Chan notes, in reaction to the actions of the Ramos Amusement Company, which had dominated the Shanghai market with stolen and "dupe" copies of film prints including UA titles since the 1910s through agents and dealers in Europe and the United States, UA registered copyrights for twenty of its films to be exhibited in Shanghai in 1922.[56] Other American studios followed suit, and by the late 1930s, eight American studios had set up their own distribution boards to "manage screening rights between theaters and to minimize disputes among themselves."[57]

Film exhibition adhered to the two-tiered colonial structure. The upscale first-tier theaters all signed exclusive contracts with Hollywood. Heavy fines were imposed when these first-tier theaters screened Chinese films. In 1939, Huguang Theater[58] ignored its contract with MGM and screened the enormously popular domestic film *Mulan Joins the Army* (Bu Wancang, 1939) for over a month. MGM took Huguang to court and won RMB 60,000 in penalties.[59] Fines were also applied to some middle-scale theaters that occasionally sneaked in a few domestic films between Hollywood films. While foreign-run first-tier theaters charged RMB 2 for cinema admission, Chinese-run theaters down the food chain charged only RMB 10–20 cents (the average monthly household income in Shanghai during the period was less than RMB 30), which was a pattern that reflected class division among cinemagoers in general at the time.[60] Meanwhile, theaters were forced to give away 30 percent to 50 percent of their revenue to foreign distributors, leaving little reserve for expansion.

Distribution of Hollywood films had moved from the triple method of exclusive contract, single purchase, and revenue sharing to revenue sharing only, which maximized income for Hollywood pictures, including less commercially viable films forced upon Chinese theaters via block booking. In actual practice, Hollywood studios only stipulated several screening times for its films and left it for the theater to decide the rest of the screenings, which provided an opportunity for theaters to screen domestic pictures. To avoid the cost of air-conditioning and heating in the theater, major Hollywood films were screened in the fall, leaving the summer market for the less popular B movies and old titles, further opening up room for domestic films to be shown in first-run theaters. Summer became the high season for domestic films long before it became lucrative, and the "summer season" became a marketing catchphrase in the 1990s. To be screened at the foreign theaters, domestic pictures must pay high rental fees and charge higher ticket prices. Anxiety over the precarious financial condition of the domestic film industry was widespread among Chinese filmmakers in the 1920s and 1930s.

Early Chinese Domestic Productions

To compete with Hollywood imports, Chinese filmmakers made efforts in the early to mid-1920s to consolidate financial and human resources.[61] The consolidation reached its peak in 1927, reducing the number of production companies from well over a hundred to only thirty-two, with Star, Dazhonghua-Baihe (Great China-Lily, or GL), and Tianyi emerging as China's big three; thus the Chinese national film industry took its initial shape. Founded in 1925, Great China-Lily produced chiefly contemporary urban dramas emulating D.W. Griffith's melodramas popular in China, including *Way Down East* (1920), *Orphans of the Storm* (1921), *The Birth of a Nation* (1915), and *Broken Blossoms* (1919). Second only to Star in production scale and output during its heyday, GL's films promoted free love and women's rights, introducing to Chinese cinema the theme of the May Fourth modernization movement, an antitradition cultural movement in China from 1917 to 1920 that advocated individual emancipation and the creation of a new culture merging Chinese heritage and Western civilization, all at the service of a nation in crisis. Taking its name from an anti-imperialist demonstration on May 4, 1919, the May Fourth Movement and its discourses on enlightenment, modernity, and modernization exerted a long-lasting influence on the development of Chinese nationalism and national cinema.

Though the impetus for developing a Chinese national cinema had more to do with building a stronger China than with building a more profitable film industry, studios including Great China-Lily produced films not without profits in mind. GL was absorbed into Lianhua cofounded by Li Mingwei and Luo Mingyou in 1930, making Lianhua one of the new big three from the early 1930s. Among the big three, Star had the longest production history, the largest production capacity, and the best distribution network. Star productions tried to strike a balance between enlightenment and entertainment as it sought to make socially responsible whilst financially profitable films. The solution was social realist melodramas catering to the popular taste while simultaneously preaching the value of traditional Chinese moral codes.

STAR (MINGXING, 1922–1927) AND SOCIAL REALIST MELODRAMAS

Star was founded in Shanghai in March 1922 by five cinema aficionados who wanted a film company that would be wholly owned and operated by the Chinese. The five all-male founders came to be known as "Star's Five Tiger Generals." Among the tigers, Zhang Shichuan had directed several short films for the now defunct Asia Film Company; Zheng Zhengqiu, Zhang's longtime collaborator, was a playwright turned director with a few film credits under his belt; Zheng Zhegu was a stage actor with some business background; Zhou Jianyun came from the publishing industry; and Ren Jinping came from an educational background. They named the newly formed company Mingxing, meaning Bright Star (hence Star), the name of a popular fan magazine in Shanghai at the time. Settling into Avenue Joffre in the French Concession, Star soon emerged as the dominant player in Shanghai's flourishing movie indus-try. The careful planning that went into the venture and the diverse, yet relevant, backgrounds of its founders contributed to Star's success.

The founders set up an affiliated film school to cultivate its own talent pool while publishing a film magazine to educate the masses about film. Zhang Shichuan and Zheng Zhengqiu were the creative talents behind the studio's production slates. Zheng wrote screenplays and Zhang di-rected. The Shanghai-born Zheng also directed and served as a studio manager and producer, personally scripting and directing fifty-three films by the time he passed away in 1935. Like many of his colleagues during the period, Zheng was attracted to leftist ideas and to issues of equality and social justice, themes that were repeatedly explored in many of his works. Zhang was more profit-minded while Zheng wanted their movies to have a positive impact on social change. The resulting collaboration found its niche for socially conscious popular films. Through-out their collaboration, the two paradoxically made left-wing progressive films, sensational crime films, and the longest running martial arts ghost film series, *Burning of the Red Lotus Temple*. Zheng's filmmaking is em-blematic of Chinese cinema's overall push-and-pull trajectory, striving to maintain a balance between multiple demands. Zhang and Zheng remained close friends up until Zheng's death, two years before the stu-dio was forced to shut down amidst the chaos of the second Sino-Japanese War.

An avid consumer of American films, Zhang Shichuan learned the craft of filmmaking and the skill of running the film business by actively seeking out foreign experts. Zhang famously invited Mary Pickford and Douglas Fairbanks to the production site of *Burning of the Red Lotus Temple* when the couple stopped by Shanghai in 1929 on their global tour.[62] The company was said to have benefited from Fairbanks's talk on sound devel-opment. The same year, Star received James Wong Howe (1899–1976), a Chinese-born American cinematographer with over 130 films under his belt. Howe gave a talk on new inventions in cinematography and demon-strated several new-style cameras he brought along. Howe filmed several short skits featuring Star's household actors, including Hu Die (Butterfly), one of China's most popular actresses in the 1920s and 1930s who starred in *The Burning of the Red Lotus Temple* and *Sing-Song Girl Red Peony* (Zhang Shichuan and Cheng Bugao, 1931), China's first sound film. Star screened the short films and made an extra copy of the films for Howe to take back to Hollywood.[63] Upon return to the United States, Howe continued to dispatch information to Zhang on sound development in Hollywood and new innovations in film technology. Star eventually sent a team to the United States in 1931 to learn new techniques and procure film equipment. Star named the sound recording machine it imported from Hollywood "Star Tune."[64] The introduction and installation of Star Tune at various theaters paved the way for the development of Chinese sound films.

Zhou Jianyun, another of Star's key founders, brought to film production business experience and expertise in the publishing industry and became the company's general manager, overseeing marketing, distribution, and film financing. Zheng Zhegu, a veteran stage actor with business background, became Star's stage manager while doubling as the chief administrator of the affiliated film school. He also acted in early Star productions including *The Orphan Saves His Grandfather* (Zhang Shicheng, 1923) and *The Soul of Yuli* (Zhang Shicheng and Li Chenfeng 1924). Ren Jinping came from the field of education so was put in charge of the company's publicity and public relations division, where he oversaw the publication of the studio's first film magazine, *Morning Star*.[65]

THE COMPANY OF TRADITION:
TIANYI'S COSTUME DRAMA FILMS

Tianyi was formed in Shanghai in 1925 by four financially savvy and culturally conservative brothers in the Shaw family: Runjie, Runde, Runme, and Runrun. A businessman with a law degree, the oldest brother Runjie began his adventure in the entertainment business in the early 1920s. In 1922, he formed a joint theater company with Zhang Shichuan and Zheng Zhenqiu to produce modern stage dramas. After Zhang and Zheng left to found the Star film company, Runjie established his own company, Tianyi, in June 1925. During its twelve-year history in Shanghai, Tianyi produced 110 Mandarin films and 10 or so Cantonese films, making it the most prolific and longest-standing company next to Star in early Chinese film history. Unlike Star, which fashioned a mixture of Western-style melodrama with Chinese characteristics trendy among the more upper-scale patrons, Tianyi's films were culturally conservative, catering mainly to the working-class patrons. Criticized for being reactionary and lowbrow, Tianyi persisted in its niche market and distinguished its films as bearing contemporary relevance to Chinese society.

Tianyi's signature genre in 1927–28 was the popular costume drama rooted in Chinese history and legend. The popularity of costume drama led to Chinese cinema's first full bloom entertainment wave from the late 1920s to early 1930s, a milestone in the development of Chinese cinema, which was nurtured by the political, economic, and cultural conditions in China from the mid-1920s to the early 1930s. A culturally conservative regulatory body under the KMT steered Chinese cinema away from the critical realist films of an earlier decade. The relative political stability brought economic growth in China's coastal cities, which ensured a steady capital flow for film production and exhibition. The combination of a populist, traditionalist, and pragmatic film culture welcomed films of distinctive Chinese story and flavor that catered to the taste of lower- to middle-class urban dwellers, the major patrons of domestic films. Costume drama was presented as a welcome alternative to Star's Westernized urban drama.

Classical Chinese literature and popular folklore attacked during the May Fourth Westernization movement were making their way back to the literary scene in the early 1920s, and by the mid-1920s, Westernized contemporary urban dramas had lost their appeal to both the audiences and the critics. Tianyi saw the shrinking market for Hollywood-influenced domestic films of contemporary subjects as a sign that the audiences were looking for something more traditional and rooted in Chinese history. The box-office success of imported historical epics such as *The Ten Commandments* (Cecil B. DeMille, 1923) further inspired the Shaw brothers to explore China's own cultural heritage and historical narratives. The cultural polices in Southeast Asia under colonial rule at the time further welcomed costume dramas, as such films bore no political relevance to colonial control, let alone a challenge to its legitimacy. Costume drama's popularity among overseas Chinese was crucial for the Shaw Brothers to make profits and attract investments, since prosperous Southeast Asia promised both the market and the capital. Domestically, under the reign of the politically and culturally conservative Nationalist government, costume drama provided a safer route to Star's provocative contemporary social problem films and the Western-style melodramas.

Costume drama appealed to the taste of socially and economically dis-advantaged patrons, the main target of theaters showcasing domestic films. Tianyi's strategy for less sophisticated audiences is akin to Carl Laemmle's strategy of building theater chains initially in rural areas for less sophisticated audiences. The poor and the less educated were attracted to adaptations of popular vocal and folkloric narratives that they grew up being exposed to. Costume drama evolved from adaptations of traditional Chinese performing arts chanting folktales about tragic love to literary adaptations of Chinese mythologies and classic novels and poems based on historical events. The Chinese Buddhist folktale *Pilgrimage to the West* remained the favorite source for film adaptation, while historical novels such as *Water Margin* and *Romance of the Three Kingdoms* delivered some of the most popular cinematic adaptations. Audiences' familiarity with these popular characters and plots made the film adaptations less time consum-ing and therefore more profitable. The success of costume dramas, particu-larly in Tianyi's Southeast Asia market, spurred the company to adapt more Chinese literary classics and to lavish them in costume designs. Stories of loyalty, heroism, and anti-oppression were common, together with romance between "learned man and beautiful woman," or "hero and beauty." Comic elements were added to defuse such stories' melodramatic propensity.

The profitability of costume dramas led to cheap imitations from small-scale companies with insufficient budget, talent, and technology to pull off decent productions. Over two-thirds of Chinese domestic films made in the following two years were costume dramas, which were pro-duced by seventeen out of twenty-three studios including Star and the Great China-Lily. The proliferation of cheap knockoffs soon tarnished the reputation of domestic pictures, further steering middle-class patrons away from Chinese cinema.

Star's The Burning of the Red Lotus Temple
and the Rise of Martial Arts Ghost Drama

Costume drama metamorphosed into the martial arts ghost drama in 1928. As the name suggests, martial arts ghost drama was the combina-tion of martial arts and ghost story. Emerging as separate subgenres of costume drama, the two soon found strength in each other. Martial arts stories depicted the lives of kung fu legends and were typically formulaic, combining heroic themes with predictable plot structure and characterization. The martial arts story had been a popular genre long before it was adapted to the big screen. The newspaper adventure serial and its derivative comic books had regularly featured stories of kung fu masters. Martial arts stories were also popular resources for various traditional Chinese stage performances, and the martial arts novel as a literary genre occupied a special position in the history of Chinese literature. The popularity of kung fu stories made martial arts film easily accessible.

The Chinese martial arts film was firmly rooted in Confucian principles of filial piety and loyalty to one's country. Kung fu film was praised for its demonstration of Chinese people's physical ability, countering the perception of Chinese as the "patients of East Asia," as seen in the more sentimental urban melodrama with neurotic characters of "weak physiques." The Chinese critic Lu Mengshu publicly advocated martial arts drama for its embodiment of his "new heroism" ideal that called for a new kind of national hero who defied oppressive forces and elevated the public. Other critics echoed his call, and "the new heroism cinema" became a slogan in the mid-1920s. The popularity of imported films such as *Robin Hood* (Allan Dwan, 1922) and *The Three Musketeers* (Fred Niblo, 1921) with their egalitarian tone further facilitated the ascendancy of martial arts films.

Martial arts pictures fought for their niche market amidst the costume drama craze in 1927 and received a boost after they absorbed supernatural elements from ghost stories. The combination of kung fu and ghost stories resulted in martial arts ghost films in which the kung fu legends, with their raw physical power, were now endowed with supernatural ability. Old Buddhist temples were added to the kung fu drama's usual settings of barren mountains and remote countrysides. Naked women and men wearing grotesque masks were also added, together with special effects that created the illusion of characters flying and disappearing. Both martial arts and ghost stories were popular genres in the 1920s, which made readily available material for film adaptation and genre merging. What mattered most to martial arts ghost drama was not its originality but the visualization of the already familiar story and characters.

Star's *The Burning of the Red Lotus Temple* (Zhang Shichuan) kick-started the wave of martial arts ghost dramas in 1928. From 1928 to 1931, martial arts ghost dramas swamped the domestic and overseas Chinese markets, prolonging Chinese cinema's commercial entertainment trend. The most common martial arts ghost story focuses on competition between opposing kung fu schools, which would become one of the most popular prototypes for kung fu films for years to come. The multiepisode *The Burning of the Red Lotus Temple* (*BRLT*), for instance, was about factional strife among various kung fu schools.

With its 1928 premiere of *The Burning of the Red Lotus Temple*, Star became the innovator and the leader in producing martial arts ghost genre. The company's established genres—the social problem drama and the urban melodrama—were not faring well against the ascendancy of Tianyi's costume drama. Anxious to regain its footing, Star turned to making martial arts film as an alternative to cheap knockoffs of Tianyi's costume drama, which were in wane by 1928. Zhang Shichuan had his eye on the popular kung fu novel *The Tales of Kung fu Legend* with its embedded supernatural elements and suggested to his collaborator Zheng Zhengqiu that he flesh out a screenplay based on the novel. The resulting film was *The Burning of the Red Lotus Temple*, the debut of the martial arts ghost genre. Star's in-house actors were not known for their martial arts prowess, so the supernatural elements made up for actors' lack of real kung fu skills. The utilization of special effects served as a harbinger for the arrival of a new breed of martial arts film combining kung fu with supernatural (ghosts). Supernatural power made Star's anchoring actor Hu Die (Butterfly) a female kung fu legend, despite her ineptitude in any real kung fu skill.

Overall, martial arts ghost drama had a much narrower yet arguably more creative focus than costume drama in terms of its literary resources and its themes. Only a small number of martial arts ghost stories were adaptations of classical novels, folklore, and stage performances, and most of the scenarios were of the filmmaker's own creation. The heroes of martial arts ghost drama were all chivalrous swordsmen/women with super and indeed supernatural martial arts skills. There was a fair amount of sexual tension between heroes and heroines, though the Buddhist vow of celibacy prohibited consummation.

The success of *BRLT* encouraged Zhang to make eighteen sequels from 1928 to 1930, generating enough revenue for the company to bounce back and even expand. The success also compelled medium-sized companies to follow Star's lead, creating a wave of martial arts ghost pictures. Most martial arts ghost drama films were made on shoestring budgets in a short period of time, utilizing outdoor settings with limited props and natural lighting. Actors' martial arts skill was prized over their acting talent and physical chop over their psychological complexity. The success further spawned a series of cheap, copycat "Burning" films including *The Burning of Black Dragon Temple* (Ren Yutian, 1929), *The Burning of White Flower Terrace* (Li Pingqian, 1929), and *The Burning of Sword-Peak Fortress* (Yu Boyan, 1930), hurting the quality and hence the reputation of martial arts ghost films. The production of martial arts ghost films reached its apex in 1929, with an annual output of eighty-five pictures, far exceeding the market demand.

By the early 1930s, the quality of martial arts ghost films had seriously deteriorated. The low quality and high quantity led to price cuts, draining studios' production investment. It also gave the foreign-controlled theater chains in big cities excuses to reject Chinese native productions. Many domestic production companies went bankrupt. The genre's superstitious elements attracted much derision from Chinese critics, which soon led to an outcry for the government to ban martial arts ghost pictures. A ban was issued in 1931 by the KMT government, officially ending Chinese cinema's first wave of entertainment films initiated by Tianyi's costume drama films in 1927. *The Ten Commandments* would be banned in 1932, together with *Ben Hur* (Fred Niblo, 1925), on the ground that religious films with gods and deities fit into the censored category of "superstitious films,"[66] which also included films with "unscientific elements" such as *Alice in Wonderland* (Bud Pollard, 1931) and *Frankenstein* (James Whale, 1931).[67] Star's domestic hit *The Burning of the Red Lotus Temple* also became a casualty of the ban.

The cycle of boom and bust in Chinese cinema was short during the Republic era. The Chinese film industry benefited initially from the Westernization movement and then the sinicization movement in the 1920s. Western technologies and ideas were an important component of early Chinese cinema. When the nationalist sentiments of the Chinese public ran high, the film industry turned to costume dramas and martial arts genres rooted in Chinese literary tradition. Meanwhile, patriotism continued to be the driving force for Chinese cinema. More than half of the film output from 1927 to 1931 fit one of the two genres. Except for the first Chinese sound novelties, such as *The Sing-Song Girl Red Peony* (Zhang Shichuang, 1930) featuring Star's Butterfly Wu, all the financial successes during the period came from either costume or martial arts ghost dramas. Though boosting the popularity of domestic pictures, Chinese cinema's first entertainment wave fell short of curbing Hollywood's dominance.

2

Into the 1930s and 1940s: Hollywood's Global Expansion and Chinese Cinema's Local Buildup

It is absolutely necessary that a work of art have national style. Only through a specific national style, can the ideas and feelings of a nation be expressed.

—Ge Yinghong, "On National Style,"
Literature Monthly 1, no. 2 (1940)[1]

When Harold Lloyd's first talkie, *Welcome Danger*, premiered in the United States on November 22, 1929, the Chinese consulate in San Francisco received complaints from the local Chinese Chamber of Commerce about the negative image of Chinese depicted in the film and how it would harm the already fragile relationship between white and Chinese people and further hurt Chinese businesses in the United States. *Welcome Danger* featured stock low-life Chinese characters stealing, robbing, and kidnapping their way around Chinatown. The Chinese deputy consul general Li Zhaosong promptly dispatched a letter to San Francisco's mayor on November 26, urging him to consider banning the film. The mayor's intervention led to the cutting of an indoor scene in a Chinese household where opium was discovered. Paramount Studio, which distributed the film, promised not to make films that would harm China's and Chinese Americans' images in the future. Yet when the cut version of the film debuted in China in February the following year, it caused another stir. During a February 22, 1930, screening at Shanghai's Grand Theater, Hong Shen, a U.S.-trained playwright and filmmaker, was so enraged by the Chinese images on-screen that he interrupted the screening and pleaded for the audiences to leave and demand their money back.

A native of Jiangsu Province, Hong attended secondary schools in Shanghai and Tianjin before entering the newly founded Tsinghua School (now Tsinghua University) in 1912. After graduating from Tsinghua in 1916, Hong left for the United States to study ceramic engineering at Ohio State University (OSU) on a Boxer Indemnity Scholarship. He wrote and produced two plays in English while at OSU. *The Wedded Husband* was performed at Oberlin College in April 1919 before an audience of 1,300 in the college chapel. It was likely the first play written by a Chinese citizen that was performed in the United States. Hong transferred to Harvard University in the fall of 1919 and was selected as one of "Baker's Dozen" to study drama under the renowned theater professor George Pierce Baker.[2] Hong Shen returned to China in 1922 and taught Western Literature at Fudan University, an elite Chinese university founded in Shanghai in 1905. He directed his first film, *Young Master Feng*, at the Star Film Company in 1925, and later wrote the script for the 1931 film *Sing-Song Girl Red Peony* (Zhang Shichuan), the first Chinese sound film.

Hong stumbled upon the screening of *Welcome Danger* in 1930 by accident. He was supposed to go to the Carlton Theater with a friend to see *The Thief of Bagdad* (Raoul Walsh, 1924), which was causing consternation among the Chinese over its Orientalist representation of the Mongol prince in the film. Chen Dezheng, the secretary of education and chair of the Film Censorship Committee, had issued a series of public statements in 1929 to echo public anger over China humiliation films including *The Thief of Bagdad* by invoking international precedent: "I recall that *Broken Blossoms* was banned by the British in the foreign concessions because it depicts the superiority of Chinese women over British women. . . . According to international law (*guoji gongfa*), a national of any country cannot humiliate a national of any other country."[3] At any rate, Hong decided to shun *The Thief of Bagdad* and watch *Welcome Danger* at the U.S.-registered Grand Theater run by a Chinese manager in the heart of the Shanghai foreign settlements. But *Welcome Danger* offered no relief, and the depiction of Chinese offended Hong. Disturbed by the images of Chinese on-screen, Hong rose to protest and was promptly led out and detained by the Shanghai foreign police.

From Welcome Danger *to* The Good Earth
(Sidney Franklin, 1937)

Hong's detention led to a public outcry that quickly snowballed into a campaign against "China-humiliation films."[4] The Shanghai Film Censorship Committee reacted swiftly, issuing an order for the Grand Theater to immediately halt all screening of *Welcome Danger*. The committee further ordered all newspapers to cease running ads for the film and demanded that the two theaters screening the film "apologize to the public, discontinue and burn the film prints."[5] The KMT government reached out to the Chinese consulate in San Francisco to demand an apology directly from Harold Lloyd, one of the most popular Hollywood stars in China. Lloyd initially demurred, arguing that "all countries have bad men, but that doesn't mean a whole race is bad," and that "if we start apologizing, who'll we have left to poke fun at?"[6] Lloyd's response led to a nationwide ban on the film on March 31, essentially pushing the film out of circulation except at a few theaters in foreign concessions. Lloyd eventually backed down when the financial stakes turned high. On May 29, he telegraphed the Chinese consul general in San Francisco to offer "sincere apologies" and to reassure the "Chinese authorities of his admiration for the Chinese people, civilization and culture."[7] The Shanghai Film Censorship Committee resumed reviewing his films for approval and eventually lifted the ban on his films by the end of September, likely to the delight of theaters as Harold Lloyd films boasted top billings. The *Welcome Danger* incident led to a joint manifesto by Chinese theater and cinema professionals that denounced Western imperialism and its perceived smear campaign demonizing China and the Chinese. It led the KMT government to bar all films with negative Chinese images from being released in China.[8]

In January 1931, the KMT established the National Film Censorship Committee (NFCC) to place control of film regulation for the first time in the hands of the central government. The NFCC was created to ensure that the Chinese film industry would contribute to the party's national reconstruction project. Paramount made an offer the same year to buy out all Chinese film studios with the intention to hire Chinese actors and directors to make films in Chinese about Chinese lives for distribution in China, a harbinger of contemporary Hollywood's less ambitious effort to incorporate Chinese elements into its films targeting the Chinese market. This plan was rebuffed by the Chinese.[9] KMT censorship blocked Paramount's later films *Shanghai Express* (von Sternberg, 1932) and *The General Died at Dawn* (Milestone, 1936), Columbia's *The Bitter Tea of General Yen* (Capra, 1933), and MGM's *China Seas* (Garnett, 1935), ending the wave of China-related films in Hollywood.

The convoluted approval process of *The Good Earth* (Sidney Franklin, 1937), an adaptation of Pearl Buck's same-title novel about the tribulations of a Chinese family in a village in the early twentieth century, provides insight into how Chinese censors interacted with Hollywood studios. When the book came out in 1931, elements of its story depicting religious fundamentalism, racial prejudice, and gender and sexual oppression unnerved Chinese cultural gatekeepers and KMT officials. The book was banned in China but went on to win the Pulitzer Prize in 1932 and was quickly adapted for a Broadway play. The Broadway play intrigued MGM's production head, the "wonder boy" Irving Thalberg, who paid $50,000, a record-breaking amount at the time, to secure screen rights. The Chinese consulate in Los Angeles was alarmed upon learning this news and quickly dispatched Vice Consul Kiang Yiseng to MGM to seek assurance that the screenplay would steer clear of any objectionable elements, including opium, banditry, squalor, foot binding, and superstitions. When production started, Thalberg wanted to send his film crew to northern China for location shooting, but Chinese regulators objected. The studio turned to Willys Peck, the U.S. counselor of legation at Nanjing, for help. After several failed attempts to persuade Chinese censors, Peck resorted to name-dropping, hinting that the project had the blessing of President Franklin D. Roosevelt.[10]

MGM further lobbied the U.S. State Department for Chiang Kaishek's endorsement. Chiang reportedly sent a telegram to the KMT's Film Censorship Committee to encourage approval. Perhaps because the censors realized that MGM would make the film regardless of their approval and that images of a real China would be better than what Hollywood might conjure up in its back lot in the San Fernando Valley, and that some influence over the filming process would be better than none, the Ministry of Foreign Affairs in Nanjing granted permission in December 1933 for the MGM crew to enter China. The KMT's publicity department nonetheless demanded various modifications to the script, including changing the title to disassociate the film from the controversial novel and adding a prologue stating that the film did not follow exactly the story from the original novel. The studio rejected the title change but reaffirmed its willingness to make reasonable modifications to the original story. The movie script was more sympathetic to China than the novel had been. The Chinese government further demanded that representatives from the NFCC be present during production in China and in the United States. The United States strongly opposed hosting a Chinese censor in Hollywood, fearful that it would encourage similar demands from other countries. It also worried that the censor could pass Hollywood trade secrets on to China's own film industry, and that such an arrangement would make MGM more susceptible to the KMT's propaganda effort. The concern about trade secrets speaks volumes about the competitive nature of national film industries. At the time, MGM, a minor studio relying on low-risk products appealing to independent and overseas distributors, had to make sure that the final product would be completed to everybody's satisfaction, and thus consulted the Chinese every step of the way to ensure the cooperation of the Chinese government and secure a China release.

Throughout the MGM-China negotiation for *The Good Earth*, Peck mediated between Chinese government censors and MGM representatives and regularly forwarded documents to the secretary of state in Washington to report progress and solicit instructions. MGM eventually settled on a compromise approach, allowing the Chinese to send a traveling instead of resident censor at the expense of the studio. MGM further agreed to exclude content deemed insulting, and to insert a "foreword" to distance itself from the original novel. It also agreed to submit for Chinese approval footage taken in China before shipping it back to America. On their part, the Chinese showed good faith by lending their army for the filming of war scenes and by eventually allowing footage to be sent back to the United States without local inspection. In return, MGM "reduced the viciousness of the Chinese characters, including the uncle and cousin, and toned down the sexual dimension of the Lotus character," a Chinese temptress who seduced the main character and brought his family down.[11] Thalberg's initial pledge for an all-Chinese cast was quickly dropped as MGM needed its star Paul Muni to carry the film, casting him in the lead role as the Chinese patriarch. The anti-miscegenation rules in the Hays Code prevented nonwhite performers being cast as partners in a marriage to white performers, so the idea of casting the Chinese American actress Anna May Wong as the wife of Paul Muni's character was subsequently dropped.

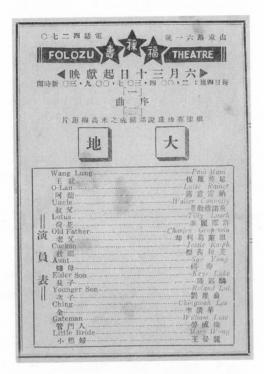

Chinese poster for *The Good Earth*.

Thalberg died before the production was completed. The film opened in the United States to sensational response and was posthumously named Thalberg's "last great achievement." *The Good Earth* passed the Chinese censors in January 1937 and was released in China with the deletion of only a few scenes depicting poverty and violence. Ironically, although the film successfully passed both the U.S. and Chinese censors in 1937, when MGM submitted it for broader overseas release in 1943, the hyper-cautious U.S. Office of War Information (OWI) objected to the film's references to slavery and concubinage, which it deemed offensive to Chinese sensibilities. To secure China's support in the United States' military campaign against the Japanese, OWI encouraged Hollywood to emphasize the nobility of the Chinese people and to refrain from portraying them as "backward illiterates." U.S. national interests dovetailed with Chinese national interest during the Pacific war, albeit at the expense of *The Good Earth*.

China's unusual demand of an in-house censor sent a chill through Hollywood, prompting studios to voluntarily consult with the Chinese consulate on all China-related projects. The Chinese consulate was able to monitor Hollywood production, and frequently alerted Nanjing for preemptive measures against "anti-Chinese" films even before prints were made available for review—so much so that Frederick Herron, the foreign manager of the MPPDA, complained frequently about the Chinese consul's meddling, calling the Chinese diplomat a "little whippersnapper."[12]

While exercising tough content regulation on imports, the Chinese government did little to curb Hollywood's China expansion and help domestic productions. By the mid-1930s, almost the entire U.S. annual output of roughly 300 features were screened in China. By the late 1930s, the eight American studios (Warner Brothers, Twentieth Century–Fox, Paramount, Radio City, Columbia, United Artists, Metro-Goldwyn-Mayer, and Universal) had all set up offices in Shanghai with a long-term China interest in mind. They had come to a unified agreement to "manage screening rights between theaters and to minimize disputes among themselves," which allowed them to "drive a hard bargain against theater owners."[13] Films generally arrived in China three to six months after their U.S. release. After sound arrived, many theaters in China continued to screen old silent Hollywood films. U.S. talkies were effectively rendered silent while being exhibited in the interior in unwired venues. Almost no U.S. releases in China carried Chinese subtitles. Instead, a printed program was handed to patrons before each screening to summarize the story.

After much lobbying by local theaters, the Chinese government passed a regulation effective July 1, 1933, that required all talkies to carry Chinese subtitles.[14] Hollywood complained, arguing that it could not afford to add subtitles at an average cost of $500 per feature in a Hollywood lab.[15] In reality, as a *Variety* reporter noted, in China "the [film] business is very profitable, at least for the Americans."[16] Nonetheless, the majors threatened a full boycott, and MPPDA representatives persuaded Chinese officials to postpone implementation of the law indefinitely. Despite the hiccup, by 1934, 78 percent of films screened came from the United

States, with Chinese domestic films taking up only 8.5 percent of the Chinese market.[17] Seeking a greater share of the local market, the Chinese film industry lobbied the KMT government to exercise more control over China's cultural and entertainment affairs.

Unlike many countries in which the exhibition of imports was heavily controlled to protect the domestic industry, the Chinese government prior to the 1930s mostly applied a laissez-faire economic policy to film exhibition. Various bureaucratic procedures actually resulted in domestic productions paying a higher tax than most foreign films did at distribution.[18] Fighting back against this unequal treatment, the Chinese film industry demanded government intervention to protect domestic production and market access. Film practitioners lobbied the government to abolish the tax-free treaty forced upon the Manchu government by Japanese and European armed forces. Zhou Jianyun, Star's business manager, published an article in 1928, titled "The right to taxation and Chinese cinema," urging the government to levy a tax on film imports.[19] Other film critics such as Ying Dou also voiced their concern over the lack of taxation on foreign films. The NFCC subsequently adopted a series of measures to safeguard the domestic film industry throughout the 1930s. It reversed an earlier mandate requesting subtitles for all imports and forbade distribution companies from subtitling foreign talkies so as to protect China's own sound films.[20] It charged foreign films reviewing fees but either completely exempted Chinese films from such charges or significantly lowered the fees applied to Chinese films. Also, "problematic" Chinese films were treated with more lenience than "problematic" imports. Chinese censorship's protective measures effectively gave the greenlight to a wave of Chinese entertainment films, most of them with inferior production values compared to imports.

Consolidation and Going Abroad: The Restructuring of the Chinese Film Industry from the late 1920s to the late 1930s

Foreign capital effectively monopolized the distribution and exhibition of films in China and was responsible for the construction of many well-equipped theaters in big cosmopolitan cities such as Shanghai and Beijing. In response, Chinese film practitioners saw the building and expansion of their own theater chains as the only path to survival and waged battles against the Western monopoly. Star took the lead in building its own distribution network and theater chain. Its Central Theater in Shanghai became a paradise for domestic films. Star also bought out foreign-run distribution-exhibition networks and reached out to several local companies with the idea of forming a consolidated exhibition network; United Film Exchange (UFE) was established in 1926 to exclusively screen films made by its affiliated companies.[21] Tianyi, which enjoyed a larger market share than UFE by relying on the popularity of costume drama, was the only big studio that refused to cooperate with UFE. UFE retaliated by publicly denouncing costume drama and endorsing films of better quality, and by demanding that its contracting distribution companies not purchase films from Tianyi.

The conflict between UFE and Tianyi became the first distribution battle in Chinese film history. The competition was kept low key, as UFE was mindful of any comparison of its monopolistic practice to Hollywood's market dominance in China. Tianyi lost part of its market share in Shanghai as a result and turned instead to expand its Southeast Asian market.

UFE's monopolistic control, spearheaded by Star, alienated many partners within UFE. A series of internal power struggles ensued, eroding UFE's financial strength, eventually leading to its breakup in July 1929. UFE's former theater chains went their own way, forming various small production companies that competed against each other, wreaking havoc on the fragile market for domestic films and prompting a call for an integrated national film industry and a united Chinese national cinema. A newcomer, Lianhua (United China Film Company), emerged as a formidable player to lead the charge toward reviving Chinese cinema in the 1930s. The expansion and restructuring in the Chinese film industry soon led to dominance by three big studios, Lianhua, Star, and Tianyi.

LIANHUA AND LUO MINGYOU

Luo Mingyou, the co-founder of Lianhua together with Li Mingwei, came from an affluent merchant family in Hong Kong with ties to high-ranking KMT officials. While a law school student at Peking University in 1919, the cinema aficionado with ample financial resources at his disposal bought the 700-seat Beijing Opera House and converted it into a modern movie theater. Luo named his theater Zhenguang, or Real Light in English translation, and screened what he considered quality Hollywood films, including two popular hits: D.W. Griffith's *Way Down East* and *Orphans of the Storm*.[22] Real Light offered lower ticket prices than foreign-owned cinemas and provided Chinese captions for all films screened, a benefit not normally accorded to imports in China. Luo also offered special student discounts every Sunday morning. Unfortunately, only half a year into its operation, a fire broke out and burned down the theater. Undaunted, Luo rebuilt the theater and opened it a year later.

Seeking to establish his own theater chain, Luo bought cinema houses from foreign owners in Beijing and Tianjin. By 1927, he had over twenty movie theaters under his belt. Luo turned Real Light into Huabei (Northern China) Company, a theater chain that by 1929 controlled film distribution and exhibition in Tianjin, Taiyuan, Jinan, Shijiazhuang, Harbin, and Shenyang, six major cities in northern China, while Star-led UFE was losing its grip on the Shanghai film market.

Despite relying on imports to attract affluent patrons, Luo objected to Hollywood's market dominance in China. Foremost a southern patriot, Luo was determined to rescue Chinese cinema from under the shadow of Hollywood. He was one of the first Chinese film entrepreneurs to appreciate Hollywood's vertically and horizontally integrated industrial structure and practice. As Luo saw it, Chinese cinema suffered from poor production quality; the separation of production, distribution, and exhibition; and race-to-the-bottom competition among production companies. Luo urged cooperation among Chinese studios and encouraged the studios to supply Chinese-run theaters with higher-quality domestic films. He also advised theater owners to consolidate domestic chains and liquidate foreign-run theaters. Akin to Star's effort in building UFE in Shanghai, Luo courted various production companies, including Great China-Lily, Star, Shanghai Cinema and Theater Company, and Hong Kong Film Company, for a possible merger under the newly named United China Film Company. With strong financial backing from his family and wealthy friends, Luo acquired shares of these companies and signed contracts with them for exclusive screening of their films in his theaters.

Following in the footsteps of theater-owner-turned-studio-moguls in Hollywood, Luo supplied his own theater chains with quality and profitable products by extending business into film production to control the final product. The coming of sound offered him an opportunity to expand, though once the initial novelty wore off, Chinese audiences lost their appetite for foreign talkies. The language barrier also made it diffi-cult for Hollywood talkies to have mass appeal in China, given that most Chinese could not understand the English language. Meanwhile, Hol-lywood had stopped exporting silent pictures, leaving Chinese theaters scampering for screening material. With one foot firmly planted in distribution as he envisioned the inevitable demand for domestic talkies, Luo ventured into production in 1929, co-writing a screenplay, *Spring Dream in the Old Capital*, with Shiling Zhu, who worked as a writer and translator for short scenarios and subtitles while at the Real Light The-ater.[23] Luo officially registered his new company, Lianhua, in Hong Kong on October 25, 1930, merging Huabei Film Company with Li Mingwei's China Sun Motion Picture Company and a few other Shanghai-based companies.[24]

Lianhua opened a management branch in Shanghai the following year to oversee three studios and one production facility in Beijing that dou-bled as the company's northern China branch. Luo consolidated theaters in Hong Kong, Shanghai, Guangzhou, and northeast China to establish a single distribution-exhibition network while scouting locations in coastal cities to build additional theaters. In May 1930, U.S.-educated Sun Yu directed Lianhua's debut film, *Spring Dream in the Old Capital* (aka *Reminiscences of Beijing*, 1930), a morality tale about an entangled relationship involving a transgressive husband, a wronged wife, and an evil concubine.[25] The silent melodrama became an instant classic, with box-office revenue during its premiere in Shanghai, Hong Kong, and Beijing equaling that of an average Chinese film's full run. The film's success heralded the beginning of the revival of Chinese national cin-ema via quality films of artistic merit as opposed to Tianyi- and Star-led commercial films, which began to lose their charm by the early 1930s. Born in Chongqing, a major city in southwest China, Sun Yu attended Tsinghua University in Beijing and continued his education in drama at the University of Wisconsin–Madison.[26] Upon receiving his degree in 1925, Sun headed to New York and enrolled at the New York Institute of

Photography, where he learned cinematography and film editing. He also took evening courses in screenwriting at Columbia University.[27] Sun returned to China in the summer of 1926. The same year Sun directed *Spring Dreams in the Old Capital*, Sun also directed Lianhua's second feature, *Wild Flowers* (1930), a melodrama about a tortuous courtship between a young man from a wealthy family and a flower girl turned singer. The film was a popular hit particularly among urban youth and intellectuals, proving the ability of quality domestic films to attract coveted elite viewers. Both films featured Ruan Lingyu, one of the most iconic Chinese film stars of the 1930s who committed suicide at the tender age of twenty-four. Sun went on to direct a series of socially conscious films in the early to mid-1930s and became a major left-wing film director working for Lianhua.

In its effort to boost Chinese domestic films, Lianhua urged Chinese audiences to "treat our domestic film like our own child."[28] The company promoted the idea that the content and style of Chinese films ought to reflect China's unique cultural heritage and display China's national merits.[29] Lianhua made twelve pictures in 1930 and 1931, most of them socially conscious melodramas. Luo lost all his northern China theaters in 1931 when the Japanese invaded Manchuria. Japanese armed forces marched into Shanghai in January 1932, damaging Lianhua's production back lot. Despite the challenge, the same year saw the arrival of Lianhua's social realist film phase with titles such as *Three Modern Women* (Tian Han) and *Wild Rose* (Sun Yu), which addressed contemporary social ills. Lianhua's turn to social realism owed much to the influence of a group of left-wing playwright-turned-filmmakers, including Sun Yu, who were affiliated with the Chinese Communist Party (CCP). At the time Lianhua launched its "revival of national cinema" movement, a left-wing film team led by underground CCP members began to systematically infiltrate the film industry. Lianhua was one of the studios penetrated by the leftist film team, which introduced themes of class struggle and anti-imperialism to Lianhua's slates.

Fearful of the CCP's growing influence, the KMT launched the New Life Movement in 1934 to promote Confucianism, Western Christianity, and Chinese nationalism as a counterforce to socialism and communism while rejecting Western-style democracy and individualism. The KMT decreed that the film industry must follow the doctrines of the

New Life Movement, which called for propriety, righteousness, honesty, and a sense of shame at a time of national emergency. Censors promptly cracked down on the leftist film movement, threatening to sabotage any production that promoted class struggle. While cherishing the creative energy the pro-CCP filmmakers brought, Luo remained close to the KMT and made an effort to balance Lianhua's political positioning. The company produced, paradoxically, Shanghai's most reactionary and most radical films. Lianhua was emblematic of a domestic film industry caught in the crossfire of competing political forces. As the company sought to strike a balance between opposite political forces, it turned inward to focus on improving production quality, nurturing in-house acting talents and training in-house directors with the most advanced cinematic techniques, raising overall production quality, and endearing Lianhua titles to students and intellectuals. "Promote arts, propagate culture, enlighten the public, and save the film industry"[30] became the company's overriding credo. Lianhua's quality progressive films such as *The Goddess* (Wu Yonggang, 1934), *Song of the Fishermen* (Cai Chusheng, 1934), and *New Woman* (Cai Chusheng, 1935) contributed to the arrival of Chinese cinema's first golden era in the mid-1930s.

Yet Lianhua's quality films began to lose their appeal amidst the chaos of the Japanese invasion. The films were criticized as elitist and out of touch with the struggles of working-class people. Luo left Lianhua in 1936 and eventually made his way to Hong Kong. Lianhua collapsed when the second Sino-Japanese War broke out in 1937. Japan took over the Chinese territory in Shanghai in August 1937 after a brutal battle at the Sihang Warehouse, which lasted over three months, in which the KMT army suffered heavy losses and eventually retreated. The fall of Shanghai after the devastating Sihang battle was captured in the blockbuster Chinese war film *The Eight Hundred* (Guan Hu), a film that restarted the COVID-19-depressed Chinese film market in the summer of 2020. In the film, a KMT general leads 452 young officers and soldiers to defend Sihang Warehouse against 20,000 Japanese troops under an order by Chiang Kai-shek to boost morale to the Chinese and rally support from the Allies, who, as depicted in the film, were able to view the battle from the foreign concession area in Shanghai across from Suzhou Creek.

The Nationalist forces withdrew from Shanghai in late 1937 and set up a wartime capital in the inland city Chongqing. Chongqing served as KMT's wartime capital during the second Sino-Japanese War and was considered, together with Washington, D.C., London, and Moscow, the world's four antifascist command centers during the period. Many Lianhua filmmakers including Sun Yu fled to Chongqing where they directed patriotic films praising the anti-Japanese war effort. The fall of Shanghai in 1937 also suspended Star's operation. A fire destroyed Star's main studio in 1938 and the company closed down permanently.

JOURNEY TO THE EAST: TIANYI'S SOUTHEAST
ASIA MEDIA EMPIRE

While Lianhua and Star looked to the West for cultural inspiration and cinematic validation, Tianyi turned southeast to seek market expansion and over time created the most sophisticated horizontal integration in the Chinse film industry during the period. Ongoing civil conflicts had weakened China's domestic market by obstructing inland expansion of film distribution networks, leaving the diasporic Chinese communities in Southeast Asia the primary overseas market for Chinese films prior to the mid-1920s.[31] Tianyi was the only company that actively cultivated the Southeast Asian market. Shaw Brothers began to integrate vertically from early on. The company engaged in cross-media ownership in the 1920s. As the film scholar Poshek Fu points out,[32] when Runme and Runrun Shaw began their cinema chain business in the early 1920s, they also entered the world of the burgeoning and increasingly popular multipurpose entertainment parks that housed cabarets, joget dance stages, bangsawan stages, Chinese opera, food stalls, magic shows, and gambling stalls. Shaw Brothers also operated their own printing house called the Shaw Printing Works, which churned out publicity materials including fan magazines. As noted by the scholar Lily Kong in Poshek Fu's book,[33] Shaw productions merged globalizing trends with local content, seeking to reterritorialize economies.

The Shaw brothers expanded their business mainly in Singapore-Malaysia, Thailand, and Vietnam. Tianyi's Southeast Asia operation struggled initially, competing with local companies and branches of other Shanghai companies. The brothers Runme and Runrun relocated to Singapore in 1928 to better manage the local business. The brothers traveled around the region, conducting open-air screenings via mobile projectors, which allowed them to bring films to previously inaccessible small towns and rural areas.[34] Runrun Shaw jokingly referred to his Chinese name in romanization, "run-run," as befitting the time he spent running around Southeast Asia doing traveling shows. Through hard work and sheer will, in less than a decade the two brothers built a regional distribution circuit in Singapore-Malaysia under the name of Shaw Brothers Ltd. to distribute Tianyi films as well as titles from other Shanghai and Hong Kong–based film companies.

With a circuit of about thirty theaters in Southeast Asia under their control, Shaw Brothers shifted gears to tailor Tianyi's productions to the predominantly Cantonese-speaking populations in the region and began to produce Cantonese-language films in 1933. The initial such film it produced was *White Golden Dragon* (Tang Xiaodan, 1933), the first sound film in Cantonese. Produced at the Shaws' Shanghai studio, the film came out to only modest success. But it led to full-blown Cantonese film production in Hong Kong the following year, when Tianyi moved to Hong Kong to expand its Cantonese production. Tianyi outpaced all other studios in sound production by the early 1930s, and its Hong Kong branch was the lead studio in making Cantonese sound films. One upshot of the transition to sound was Tianyi's shifting focus from making period costume dramas to contemporary urban dramas. As theaters equipped with sound served mostly upper- and middle-class audiences, Tianyi started to produce more politically engaging and culturally sophisticated films catering to urban audiences. By the 1930s, Shaw Brothers had linked British Hong Kong, China, and Southeast Asia into a transnational network of entertainment businesses.

The outbreak of the Sino-Japanese War in 1937 led to the closure of Tianyi's Shanghai office. Tianyi terminated its Shanghai operation in early 1937 and permanently relocated to Hong Kong, where it produced chiefly Cantonese films with a new business strategy targeting the Southeast Asian market. The studio was aptly renamed Nanyang (South Sea). Nanyang films were popular in Cantonese-speaking Guangdong and Guangxi in China as well as in Southeast Asian Chinese communities.

As pointed out by the Hong Kong–based film critic Law Kar, Shaw Brothers boasted the largest distribution network for both Mandarin and Cantonese films for Nanyang during the period.[35] Nanyang's operation depended on the steady cash flow and distribution network of

Shaw's Singapore operation, which itself relied on the constant supply of talent, skills, and equipment from Hong Kong, Shanghai, and Guangdong. Shaw's enterprise was expansive in its scale of business, beginning with regional reach and eventually extending to a global scale. By 1939, Shaw Brothers operated a chain of 139 cinemas across Singapore, Malaysia, Thailand, Indonesia, and Indochina. Shaw Brothers was also responsible for distributing and exhibiting productions from other global studios. Under the Shaw banner were films made in India, Pakistan, the Philippines, Taiwan, Japan, Indonesia, Thailand, Vietnam, the United States, and Europe, making Shaw the largest distributor of motion pictures globally at the time. Runrun Shaw's business instinct and personal ambition meshed well with his nationalistic aspiration to introduce "through celluloid images to people of different languages and races the cultural and artistic traditions of China."[36] Shaw aspired to transform Chinese cinema into a world-class production, on par with U.S. and Japanese films. The Shaw Brothers' regional entertainment business continued to expand well into World War II until the Japanese destroyed many of their properties in both Hong Kong and Singapore-Malaysia.

Chinese Cinema from the Second Sino-Japanese War to 1949

The second Sino-Japanese War temporarily disrupted film activities in China as Japan's 1937 bombing of Shanghai largely decimated China's film industry, forcing thirty small companies out of business. Sixteen out of thirty-nine theaters in Shanghai were destroyed in the bombing, most of them theaters screening Chinese films. The Japanese occupying force banned all films with anti-Japan sentiment, leading to the shutdown of many remaining Shanghai studios and a mass exodus of Shanghai filmmakers. One film studio remaining in Shanghai was the New China Film Company[37] (New China, Xinhua). Founded in 1934, New China would supplant all the existing big players to become the leading player in Shanghai's film industry.

Zhang Shankun, the company's founder, came from a wealthy merchant family in Shanghai. While studying at Nanyang University in Shanghai, Zhang ran a profitable campus movie theater. He worked as an advertising agent for a tobacco company after college and got involved in Shanghai's underworld and became a protégé of Huang Jinrong, one of the city's most notorious mafia bosses. With Huang's support, Zhang took control of two popular and lucrative entertainment centers in the city, Big World and Gong Theater. He started his real adventure in the film business by experimenting with screening movies during the intervals of theatrical performances. Upon founding New China in 1934, he released two films, *A Knight-Errant Named Hongyang* (Yang Xiaozhong, 1935) and *The New Peach Blossom Fan* (Ouyang Yuqian, 1935), both box-office hits. New China Film Company's early productions capitalized on the popularity of the leftist film movement, tackling progressive social themes. Within two years, Zhang churned out a number of socially conscious and technically well-crafted titles, including *A Sorrowful Song* (Shi Dongshan, 1936), *The Pioneers* (Wu Yonggang, 1936), *Singing at Midnight* (Ma-Xu Weibang, 1937), and *Marching Youth* (Shi Dongshan, 1937).

DOING AWAY WITH HOLLYWOOD: CHONGQING AND NATIONAL DEFENSE CINEMA

Japan's invasion of China would contribute to the eventual defeat in China of Hollywood. The war against Japan upset the commercial, urban, and Hollywood-driven characteristics of early Chinese cinema, subsequently solidifying the determination for a different style of cinema driven by patriotism and enlightenment. While films in Japanese-occupied Shanghai were either politically neutral or propaganda pictures for Japanese audiences, wartime films in KMT-controlled Chongqing and CCP-controlled Yan'an championed patriotism and Chinese resistance. In August 1937, China signed a nonaggression treaty with the Soviet Union by which the Soviets would provide much-needed military equipment to help China keep the Japanese at bay. Consequently, both the CCP and KMT aligned with the Soviet Union, leading to a call for the rejection of Hollywood in favor of the Soviet model in Chinese cinema, particularly in the Chinese government–sponsored production center of Chongqing.

The Chinese film industry at the time was geographically segmented into east (Shanghai), south (Hong Kong), northeast (Manchuria), southwest (Chongqing), and northwest (Yan'an and Taiyuan). KMT-controlled studios retreated to Chongqing in southwest China and produced documentary and feature films. Some left-wing filmmakers followed the CCP to Yan'an, the northwest inland area's high plateau. Shanghai's foreign concession area renewed commercial film production in east China, while Changchun in northeast China was Manchurian Motion Pictures' (Man'ei) base, producing propaganda films on behalf of the Japanese occupying force.

Established in Changchun in 1937 by the puppet Manchurian government and the South Manchurian Railroad Corporation, Man'ei was directly linked to Japanese-controlled distribution networks and Japanese film studios (e.g., Toho and Shochiku). The company built a new studio in Changchun with state-of-the-art equipment in 1939 and employed 900 people by December 1940 and 1,800 by November 1944. The company was prolific in churning out entertainment and educational feature films, children's programs, and newsreels in Japanese and Chinese that propagated Manchurian "national policy" and promulgated the concept of the Greater East Asia Co-Prosperity Sphere.[38] Heavily dependent upon Japanese filmmakers who had limited knowledge about China or Chinese audiences, the company could not compete with Shanghai films for market share. Manchurian audiences preferred Shanghai films. As the film scholar Zhang Yingjin noted, Shanghai films such as *Yue Fei Defends the Nation* (Wu Yonggang, 1940), *Crossroads* (Shen Xiling, 1937), and *Singing at Midnight* (Ma-Xu Weibang, 1937) were household titles among Chinese audiences during the period.[39]

In the unoccupied areas, China's locus of film production was the Central Film Studio, which started out in Wuhan and then moved to the wartime capital of Chongqing. The KMT and the CCP collaborated on film production in Chongqing under the leadership of the KMT, which strived to transcend party lines in order to present a united China.[40] The Central Film Studio (Zhongdian)[41] and the China Film Studio (Zhongzhi)[42] were the two major companies that produced films in wartime Chongqing. Chongqing cinema promoted national defense and liberation and endorsed a "national style" and a "national manner." The KMT government adopted the Soviet model of state ownership and sponsorship of the domestic film industry at the service of the interest of the party-state. In practice, Chongqing filmmakers rejected Hollywood's star system and narrative style in favor of Soviet montage theory and realism.

Debates raged among filmmakers about the future direction of film production, leading to a reappraisal of the state of Chinese cinema.

Films from the Soviet Union first appeared in China in the 1920s. The Soviet Union began supporting the KMT as early as 1921. The Comintern instructed the CCP to sign a military treaty with the KMT in 1923. A year after, China imported the first Soviet film, *The Burial of Lenin*, a news documentary screened in March 1924. The Soviet Union and China resumed their diplomatic relationship in early 1932 to form a united front against the Japanese. Access to the Chinese film market became a by-product of the diplomatic recognition. Although left-leaning Shanghai intellectuals looked with favor on films from the USSR, Soviet movies were not particularly popular among ordinary moviegoers in China. Chinese filmmakers and literary circles nonetheless embraced Soviet film for its sheer power of political persuasion, and wholeheartedly endorsed Bolshevik leaders' position on cinema's propaganda function.

Pro-KMT filmmaker and critic Pan Jienong asserted that we "must first of all cast aside the 'American style' that we have long cherished."[43] He faulted Lianhua for the veteran Shanghai studio's penchant for "a European and American style that was more economical and technical [in terms of narrative]."[44] Chongqing filmmakers deemed Western techniques deployed in many trendy Chinese films incomprehensible to Chinese soldiers and farmers who were rapidly replacing the urban petit bourgeois as dominant audiences for domestic films.[45] While Hollywood-style films were criticized as being escapist and obscuring political messages, Soviet film was perceived as adopting "an attitude of confronting reality in the face."[46] Chinese cinema was summoned to "follow the Soviet Union in nationalizing the film industry and making cinematic spiritual food for the masses of the nation. . . ."[47] Chongqing filmmakers called for a "national film style" that would cater to proletarians with limited cinematic experience and knowledge to effectively carry out propaganda missions.

THE ORPHAN ISLAND: SHANGHAI CINEMA DURING
THE SINO-JAPANESE WAR

The Japanese invasion transformed the Shanghai film industry. Chinese-controlled parts of Shanghai fell to Japan after the Battle of Shanghai, which was depicted in *The Eight Hundred*, ending in China's defeat in November 1937. Many established studios and a large number of filmmakers subsequently fled Shanghai for the relative safety of China's interior. Star and Lianhua chose to close down instead of cooperating with the occupiers. Japanese troops initially used Star's studio as a military camp and later tried to persuade the studio to produce films promoting "friendship between China and Japan." When Star refused, the Japanese burned down the studio, leading to its permanent closure. Lianhua was also decimated by the war and most of its filmmakers retreated to Chongqing with the KMT troops. The foreign concessions remained largely intact, becoming a prosperous enclave surrounded by war zones, attracting some 400,000 Chinese refugees over the next four years, until the Japanese invasion on December 8, 1941, following the attack on Pearl Harbor the day before.

Immediately following the Japanese occupation and with the retreat of Chinese film studios to inland China, film activities suffered a temporary downturn in Shanghai. The New China Film Company founded by Zhang Shankun stepped into this void. Zhang gathered nearly all the remaining influential film actors, directors, and technicians and put them on the company's payroll. New China produced four films in 1937, including the anti-Japanese film *Soaring Aspirations* (Wu Yonggang). The collapse in film exhibition in Shanghai quickly bottomed out in 1938. There were over fifty movie theaters in Shanghai at the time and nearly all of them enjoyed a full house on a daily basis. New theaters were rapidly constructed. Shi Dongshan, a veteran filmmaker, noted that "since the KMT troops retreated from Shanghai and the battle line moved inland, the Shanghai film industry has resumed normal business. Because most of the middle and upper classes from the coastal provinces and even from Central China live in Shanghai, the film business is flourishing even more than before the war."[48] Indeed, wartime Shanghai was a magnet for many Chinese who sought refuge in the foreign concessions. Nearly five million people packed into the foreign concessions. This huge population increase was a boon to show business, and all entertainment venues including movie theaters were crowded day and night. The exhibition bonanza stimulated film production. Zhang Shankun seized the opportunity and made eighteen films in 1938, most of them escapist entertainment fare catering to the tastes of "low-brow" urbanites.

That same year New China also released the patriotic film *Diaochan* (Bu Wancang, 1938), an adaption of a legendary Chinese tale about a beautiful young woman named Diaochan ("sable cicada") who marries a treacherous court official in order to save the country. Production had started before the Sino-Japanese War when Zhang Shankun vowed to make a "solemn and stirring film about national defense" in order to arouse the audience's "national consciousness."[49] War interrupted production but shooting resumed when the situation in the foreign concessions relaxed. The resulting film created a sensation in Shanghai, Hong Kong, and Singapore, ushering in Chinese cinema's second wave of costume drama films reminiscent of Tianyi's costume dramas in the late 1920s and early 1930s, though unlike Tianyi's scholar/beauty-based romantic tales, New China promoted patriotism-based Chinese legends, which appealed to wartime audiences. New China's costume drama's popularity lasted for the next two years.

As its production expanded, New China set up two subsidiary companies, Huaxin and Huacheng, in 1938 to mass-produce entertainment fare for war-torn Shanghai audiences. This escapist entertainment wave led to sharp rebukes from the Chinese film community in Chongqing. Cai Chusheng took a shot at both New China productions and its Shanghai audiences in 1938: "The pitiful five million fellow countrymen in the 'Orphan Island' who came from various occupied areas, and those people living in the occupied or non-occupied areas generally have not had a chance to see how brave KMT troops are in their fight against Japanese invaders. They are unfortunately poisoned by those films, which propagate feudalism, superstition, sex and violence. And they have forgotten the danger our country is facing and their responsibility towards our nation. What they are doing is exactly opposite to our government's call."[50]

Shanghai filmmakers defended their practices. Zhang Shankun countered that "the Chinese film industry is struggling under extremely difficult circumstances. We have unspeakable difficulties selecting historical subjects such as those in *It Happened in One Night*. Therefore, we hope audiences can forgive us and show sympathy."[51] The film in question, *It Happened in One Night* (Chen Yiqing, 1939), is a melodrama about a love affair between Zhengde, the eleventh emperor of the Ming dynasty, and a beautiful woman he met one night against the backdrop of the war against foreign invasions. It was during Zhengde's reign from 1505 to 1521 that the first direct European contacts with China occurred.

In the spring of 1939, New China released *Mulan Joins the Army* (Bu Wancang). Its theme of resistance against Japanese aggression made the film the most popular produced in Shanghai during the "Orphan Island" period. Inspired by the box-office success of *Diaochan* and *Mulan*, New China made more box-office pleasing costume dramas, though the majority of these films did not include anti-Japanese themes. The studio produced twenty-four films in 1939, the most releases of any company during the Sino-Japanese War. Zhang registered his film studio as an American business in order to avoid harassment by the Japanese.

After the Japanese entered the foreign concessions in late 1941, New China was absorbed, together with eleven other Shanghai studios, into a Japanese-controlled conglomerate, Zhonglian, with Zhang serving as the general manager of the new umbrella company. Under Zhang's management, Zhonglian produced 130 titles between 1942 and 1945, some of them propaganda pieces for the Japanese, others with covert patriotic messages. Zhang Shankun reportedly sent scripts of patriotic themes to Chongqing for advice and approval through underground KMT agents.[52] *Eternity* (Bu Wancang et al., 1943), a historical film with an antioccupation theme about the Opium War and featuring the Japanese star Li Xianglan in a secondary story line, was an instant hit nationwide. Zhang was jailed briefly by the Japanese on suspicion of association with the Chinese resistance. Ironically, Zhang was later charged by the Chinese for treason during the postwar period. Zhang fled to Hong Kong and took charge of Yonghua Film Company in an attempt to resurrect his film career. Yonghua produced several big-budget movies such as *The Spirit of the Nation* (Bu Wancang, 1948) and *Sorrows of the Forbidden City* (Zhu Shilin, 1948) by renowned filmmakers. These titles, however, did not perform well at the box office.

Shanghai remained under occupation until Japan surrendered on August 15, 1945. Several of Lianhua's directors, including Cai Chusheng, returned to Shanghai after the war. Cai had fled to Hong Kong when the war broke out, and then left for Chongqing when Hong Kong fell to the Japanese. He returned to Shanghai in 1946 to revive the Lianhua name by forming the Lianhua Film Society. Eventually, the new Lianhua was renamed the Kunlun Film Company,[53] which went on to produce many of the most memorable films of the late 1940s, including *The Spring River Flows East* (Cai Chusheng and Zheng Junli, 1947) and *Crows and Sparrows* (Zheng Junli, 1949).

Sino-Hollywood During and After the War

The Second World War interrupted Hollywood's Far East sales and changed the dynamic between Hollywood and the Chinese government. After establishing its film company Zhonglian in Shanghai in 1942, Japan rapidly took over all film activities in Shanghai and eventually enacted a ban on Hollywood films in China in 1943. Japan's ban on Hollywood led to a surge of Chinese domestic productions by Zhonglian in 1943–44, in both output and influence. Zhonglian produced twenty-four titles in 1942 and twenty-three in 1943.[54] Much to the displeasure of the Japanese censors, though, Shanghai filmmakers continued to model their productions on Hollywood melodramas. But the surge of Hollywood-influenced Chinese cinema proved to be short-lived. Rampant inflation rendered wartime cinema a difficult business to run. Production costs per feature skyrocketed from 100,000 yuan in 1940 to at least 300,000 yuan in 1942, 1 million yuan in 1943, and over 10 million yuan in January 1945. Correspondingly, first-run theater ticket prices soared from 8 yuan in 1942 to 60 yuan in 1945.[55] As economic pressure mounted, Zhonglian merged with the Japanese film producer Nagamasa Kawakita's China Movie Company and Japanese-controlled Shanghai Movie Theaters Company in May 1943 to become United China Motion Picture Company (Huaying). From 1943 to 1945, Huaying produced eighty features, most of them popular entertainment fare.[56] In its comprehensive vertical and horizontal integration, Huaying presaged the nationalization of the entire Chinese film industry pursued by the KMT in the postwar era. This total nationalizing effort would be completed by the CCP in the 1950s.

After the war, the Nationalist government confiscated the production equipment of both Zhonglian and Manchurian Motion Pictures. The KMT government had established the Central Film Service (CFS) in Chongqing in 1943 to control film distribution and screening in nonoccupied areas. The government moved CFS from Chongqing to Shanghai to start the process of nationalization by taking over distribution companies and theaters previously under Japanese or collaborators' control. In allocating resources, CFS typically gave favorable treatment to affiliated studios or studios that had a relationship with the government. One unintended consequence of CFS's favoritism promoting films from affiliated studios and studios that extolled the KMT was to reduce theaters' incentives to screen imported films, which benefited the growth of Chinese domestic pictures.

Japan's defeat in August 1945 allowed a brief comeback of Hollywood films, which quickly took up a 92 percent share of screenings.[57] Hollywood enjoyed its best year ever in 1946, coasting on pent-up demand created during the war.[58] In the United States, cinema-going surged after the war, as millions of returned servicemen sought female companions, with cinema-going as one of the popular dating rituals. Boosted by its domestic surge, Hollywood returned to China with a vengeance immediately after the war. In Shanghai alone, from August 1945 to May 1949,[59] a total of 1,896 American films, including newly imported ones and those that were blocked in China during the war, were available for public screening. During this period, Shanghai's first-run theaters showed 1,083 Hollywood titles, most of them from the eight major studios. In 1946 alone, 352 out of 383 films screened in Shanghai's first-run theaters were American films; only 13 were Chinese titles, while British films numbered 15 and 3 were Soviet titles.[60] In 1947, *Gone with the Wind* (Victor Fleming, 1939) sold 170,000 tickets, and *Arabian Nights* (John Rawlins, 1942) sold 220,000 tickets from two Shanghai theaters alone.

But Hollywood soon suffered financial setbacks amidst skyrocketing inflation in China during the postwar era. China after World War II plunged into a devastating civil war between the reigning KMT government and the rebel CCP. The economy had already been in a downward trajectory during the war; the civil war further decimated the economy, leading to intense inflation. To combat rising prices, the KMT government imposed price restrictions, which prevented Hollywood studios from raising ticket prices just as costs soared amidst the inflation. Government's price controls unintentionally benefited domestic films as movie tickets became relatively more affordable, drawing to theaters a disproportionate share of spectators from lower social strata who traditionally favored Chinese domestic productions.

When the war ended in 1945, fewer than ten Chinese domestic production companies were operating, but over eight hundred theaters were hungry for movies. Consequently, suppliers had an upper hand. Though foreign distributors continued to monopolize first-run upscale theaters, domestic distributors surreptitiously developed alongside imports. There were four private domestic theater chains in China at the time: United China Film Management, which distributed official, traditional, and more artistically inclined films; Shanghai Light, which oscillated between screening imports and domestic pictures; Hong Kong, which specialized in commercial fare; and the Liu brothers' Cathay, which screened its own productions as well as Hollywood imports and Hong Kong–produced Mandarin films. The four chains competed against each other for domestic pictures, helping to stimulate local output. Chinese cinema entered what film historians now call its second golden era.

The postwar rally of Chinese domestic films owed more to fierce competition among the domestic studios than to the Chinese film industry's conscious effort to battle Hollywood.[61] With little ability or will to compete with imports for the first-run theaters, domestic studios fought against each other for star actors, writers, and directors to feed their own distribution and exhibition networks. Prominent domestic studios during the period were all newcomers, such as Wenhua, Kunlun, and Zhongdian, all emerging in 1946–47 and most of them reconstituted from the ravages of old Shanghai studios. Responding to market demand, a few new production companies were formed alongside the rebuilt old companies, both settling into routine production starting in 1947, the same year that domestic distributors began to utilize Hollywood's blanket booking strategy to schedule simultaneous screenings of the same film in multiple theaters. The saturation or blanket release strategy and intensified marketing campaigns for domestic pictures thrust homegrown productions onto the center stage in Shanghai.

Hollywood majors suffered as a result. In a concerted effort to reclaim the Chinese market, eight Hollywood studios with interests in China formed the Film Board of Trade in 1947 in an attempt to relegate Chinese domestic films to the Chinese-language market. The cartel controlled 95 percent of the film business in Shanghai, while also dictating film scheduling. Hollywood blockbusters regained ground, with the belated showing of *Gone with the Wind* (Victor Fleming, 1939) and *Arabian*

Nights (John Rawlins, 1942) topping box-office charts. Hollywood's effort to recapture its old glory in China enraged the Chinese film community. Battles began between Chinese and Western firms for first-run movie houses. Local companies lobbied for favorable government policy as they set up their own film distribution chains to control and expand their market share. Chinese films of better quality entered theaters specializing in imports in 1947, splitting screen time equally with Hollywood films. Many second-tier theaters that previously screened predominantly foreign imports shifted gears to showcase domestic pictures.

Prospects for Hollywood in China looked increasingly grim. Deteriorating economic conditions in China were dramatically impacting Hollywood's profits. Skyrocketing inflation meant that there could be no guarantee of profit in Hollywood's share of film proceeds. Worsening inflation led to the unstable foreign exchange rates, which disrupted the regular revenue-sharing cycle for imports. Reacting to this unfavorable business environment, Hollywood studios began to reduce their releases in Shanghai. Hollywood imports dwindled from 881 in 1946 to 393 in 1947 and 272 in 1948. The vacuum created by this reduced Hollywood presence further opened up space for domestic films. While all films with over 100,000 viewers came from Hollywood in 1946, six Chinese titles posted viewership over 100,000 in comparison to seven Hollywood films in 1947.

As domestic output rose, market dynamics turned to favor the demand side, forcing studios to compete for theaters and screening slots. Theaters that showcased domestic pictures became more selective and refused to sign exclusive distribution agreements with production companies, which propelled Chinese studios to make films of better quality and entertainment value. Thus 1947–49 saw an unprecedented revival of Chinese cinema, as domestic distributors expanded their market share. More popular Chinese films entered the market beginning in 1947, with *Code Name Heaven No. 1* (Tu Guangqi, 1946) selling 150,000 tickets at the Empress alone, and *Long Live the Mistress!* (Sang Hu, 1947) scoring the same box office at the Empress and Jincheng. *Phony Phoenixes* (Huang Zuolin, 1947) was the top performer at the Grand Theater, selling 165,000 tickets.[62]

The Spring River Flows East, a landmark Chinese leftist film hailed as "China's best film of 1947" by the veteran leftist critic Xia Yan,[63] swept through several Shanghai theaters, selling 712,874 tickets between October 1947 and January 1948, with total audience figures likely to have exceeded 1 million.[64]

Hollywood's Domestic Decline and China Retreat[65]

Just as the Chinese film industry entered a "golden era" with unprecedented output of films of diverse political and stylistic persuasions amidst the chaos of the civil war, in the United States the House Un-American Activities Committee (HUAC) began to target Hollywood's writing community for subversive activities and Communist influence in the movie industry. By the fall of 1947, HUAC held a series of formal hearings and sent subpoenas to nineteen "friendly" and nineteen "unfriendly" witnesses from the industry. A group of Hollywood luminaries formed the Committee for the First Amendment and traveled to Washington to support the constitutional rights of the nineteen unfriendly witnesses and to voice their collective disapproval of the hearings. But the hearing went on and eleven of the nineteen were called to testify. Ten, however, refused to cooperate. The infamous "Hollywood Ten" were cited for contempt of Congress. They were soon abandoned by their studios and guilds and blacklisted for being suspected Communists and were thus denied employment in Hollywood. Blacklisting removed dozens—and eventually hundreds—of top artists from active production, creating a climate of fear and repression throughout an already weakened industry. The Big Eight's combined profits fell from an all-time high of $122 million in 1946 to $89 million in 1947, and the decline accelerated in 1948 with revenues and theater attendance falling sharply. Ironically, Hollywood under suspicion of Communist influence would be cut off completely from the Chinese market when the Communist Party took over China a year later.

Hollywood majors suffered an even heavier blow in May 1948 when the Supreme Court handed down a major decision, the so-called Paramount Decree, that effectively abolished the Hollywood studio system by banning block booking, blind bidding, price-fixing, and all privileged arrangements between studios and theaters. In addition, the integrated majors were ordered to divest themselves of their theater holdings so that they would function only as production-distribution companies. This brought an end to the studio-based production system with its contract personnel, steady cash flow, and regulated output. A domestically defeated Hollywood struggled further in China.

Emboldened by the positive outlook for domestic pictures, fourteen Chinese production companies lobbied the KMT's propaganda minister Li Weiguo on January 11, 1948, to encourage theaters to screen more domestic pictures and expand Chinese films globally. Studios in Shanghai further requested that the government issue a policy to reserve sixty days exclusively for domestic pictures, and to reduce the overall number of imports.[66] While 21 percent of Shanghai theaters exhibited domestic films in 1946, the number rose to 66.7 percent in 1947, roughly the same rate as in the prewar era. The number jumped to 84 percent in 1948. A 1948 sampling indicated that domestic films took up all cinema screens across the nation on certain dates: in all four theaters in Fuzhou on January 25, in all eight theaters in Nanjing on February 20, and in all five theaters in Xi'an on August 15.[67]

As the Chinese Civil War drew to an end, with the U.S.-backed KMT ceding ground to the CCP, Hollywood increasingly became disillusioned with China's political and economic instability and the looming defeat of the KMT. To add to the insult, the KMT government dramatically increased the customs duty on imported movies from $250 to $1,200 per feature in 1948 amidst stagnant ticket prices and with raging inflation. With no guarantee of monetary value in its share of box-office proceeds, Hollywood studios reduced their China releases. By 1948, Hollywood was losing market share in China. In Beijing, its share dropped from 60 percent in 1937 to 22 percent in 1948. In Shanghai, the majority of first-run theaters in 1948 showed Chinese features for the first time. To make matters worse, the KMT government mandated a price ceiling for what Hollywood could take from revenue sharing, making it difficult for Hollywood to profit from the Chinese market. Hollywood threatened to withdraw from the Chinese market.

In May 1948, the KMT's Social Security Bureau mandated that 30 percent of the seats at any given theater must be kept affordable. After several failed attempts at negotiating, the United China Film Board of Trade stopped supplying films to Shanghai's first-run theaters and provided only B movies to the second-tier theaters. The Hollywood cartel eventually retaliated against the KMT government by boycotting the Chinese market altogether. By October 1948, the United China Film Board of Trade ceased its operation in Shanghai, and left Shanghai in December. Only one Warner Brothers film was in circulation in Shanghai from December 1948 until the Communist takeover in October 1949.

The Chinese Civil War ended in the fall of 1949 with the KMT retreat to Taiwan, ceding the mainland to the People's Republic of China (PRC). Not long after the CCP took over Shanghai, U.S. films were criticized as vehicles for spreading "imperialist poison" and for "doping" the minds of Chinese audiences with "sex and legs." Hollywood's presence in China came to an abrupt halt in 1950 once the newly founded PRC banned Hollywood imports. Just before the Communist takeover, of the 211 movies shown in Shanghai, 142 (67 percent) were American. Soon thereafter, China became a closed market to Hollywood.

Hollywood's China run officially ended one year into the Chinese Communist Party's takeover of China when the Korean War pitted the U.S. army in deadly military confrontation against the Chinese volunteer army. The founding of the People's Republic of China at the end of the civil war would lead to the nationalization and centralization of the Chinese film industry in the early 1950s, under Communist Party directives. Film production in China from then until the mid-1980s followed Soviet-style centralized planning, with state ownership and subsidized production and churning out propaganda-driven films according to the state's production targets. China's once vibrant cinema dwindled as the endless political turmoil of the Maoist era wreaked havoc on China's cultural scene.

3

From Hollywood to Soviet Model: Building a Socialist Cinema

The Shanghai community has launched a campaign to denounce the poisonous films of the American and British imperialists. . . . People from all walks of life have launched various discussion forums to severely criticize the American and British films shown in Shanghai cinemas. The current market is said to have been flooded with these ridiculous films of low quality and negative impact, which seriously poison the Chinese people. The imperialists use these reactionary films to propagate their imperialist power, promote racial discrimination, distort class concepts, sell abnormal lifestyles, induce pornographic fantasies, and paralyze our will to fight, etc.

—"The Purge of the American and British Poisonous Films;
Shanghai People Demanding Governmental Censorship"
(published in *People's Daily*, September 21, 1949)[1]

From late 1932 to early 1933, the Isis Theater,[2] located in the Chinese part of Shanghai just 500 meters north of the international settlement boundary, became a designated place to showcase not Hollywood but Soviet movies. A total of 10,856 Russians relocated to Shanghai from Harbin, China's northeast city once known as the "Oriental Moscow" amidst the Japanese invasion of Harbin and the establishment of Manchukuo in 1932. The Russians became the second largest foreign population in Shanghai, making the city a major market for Soviet films from 1934 to 1937. Yet cinemas located in the foreign concessions in Shanghai were not under Chinese jurisdiction and foreign-controlled theaters did not welcome Bolshevik films. The foreign-controlled Municipal Council of the Shanghai International Settlement explicitly stated that "any film that carries a political message" should be handled carefully. In practice, many Soviet films were banned in Shanghai's foreign concessions. As a result, the commercially bustling location of the Isis Theater, with convenient public transportation bordering the international settlement, emerged to be the ideal place to evade "foreign censorship"[3] by showcasing Soviet films.

The debut Soviet film shown at the Isis was *The Road to Life* (*Putiovka v zhizn*, Nikolai Ekk, 1931), the first Soviet film in sound that featured Nicolai Sergeev, a Communist educator who transformed Moscow's homeless juvenile delinquents into meaningful members of the society. Winner of the Best Director award at the First Venice International Film Festival in 1932, the film was screened at the Isis Theater between February 16 and 24, 1933. An advertisement in *Shenbao*, a foreign concession–based moderate-to-liberal newspaper, pitted the film against Hollywood films by noting approvingly that the Soviet film had "no depictions of women's legs and gentlemen's top hats," seen as decadent and vulgar. As a marketing gimmick to draw in curious spectators, Isis billed Soviet films as "banned by foreign censors." But the once-banned Soviet films would sweep Shanghai and China once the CCP took over China. The founding of the People's Republic of China in October 1949 would soon lead to the banning of Hollywood films a year later, with the aim of erasing traces of American culture in China. To fill the gap and to inculcate a new socialist spirit in the newly established PRC, the party promoted Soviet films as it aggressively campaigned to rid China of the U.S. influence.

De-Americanization and the Conversion from Hollywood to Soviet Films

One of the concerns for the CCP regarding U.S. influence was the popularity of Hollywood films, which the CCP blamed for the widespread worship of America and the popularity of the American lifestyle in urban centers, especially in Shanghai, a city that seemed more receptive to American influence than to the CCP's indoctrination. A survey conducted at the University of Shanghai in December 1948 indicated that only 3.7 percent of university students and faculty favored the Communist government.[4] The prevailing pro-American sentiment was seen by the CCP as the result of the impact of U.S. films, and thus the most militant anti-U.S. effort was geared toward Hollywood films.

But an immediate Hollywood ban was not in the party's plan. The newly appointed Shanghai mayor, Chen Yi, speculated that it would take up to ten years to wean Shanghai audiences from Hollywood films. They were mindful of Chinese movie theaters' dependence on Hollywood films and of the potential revolt of Hollywood fans if American films were to be banished overnight. So a hard-line position against Hollywood was not yet on the table. The Cold War had not yet solidified around a pair of mutually hostile blocs in early 1950.[5] The critique of Hollywood films by Chinese media was mild and indeed mostly came from nongovernment entities. Theaters were put on notice mainly to not screen Hollywood films that might be detrimental to the new socialist government, which meant that films with anti-Soviet, anti-Communist messages, or films showing the American military in a favorable light, would not be permitted.

The outbreak of the Korean War in June 1950 put pressure on the government to immediately ban Hollywood films. But *People's Daily* warned that a coercive policy banning Hollywood would backfire.[6] The government instead pushed to increase the production output of progressive domestic films and to decrease ticket prices of these films so as to make domestic films a viable alternative. The plan by the Chinese government was to gradually decrease movie theaters' reliance on Hollywood films and thus let Hollywood die a quiet death on its own.

In July 1950, just after the outbreak of hostilities in Korea but well before Chinese military forces entered the conflict, Beijing's Ministry of Culture issued documents calling for a weakening of Hollywood's China dominance, but not total eradication of Hollywood. Yet the ground was shifting rapidly. In September 1950, the more militant Shanghai press called for an immediate wholesale ban on American films. As rumors spread about an impending ban, anxious Hollywood fans rushed to cinemas to catch the last picture show from the U.S.[7] Concerned that an abrupt end to Hollywood's presence might threaten social stability, official directives from the central government remained cautious. Policy makers devised a strategy to limit the days Hollywood imports were allowed screening and to aggressively promote Soviet imports in place of Hollywood's.

But the transition from Hollywood entertainment films to Soviet propaganda films was not an easy one, as it took some convincing and coaxing, if not coercing, for the Hollywood-addicted urban audiences to warm up to Soviet films. The CCP used a variety of strategies to curb Hollywood's market share while pushing for more screening of domestic and Soviet films. Discount tickets and even free screenings were offered for Soviet films.[8] Policy makers in Shanghai employed such tools as using preferential screening permits, low ticket prices, and low taxes and even tax exemptions to boost the fortunes of the politically preferred movies.

Yet Hollywood films remained popular and continued to serve as the yardstick against which other imported films were measured in the popular eyes. In Beijing, it was reported that the discount tickets given to the members of the film community, including the China-Soviet Friendship Society and the military, that were meant for Soviet and progressive Chinese films were mostly utilized to watch "regressive" Hollywood films.[9] The theater union had to adjust its policy to spell out that discount tickets were available only for domestic and Soviet film screenings.[10]

Mao, the Chinese Communist Party chairman, was losing his patience and was determined to cleanse any residual U.S. influence from China. The opportunity arose in the fall of 1950 when China officially entered the Korean War on October 24, which led to the U.S. declaration that Taiwan would be under U.S. protection. This became the straw that broke the camel's back, and the move to rid Chinese screens of all remnants of Hollywood films and "unhealthy" domestic pictures went into full gear in late 1950. A massive campaign was launched not only to discredit Hollywood films but also to deem watching American films unpatriotic and reactionary. As the political campaign got going, confessions of former fans were published, pointing to the corrosive impact of Hollywood. Shanghai's Dahua Theater, which had an exclusive contract with MGM, quietly stopped showing American films. The Paris Theater, which was later renamed Huaihai Theater, followed suit a few weeks later, ending its run of Hollywood films on a louder note on November 10, with employees raising a big banner that read "Resisting American Films."[11] The day after the Paris Theater's grand gesture, the Shanghai Movie Theater Association, representing over forty cinemas, called for an emergency meeting to hash out a plan to halt the screening of American films in affiliated theaters. By November 14, all theaters in Shanghai stopped screening American films. When the ban was officially announced later in the month, audiences rushed to purchase tickets for the few remaining screenings of Hollywood oldies, which led to the dramatic hike of ticket prices and the subsequent complaints about the elimination of Hollywood films. The complaints were drowned out by the louder voices denouncing Hollywood.

In early December 1950, as a retaliation against the Chinese intervention in the Korean War, the U.S. government froze Chinese assets in the United States and declared economic sanctions against the PRC. As a tit for tat, the PRC government announced on December 28 that it would freeze all U.S. assets in China and ordered all cultural, educational, humanitarian, and religious organizations receiving U.S. aid to sever their relationship with the United States.[12] The Chinese government enacted favorable tax schemes to help wean these organizations from U.S. support. Religious practices were harshly denounced while almost all missionaries accused of antirevolutionary conspiracy from January 1951 onward were Americans, and many were expelled from China.[13]

To counter the U.S. influence, the CCP began to draw even closer to the Soviet Union. Hollywood films were now denounced publicly as "poisonous weeds" that reflected American imperialism and capitalism. The denunciation of Hollywood, coupled with the aggressive promotion of Soviet films, functioned to kill two birds with one stone.[14] While filling up screening slots, Soviet films also helped drive home socialist ideas and images much needed for the party to formulate and propagate a coherent ideology.[15] Revolutionary Soviet films such as *Private Aleksandr Matrosov* (Leonid Lukov, 1948), *The Russian Question* (Mikhail Romm, 1948), *The Turning Point* (Fridrikh Ermler, 1945), *The Battle of Stalingrad* (Vladimir Petrov, 1949), *The Fall of Berlin* (Mikheil Chiaureli, 1950), *Lenin in October* (Mikhail Romm and Dmitriy Vasilev, 1937), and *Zoya* (Lev Arnshtametc, 1944) began to flood Chinese screens.[16]

Soviet films helped fan anti-American sentiment during the Korean War. A student at a Shanghai all-girls middle school remarked how watching the Soviet film *The Fall of Berlin* was akin to taking a crash course in political awareness, as the film taught her the importance of "fighting American imperialism in Korea."[17] The Chinese fan magazine *Popular Cinema* published audiences' letters calling Soviet films inspirational in China's fight against American imperialism. *Private Aleksandr Matrosov*, the first Soviet film translated and dubbed into Chinese in 1950, was said to have inspired Chinese People's Volunteer (CPV) soldiers on the battlefield during the Korea War.[18] In a letter to the fan magazine, a CPV soldier singled out repeated viewing of war films such as *The Fall of Berlin*, *Chapayev*, and *She Defends the Motherland* in strengthening his resolve in fighting the enemies during the Korean War. In October 2021, the year marking the one hundredth anniversary of the CCP, an epic Chinese film about the Korean War commissioned by China's central propaganda department, *The Battle at Lake Changjin* (Chen Kaige, Tsui Hark and Dante Lam, 2021), stormed Chinese theaters to enormous popularity, reopening the old wound and rekindling anti-American sentiment. The film depicts the historical 1950 battle around the high-altitude Lake Chosin Reservoir where an underequipped Chinese army on a deadly mission managed to triumph over a division of top-tier U.S. Marines. It shines the spotlight on the valor of Chinese soldiers and the role China played in what the Chinese official narrative calls "the war of resistance against the United States and aid Korea." The historical battle was one of the harshest in the history of modern warfare, with the United States and the ROK Corps reporting a total of 10,495 battle casualties[19] and the official Chinese casualty number at the staggering 48,156[20] and unofficial outside estimation at 60,000.[21] Some on Chinese social media questioned the wisdom of China's intervention in Korea; their chatters were quickly scrubbed clean. Luo Changping, a muckraking journalist who openly challenged the official patriotic narrative concerning China's involvement in the Korean War, was promptly detained by the Chinese authorities.[22]

Back in 1950, the year when the actual battle occurred, the anti-American fervent ran high in China, paving the way for the eventual eradication of Hollywood films. The CCP during the early years of the PRC relied heavily on imports from the Soviets to fill the void left by Hollywood at a time when domestic pictures were in short supply. Yet overall, Chinese audiences did not immediately warm up to Soviet films. Audiences in urban centers were not thrilled by them, and private cinemas did not always actively promote Soviet films. Private theater owners in the more pro-commerce Canton avoided Soviet films on the grounds that the dubbed imports with Soviet voice actors were hard for Chinese audiences to follow. In 1950 and 1951, on average a theater could roughly manage to screen two Soviet films per day, with an average number of 472 viewers in attendance.

Enticing audiences to come to cinemas for Soviet films became a political duty of Chinese distribution and theater chains. To encourage more viewing, Guangzhou and its neighboring cities in Canton initiated a USSR Film Week to commemorate the victory of the Soviet revolution.[23] There were also organized student viewings of Soviet films, though reception was lukewarm. In Shanghai in 1951, the municipal government divided films into five categories: films made by state-run studios, imports from the USSR, imports from other liberated countries, progressive films made by private studios, and "regressive" films made by private studios. Among the ninety-one films screened in 1951, seventy-one were Soviet films, which far exceeded "regressive films" made by private domestic studios.[24] According to the Shanghai government, attendance for regressive films was much smaller than for films made by national studios or progressive films made by private studios. The assessment is highly doubtful, given audiences' resistance to Soviet films, though the lack of good alternatives might buttress the claim. Yet a survey done in 1951 by the Shanghai branch of the Chinese Youth League indicated that students considered Soviet films too political and not as relaxing as Hollywood films and that the actors/actresses in Soviet films were not as attractive as Hollywood stars.[25] Hollywood films continued to serve as a yardstick for these students to measure a given film's worthiness.[26] As a result, movie theaters lost patrons.

Nevertheless, the push for Soviet and domestic films continued. By the end of 1950, both the amount of time devoted to domestic and Soviet films and the size of audiences watching such films had grown to exceed the numbers applied to American and British offerings. Between 1949 and 1957, China imported 1,309 films, almost two-thirds from the Soviet Union. Nationwide, by 1957, 468 Soviet films were translated and shown to a total audience of 1,397,289,000.[27] Nine of these Soviet films attracted audiences of more than 25 million.[28] Seen as a political-aesthetic model worthy of emulation, Soviet films would exert a long-lasting impact on Chinese cinema during Mao's era. As cultural historian Tina Chen puts it, "Soviet film provided visual imagery, language, and a comparative framework central to China's understanding of its own future."[29] Soviet experience, expertise, plot lines, and images began to occupy an important position in Chinese people's moviegoing experience throughout the 1950s. New theaters and mobile projection units were employed on a massive scale to bring Soviet film and the attendant party ideology to inland rural areas and factories for open-air screening.[30] The Soviets provided both the projection units and technical training. Statistics show that among a total of 860 foreign films imported from 42 countries between 1949 and 1964, 421 were from the USSR. Soviet films thus occupied nearly half of all imports between 1949 and 1964.[31] During the same period domestic productions numbered 564.

Building a National Film Industry: From Hollywood to the Soviet Model

As part of a wholesale embrace of Soviet theory and practice, the CCP further imported a Soviet-style centralized national film industry model. CCP members had been systematically dispatched to the Soviet Union since the Yan'an era to learn how to run a socialist country. The left-wing filmmaker Yuan Muzhi was sent to the USSR in 1940 and stayed there until 1946. A veteran Shanghai actor and director, Yuan gained prominence in participating in the production of a series of socially conscious films of the 1930s, including *Plunder of Peach and Plum* (Yunwei Ying, 1934), which he wrote and in which he starred; *Children of Troubled Times* (*Fēngyún Érnǚ*, Xingzhi Xu, 1935), for which he sang the theme song that later became China's national anthem, "The March of the Volunteers"; and *Cityscape* (1935), which he directed and for which he wrote the screenplay. The films were all produced by Diantong Film Company founded in Shanghai in 1934 by Situ Huimin, a major leftist filmmaker and intellectual with close ties to the CCP. Diantong was shunned by most of the established filmmakers in Shanghai for its left-leaning politics and its connection with the CCP. The company resorted to recruiting local theater talents and turning them into first-time filmmakers. Situ Huimin was responsible for bringing to the company left-leaning screenwriters such as Tian Han (author of the lyrics of "The March of the Volunteers") and Xia Yan, who would later play key roles in managing the PRC's cultural affairs. Yuan Muzhi was one of such new recruits, together with Chen Bo'er, who co-starred with him in *Plunder of Peach and Plum* and later married him.[32] Both Yuan and Chen would become major players in building a new cinema in China under the CCP.

One of the earliest sound films in China, *Cityscape/Scenes of City Life*, was Yuan Muzhi's directorial debut. A morality tale of money and lust, the film deftly blended screwball comedy and musical to satirize the frivolous charades of a bourgeois love triangle in the bustling metropolis of Shanghai. The film's much-admired opening scene featured an extended montage of Shanghai's modern cityscape that captured the urban metropolis' landmark neon signs, theater marquees, and the neo-Gothic-style St. Ignatius Cathedral designed by the English architect William Doyle and built by French Jesuits between 1906 and 1910. Hailed as "the grandest church in the Far East" at the time, the St. Ignatius Cathedral was severely damaged during the Cultural Revolution and used during the period as a state-owned grain warehouse. Yuan's film preserved the iconic cathedral in its original glory.

The film also featured Lan Ping, the future wife of Mao Zedong, in a minor role, which would become Yuan's liability later, when Madame Mao—who by then had a new name, Jiang Qing, bestowed by Mao—tried to cover up her old tracks by attacking many of her contemporaries in the Shanghai filmmaking scene. An idealistic young theater lover attracted to left-wing ideas in the 1930s, Lan Ping joined the CCP in 1933 and became known for playing the leading role in Ibsen's *A Doll's House*, opposite the popular actor Zhao Dan. Lan Ping left Shanghai for Yan'an when the Sino-Japanese War broke out, where she met Mao and became his fourth wife.

Financial woes and political pressure under the KMT led to Diantong's collapse in 1935. Situ joined the more established Lianhua Film Company in Shanghai and then moved to Hong Kong during the Sino-Japanese War to make anti-Japanese films. After the war, several of Lianhua's directors returned to Shanghai to form the Lianhua Film Society in an attempt to revive the old Lianhua. The new Lianhua later became known as Kunlun Film Company, producing several memorable titles of the postwar 1940s, including *The Spring River Flows East* and

Crows and Sparrows, two films that depicted China during the war-torn era, with the former chronicling the trials and tribulations of one family during and immediately after the second Sino-Japanese War and the latter exposing the hardship of ordinary Shanghainese on the brink of the KMT's defeat.

While Situ joined Lianhua, many of Diantong's top talents, including Yuan Muzhi, joined Star, the veteran production company. Star's newly formed Studio 2 focused on producing socially conscious films then popular in Shanghai. While at Star, Yuan made his most renowned film, *Street Angel* (1937), considered by film historians as one of the most important Chinese films of all time and a highlight of the "second generation" Chinese cinema. Released in summer 1937 shortly before the Japanese invasion of Shanghai, the film was a massive hit, marking it one of the last titles of the "golden era of Chinese cinema." Filmmakers were soon forced to leave Shanghai or retreat to Shanghai's foreign concessions. *Street Angel* featured the then-unknown actress Zhou Xuan, whose singing of "Song of the Four Seasons" and "The Wandering Songstress" would make her one of the screen icons in China.

Yuan Muzhi left for CCP-controlled Yan'an when the Japanese entered Shanghai in 1938. He started to work on a feature-length documentary film, *Yan'an and the Eighth Route Army*, while in Yan'an and joined the CCP in 1940. The same year, Yuan was sent to the Soviet Union to learn about filmmaking in the USSR and to work on the postproduction of his documentary feature.[33] While in Russia, Yuan worked as Sergei Eisenstein's assistant and participated in the production of *Ivan the Terrible* (Sergei Eisenstein, 1944). He returned to China in 1946, with the conviction that cinema was essential to building a new socialist China. Yuan would be put in charge of building a nationalized Chinese film industry. The same year Yuan returned from the Soviet Union, Situ left for the United States to study film technology and management. He returned in 1952 to work in the film industry as a ranking technical and cultural gatekeeper, holding positions as the vice minister of the Ministry of Culture, director of the technology committee under the Ministry of Culture, and vice chairman of the Chinese Filmmakers Association. Yuan and Situ, together with a few other former Diantong colleagues, were poised to lead Chinese cinema into a new era.

The foundation of a CCP-led national film industry was laid in the late 1940s with the establishment of three state-sponsored studios: Northeast Studio, Beiping Studio, and Shanghai Studio. The Northeast Studio, which would be renamed Changchun Film Studio in March 1955, was founded on October 1, 1946, using the space and equipment abandoned by the Japanese-controlled Manchurian Motion Pictures.[34] Yuan Muzhi served as the head of the newly founded studio upon returning from Moscow in 1946.[35] Beiping Film Studio, which would be renamed Beijing Film Studio on October 1, 1949, was established on April 20, 1949, following the CCP's takeover of the city at the end of January.[36] In May 1949, with the People's Liberation Army rolling into Shanghai, party leaders dispatched veteran left-wing literary figures including Xiao Yan to Shanghai to overtake film operations in the city, leading to the founding of Shanghai Studio on November 16, 1949, consolidating several formerly KMT-controlled studios. To streamline productions, the newly formed Shanghai Studio set up internal divisions, including News Production, Translation, and Animation, to produce newsreels and documentary films as well as re-voiced imports. The Translation Division of the Shanghai Studio became the foundation of the Shanghai Translation and Re-voicing Studio, commonly known as Shanghai Dubbing Studio, in 1957. Shanghai Studio's animation division absorbed the animation division of Northeast Studio in early 1950 to produce animated films.

Making as many films as possible for socialist China was the main task for the newly established state-run studios. The CCP also mobilized existing private studios to make films in support of the new government. Twenty-one private studios were in operation when the CCP took over China. Two major preliberation studios, Kunlun and Changjiang, were chosen to receive direct investment from the state and became public-private joint-venture companies, which formed the third model. The party put Yuan Muzhi in charge of phasing out the coexistence of all three models and nationalizing and centralizing the entire Chinese film industry. While in Russia, Yuan did not actually learn much about how the Soviet film industry operated, as the chaos of the war made it impossible for the Soviet film industry to carry on its routine functioning. But Yuan did bring back from Moscow the book *Party's View on Cinema* and had it translated into Chinese. The book made it clear that cinema is a tool for promoting Communism: "It must not be allowed to turn films into a purely entertaining pastime unrelated to politics."[37]

In building a film industry at the service of the new China, Yuan relied on his professional hunch and instinct, which was shaped by his experience as a commercial filmmaker during the KMT era. Mindful of the industry's bottom line, Yuan proposed in September 1948, while still heading the Northeast Studio, to build a centralized commercial film industry, modeled more or less on Hollywood in its market practice. Yuan envisioned an economically sustainable Chinese film industry capable of supporting itself financially. The industry was to be self-reliant and profitable despite the propaganda mandate. Yuan's vision of a state-controlled commercial system actually echoed the USSR's initial model for the film industry. As noted by film scholar Kristin Thompson, Soviet film policy in the 1920s was "to create a central organ which could regulate and coordinate the activities of the various private and regional film companies and which could itself make and distribute films with the type of ideology desirable for the new Soviet society. . . . The goal was for the Soviet film industry to become self-supporting and to make a profit."[38]

YUAN MUZHI AND THE BEIJING CINEMA VILLAGE

The concrete idea for a self-sufficient yet effective propaganda machine materialized with the proposed construction by Yuan of Beijing Cinema Village, a massive production site akin to the Hollywood-style production back lot, with on-site postproduction facilities on the outskirts of Beijing, to the north of the Summer Palace.[39] Unlike Hollywood, where numerous private studios carved out space and competed with each other, the Beijing Cinema Village was to host all major productions under one nationalized and centralized Chinese film industry; it was also at the beating heart of China's political and cultural nerve center. The CCP's Propaganda Department responded positively to Yuan's idea, issuing directives in November and December 1948 to designate the site on the outskirts of Beijing as the headquarters of a nationalized film industry. Yuan relocated to Beijing from Changchun on February 14, 1949, only two weeks after Chinese Communist armies took control of the city, to lead the effort. In April 1949, Yuan established, under the auspices of the Propaganda Department, the Central Film Bureau (CFB), which would be moved to the Ministry of Culture in November 1949. Yuan was appointed as the inaugural director of the Central Film Bureau in 1950.[40]

Upon assuming the role of the head of China's Central Film Bureau, Yuan envisioned a gradual transition of both film content and studio ownership and sought to rely on market competition in transforming private ownership to state ownership. There was no indication, in 1950, that the private studios would be seized anytime soon, so long as they supported the initiatives of the state-run studios. When it came to the transitioning of filmmakers from making popular films in the humanistic tradition to films carrying political water, Yuan Muzhi understood that it would be difficult for the veteran Shanghai filmmakers to make the adjustments overnight and cautioned against heavy-handed approaches that could dampen filmmakers' enthusiasm in making quality films.[41] But it was clear from the beginning that state studios would receive the lion's share of resources. In his proposed film budget to the Ministry of Culture for 1950, roughly 70 to 80 percent of the total funding was allotted to the Film Bureau and the three national studios, though the production output of the three studios took up only a small portion of the market share at the time. The Chinese film industry established a national distribution network in 1950, in the form of regional film management companies in the Northeast, Beijing and Shanghai, and the south-central, southwest, and northwest military administrative regions.[42]

A year later in 1951, the China Film Distribution and Exhibition Company (China Film)[43] was established under the Ministry of Radio, Film, and Television (MRFT) to take over film distribution at the national level. China Film purchased complete film prints from studios at the rates based on length rather than quality or projected popularity. At the provincial level, local film bureaus established their own management organizations to control local film distribution and exhibition. Central control over local activities was not always effective, and local exhibitors sometimes altered the length of exhibition cycles to meet the demand for more popular films. For instance, a few cinemas in Changsha, the capital city of Mao Zedong's native Hunan Province, scheduled politically charged Soviet films for shorter runs while granting entertainment-oriented domestic comedies longer runs.[44]

The Ministry of Culture recruited Soviet experts in the early 1950s to work on the "Proposal for Cinema" for the PRC's first Five-Year Plan. The same year, Yuan Muzhi commissioned Czechoslovakian film experts and architects to draw a plan for the construction of the Beijing Cinema Village. The ambitious blueprint envisioned the building of fourteen sites, including a fully equipped production studio, a large post-production facility, and an animation studio capable of producing five feature-length films or forty short animations per year. A documentary studio with the capacity of producing fifteen long films or fifty-two short films per year would also be built, together with an education film studio with an annual target of ten science education film or eighty short films. The plan also envisioned the construction of a film academy, a screenwriting institute, a film engineering research institute, administrative buildings, canteens, car garages, a sports stadium, and a residential area with day care centers, kindergartens, elementary schools, stores, and movie theaters to accommodate the daily living of 20,000 employees and their families. Despite the idea's Hollywood lineage, Beijing Cinema Village was essentially a company town, with working and living quarters and relevant amenities all within a walkable distance, a typical example of the model of industrial plants from the USSR and of the corresponding Chinese socialist workplace or work unit that provided essential social resources to its members.

In May 1950, just as Yuan thought he was given free rein to run the film industry, Premier Zhou Enlai ordered that the Central Film Bureau establish an independent Film Steering Committee to strengthen the party's ideological guidance and control of the film industry. The move took away some of Yuan's decision-making power. Two film incidents triggered Premier Zhou's push for tightened control, one concerning *Spring in Inner Mongolia* (Sue Wei Gan, 1950),[45] the first PRC film featuring ethnic minorities and the party's ethnic policy, and the other concerning *Life of Wu Xun* (Sun Yu, 1950), a pacifist film that triggered a political firestorm.

Spring in Inner Mongolia captured historical events leading up to the founding of the Inner Mongolia Autonomous Region in China. It was initially warmly received by the party's rank and file. However, comments made by an Inner Mongolian representative at a meeting of the party's United Front Work Department raised concern over the film's less than flattering depiction of Inner Mongolia's ruling class, one of the targets of the party's united front effort. Reporting directly to the Party Central Committee, the United Front Work Department is a party body that functions to co-opt non-CCP-affiliated intellectuals, business elites, and special interest groups into the party's orbit. The member representing Northeast China at the United Front meeting objected to the film on the grounds that it demonized the Mongolian prince figure by portraying him as hostile to the CCP while colluding with the KMT to sabotage the CCP's effort in establishing an autonomous Inner Mongolian region. The party leader in the film was said to have treated the Mongolian prince figure as an enemy rather than a potential ally of the United Front. The representative worried that the story would alienate Inner Mongolian elites. The comments caught the attention of Ulanhu, the head of the United Front Work Department and an Inner Mongolian native and former army general. A member of the Mongolian elites himself, Ulanhu was also the inaugural chairman of the Inner Mongolia Autonomous Region and served in the position from 1947 to 1966.[46] The attention from Ulanhu led the screenwriter Wang Zhengzhi to publish a self-criticism letter in the *People's Daily*, expressing regret for not fully comprehending the party's policy on ethnic minorities and thus misrepresenting the constructive partnership between CCP and local elites. The film was pulled out of theaters for revisions, and major figures in China's arts and culture community were involved in making changes. The revised final cut had to obtain approval from Premier Zhou Enlai. Even Mao Zedong became involved, by giving a revolutionary new title to the film: *The Victory of the Inner Mongolian People*.[47]

The incident made clear to Zhou the necessity of setting up a Film Steering Committee to safeguard the political and ideological correctness of future productions. Composed of thirty-five members, the Film Steering Committee included party leaders and representatives from diverse organizations. A smaller executive committee within the Film Steering Committee was set up to carry out the core task of evaluating films for political correctness. Members of this executive committee included renowned novelists and playwrights as well as filmmakers. Both Yuan Muzhi and Mao's wife Jiang Qing were on the committee.

Another incident that led to the tightened ideological control was more sinister and had to do with *The Life of Wu Xun* (Sun Yu, 1950), a film produced by the private Kunlun Studio. The film tells the story of the historical figure Wu Xun (1838–96), a Chinese education reformer who pioneered free education by raising funds from saving, begging, and appealing to wealthy landlords. Wu Xun was a hero to the liberal-minded Chinese intellectuals of the 1930s and 1940s. Though released in 1950, one-third of the film was shot back in 1947, the year when Kunlun debuted one of its most memorable films, *A Spring River Flows East*.[48] A product of the humanistic tradition of the late 1940s Shanghai cinema, *The Life of Wu Xun* was well received upon its initial screening in 1950, being hailed as one of the ten best films of the year. Party leaders including Zhou Enlai all sang its praises before the film's public rollout in Beijing, Tianjin, and Shanghai in February 1951, the very month in which the Central Film Bureau met to settle on a five-year construction plan of the Beijing Cinema Village. But on May 20, 1951, Mao surprised everybody by publicly denouncing the film for "publicizing feudal culture." Mao attacked the film "for slandering the peasant revolutionary" and called the lead character a "reactionary feudalist ruler" in an op-ed piece on May 20, 1951, in the *People's Daily* headlined "Must Pay Attention to Discussion on *The Life of Wu Xun*."[49] Mao lashed out at the filmmakers for denying "the right of class struggle by the oppressed" and took issue with the critics who endorsed the film.[50] A chorus of Mao's followers including his wife quickly lined up behind him, discrediting the film for its "liberal" tendencies. Madame Mao went so far as to make a trip to Wu Xun's hometown in Shandong, the province from which she herself came, to collect negative information about him. Wu became a "big hooligan, big creditor and big landlord" overnight. The party launched a lengthy political campaign against the film, marking it the first large-scale excoriation of a single film in PRC history and foreshadowing harsh political campaigns against filmmakers that would come periodically throughout Mao's era and beyond. *The Life of Wu Xun* became the PRC's first banned film. The attack on the film would be rekindled during the Cultural Revolution when Wu Xun's former home and his tomb were damaged and the members of the production team that had worked on the film were persecuted.

Mao's reaction to the film in the early 1950s was hardly surprising, given the film's reference to two leaders of violent peasant uprisings in Chinese history, Li Zicheng and Hong Xiuquan. Li, who led a peasant uprising that overthrew the Ming dynasty in the seventeenth century, was born in Yan'an, the CCP's revolutionary base. Hong, who ignited and led the Taiping Rebellion against the Qing dynasty in the mid-nineteenth century, was much admired by Mao. In the film, a peasant called on Wu Xun to help kill evil officials and local landlords. Wu replied that "Li Zicheng killed many people but failed in the end. Hong Xiuquan became emperor five years ago, but quickly forgot the poor. What's the point of killing people?" Mao took the exchange as a personal offense and an attack on the violent Communist revolution he led.

Mao's criticism of Wu Xun opened the floodgate to a political purge of China's cultural elites. The government began to aggressively weed out films and filmmakers not conforming to party directives. It was speculated that Mao might have nursed personal grudges against elite intellectuals who failed to take notice of him when he was working at the Peking University library in 1919 as an assistant to the university librarian Li Dazhao, the co-founder of the Chinese Communist Party in 1921. The elites ignored a future emperor at their own peril!

In November 1951, as the attack on *The Life of Wu Xun* was under way, Yuan lost his beloved wife, Chen Bo'er, to a heart attack. A long-term collaborator who initiated China's first training school for film professionals in 1950, Chen died suddenly while on a business trip. Chen joined the CCP and worked on the leadership team of the Northeast Studio alongside Yuan. The film training school she launched became the predecessor to the Beijing Film Academy. Chen was savvier politically than Yuan and the two were each other's confidant. Together, they made a perfect "power couple" in China's elite film circle. Yuan was devastated by the loss and struggled to keep up with the shifting political winds. He sank into depression and had to take an official sick leave from the Film Bureau starting in January 1952. Wang Lanxi was put in temporary charge of the Film Bureau in May 1952. Wang would soon be appointed as the inaugural president of the Beijing Film Academy, a legacy of Chen Bo'er's.

While Yuan was on leave, the Beijing municipal government officially approved the five-year construction plan in June 1952. Yet the political tide was changing, and China, after severing its relationship with the United States, was ready to cut its film industry's symbolic ties to Hollywood. In July 1952, a film unit was established under the Central Propaganda Department, replacing the Film Steering Committee under the

Film Bureau, to further strengthen the party's oversight of film activities. On October 23, 1952, Premier Zhou officially vetoed Yuan's Beijing Cinema Village plan because of its resemblance to Hollywood. Instead, Zhou instructed the Chinese film industry to look to the Soviet film industry for inspiration and encouraged a localized and diffused approach that would build studios in various provinces so as to ensure, to use his term, "the blossoming of one hundred flowers."[51] Wang Lanxi, the acting Film Bureau chief, convened a meeting from October 29 to October 31 to peruse and carry out Zhou's directives. In a remarkable reversal of fortune and course typical of Mao's era, a group criticism session ensued, attacking the idea of a cinema village. Yuan was soon cast aside, and eventually put on permanent convalescent leave, citing health reasons. The so-called convalescent leave was a euphemism for when the CCP sent away politically problematic ranking party cadres. On November 18, 1952, at a Ministry of Culture managerial meeting on Chinese cinema's first Five-Year Plan (1953–57), Premier Zhou's criticism of Cinema Village was thoroughly studied, and the Ministry of Culture turned to Soviet experts for help in drafting a revised first five-year film plan. The Central Propaganda Department also established a film unit in 1952 to ensure that the film industry's political path would follow the party's lead. Between 1951 and 1952, the film unit under the Propaganda Department "banned more than four hundred proposals, eighty finished films, and forty scripts."[52] Domestic film output plummeted from twenty-three films in 1951 to eight in 1952.

The nationalization and centralization of the film industry went into even higher gear in 1952, forcing all private studios in Shanghai to merge and form the state-run Shanghai United Studio.[53] In February 1953, Shanghai Studio acquired Shanghai United, completing the Chinese film industry's nationalization process.[54] The film industry now came under the direct guidance of Soviet film experts who applied a command economy model in which investment in production responded to government planning rather than market demands. The nationalized studio system produced films dictated by the government's political agenda, and film production functioned to disseminate Communist ideology and bolster the party's leadership. Production resources and quotas, film licensing, film distribution and exhibition, and film export were all planned annually, with the Film Bureau under the Ministry of Culture in charge of the planning. The Film Bureau was also responsible for managing film studios and allocating production quotas among studios in terms of both quantity and types of films.

Production funding and targets were allocated according to each studio's production capacity and specialties.[55] The largest ones, including Changchun, Beijing, Shanghai, and the People's Liberation Army's August First Studio, received the lion's share of resources. Studios were generally well stocked with 35mm equipment, and larger studios even built their own exterior "back lot" generic streets, the Chinese equivalent of the frontier towns in American Westerns. Instead of adopting a Hollywood-style consolidated model, the first Five-Year Plan for the Chinese film industry adopted the Soviet model, with film studios being built around the country, each with its own complete production and postproduction facility. Each studio maintained a full staff of actors, writers, directors, cinematographers, and technicians. Most were overstaffed, following the general pattern of Chinese state-controlled enterprises.[56] The entire system, built on Soviet concepts, ultimately proved to be impractical, redundant, and hugely wasteful.

Chinese Cinema's Tortuous Relationship with Soviet Films

The political wind would change yet again just as the Chinese film industry settled into its Soviet-inspired operational model with rigid party control and planning. The USSR started to experience "the Khrushchev Thaw" from the early 1950s, following the death of Stalin in March 1953 and the subsequent denunciation of Stalin and Stalinism in February 1956 in Nikita Khrushchev's speech "On the Cult of Personality and Its Consequences." The Khrushchev Thaw relaxed political repression and censorship in the Soviet Union, leading to sweeping political and cultural liberalization that would last until the early 1960s, breathing fresh air into film production and thus ushering in new forms of cinema free from a propaganda mandate. Films of artistic self-expression and innovation reemerged, and Soviet filmmakers reconnected with their international counterparts. Some successfully competed at major international film festivals.[57] Mikhail Kalatozov's 1957 war drama *The Cranes*

Are Flying, for example, won the Palme d'Or at the Cannes Film Festival in 1958, being hailed as "the first indisputable masterpiece of post-Stalin cinema."[58]

Released in October 1957, *The Cranes Are Flying* received a mostly positive reception from Soviet critics and audiences. The film breaks several Stalinist taboos. In one scene, when the hero, Boris, volunteers for the front after Germany invades the Soviet Union on June 22, 1941, a farewell tribute is paid to him by his co-workers. Boris's father cuts short the ritual, indeed rudely mocking the clichés of patriotism. The film astonished further with its bold stylistic approach. It did not take long for the film's artistry to gain international recognition. The following year, *Cranes* competed at Cannes, winning the Palme d'Or for the virtuosity of its camera work by Sergey Urusevsky, known for his relentless movement with a handheld camera, jarring diagonals, and low- and high-angle shots. Urusevsky coined the phrase "off-duty camera" to describe the freedom he gained by taking the camera off its tripod. As he put it, "The camera can express what the actor is unable to portray: his inner sensations. The cameraman must act with the actors."[59] The unmooring of the camera is evident in the opening scene where the camera dashes ahead of our leading man Boris around the open well of a staircase as he runs up several flights after Veronica, his love interest. Urusevsky's work drew influence from Eduard Tisse, the cinematographer known for his work with Sergei Eisenstein on the film *Strike*. The cinematography of *The Cranes Are Flying* with the handheld mobile camera and POV shots is a legacy of Sergei Eisenstein's subjective cinema.

The film made a strong impression on two filmmakers in China who went on to make *Early Spring in February* (Xie Tieli, 1964), a poetic film about the struggle and disillusionment of May Fourth intellectuals in the 1920s—a rare cinematic gem made at the dawn of the Cultural Revolution. It offered a sympathetic portrayal of Xiao Jianqiou, a May Fourth intellectual torn between his attraction to a young progressive woman and his sense of duty and obligation to the widow of a comrade in a small town where he teaches. Frustrated by his inability to effect change, the dejected Xiao leaves the small town to join the revolution. The film was much praised for its poetic quality. Li Wenhua, the cinematographer, attributed lyricism in the film to the direct influence of Sergey Urusevsky.[60] In an iconic sequence in *Cranes*, one of Veronica's suiters,

Mark, plays a piano in a cavernous apartment lit by the flashes of an ongoing aerial bombardment, with curtains billowing around. This scene was said to have inspired the piano playing scene in *Early Spring in February*.

Li and the film's director Xie were particularly taken by the visual exuberance of *The Cranes Are Flying*, which actually bears imprints from Hollywood films. The director of *Cranes*, Kalatozov, spent a year and a half in Los Angeles during World War II on a diplomatic assignment, an experience that allowed him to see Hollywood films that were unavailable in the Soviet Union.[61] The complexity, fluidity, and audacity with which Kalatozov approaches what is essentially a melodrama about love torn by war recall the peak moments of certain films by Frank Borzage, King Vidor, and Vincente Minnelli. In spite of their lack of access to Hollywood films at the time, the Chinese filmmakers unknowingly and indirectly absorbed Hollywood styles via the Soviet master.

One of the highlights of *The Cranes Are Flying* is the long take in which Veronica, having arrived too late for the farewell gathering at Boris's apartment, joins the crowd of people seeing new recruits off to the front as she scanned crowds for Boris. As recounted by the film critic Chris Fujiwara in his notes to the film's 2020 Criterion Collection edition, the sequence begins with Veronica in close-up, looking tensely out the window of a moving bus: "when she descends from the bus on the opposite side, Urusevsky's camera gets off with her, and it continues to follow her, without a cut, as she winds her way through the massive crowd. Miraculously, as she dashes between moving tanks to cross an avenue, the camera ascends into the sky and looks down at her."[62] The epochal event is done in one elastic and elaborate long take, communicating to the viewer in breadth and depth Veronica's urgency in bidding farewell to a lover who might not and indeed would not return. The long takes were utilized amply in *Early Spring*, though nowhere near as elaborately as in *Cranes*. The last sequence in *Early Spring in February* witnesses the leading female character running after the departing leading man. The much commented upon long crane shot of the female lead running behind a bamboo fence and stumbling through a variety of "barring devices" and eventually reaching a bridge—a passage to a new world—was frequently compared with the long take of the lead character running behind a metal fence in *Cranes*.

The Cranes Are Flying was never officially distributed in China, as only Stalinist films were allowed for public screening under Mao. But the wife of the director Xie Tieli was working at the China Film Distribution Company in the early 1960s and had access to "pass-through" Soviet films for internal screenings at the company's small screening room. Pass-through films were the films available for inspection but never distributed officially in China. Many of the pass-through films were obtained through the Hong Kong branch of the Xinhua News Agency, the Central Government's propaganda organ. The films circulated among ranking party leaders and cultural workers and were returned within a week. Xie and Li took advantage of the spousal privilege and watched a fair number of Soviet films made during the Khrushchev Thaw. While Xie was mostly self-taught as a young revolutionary growing up in the Red Army's cultural division, Li actually underwent professional cinematography training at the Beijing Film Academy from 1955 to 1957. The Ministry of Culture invited a team of Soviet experts to China in 1955 to offer training classes on directing, acting, cinematography, and production at the Film Academy.[63] The experts brought with them award-winning films including *The Cranes Are Flying*, which absolutely astonished the Chinese trainees who had little exposure to films beyond the socialist norm, Li among them. The range of emotional, psychological, and ideological shadings registered in the film came as a shock to the young Chinese filmmakers. In the movie, Boris and Veronica are madly in love. To enhance the two lovers' soon-to-be-shattered moments together, the filmmaker places the lovers' early-morning idyll on the empty streets of Moscow and films them from alternating high and low camera angles to capture the peaceful city and the sky. Sequences like this created a collective ecstasy among the young trainees at the Beijing Film Academy.

Li was blunt about imitating shot-by-shot *The Cranes Are Flying* while making *Early Spring in February*. He was particularly impressed by the scene of Boris being hit by a sniper's bullet and dying. As Boris slowly collapses, the camera gazes up from him at a swirling skyscape of wintry birch trees, which dissolves into an elaborate hallucination of his wedding to Veronica as they descend stairs accompanied by flowers and cheering crowds. In the windswept gauze of Veronica's veil, the montage echoes the billowing curtains of the scene of Veronica being forced upon by another suitor earlier in the film, and the bare birch branches that loom over the dying Boris are turned into clouds of translucent leaves. The hyperbolic lyricism shocked the Chinese trainees at the Beijing Film Academy. Li was particularly touched by the way the cinematographer visualized emotion for maximum effect in Boris's death scene, what Li called "film for emotional impact."[64] *Early Spring in February* evokes the same lyricism, wonder, and romanticism.[65]

THE WEANING OF SOVIET FILMS

The mid-1950s was a time when the Chinese film industry was finally picking up its own production, paving the way for the weaning of Chinese cinema from Soviet films. The importation of Soviet films gradually declined. Stalin died in 1953, leading to the Khrushchev Thaw starting in the mid-1950s. Mao was not happy with the turn of events in the USSR. Concerned about the impact on China of Khrushchev's policy changes, Mao called for the Chinese Communist Party to chart an independent path and reaffirm China's version of the Stalinist policy. The Chinese Communist Party vilified Khrushchev's de-Stalinization policies as ideological revisionism of orthodox Marxism. Political and ideological differences between Mao and Khrushchev threatened to destabilize the harmonious relationship between the Soviet and Chinese film industries. It became imperative, Mao argued, for China's filmmakers to reenergize and chart their own path.

Mao launched the policy of "letting a hundred flowers bloom and a hundred schools of thought contend" to "promote the flourishing of the arts and the progress of science" in 1956.[66] The first Hundred Flower liberalization period proved to be short-lived, as Mao had no real stomach for dissenting voices. A crackdown on those who criticized Mao turned into the Anti-Rightist Campaign from 1957 to 1959. As the Anti-Rightist Campaign got under way, Mao launched the Great Leap Forward campaign in 1958 to accelerate the industrialization process, which led to the great famine with the death of millions. "Let one hundred flowers blossom, one hundred schools of thought contend" was the beginning of a series of political loosening-ups and crackdowns in China's film industry that would continue well past the Mao era, establishing a pattern of political control that helped to ingrain habits of socially purposeful filmmaking and the attendant self-censorship which now affects Chinese cinema's "brand" and competitiveness in the global market.

As Sino-Soviet tensions mounted, negative reports on Soviet films started to appear in 1957. Ironically, on August 1, 1957, Yuan Muzhi was summoned back to Beijing from his sick leave, not to be vindicated for not adhering to a pure Soviet model, but to write self-criticism of his alleged attachment to the Hollywood model. Though Soviet films were now out of Mao's favor, the link to Hollywood continued to be stigmatized, and the fear of being associated with Hollywood lingered among the Chinese cultural elites, even though Chinese cinema during the Mao era carried on the legacy of a Hollywood-style narrative formula, albeit substituting morality with political correctness, individual conflict with class struggle, and domestic drama with national allegory. As China asserted its autonomy in the realm of film imports and distribution, the number of new Soviet imports to China dropped dramatically after 1957. The Chinese film industry introduced import quotas in the late 1950s and began to take control of Sovexportfilm's data collection, requesting that the statistics collected by China's Board of Film Distribution become the official document upon which decisions on Soviet films were to be made.[67]

While cutting the umbilical cord with the Soviets, the Chinese government turned its focus to boosting domestic productions. Domestic productions increased exponentially by the late 1950s, especially with the launching in 1958 of the Great Leap Forward campaign, whose obsession with growth targets extended even to film production. From the late 1950s to the mid-1960s, China's isolationist film policy, fashioned more out of political than economic concerns, kept at bay imports from most of the countries, leaving China's large film market exclusively for the domestic industry. Domestic outputs overtook Soviet imports in 1961 when the Sino-Soviet split officially occurred. By the early 1960s, very few new Soviet films were imported to the PRC and screenings of Soviet films stuck to a few old classics such as *Lenin in 1918* (Mikhail Romm, 1939) and *Lenin in October* (Mikhail Romm and Dmitri Vasilyev, 1937). Mao formally denounced Khrushchev as "revisionist traitor" in 1961. A list of Soviet films deemed revisionist at a China Film Workers Association forum in Beijing on January 1, 1963, included *The Cranes Are Flying*.[68] Coming out a year later, *Early Spring in February*, with no clear-cut closure nor standard triumph narrative of the CCP, met a similar fate.

THE UPS AND DOWNS OF EARLY SPRING IN FEBRUARY

The year 1961 saw the beginning of what scholar Zhuoyi Wang termed "the second Hundred Flower period," a resurrection of the initial Hundred Flower Campaign in 1956, when citizens were encouraged to openly express their opinions of the party.[69] The catastrophe of the Great Leap Forward forced the party to adjust its policies in late 1960 and throughout 1961, during which time policy meetings and talks were held in the film industry to encourage criticism, leading to the announcement by the Film Bureau in 1961 of a series of new directives to reverse the Great Leap Forward policy. That same year the Ministry of Culture held a national meeting in Beijing to discuss feature film production.[70] At the meeting, Premier Zhou Enlai delivered a speech advocating stylistic diversity, creativity, and a more democratic atmosphere within the filmmaking community. Xia Yan, the deputy culture minister, gave a speech at the same meeting that registered his discontent with the recent film policies, and charged that contemporary filmmaking was too "direct, un-nuanced, excessive, crude"[71] and called for a humanistic approach to filmmaking to improve artistic quality and professional competence.

In January 1962, a Seven Thousand People Conference was launched by leading cadres at the CCP's county level and above to allow people to vent their frustrations. The conferences turned into a platform for criticism, which pushed CCP authorities to carry through with policy changes. The film industry became one of the first sectors to implement the changes in policy. The term "star," which had attained a negative connotation immediately after the establishment of the PRC, was miraculously rehabilitated. Large posters of "22 Big Stars of New China" appeared in movie theaters all around China in April 1962.[72]

With the change of political wind, the film industry witnessed a brief commercial turn, leading to a wave of popular comedies in 1962 that danced between political correctness and artistic transgression. *Early Spring in February* was produced during the brief liberalization of the second Hundred Flowers period. A perfect poster boy for what Xia envisioned as a humanistic film, *Early Spring in February* was well received when it came out in 1963. But the cultural tide soon changed again, and the relaxation proved short-lived. In early 1964, Mao started two rectification campaigns in the cultural sector that brought down as "capitalist roadrunners" two chief cultural bureaucrats in charge of the film industry. The posters of the new stars were removed from movie theaters in September 1964 and dozens of films were condemned as "poisonous weeds," including *Early Spring in February*, which was widely circulated. The wide distribution accorded to the film was solely for the purpose of mass criticism in the lead-up to the Cultural Revolution. In August 1964, Mao wrote a personal note demanding large-scale condemnation of the film as an example of a cinema of "poisonous weeds." The film was denounced for espousing "bourgeois humanitarianism" and for being excessively sentimental, pessimistic, and nostalgic about an old era, though Jiang Qing apparently privately praised the cinematographer for the film's beautiful composition and color scheme.[73] Mao used *Early Spring in February* as a springboard to launch a massive national purge of "antirevolutionary" feature films.[74] During the Cultural Revolution, in 1968, the actress Shangguan Yunzhu, who played the tragic widow character in *Early Spring*, was persecuted in real life and met her own tragic death by leaping from a Shanghai building.[75]

Stalinist-era films acquired new significance in China in the mid-1960s as a way for Mao to legitimize continued draconian film policy in China. At a 1965 film festival dedicated to victory over Nazi Germany, only films made in the Stalinist era, including Stalinist productions banned under Khrushchev, were shown. Repeated screening of the old classics made a long-lasting impression on viewers coming of age during the period, indeed spurring imitations on and off the screen. Recitation and reenactment of memorable moments from the Lenin film series was a national pastime for youth during the era, which has been captured in post-Mao Chinese films depicting life in those days. In a riotous sequence in *In the Heat of the Sun* (Jiang Wen, 1994), the juvenile delinquent Ma Xiaojun and his comrades fluttered about in their parents' PLA uniforms to dance *Swan Lake* in imitation of the ballet scene in *Lenin in 1918* (*Lenin*). Elsewhere in the film, an audience was seen during an open-air screening reciting a famous line from *Lenin* before the line was spoken by the character on-screen: "There will be bread, and there will be milk, there will be everything."[76]

With Soviet films out of favor and domestic output hampered during the Cultural Revolution, available films for screening became limited and repeated viewing became more of a norm. During the height of the Cultural Revolution, accessible films dwindled to only eight so-called "model opera" films, which were experimental theatrical works attaching revolutionary flare to the ballet forms of Western origin and augmenting the traditional art of Peking Opera, with string and percussion band. Workers, peasants, soldiers, and other revolutionaries replaced ancient emperors, aristocrats, scholars, gods, and fairies in the traditional operas. The most popular of these Peking operas included *On the Docks*, *Raid on the White Tiger Regiment*, *The Red Lantern*, *Shajiabang*, *Song of the Dragon River*, *Taking the Tiger Mountains by Strategy*, *The Dujuan Mountain*, and *Fighting on the Plains*. Most people coming of age during the period can hum a few or more bars of arias or melodies from these operas. Among the favorite roles was Ke Xiang, a Communist heroine in *The Azalea Mountain* who led a group of local peasant rebels to victory in the fight against landlords and the KMT army. It was reported that Madame Mao changed the lead character's last name from He to Ke, as He is the last name of Mao's second wife. The play was later made into a movie with the same title[77] featuring as the lead actress Yang Chunxia, a charming and affective young opera singer. Yang Chunxia shot to fame overnight and her signature song, "I'm from Anyuan,"[78] was widely performed. The character Ke Xiang became something of an idol through Yang's vivid portrayal, and Ke Xiang's bob cut became trendy throughout the country. The model operas witnessed a comeback in the mid-2000s amidst Maoist nostalgia. In 2005, three of the operas were restaged by the National Peking Opera Theatre of China.[79]

The Lone American Film

It is worth noting that the lone U.S. film imported to China amidst Soviet film promotion was *Salt of the Earth*, a 1954 feature written by Michael Wilson, directed by Herbert J. Biberman, and produced by Paul

Chinese poster for *Salt of the Earth*.

Jarrico.[80] All three men had been blacklisted in Hollywood due to their suspected Communist sympathies. In 1947, Herbert Biberman was one of the ten Hollywood screenwriters and directors who refused to answer the House Un-American Activities Committee's questions on their Communist Party of the USA affiliation. Biberman was cited for contempt of Congress and was put away in the Federal Correctional Institution at Texarkana for six months. He directed *Salt of the Earth* upon his release. Hailed later as one of the first pictures to advance a feminist social and political viewpoint, the film features a long and difficult strike based on a real-life strike against the Empire Zinc Company in Grant County, New Mexico, in 1951. Sponsored by the International Union of Mine, Mill and Smelter Workers, the film was shot in neorealist style, using actual miners and their families as actors. The film was denounced by the U.S. House of Representatives for its alleged Communist sympathies while the FBI investigated the film's financing. The American

Legion, an organization of U.S. war veterans, called for a nationwide boycott of the film. The *Hollywood Reporter* charged at the time that the film was made "under direct orders of the Kremlin."[81] Critics' reviews of the film were mixed.

But Bosley Crowther, the film critic for the *New York Times*, responded favorably, calling the film "a calculated social document." Crowther wrote that "in the light of this agitated history, it is somewhat surprising to find that *Salt of the Earth* is, in substance, simply a strong pro-labor film with a particularly sympathetic interest in the Mexican-Americans with whom it deals. . . . But the real dramatic crux of the picture is the stern and bitter conflict within the membership of the union. It is the issue of whether the women shall have equality of expression and of strike participation with the men. And it is along this line of contention that Michael Wilson's tautly muscled script develops considerable personal drama, raw emotion and power."[82] Wilson, the screenwriter who was blacklisted and had to work under a pen name for some years afterward, later won an Academy Award for the screenplay of *The Bridge on the River Kwai* (David Lean, 1957). *Salt of the Earth* found an audience in both Western and Eastern Europe a few years after its slim American release. The film's depiction of the suppression of the labor movement is said to have inspired underground devotees of "unionists, leftists, feminists, Mexican Americans, and film historians."[83] The film made its way to China in 1960 from a third country.[84]

4

Internal Reference Films and the Never Vanishing Hollywood Presence in China

[The] 1930s–40s was the period when capitalism was on the rise, so the films made during the time were more enjoyable.

—Jiang Qing[1]

In his directorial debut, *In the Heat of the Sun* (1994), Jiang Wen, famous for his lead role in *Red Sorghum*, chose a coming-of-age story set in the period toward the end of the Cultural Revolution. The film captures the fond and idyllic memories of a group of juvenile delinquents as they loiter around, chase girls, and look for trouble. Though nostalgic in its overtone, the film is not a celebration of the Cultural Revolution but an affirmation of the liberating power of being young and alive with boundless imagination and creativity even under the harshest political climate. *In the Heat of the Sun* is an adaptation of a popular 1991 novel, *Wild Beasts*,[2] by the satirical Beijing author Wang Shuo. In Wang's rendition of life during the period, the carefree and lackadaisical attitude of youth made for an exhilarating coming-of-age journey. Youth were relatively free during the period, with adults mostly absent, carrying out Mao's revolutionary tasks. Wang's fiction works, many of which have been adapted into films and TV dramas, are known for their biting satires and irreverent antiheroes. The teenage clique in *In the Heat of the Sun* is one such instance.

One of the group's most intriguing routine shenanigans is to sneak into a movie theater to watch foreign films. The forbidden film fruits are enticing to the roguish youth in Jiang's film. To impress a girl on whom he has a crush, the lead character brags about his ability to sneak everybody into the theater. The night when the group does sneak into the theater, the film on screen is *The Last Roman/Kampf um Rom I* (Robert

Siodmak, 1968), a scandalous West German–Italian co-production starring Laurence Harvey, Orson Welles, Sylva Koscina, and Honor Blackman. Depicting the sixth-century power struggle between Byzantine emperor Justinian and the Ostrogoths, the historical epic received lukewarm reviews in the West but was fast-tracked for dubbing in China in 1971, apparently upon a request from Lin Biao, the Chinese army general who would carry out a failed coup against Mao soon after. Lin was said to have been intrigued by the murders and coups that enlivened the imperial politics of sixth-century Rome.[3] Another scandalous aspect of *The Last Roman* was its provocative nude scenes involving two rival sisters, which created a stir among the few Chinese with access to "internal reference" films.

In the Heat of the Sun captures the transfixed expressions of the teenagers upon their sighting of naked female bodies as they hide at the back of the movie theater sneaking peeks at the film. The lights suddenly switch on, exposing the youngsters. The screening is halted. An elderly army statesman in the front row with a beautiful female companion by his side stands up and makes an impromptu speech, telling the kids that this film is seriously poisonous and that they will be led astray if they watch it. The purpose of adults watching this film is to criticize it, he says. The kids are ushered out, and the adults promptly resume the serious business of reviewing films.

After decades of successful screening in China, Hollywood films vanished from the Chinese screen during the Mao era. Yet, hidden from the public eye, many Western films, including classic Hollywood films, were available to the party rank and file as well as to key film professionals. These became known as "internal reference films." The phenomenon of clandestine viewing of Hollywood films lasted until the end of the Mao era; watching poisonous films was a common ritual among the privileged few with access. The studio responsible for the translation of many such internal reference films was the Shanghai Dubbing Studio.

The Shanghai Dubbing Studio

Despite the ban on Hollywood films early on, and on Soviet films later, foreign films became available through restrictive internal screening to

Shanghai Dubbing Studio's recording room on the rooftop. Source: Pan Zheng,
Peng Li Peng Wai: Shanghai Dianying Yizhichang de Huihuang yu Beichuang
[In and out of the Studio: The Glories and Frustrations of Shanghai Dubbing Studio]
(Beijing: SDX Joint Publishing, 2016).

film practitioners for professional needs and to an exclusive group of
ranking party officials led by Mao Zedong's fourth wife, Jiang Qing. A
second-rate movie actress herself during the Republican era, Jiang Qing
was a closeted Hollywood devotee with a trove of Hollywood films,
mostly dubbed but some in original versions, at her private disposal, even
when she was attacking Hollywood in public. She reportedly had a fondness for classic Hollywood films of the 1940s, including *Bathing Beauty*
(George Sidney, 1944), *Jane Eyre* (Robert Stevenson, 1943), and *The Red
Shoes* (Emeric Pressburger and Michael Powell, 1948), which were housed
at the China Film Archive, a Beijing-based archive established in 1958
under the direct administration of the central government's Department
of Propaganda.[4] Jiang told people around her that "the 1930s–40s was the
period when capitalism was on the rise, so the films made during the time
were more enjoyable."[5] She reportedly made Hollywood titles available
for internal viewing so that ranking film professionals could learn advanced production techniques from Hollywood, never mind the "decadent" nature of Hollywood productions. A 1965 production plan issued
by the Propaganda Department at the end of 1964 permitted the appro-
priation of Hollywood techniques in the production of socialist films.

Shanghai Dubbing Studio emerged as the major provider for dubbed internal reference films from the West.

Established on April 1, 1957, Shanghai Dubbing Studio was the successor to the Shanghai Studio's Translation Unit led by Chen Xuyi, a veteran translator of English-language stage plays.[6] The Translation Unit re-voiced exclusively Soviet films in 1950–52. Films from Eastern Europe were added to the list in 1952–53. Starting from 1954, efforts were made to introduce a diverse range of films from Asia, Africa, and Latin America as well as progressive titles from the West, including Western adaptations of world-renowned literary works and films of diverse styles and trends, many of which were world classics. The Translation Unit re-voiced several memorable films in the 1950s, including *Rome, Open City* (Roberto Rossellini, 1945), which was dubbed for public viewing in 1954.

Translation and dubbing originated in 1930s when France, Italy, Germany, and Spain started using local actors to re-record dialogue for imported American films. The process of replacing the original audio with translated voiceover is known as dubbing or "re-voicing." Similar to creating translated subtitles, where literal translation is usually replaced with a translation that captures the basic meaning and intent of the original dialogue, the audio in dubbing must be translated into the local language and the sounds of words must match the shapes the actors on screen make with their mouths. The voice actors' voice performance must also match the tone and rhythm of the original audio. In the quintessential dubbing method called lip-sync dubbing, the original audio is completely removed, translated, and re-recorded in order to match the mouth movements with the local-language sounds. In China, the re-voicing pioneers knew little of this, and with no access to European practices they turned to the Soviets for techniques. But the quality of Soviet dubbing, as shown in Soviet films with Chinese re-voicing done by Russian actors, was not up to par, so the Shanghai team experimented with various methods on its own. One advanced technique, known as "looping," consisted of playing short pieces of the original dialogue over and over with a special machine until a proper audio recording was done. A less expensive way was lock-to-picture recording, where the voice actors just watched pieces of the film over and over and recorded their audio until it matched perfectly with the original performance. The Shanghai team could not afford the expensive machinery needed for looping, so they had to make do with the more labor-intensive lock-to-picture recording. To ensure quality delivery, Chen Xuyi assigned each film a director to work with voice actors to rehearse and do multiple recording takes. The studio also obtained original scripts from overseas to do the translation before re-voicing.

In 1957, the Translation Unit's office in the Hamilton Building (now Fuzhou Mansion) in Shanghai's Jingan District became the base for the newly established Dubbing Studio.[7] Headed by the same Chen Xuyi, the newly independent Dubbing Studio served at Madame Mao's pleasure by translating and re-voicing foreign films on demand. The dubbed films were made available for internal viewing ostensibly to detect and ward off unhealthy cinematic undercurrents, but these closed viewings at the same time helped Madame Mao reach decisions on what foreign films should be emulated.[8]

Internal Reference Films for the Rank and File

Between 1949 and the beginning of the Cultural Revolution in 1966, internal reference films were only accessible to party rank and file at Zhongnanhai, the exclusive party compound adjacent to the Forbidden City. Once a Qing imperial garden, the place has served as the central headquarters for the CCP and the State Council since the founding of the People's Republic of China. It houses the office of the president and premier of the PRC. Screenings of internal reference films frequently took place at the Western Hall of the compound, with the highest security clearance. A special pass signed by Yang Shangkun, then director of the CCP Central Committee, was required to enter the Western Hall. Party leaders who frequented the internal reference film screenings included CCP secretary-general Deng Xiaoping and Liu Shaoqi, chairman of the National People's Congress Standing Committee from 1954 to 1959; it was said that Liu and Deng were among the most devoted attendees at these private weekly screenings. Other attendees were the dancers who came to Zhongnanhai to serve as CCP leaders' partners during the compound's frequent ballroom dance parties.

Jiang Qing also held secret screenings of so-called "workshop films." Mao's wife was keen to keep abreast of new cinematic trends around the world, and her personal taste dictated national choices.[9] Internal memos dispatched to production studios carried Jiang's frequent instructions to the Chinese film community, ranging from making film prints green instead of red, which was more routinely used in Chinese production, and to use more "long takes" that were in vogue in both Hollywood and Soviet cinemas as well as European cinemas, which explained the stylistic choice of Chinese films made during the period, including *Early Spring in February*, which utilized long takes to capture the stillness of life in a small town.

In the late 1950s and early 1960s, to improve Chinese filmmakers' professional skills, internal reference films were organized at the building that housed the China Filmmakers' Association in Beijing. The association showed films at its 200–300-seat screening room every Sunday,[10] and many of the films screened were pass-throughs. Instead of returning to the distributors right away, Chen Huangmei, the deputy head of the Ministry of Culture, made these films available for "sneak previews" to filmmakers with little exposure to world cinema.[11] Some pass-through films, including political films from Eastern Europe, had no dubbing or subtitling and required on-site translation; in these cases, language experts were brought in for simultaneous translation. The association ran a snack bar at 4:30 p.m. every Sunday for people to gather and discuss films before the 6:30 p.m. screening. These weekly Sunday screenings and discussions essentially functioned as a salon for Western films.[12] Titles screened were eclectic, ranging from *Dracula* (Terence Fisher, 1958) to *Pickpocket* (Robert Bresson, 1959);[13] many were award-winning or festival-nominated films.

During the early days of the Shanghai Dubbing Studio, the studio would screen internally the rough cut of its dubbed version before submitting the film to Jiang Qing's people for approval. Studio staff could receive four complimentary tickets per week. That special viewing privilege brought esteem and conferred power. Family members of Shanghai Dubbing Studio staff used tickets to bribe schoolteachers, canteen servers, and food venders. Going to the Dubbing Studio to watch re-voiced films became a sought-after event. As Pan Zhen, the son of the renowned voice actress Liu Guangning, recounts, his family used tickets to exchange for meat and other food ration coupons.[14]

Access to internal reference films actually widened during the Cultural Revolution, particularly for key film practitioners and cultural gatekeepers whom Madame Mao deemed essential to her effort to launch quality domestic revolutionary film production. The Proletarian Command Centre Jiang Qing set up in Beijing to facilitate the Cultural Revolution issued an order in 1970 for the Shanghai Dubbing Studio to re-voice eight films for internal circulation. Code-named "Shanghai Internal One to Eight,"[15] the films included the French film *The Red and the Black* (Claude Autant-Lara, 1954), a co-produced film shot in Vienna titled *Bel Ami* (Louis Daquin, 1955), the British film *The Red Shoes* (Michael Powell and Emeric Pressburger, 1948), the Hollywood musical *The Unfinished Dance* (Henry Koster, 1947), and several British documentary films.

Hollywood for a Private Stash

During the Cultural Revolution, Jiang built a private film collection at the exclusive Diaoyutai (fishing platform) Guesthouse, a historic hotel and guesthouse complex in Beijing so named because the site had been a favorite imperial fishing spot in the eleventh century. Frequently housing visiting foreign dignitaries and provincial government officials, the site was used as the office of the Central Cultural Revolution Group as well as Mao and Jiang's residence. An ardent viewer with a particular fancy for Hollywood films, Jiang routinely ended her workday by watching films there well past midnight, often in the company of her "Gang of Four" coterie.[16] Seasoned language experts provided simultaneous translations for Jiang and her cohorts for the films that were not dubbed.[17] The highest ranked party leaders also enjoyed tiny private screening rooms that came with only three to four rows of seats. As recounted by Dai Guangxi, a regular translator of Russian-language films, the party leaders normally settled into film screenings past midnight, with Jiang frequently showing up around 2 a.m.

Jiang and Wang Hongwen, the youngest member of Jiang's political clique, were said to be the most avid viewers in the weekly film group. While Wang preferred Hollywood musicals from the 1930s and 1940s, Madame Mao did not usually revisit those Hollywood classics, as she had already watched them in theaters during the Republican era. The 1930s Hollywood films, however, remained her favorites, and she paid particular attention to the camerawork, performance, scenery, and soundtrack in classic Hollywood films. While Jiang did watch films from the Eastern Bloc, including Soviet films, Dai Guangxi would sit next to Jiang and whisper simultaneous translations. Dai notes that Jiang generally preferred Hollywood films over Soviet films and fancied the U.S. version of *War and Peace* (King Vidor, 1956) featuring Audrey Hepburn and Henry Fonda over the Soviet *War and Peace* (Sergei Bondarchuk, 1966).[18] *The Dove*, a 1974 Hollywood biopic directed by Charles Jarrott, was rumored to be one of Jiang Qing's favorite films. Produced by Gregory Peck, the film told the true story of Robin Lee Graham, a young man who spent five years sailing around the world solo, with his girlfriend cheering him from port to port. Jiang was said to have a particular fondness for the climactic scene when the two lovers jump into the ocean before the boat docks and swim toward each other, he from the boat and she from the riverbank. As the two love birds embrace each other with a wet kiss while still in the water, Jiang was heard to have remarked that "I would have jumped into the ocean if I were her."[19]

While alone, Jiang watched films to unwind. She apparently suffered from insomnia, which she attributed to the demanding job of leading the Cultural Revolution. For better sleep after a long day of making revolution, Jiang needed a good distraction. Occasionally her hobby turned out to be counterproductive. Albert Lewin's 1945 gothic horror film *The Picture of Dorian Gray* caused considerable distress when Jiang watched it one summer night in 1968. Adapted from Oscar Wilde's 1890 novel of the same title, the film tells the story of a vain and narcissistic man attempting to preserve his youthful good looks by making a devil's bargain to let his portrait instead of his real self age as he pursues a life of vice. When his appearance in real life remains unchanged, his portrait ages, capturing his degeneracy. Horrified by the withered and wrinkled visage of his portrait that reflects his sins, he stabs the portrait in the heart and winds up stabbing his own heart. One can only imagine how Jiang Qing would react to such a film. The insomniac Jiang reportedly went hysterical after watching the film, and no amount of sleeping pills and other tranquilizers could calm her down. It took another film to sedate her. That movie, *The Red Shoes*, was her security blanket, particularly a few segments in the film that later become her frequent bedtime screening.

Written, directed, and produced by Michael Powell and Emeric Pressburger, *The Red Shoes* tells the story of a promising ballerina who must choose between her career and her love affair with a composer. Most of the cast were professional dancers. The film was initially sent to Beijing for translation, but the quality of the dubbing did not meet Jiang's standard, so a copy was dispatched to Shanghai Dubbing Studio to redo the voices. By then many of the veteran voice actors, including the head of the studio, had all been sidelined, so the re-voicing was done by second-rate actors, not to Jiang Qing's satisfaction. The film was sent back to Shanghai for a do-over, and the Worker's Revolutionary Team, which took over the Dubbing Studio during the Cultural Revolution, had to summon the sidelined veteran studio head Chen Xuyi back to handle the task. Chen cast Qiu Yuefeng in the voice of the imperious ballet instructor Boris Lermontov, whose jealous rage over his leading lady's love affair with his composer leads to her death. Jiang's favorite scene in the film was Lermontov's angry outburst upon reading Vicki's letter resigning from the ballet troupe to be with her lover.[20] The film was released for public viewing after the Cultural Revolution.

Featuring a seventeen-minute ballet sequence not in one continuous performance, *The Red Shoes* uses a variety of shots and editing techniques to piece together the long ballet vignettes, offering an enhanced experience of the ballet centerpiece.[21] A technical feat, the film likely provided inspiration to Jiang and her film team as they sought to turn the ballet version of the revolutionary opera *Red Detachment of Women* into a model film. Jiang was developing revolutionary ballet operas at the time when she became infatuated with *The Red Shoes*. To push Chinese stage arts closer to the masses, she commissioned new, revolutionary works, eventually assembling five operas, a symphony, and two ballets, including *The Red Detachment of Women*, a revolutionary ballet featuring a fierce young peasant woman fighting for liberation. The film version of the ballet first appeared in 1972, and Li Wenhua, the cinematographer of *Early Spring in February* (Tieli Xie, 1963) a decade earlier, was the chief "snowrunner," cinematographer, and director of the new film. Liu Qingtang, a ballet dancer, shot to fame by performing the part of Hong Changqing, the party commissar in the film. In 1975, Liu was promoted to vice minister of the Ministry of Culture under Jiang and was then appointed as the head of the Film Subcommittee of the Cultural Revolution Committee to lead a team to select internal reference films for party leaders.[22] Liu tasked the Shanghai Dubbing Studio with re-voicing the chosen films.

While Liu made the selections for the rest of the party leaders, Jiang Qing relied on her personal secretary and security detail and nurses, who knew her preference by heart, to select bedtime films for her. The broad instruction she gave was: no horror films, no pornography, and no reptiles.[23] During the screening of *The Dawns Here Are Quiet* (Stanislav Rostotsky, 1972), a Soviet war drama featuring a garrison of Russian female soldiers in World War II, a group bathing scene with female nudity apparently agitated Jiang, who denounced the film as obscene. The film was nominated for an Oscar in the Best Foreign Language Film category and became a popular hit in China when it was officially released for broadcast on China Central Television in November 1993.[24] Other titles that received repeated bedtime viewing by Jiang included *Humoresque* (Jean Negulesco, 1946), *The Farmer's Daughter* (H.C. Potter, 1947), *Great Expectations* (David Lean, 1946), *Gaslight* (George Cukor, 1944), *Waterloo Bridge* (Mervyn LeRoy, 1940), *Random Harvest* (Mervyn LeRoy, 1942), *Queen Christina* (Rouben Mamoulian, 1933), *Camille* (George Cukor, 1936), *Suspicion* (Alfred Hitchcock, 1941), *Fiesta* (Richard Thorpe, 1947), *Rebecca* (Alfred Hitchcock, 1940), *Letter from an Unknown Woman* (Max Ophüls, 1948), *The Great Waltz* (Julien Duvivier, 1938), *The Yearling* (Clarence Brown, 1948), *Heartbeat* (Sam Wood, 1946), *The Hunchback of Notre Dame* (Jean Delannoy, 1956), *Roman Holiday* (William Wyler, 1953), *The Million Pound Note* (Ronald Neame, 1954), and *Notorious* (Alfred Hitchcock, 1946). Jiang occasionally called for films by particular stars, and Ingrid Bergman, Paul Newman, Gary Cooper, Joan Fontaine, Tyrone Power, Vivien Leigh, and Shirley Temple were among her frequent summonses.

Hollywood as a Model for Revolutionary Operas

To prepare for the making of revolutionary model opera films, Jiang made her private collection available for internal viewing to a few hand-picked filmmakers to expose them to the more sophisticated Hollywood filmmaking. Zhou Enlai too encouraged Chinese filmmakers to watch quality Hollywood films and learn advanced filmmaking techniques and technologies.[25] As Li Wenhua recounts, Jiang invited a handful of film-makers to the Diaoyutai, among them Li and Xie Tieli, to watch Hollywood films with her. During the frequent late-night double-feature screenings, Jiang parked herself in the front row and left the rest sitting in the back, commenting frequently and quizzing the group behind her while the film was in progress.[26] Xie, Li, and the few selected fellow filmmakers paradoxically had more access to Hollywood films during the Cultural Revolution than during the earlier period. Li went on to make *Red Detachment of Women* (1970) while Xie went on to make *Taking of the Tiger Mountain* (1970), another model opera film. Groomed to make model revolutionary films, the group was instructed to be critical of Hollywood content but to learn from sophisticated Hollywood techniques including costume, lighting, character building and blocking, and scene design. In practice, it was a tall order for the Chinese film-makers to separate the influence of Hollywood technology and style from its story and worldviews.[27]

Jiang kept her favorite films in her private archive at her Diaoyutai residence.[28] The private archive was dismantled in the summer and fall of 1975 and Jiang returned all film prints to the China Film Archive in Beijing. But Jiang subsequently set up a top-secret Special Cultural and Art Archives[29] to hoard a separate collection, which became known as the Thirteenth Vault.[30] Together with Yu Huiyong, a music faculty member at the Shanghai Conservatory and one of the early participants in Jiang's model film experimentation, Vice Culture Minister Liu, the former ballet dancer, took charge of guarding the secret vault. Permission to sign out any print required the signatures of both Liu and Yu.

In the early 1970s, Zhu De, one of the Politburo Standing Committee members and a marshal of the People's Liberation Army, asked that the internal reference films be sent to the CCP's Internal Liaison Department so that cadres cast aside by the political winds, including many good friends, could enjoy watching films with him together. Deng Xiaoping frequented these screening occasions. In fact, Deng participated in a film screening two weeks before being purged a second time in 1976 when Jiang's "Gang of Four" clique started the "Criticize Deng and Oppose the Rehabilitation of Right-Leaning Elements" campaign. Deng was subsequently removed from the party's power apparatus and his film viewing privilege was revoked.

A special team at the China Film Archive oversaw selecting films for Mao in the early 1970s. The team purchased a few dozen Hollywood films made in the 1940s and 1950s and had them dubbed for Mao. These films formed the main collection of Hollywood films in the mid-1970s at the China Film Archive. Mao reportedly admired Greta Garbo's acting skill and particularly loved Bruce Lee's martial arts films such as *The Big Boss* (1971) and *Fist of Fury* (1972) by Lo Wei and *Way of the Dragon* (1972) by Bruce Lee. On May 22, 1976, a few months before Mao's death in September, Liu directed the China Film Company to establish a film reference division devoted exclusively to selecting films for central party leadership including Mao.[31]

During the Cultural Revolution, Shanghai Dubbing Studio re-voiced a number of Hollywood classics from Jiang's personal collection; among them were *The Sound of Music* (Robert Wise, 1965), *Patton* (Franklin J. Schaffner, 1970), *Bathing Beauty* (George Sidney, 1944), *The Ten Commandments* (Cecil B. DeMille, 1956), *Notorious* (Alfred Hitchcock, 1946), *Tomorrow Is Forever* (Irving Pichel, 1946), *Queen Christina* (Rouben Mamoulian, 1933), *Random Harvest* (Mervyn LeRoy, 1942), and *Waterloo Bridge* (Mervyn LeRoy, 1940). Many of these films had been popular in Chinese theaters, without subtitles, in the 1930s and 1940s, but were banned after 1950. *Queen Christina* (Rouben Mamoulian, 1933), *Random Harvest* (Mervyn LeRoy, 1942), *Pride and Prejudice* (Robert Z. Leonard, 1940), and *The Valley of Decision* (Tay Garnett, 1945) were all dubbed in 1975, shortly before the end of the Cultural Revolution, from the original English prints available during the Republican era. Most of the dubbed versions were never publicly screened.

Among the few that received public screening, *Waterloo Bridge* was dubbed in 1975 and released in the 1980s. The film was said to have been one of the favorites of Jiang Zemin, the CCP leader who came to power following the 1989 Tiananmen Square crackdown.[32] Another one of Jiang Zemin's favorites was *The Great Waltz* (1938). Jiang Zemin reportedly sang the theme song, "One Day When We Were Young," on multiple occasions while meeting with foreign diplomats. The year 1976 saw the re-voicing of *It Started with Eve* (Henry Koster, 1941) and *The Sound of Music* (Robert Wise, 1965), both done by the Shanghai Dubbing Studio. Since one-third of the dubbed films were from Hollywood, the period essentially saw an internal revival of classic Hollywood.

Dubbing and the Expansion of Internal
Reference Films in the 1970s

The dawn of the 1970s saw relaxation on the cultural front, owing partly to China's pivot to the West. Henry Kissinger flew on secret diplomatic missions to Beijing in 1971 to meet with Premier Zhou Enlai. On July 15, 1971, Richard Nixon shocked the world by announcing on live television that he would visit the PRC the following year. As the world awaited Nixon's China visit, the highly limited access to internal reference films was relaxed. Organizers of numerous conventions and conferences managed to book internal reference films, usually two films per night, as special treats and also incentives for attendees to sit through otherwise exhausting marathon party meetings.[33] Frequent overnight screenings at military compounds could run for seven to eight hours straight in the early 1970s.[34]

As the demand for internal reference films grew, the Ministry of Culture issued a memo on January 12, 1972, to curb unauthorized screenings by taking to task the problematic screening of "poisonous films without post-screening criticism sessions."[35] A month after the memo was issued, Nixon embarked on his seven-day historic trip to China, ending twenty-five years of hostile relations between China and the United States. The trip planted the first seeds of China's opening to the world, and Nixon became a hero to the Chinese, in spite of the downturn of his political fortunes in the United States only two years later. Nixon's memoir would become a popular item when it was translated into Chinese and published in China.

In May 1972, Premier Zhou Enlai invited the Italian leftist filmmaker Michelangelo Antonioni to China to make a film that would introduce China to the world. Antonioni visited China from May 13 to June 16, and the resulting 217-minute travelogue *Chung Kuo, Cina* came out in December 1972, capturing in an unembellished, rambling observational style the lives of ordinary Chinese in drab Mao-era clothing against the backdrop of equally drab socialist apartment complexes and streetscapes. Jiang Qing—who had by 1973 become Zhou Enlai's political rival—attacked the film as slanderous to the Chinese. The film received restricted showing in China for the purpose of critiquing,[36] echoing the call from the Ministry of Culture in its January 1972 memo of the need for organized criticism of "poisonous films." Jiang continued her assault on the film throughout 1973 and into 1974.[37] At a January 25 speech in 1974, Jiang declared that the film was orchestrated by a spy-cum-traitor, insinuating that Zhou was conspiring with Antonioni to destroy Mao. An opinion piece appeared in the *People's Daily* on January 30 to further denounce the film. *Chung Kuo, Cina* was subjected to relentless attacks in the state media, and the director whom Jiang called "the clown from Rome"[38] was branded an enemy of the Chinese people.[39] Antonioni was denounced as a lackey of both Benito Mussolini and the Soviet leader Leonid Brezhnev. Wall posters in Beijing covered his face with swastikas, and his films were soon banned in China. The incident left Antonioni traumatized.

Films from the Socialist Bloc

Movie theaters gradually resumed regular public film screenings in the late 1960s. Following seven years of mostly model films, the eager public treated every new release as a holiday. Whenever a new film became available for public screening, schools and work units reserved tickets at the group rate and treated students and employees to complimentary screenings. Free movies, cash bonuses, and company-sponsored yearly banquets became the main fixtures in China during holidays. In 1973, at the height of the critique of poisonous films, the production of feature films resumed.

New imports, chiefly from Vietnam, Romania, Albania, Yugoslavia, and North Korea, appeared publicly alongside new domestic titles. Many of the 200 internal reference films in circulation in the 1970s were from the socialist bloc. A total of seventy feature films were distributed publicly in China from 1966 to 1976, and among them thirty-six titles were dubbed foreign films. Of the imports available for public screening, eight came from North Vietnam and eleven from Albania. Albanian and North Korean films were particularly popular. Beijing audiences even came up with shorthand characterizations of these foreign films: "A Korean film: weep and smile; a Vietnamese film: rifles and artillery; an

Albanian film: all hugs."[40] The "all hugs" Albanian films such as *Victory Over Death* (Piro Milkani, 1967), *Clear Horizons* (Viktor Gjika, 1968), and *The Guerrilla Unit* (Hysen Hakani, 1969) featured intimate physical contacts between lovers and comrades on-screen that were particularly popular in China, and viewing these films served as a rite of sexual awakening for otherwise chaste Chinese youth. Joan Chen, the Chinese American actor born and raised in China known for her role in *The Last Emperor* (Bernardo Bertolucci, 1987) and the TV show *Twin Peaks*, recalled her "sexual awakening" while watching the Albanian film *Victory Over Death* as a teenager.[41] The Albanian films are available through online portals in China now but are banned in Albania. The director of Albania's Institute for Communist Crimes calls most Communist-era Albanian films "a massive brainwashing tool" and "an ethical and aesthetic catastrophe" for the younger generation. The Albanian Cinema Project, which dedicates itself to the preservation and restoration of the country's films, argued otherwise, emphasizing that these movies address the "rich and complex legacies of Communist-era film production," and are thus vital for both Albanian and international audiences "to confront and come to terms with this past."[42]

In 1972, the North Korean melodrama *The Flower Girl* (Choe Ik-gyu and Pak Hak) created a sensation in Beijing, with ticket lines stretching around the block at the movie theaters.[43] Theaters had to adopt a twenty-four-hour screening cycle to meet the high demand.[44] In all, close to one-third of Beijing's population reportedly watched the film in 1972–1973.[45] Based on a popular play written by Kim Il-sung while he was imprisoned by the Japanese, the story of *The Flower Girl* is set during the anti-Japanese guerrilla movement of the 1930s.[46] In the film, a poor rural girl picks wildflowers to sell at the market in order to care for her ill mother and blind sister. Her father is deceased, the brother leaves to join the revolutionary army. The film puts the main character through heart-wrenching ordeals including the death of her mother, until the brother returns to rescue the two sisters. The film was dubbed by the Changchun Studio in only seven days.[47] The opera version of the same stage play was performed in more than forty countries,[48] mostly in the Eastern Bloc, although France, Italy, Germany, Algeria, and Japan have also hosted performances.[49] The film is banned in South Korea under the national security law.[50]

Film Dubbing After the Cultural Revolution

Jiang's demise in 1976 did not interrupt the dubbing of foreign films. Dubbed foreign films were enormously popular, ushering in a golden era for the Shanghai Dubbing Studio. An assortment of available films from different periods, including *Les Misérables* (Jean-Paul Le Chanois, 1958), *Futureworld* (Richard T. Heffron, 1976), *Night Flight from Moscow* (Henri Verneuil, 1973), *Guess Who's Coming to Dinner* (Stanley Kramer, 1967), *Julia* (Fred Zinnemann, 1977), *It Started with Eve* (Henry Koster, 1941), *The Sound of Music* (Robert Wise, 1965), *The Great Dictator* (Charles Chaplin, 1940), *Nightmare in Badham County* (John Llewellyn Moxey, 1976), and *Death on the Nile* were all dubbed in the late 1970s, after the fall of the Gang of Four.[51]

In fact, newly dubbed films were now available for public screening instead of the restricted internal screenings. An incongruous buffet of films, including black and white Chinese left-wing films from the 1940s such as *The Spring River Flows East*; Italian neorealist films of the 1950s; Soviet films of the 1930s–1950s; genre films from Western Europe such as *The Hunchback of Notre Dame* (Jean Delannoy, 1956), *Evil Under the Sun* (Guy Hamilton, 1982), *Murder on the Orient Express* (Sidney Lumet, 1974); the golden era Hollywood classics; and third-world films such as *Insan Aur Aadmi* (Shabab Keranvi, 1970), *Mera Naam Hai Mohabbat* (Shabab Keranvi, 1975), *El-Soud Ela Al-Hawia* (Kamal El Sheikh, 1978), *Noorie* (Manmohan Krishna, 1979), *Caravan* (Nasir Hussain, 1971), *Awaara* (Raj Kapoor, 1951), and *Yesenia* (Alfredo B. Crevenna, 1971) all entered theaters for circulation. Audience enthusiasm saw no signs of waning and tickets were hard to come by, so much so that young bachelors would attract dates by showing off movie tickets. Theaters were packed for each screening.

As the demand for internal reference films surged, the boundary between internal and public became increasingly blurred. In 1979, the China Film Archive (CFA) started to work with local cultural institutions to organize public viewings of selected internal reference films. The same year, the CFA initiated a biannual Special Film Exhibition that utilized existing film prints for retrospectives of Japanese, Italian, and French films.[52] On such occasions, bilingual foreign experts were invited to do live translation for the undubbed films. The end of the 1970s and the beginning of the 1980s saw the initiation of Foreign Film Week, part of China's international outreach effort after decades of isolation. *Futureworld*, the first officially imported U.S. sci-fi film, was dubbed and released for public viewing during American Film Week in 1979 and became enormously popular.[53]

Among the films dubbed in 1979 was the Japanese pulpy thriller *Manhunt* (Junya Sato, 1976) starring Ken Takakura, the "Japanese Clint Eastwood," known for his brooding style and stoic presence. The China release of *Manhunt* made Takakura a household name in China. One of the first foreign films officially distributed in China when the Cultural Revolution ended,[54] the hard-boiled genre film received little notice in Japan but became a sensation in China for its sheer novelty for the long-deprived Chinese audiences. The film became the yardstick for China's emerging action genre, and its lyric-free theme song—a simple yet catchy vocal of la-las and da-das accompanied by a zippy and snazzy guitar track—was a hit. The sunglasses and the trench coat Takakura's character wears in the movie became all the rage in China.[55]

From Internal to Public via the Voices of Dubbing Actors

Chinese audiences' lovefest with dubbed films led to the founding of more state-owned dubbing studios in the late 1980s.[56] Until *Titanic* (James Cameron and Jon Landau, 1997) came along, all foreign films reaching Chinese movie theaters were invariably dubbed, with several major dubbing actors/actresses assuming considerable star status and the films leaving long-lasting impressions on devoted fans.[57] "The voice actors at that time almost commanded the same star power as that of today's Hollywood megastars and popular Hong Kong singers and actors," reminisced a female audience member who watched, repeatedly, the dubbed British tele-film *Jane Eyre* (Delbert Mann, 1970) starring George C. Scott and Susannah York. As a university student in the late 1970s, she had memorized many of Jane's lines in Chinese. "These lines are thought-provoking, moving and encouraging and expressed my own feelings when I was a young girl trying to recognize myself as a mature and independent-thinking woman," she told a *China Daily* reporter.[58]

The practice of dubbing and the concomitant phenomenon of internal reference films continued well into the late 1980s, during which Shanghai Dubbing Studio translated several U.S. films and TV shows, paving the way for the eventual return of Hollywood. The Dubbing Studio's *Spartacus* (Stanley Kubrick, 1960) won the Chinese Cultural Ministry's Best Dubbed Film Award in 1986, and the dubbed version of *Charade* (Stanley Donen, 1963) won the same award in 1989. Both are American films, an early sign of Hollywood's return to China, in public instead of as internal reference films.

The Return of U.S. Popular Culture

Deng Xiaoping signed a series of cultural exchange agreements in 1979 to allow U.S. entertainment programs to enter China. Popular films and TV shows from the United States appeared sporadically in China throughout the 1980s, after the successful release of *Futureworld* in 1979. The China debut of NBC's 1977 science fiction serial drama *Man from Atlantis* in 1980 secured a prime-time slot on China Central Television every Thursday evening at 8 p.m. In the show, Patrick Duffy starred as an amnesiac believed to be the only survivor of a lost civilization called Atlantis. A government agency recruits Duffy to conduct top-secret research and explore the depths of the ocean. The first science fiction TV drama the Chinese ever encountered, *Man from Atlantis* found enthusiastic response in China. In the United States, the show was dismissed for having a plotline that was "thinner than water" and thus lacked "adult appeal," as "the heroics and special effects" would only appeal to kids.[59] It did draw large youth followers in China. The lead character Mark, played by Duffy, became a youth icon, and the sunglasses he wore, the symbol of fashion and hip. The young in China adored U.S. film and TV programs for their irreverent attitude and the sheer viewing pleasure without the usual burden of political indoctrination.

GARRISON'S GORILLAS AND URBAN YOUTH CRIME

Another U.S. TV serial, *Garrison's Gorillas* (1968), met the same fanfare when it debuted on China Central Television in October 1980. The show featured four commandos with special skills who are recruited from stateside prisons to fight against the Germans in World War II. Led by West Pointer and First Lieutenant Craig Garrison, the group of rugged individuals carries out their exploits all over Europe, often violent and behind enemy lines. The popularity of the show caused concern among China's cultural gatekeepers, who had grown wary of the impact of sex and violence in U.S. popular culture on China's urban youth, especially the combustible unemployed young men.

The early to mid-1980s was a period in China when inflation and urban youth unemployment ran high, leading to a spike in youth crime. Urban youth unemployment was nothing new to the CCP. Back in the 1950s, the newly established People's Republic had tackled the problem by launching a rustication movement to disperse urban youth to remote rural towns and countryside. The *People's Daily* published an editorial, "Organize school graduates to participate in agricultural production labor," in 1953 to sugarcoat the massive dislocation practice. In 1955, Mao's message to Chinese youth that "the countryside is a vast expanse of heaven and earth where we can flourish" became the slogan for the so-called "Down to the Countryside Movement." The Communist Youth League took to action the same year by initiating organized farming for the youth to cultivate the land in rural areas. The tactics worked in lessening the burden of youth unemployment on the newly established socialist economy. But the Cultural Revolution disrupted the delicate equilibrium, as Red Guards from 1966 to 1968 unleashed chaos and instability in the urban centers. It became clear by late 1968 that the earlier youth relocation movement might help restore order. The *People's Daily*, under Mao's directive, published a piece entitled "We too have two hands, let us not laze about in the city" on December 22, 1968, quoting Mao's call that "the intellectual youth must go to the country, and will be educated from living in rural poverty."[60] More youth were rusticated starting in 1969.

With universities stopping college entrance exams and halting all classes, high school graduates were organized and assigned to the countryside at a national level. In total from 1962 to 1979, no fewer than 16 million youth were mandatorily displaced.[61] While the usual destinations for the sent-down youth were rural counties in neighboring areas, many were dispatched to far-flung provinces such as Inner Mongolia.

The government tried to amend its harsh policies after the Cultural Revolution. Hu Yaobang, then general secretary of the Central Committee of the Communist Party, proposed on March 8, 1980, to end the vastly unpopular and inhumane rustication movement. The movement officially ended on October 1 of that year and the youth were allowed to return to the cities. Yet homecoming was not easy, as the young men and women struggled to reacclimate to city life. The lack of immediate job opportunities for the returnees presented challenges for the central and local governments. Adept at the art of labeling, the government shunned the term "unemployment" and instead coined the phrase "waiting to be employed" to use to discuss the problem of youth unemployment in the early 1980s. The number of "waiting to be employed" reached a record of 20 million in China's urban centers. Four hundred thousand idle youth, roughly 8.6 percent of the Beijing population, loitered in Beijing alone. Rising crime rates and social instability became a major challenge by the end of the decade.

It was during this precarious period that *Garrison's Gorillas* debuted in China.[62] The first sixteen episodes of the twenty-six-episode show were screened every Saturday at 8 p.m. on CCTV in 1980. A sensational success, the show achieved a cult status in China, even reportedly receiving a Public Security Award from the Shanghai Public Security Bureau for helping to reduce the crime rate by keeping potential criminals glued to their TV sets instead of leaving them free to roam the streets of Shanghai.[63] But the goodwill toward the show did not last. The show's English title was cleverly translated into Chinese as "Dare to Die Squad," a name linked to the volunteer revolutionary fighters during the 1911 Chinese Revolution known as the Xinhai Revolution that ended China's last imperial dynasty, the Qing dynasty. The Chinese title stuck and some of the unruly youth invoked the show's Chinese title while terrorizing the streets. There was a notorious Kitchen Knife Squad in Tangshan, a city that four years before had suffered a devastating earthquake, and an Axe Gang in Hunan, Mao's home state. The crimes led to China's first "strike hard" campaign to root out youth violence. *Garrison's Gorillas* was blamed for spurring a wave of copycat urban crimes. The broadcast of the show was abruptly pulled after sixteen episodes, with black and white captioning on the screen announcing that the entire show had been completed. Refusing to believe that the show had finished its entire run, fans of the show wrote to CCTV, demanding an answer. The answer never came.

The banning of *Garrison's Gorillas* put a pause to U.S. TV imports. A Chinese book on the history of China Central Television published in August 2003 revealed that the show was pulled ostensibly for lack of artistic value.[64] The remaining ten episodes of *Garrison* were shown many years later, after 1992.[65]

FROM RAMBO TO *FUGITIVE*

Not long after the *Garrison's Gorillas* debacle in late 1980, *Rambo: First Blood* (Ted Kotcheff, 1982) made its way to China in 1985 and immediately became another U.S. hit.[66] New feature films from the United States were rare in China at the time. *Rambo* came just three years after its U.S. release so was proudly billed as a new film. *Rambo's* sheer violence and brutality dazzled Chinese viewers new to Hollywood action films. At first glance, it might seem curious that a film this violent managed to pass China's censor. But surely a simple narrative critical of U.S. imperialism that pitted a Vietnam War veteran against the U.S. government could be a welcome gift to the Chinese. Still, given the import criteria that forbids sex and violence, the selection of *Rambo* seemed odd. Ultimately financial considerations dictated film choice for the cash-strapped China Film Import and Export Corporation. At the time, the licensing fees for real blockbuster films in Hollywood were beyond China's reach. A B movie with mostly negative reviews in the United States when it first came out, *Rambo* was relatively cheap to purchase with a flat fee. A huge box-office success in China, *Rambo* was a lucrative import that generated revenues far beyond the flat fee. In comparison, another Hollywood import released earlier during the same year, *Tender Mercies* (Bruce Beresford, 1983), a Robert Duvall vehicle about a down-on-his-luck country singer, proved to be too distant and dull for the thrill-seeking Chinese audiences. *Tender Mercies* generated little enthusiasm and box office, which showed that Chinese audiences' embrace of Hollywood was not nondiscriminatory.

While Rambo's mental anguish and physical destruction came as a shock to many Chinese viewers, violence was not exactly a novelty to the Chinese audiences who were familiar with raw fistfights in kung fu films. The early 1980s saw a revival of martial arts films led by *Shaolin Temple* (Hsin-yan Chang, 1982), featuring the kung fu master turned martial arts actor Jet Li. But Rambo's high-tech violence utilizing helicopters, four-wheel-drive vehicles, and big guns offered something novel to the Chinese audience. While critics in the West objected to the film's fascist undertone, most Chinese viewers were in awe of the film and considered it far superior in cinematic quality and imagination than domestically produced films. American expatriates living in China, on the other hand, were dismayed to see "Hollywood trash" being revered by the Chinese.

But not all Chinese viewers embraced the film with open arms. One viewer in the summer of 2016 recalled her experience as a teenager watching *Rambo*, the first Hollywood film she'd ever encountered, in the mid-1980s. She went to *Rambo* partly to see "what the fuss was all about."[67] "Stallone was surreal, unlike any male lead I had ever encountered in any films I had seen up to that point," she said.[68] She went in for novelty but came out confused and frightened. The tormented and misguided Vietnam veteran on-screen proved too much for her. As she put it, "I was not able to follow the story. The entire film seemed to be one bloody escape after another and there is not much else beyond violence." She described how the image of the hollow-eyed and big-muscled Sylvester Stallone, whom she initially mistook for Arnold Schwarzenegger, hiding in a tree staring at her (via the camera) spooked her, haunting her in her dreams.[69] "Till this day, the first thing I remember whenever someone mentions this film is this image of John Rambo staring at me from in the tree."

In terms of the story itself, *Rambo*'s connection with the Vietnam War was not of any particular significance to the Chinese, though some audiences did compare John Rambo's postwar struggle with the struggles to adjust to civilian life of the veterans of the 1979 Sino-Vietnamese War, a subject that was not touched upon in Chinese films until *Youth*, a film by the veteran Chinese filmmaker Feng Xiaogang, came out in 2018.

Another Hollywood film that created a sensation, especially among youthful Chinese, was *Breakin'* (Joel Silberg, 1984), a story about a group of Los Angeles youths at a multiracial hip-hop club with a shared interest in break dancing. Released in China in 1987, two years after the sensational success of *Rambo*, the film spurred a wave of imitation, with young men twirling and spinning in public parks to the beat of rock music that blasted from portable cassette players. Break dancing became part of the distinctive urban scene in China in the late 1980s. A national break dancing contest took place in September 1988 in Beijing's venerable Workers' Gymnasium, with twelve thousand spectators in attendance.

Most of the imported U.S. film and TV shows in the 1980s were dubbed by the Shanghai Dubbing Studio. The advent of VHS and DVDs made pirated copies of foreign films readily available, thus reducing the demand for dubbing. Both dubbing and internal reference film phased out completely once China started to distribute foreign films officially and regularly in the early 1990s. The changing audience tastes, with a preference for the original soundtrack with subtitling, together with the shifting aesthetics of translation meant that authenticity was now valued over re-creation, which was the trademark of Shanghai Dubbing Studio. By the dawn of the 1990s, veteran actors at the Shanghai Dubbing Studio were either retiring or no longer living. The death of Chen Xuyi, the veteran head of the studio, in 1992 marked the turning point in the downward slide of the studio.[70] In 1994, the studio's last major dubbing, *The Fugitive*, became the first revenue-sharing Hollywood film to be shown in the PRC. Despite its historical significance and the enormous box-office success, *The Fugitive* became the swan song for the Shanghai Dubbing Studio. *The Fugitive* would open the floodgates of Hollywood's resurgence in China, with the less costly subtitling replacing revoicing. The success of *Fugitive* spurred simultaneously rejection, admiration, and the fear of Chinese cinema becoming the fugitive in a Chinese film market being taken hostage, literally and figuratively, by Hollywood.

A Course in Reversal: Decentralization and Marketization[71]

The China Film Corporation (China Film/CFC) had since 1951 been purchasing original prints from studios at a mandatory price of 9,000 yuan per print, regardless of each film's individual market value.[72] The company was renamed China Film Distribution and Exhibition Corporation in 1958. It then merged with China Film Archive and China Film

Equipment Corporation and reverted its name back to China Film Corporation in 1971. CFC acted as a wholesale agent in acquiring all domestic films and covering the cost of making prints for nationwide circulation. It also functioned as China's sole distributor by releasing films through its multilayered distribution system while handling film promotion. CFC was then made responsible for film importation and exportation, including promoting Chinese films abroad at festivals, art houses, and educational institutions.

Up until the mid-1980s, studios were able to sell their entire production output to China Film, receiving payment for their unpopular films on the strength of the popular ones, or sometimes even in the absence of popular films. Such a distribution system resembled the blanket-booking practice of the Hollywood majors during the height of the studio era, except that in China the studios did not need to exert any pressure on the distributor. As the popularity of cinema continued to rise, studios lobbied for a cut of the box-office receipts.[73]

China's economic reform in the mid-1980s shook the very foundation of the state-run studio system. Economic reforms emphasized the financial accountability of individual production units. This played a significant role in determining the parameters and possibilities of Chinese cinema as both an economically viable and politically motivated institution. In January 1986, a structural overhaul at the central level put the Film Bureau under the leadership of the Ministry of Radio, Film and Television (MRFT). The restructuring sought to consolidate and coordinate the three major sectors of China's audiovisual industry, i.e., production, distribution, and exhibition. In 1987, both the studios and the local distribution companies demanded further autonomy from China Film. The studios and the distribution-exhibition companies courted each other, agreeing to collaborate directly in film distribution to bypass China Film altogether. The MRFT issued "Policy Document 975" the same year, doing away with the mandatory price limits and allowing studios to share box-office profits with distributors.

Overall, film reform in the 1980s focused mostly on the distribution-exhibition sector, granting distributors and exhibitors a better share of the profits and more managerial autonomy. This partial reform reflected policy makers' unwillingness to come to terms with the inefficiencies of the state-run studio system, which had long been out of touch with the market. Apprehensive of a market-driven economy, the Chinese film industry had become one of the most conservative state-run sectors in China by the end of the 1980s.

The 1989 Tiananmen Square crackdown put China's overall reform policy on hold, but the stoppage did not last long. Deng Xiaoping's Southern Tour in early 1992 propelled a thorough structural overhaul of state-run enterprises, including film studios. With the studios' financial crisis exposed, a consensus emerged that Chinese cinema's state-run studio system was long overdue for a fundamental overhaul. The problems of overstaffing, especially of administrative personnel, and the aging of creative personnel and production equipment had persisted. The studios adopted measures including downsizing, internal restructuring, talent outsourcing, and linking bonuses with profits to address these challenges. However, production reform in the early 1990s did not lead to better box-office performance. Chinese cinema continued to lose audiences, revenues remained slim, and production money remained meager. The film industry was in a prolonged crisis. Hoping to improve the situation, the MRFT issued yet another policy revision in early 1994, approving the importation of ten international blockbusters annually, primarily big-budget Hollywood films. Hollywood's reentrance to the Chinese market would profoundly shape the course of Chinese cinema from this point forward.

Hollywood Reacquainted

The MRFT required imported blockbusters to represent the state-of-the-art in global cultural achievement and to display excellence in cinematic art and technique. In practice, cultural achievement and artistic and technological excellence were apparently measured by a prospective film's budget, its star power, and/or its box-office returns. Thus, as much or even more than ideology, economics determined the selection of imports. As a result, after 1995, star-studded, big-budget, and high-tech Hollywood blockbusters such as *Natural Born Killers* (Oliver Stone, 1995), *Broken Arrow* (John Woo, 1995), *Twister* (Jan De Bont, 1997), *Toy Story* (John Lasseter, 1995), *True Lies* (James Cameron, 1995), *Waterworld* (Kevin Reynolds, 1995), *The Bridges of Madison County* (Clint Eastwood,

1995), and *Jumanji* (Joe Johnston, 1995) entered the Chinese market under the revenue-sharing methods. The imports generated huge box-office revenues, totaling 70–80 percent of the Chinese film box office in 1995. As intended, the ten big imports restored Chinese audiences' theatergoing habit. "Going to the movies" once again became a leading entertainment choice.

The returning Chinese audiences took notice of domestic films, discovering some of China's own big-budget and high-tech entertainment pictures—what the Chinese called "domestic big pictures" (*dapian*). These included international co-productions with majority creative contributions from the domestic partners. The domestic big pictures all became blockbusters in 1995, with the box office of *Red Cherry* (Ye Daying) even topping the big imports. Chinese cinema made a quick recovery, with total box-office returns in 1995 15 percent higher than in 1994. With ten big imports and ten big domestic pictures, 1995 became known as "the year of cinema."

By the end of 1995, it seemed that the imports, by triggering policy changes and restoring the theatergoing habit, had together restored Chinese domestic film production. However, a closer examination reveals that the domestic box-office success mostly came from productions involving private investment. The majority of the state-run studios continued to fall behind in making marketable films. Two-thirds of the domestic films produced in 1995 were cheap knockoffs of Hollywood and Hong Kong–style entertainment films. The majority were box-office "turkeys" made by either the financially ailing state-run studios or profit-conscious private investors inexperienced in film production and distribution. The proliferation of low-budget and low-production-value entertainment pictures failed to generate profits and instead provoked tough sanctions from the government.

Meanwhile the commercial boom had other consequences. Risqué literature, politically explicit and exploitative artwork, and pirated rock music were proliferating. The government launched a campaign in 1996 to attack "spiritual pollution" and to rein in these markets. In March, the MRFT held a national film workers' conference in Changsha to address the ministry's concern about the quality of Chinese cinema, particularly low-budget entertainment films featuring gratuitous sex and violence. At the "Changsha Meeting," cinema's pedagogical function and social impact were once again foregrounded. Policy makers demanded that the industry produce and promote ten quality domestic pictures a year for the next five years. What qualified as "quality" remained vague, prompting considerable discussion among industry practitioners. As usual, the studios retreated to self-censorship, slating predominantly safe, mainstream propaganda films.

Not surprisingly, Hollywood-influenced Chinese audiences were not enthusiastic about Chinese cinema's renewed passion for the socialist genre. Film revenue fell and the number of films produced also decreased in 1996, which led to another downturn in Chinese cinema, raising doubts about whether the film market could survive without the big imports. The looming danger of a domestic film market dependent on imports propelled the state to adopt yet more protectionist policies, requiring that two-thirds of the films distributed and exhibited must be domestic productions, and two-thirds of screening time must be reserved for domestic pictures. The state's conservative turn steered many private investors away from film and toward investing in the more profitable field of television drama production.

In the Shadow of Hollywood

The Chinese film industry witnessed yet another downturn during the second half of the 1990s. While ten domestic blockbusters accounted for $3.1 million at the box office in 1995, the remaining 135 Chinese films produced the same year earned an average of only $15,000 each. At the same time, while the ten big imports (six from Hollywood) accounted for just 3.3 percent of the 269 films exhibited in Beijing in 1995, they took in 40 percent of Beijing's box-office receipts of RMB 92.6 million ($11.4 million). Hollywood blockbusters continued to dominate the Chinese market throughout the late 1990s, owing primarily to the performance of *Titanic* (James Cameron, 1997) and *Saving Private Ryan* (Steven Spielberg, 1998), which together accounted for about one-third of the total box office in Beijing and Shanghai. *Titanic* alone set a box-office record in China, taking 21 percent of Shanghai's total (RMB 38 million) and 28 percent of Beijing's total (RMB 36 million).

To boost screenings of domestic films, the Chinese Film Distribution and Exhibition Association launched a national-level theater chain, China Theater Chain, by consolidating three hundred theaters in big urban areas to guarantee that quality domestic films received the most favorable screen times. But the state's ideological impositions continued, hampering film practitioners' creative imagination, and contributing to Chinese cinema's lackluster performance at home and its scant appearance abroad. With no concessions on creative freedom, the protective measures failed to boost attendance at domestic pictures; rather, they cut into overall revenue by reducing the profit margin of the big imports in 1998. Box-office receipts for the periods allowing only domestic films were consistently lower than those during open screening periods.

The Film Bureau and the Film Distribution and Exhibition Association continued to restrict the release of Hollywood films in 1999. The entire months of May and June and September and October were blacked out. The occasions cited for the blackouts were the tenth anniversary of the June 4, 1989, Tiananmen Square crackdown and the fiftieth anniversary of the PRC's founding on October 1, respectively. The accidental U.S. bombing of the PRC embassy in Belgrade on May 1, 1999, led to a complete shutdown of Sino-American relations throughout the summer. An official decision stated that any Hollywood films released in 1999 would be permitted only "low-key" promotional campaigns, while distributors would be required to aggressively promote domestic films, particularly films made to commemorate the PRC's fiftieth anniversary. Many in the distribution-exhibition sectors expressed doubts as to whether such an antimarket practice was feasible in the long run.

The protectionist measures chiefly benefited state-supported propaganda films, what the Chinese film community calls "leitmotif films," achieving the ironic result of effectively "renationalizing" Chinese cinema in the age of globalized markets, sending "hypernationalist" productions out to compete against the wide world of glittering escapist entertainment. The vast majority of domestic pictures, mostly mediocre entertainment fare, were left to fend for themselves. Pushed against the wall, the film industry initiated a new round of vertical and horizontal consolidation to reorganize and expand the motion picture business, all with the goal of competing with Hollywood for a domestic market share.

The consolidation pushed the film industry into the era of conglomeration, leading to the founding of China Film Group Corporation (CFGC).

China Film Group Corporation and Monopoly, Chinese-Style

As the battle with Hollywood intensified, the Chinese government introduced further structural overhauls to align its film industry with the global benchmark. Film reform since the late 1990s pretty much followed the New Hollywood model, ushering the Chinese film industry into the age of conglomeration. The first stage in the consolidation push was to turn the state-controlled China Film Corporation (China Film/CFC) into China Film Group Corporation (China Film Group/CFGC) in 1999, by merging China Film Corporation, Beijing Film Studio, China Children's Film Studio, China Film Co-Production Corporation, China Film Equipment Corporation, China Movie Channel (television), Beijing Film Developing and Printing and Video Laboratory, and Huayun Film and TV Compact Discs Company into one horizontally and vertically integrated company. CFC was entirely subsidized by the government until the mid-1990s, when the huge profits it generated as the monopoly distributor of revenue-sharing imports led to its financial independence.

The founding of China Film Group Corporation emulated a Hollywood-style corporate structure, effectively extending the power of the state into the booming capitalist market economy. As China's largest state media operator entrusted with executing state policy concerning import quotas, CFGC also has the rights to distribute the most popular domestic productions. By controlling market entry and regulating distribution, CFGC quickly established a dominant position in the newly expanded marketplace. The company also enjoyed a monopoly in co-productions, which was handled through its subsidiary China Film Co-Production Corporation (CFCC), a state company established in 1979 to administer, coordinate, and promote co-productions in China. In the mid-1990s, during the negotiations for the Sino-U.S. Agreement on China's accession to the WTO, the U.S. side pushed hard to eliminate China Film Corporation's monopoly over film imports and to engage directly in film distribution in China, but the Chinese refused to budge on this particular front. China was committed to solidifying CFC's control and dominance in China, not tearing it down. And it further strengthened the state monopoly by transforming CFC to the even more powerful CFGC by the end of the 1990s.

Yet Hollywood imports continued to dominate the Chinese market despite the control by CFGC. Hollywood's enduring popularity in China tells us that Chinese audiences are a lot like global audiences when it comes to consuming popular entertainment. Chinese cinema must now compete with Hollywood for a domestic market share. Would China open its theatrical market completely by adopting the model in developed markets such as France, the United Kingdom, and Germany where there is scant limitation on theatrical releases and where film rental remittance is around 40 percent? Can the Chinese government manage Hollywood? Or can Hollywood manage China? The person who emerged to be one of the key players in the Sino-U.S. relationship was Jack Valenti, the seasoned Hollywood lobbyist.

5

Wolves at the Doorstep:
Hollywood Reenters China

That every major metropolitan area on the planet is playing mostly American movies is a monument to Jack Valenti.

—Douglas Gomery, film historian[1]

On April 26, 2007, Jack Valenti, president of the Motion Picture Association of America (MPAA) from 1966 to 2004, passed away at his home in Washington, DC, at the age of eighty-five. One sentence in his obituary in the *New York Times* read "Valenti also travelled worldwide seeking to thwart movie piracy and boost film exports to reluctant countries such as China"[2]—the only China connection noted in the recounting of his long and illustrious career as a Hollywood's spokesperson. And yet China has become indispensable to Hollywood, and Valenti played a crucial role in reestablishing Hollywood's relationship with the Middle Kingdom, now the world's largest market.

A veteran lobbyist on Capitol Hill for the Hollywood majors, Valenti served as a special assistant to President Lyndon Johnson before taking over the position as the president of the MPAA. Like his predecessors, he used his vast Washington, DC, network to lobby the U.S. government to aid Hollywood's international expansion. China emerged as one of the most promising film markets under his watch and he lobbied diligently for the U.S. government to pressure China to open its market while simultaneously cracking down on piracy, one of the thorniest issues in the olden days of Sino-Hollywood negotiation.

Market and Piracy

When Sino-U.S. bilateral diplomatic relations were officially established on January 1, 1979, Jack Valenti paid a visit to China as the president of the MPAA that same year. While in Beijing, he discussed distributing U.S. films in China with the Ministry of Culture and China Film Bureau.[3] China was a brave new world to Hollywood, which had been shut out of the PRC market for nearly three decades; the China that Hollywood knew during the Republic era was now ruled by the Chinese Communist Party. Considering the country's meager household income and underdevelopment after decades of isolation, Valenti was initially quite skeptical about China's attractiveness as a film market. As he put it, "the kind of price the Chinese want to offer for films, at this point, I think I can say, does not measure up to what our people believe is the intrinsic market value of those films."[4]

This was the same reaction Hollywood had shown toward China in the 1920s and 1930s when box-office receipts from the vast yet primitive Chinese market were only a fraction of what it could earn from the smaller, but more affluent, Japanese market. Valenti and the Hollywood majors nonetheless saw potential in cinema's unprecedented popularity and the pent-up demand by eager-eyed moviegoers in China. China's total movie attendance in 1979 was 29.3 billion, which meant that on average each Chinese citizen watched movies twenty-eight times that year. The choices were limited, and films were in short supply, so people made do with repeated viewing of a few old movies.

Deng Xiaoping announced his "open door policy" in December 1978 to reopen China's doors to the outside world and to let in foreign business interested in setting up shop in the Middle Kingdom.[5] The policy led to trade with the outside world and China started to experiment with a market economy, effectively abandoning the Soviet-style economic model and instead looking to the United States for inspiration. In 1980, the China Film Bureau sent a delegation to the United States to learn firsthand how the capitalist U.S. film industry operated.[6] The delegation met with Valenti and affirmed China's interest in importing U.S. films. The MPAA reciprocated the visit and toured China later in the same year, bringing with it a few Hollywood films to be shown in twenty Chinese cities. The head of the China Film Bureau, Chen Po, later told the

Americans in 1981 that China would love to buy more American films if they were not so expensive.

Valenti envisioned an "overall arrangement" for Hollywood to reenter the Chinese market, which meant exporting films through a standard revenue-sharing formula, essentially rejecting the flat-fee arrangement that China preferred and could actually afford at that time.[7] This proposal did not sit well with the Chinese government. Cinema-going in China, like everything else under the socialist sky, was mostly a state-subsidized event at the time. Going to the movies, together with holiday banquets and cash bonuses and even meats and fresh produce, were perks paid for by employers especially during holidays. For regular paid cinema-going, the ticket price was set way below market value. Making a profit was not the goal of movie theaters, nor of the studios that produced movies.

Chen Po, the frugal head of the China Film Bureau, vetoed any revenue-sharing rental proposal and only endorsed purchasing Hollywood films at a flat rate. As a result, and with a long-range plan to reestablish a foothold in China by exposing their films to a new generation of Chinese audiences with little to no exposure to Hollywood, the two veteran Hollywood studios, Paramount and Universal, signed a flat-fee deal with the China Film Corporation (China Film/CFC) in 1986, the Chinese state-run film firm established in 1979 to represent China in international negotiations.

At the time, China Film handled an average of ten film imports annually from U.S. independent studios at a low price of around $30,000 each. While the amount was negligible, the meager budget for Hollywood imports actually amounted to one-third of China's total import allowance. Throughout the 1980s, China Film managed to import a small number of dated independent U.S. films critical of the U.S. government, such as *Rambo: First Blood* and *Harry's War* (Kieth Merrill, 1981).

The sporadic importation of small independent films continued well into the early 1990s, a time when China's domestic film industry struggled to keep up with the pace of marketization and commercialization set by the central government. For Valenti, pushing revenue-sharing Hollywood films into the Chinese market was only one part of his China mission. The other part was to tackle piracy, which was running rampant in China, posing a major challenge to Hollywood's revenue.

With burgeoning demand for pirated copies of Western movies and TV shows, China was one of the world's most prolific audio-visual counterfeiters of VHS in the 1980s and VCD and DVD in the 1990s.[8] At the price of roughly US$1–$2, cheap pirated copies of U.S. films usually hit Chinese streets within a week or so of their U.S. cinema debuts. Pirates even released low-quality camcorder-filmed versions within days of their U.S. openings. As he plotted for Hollywood's full-fledged return to China, Valenti pushed aggressively for the U.S. government to ensure that China enforced intellectual property rights (IPR).

The United States began pressuring China to adopt stringent intellectual property laws to protect foreign rights as soon as Deng's reform policy opened the door for Western goods to come in, albeit not always through proper channels. In 1988, the U.S. Congress passed Special 301 of the 1988 Trade Act, giving the United States an effective tool to deal with nations that imposed barriers against U.S. film and entertainment products while also forbidding piracy of U.S. audio-visual products. Countries identified by the U.S. trade representative (USTR) under Special 301 could face a variety of retaliatory actions. Those with potentially the greatest adverse impact on U.S. products were designated as "Priority Foreign Countries," which were subject to trade sanctions. Valenti termed Special 301 "an essential weapon in the war against worldwide piracy and market access barriers."[9] In addition to the list of "Priority Foreign Countries," "Priority Watch List" and "Watch List" were lesser categories that would not incur immediate trade sanctions.[10] The USTR placed China on the Priority Watch List in 1989 and 1990 consecutively as it coaxed China to pursue IPR legal reform.

China promulgated the country's first copyright law in 1990, but the new law did not adhere to international standards. The USTR promptly named China a Priority Foreign Country on the grounds that China's newly devised law was not compatible with the Berne Convention, an international agreement governing copyright adopted in Berne, Switzerland in 1886.[11] China and the United States entered into a Memorandum of Understanding in January 1991 with China pledging to comply with its commitment to adopt Berne-compatible copyright regulations by joining the Berne Convention and adhering to the Geneva Phonograms Convention within the next two years. Under Valenti's close watch, China agreed to make U.S. products including Hollywood films "fully eligible for protection." Valenti was making a name for himself as a crusader against film and video piracy in unruly China.

Yet film piracy continued to rage in China as Hollywood products became increasingly popular, making the low-capital piracy business an ever more lucrative enterprise—anyone could afford to counterfeit, and no one in China at the time considered selling counterfeited goods a serious crime. The MPAA under Valenti loudly complained about the lack of enforcement of China's own laws.[12] Pressure escalated after Deng Xiaoping's Southern Tour in early 1992, which accelerated economic reform, making China an ever more attractive destination for foreign investment and products.

China's Struggling Domestic Film Industry

China's film market was shrinking by the early 1990s, losing out to more robust TV and video markets as well as other alternative entertainment options. Movie attendance in 1992 hit a historical low of RMB 10.5 billion as opposed to RMB 29.3 billion in 1979.[13] Movie attendance in Shanghai in 1992 dropped 41.7 percent from the previous year. Film attendance in Beijing in April 1993 declined 78 percent from the same period in 1992. That same year, state-owned film studios' financial losses reached RMB 70 million. As the domestic film industry struggled with the deadweight of a financially egalitarian and ideologically authoritarian system, production reform revealed studios' inflated overheads, low productivity, and lack of creativity. While mandatory profit-sharing quotas could be adjusted through tax reform and marketization at a macro level, problems with egalitarian pay scales and overstaffing could not be solved easily, since they cut deep into ideological, cultural, and political norms. The challenges of overstaffing, especially of administrative personnel, and the aging of both creative talent and production equipment persisted. Money-strapped studios were compelled to adopt a number of measures, including downsizing, talent outsourcing, and linking bonuses with profits to break the decade-old iron rice bowl mentality and to introduce market competition.

Studios cultivated multiple revenue streams by leasing out idle talent as well as equipment and studio back lots to shoot commercials and TV programs. Several entrepreneurial studios even ventured into the restaurant and discotheque business, what the Chinese called "plunging into the sea," a term apparently originating in the early twentieth century in Shanghai as a pejorative expression for young female streetwalkers.[14] The phrase was resurrected around the time of Deng's Southern Tour to capture the entrepreneurial fervent that was sweeping the entire nation, which glorified "making money" or "getting rich"—a sharp departure from Communist doctrine. Resourceful and adventurous individuals were quitting their secure state jobs en masse to start private businesses.

The number of registered private companies in China soared 88 percent in 1992, rising to 486,000.[15] Registered capital of private enterprises surged 79 percent in 1993, to $3.9 billion. Film studios giddily joined the fray to explore ways of making cash to offset budget shortfalls and to hopefully make profits. Studios were able to leverage their trademark fashion and glamour to open retail stores that sold beauty products and to form other film-related companies. Liu Xiaoqing, the lead actress in the critically acclaimed film *The Hibiscus Town* (Xie Jin, 1986) and China's most famous movie star at the time, established the Xiaoqing Industrial and Commercial Company, with business interests varying from cosmetics to real estate. Liu was later punished for tax evasion and became the first entertainment figure who went to prison as the result of "plunging into the sea."

But production reform in the form of venturing beyond studios' core businesses did not lead to better box-office performance. Chinese cinema continued to lose audiences while revenues remained slim and budgets for production remained meager.[16] Roughly 6,000 film-related companies either went bankrupt or transitioned to other businesses.[17] Pessimism prevailed regarding the long-term sustainability of not only domestic studios but the domestic film market itself. To give a quick boost to the film industry, Chinese film regulators looked beyond China's own borders and reached out to Hollywood for a quick fix.

Hollywood to the Rescue

At the annual national film distribution and exhibition convention in January 1994, Tian Congming, the vice minister of MRFT, announced that China Film Import and Export Company (CFIEC) under the China Film Bureau would import ten "excellent" foreign films that "basically reflect the finest global cultural achievements and represent the latest artistic and technological accomplishments in contemporary world cinema."[18] Tian did mince words when he added the noncommittal adverb "basically" in front of the listed criteria. The films China elected for importation were mostly commercial fare from Hollywood, catering more to the bottom line than to the lofty goal of representing "global cultural achievements." Wu Mengchen, then president of CFIEC, revealed that the importation of ten blockbuster imports benefited the company's financial well-being while also ensuring job security for 500,000 film practitioners nationwide.[19] Elsewhere, Wu reiterated on several occasions that the ten imported foreign films would not be confined solely to the top box-office movies, nor would they be limited to Hollywood films. Yet in practice the imports were almost exclusively big-budget and high-box-office megapictures, tantamount to "Hollywood blockbusters."

HOLLYWOOD'S TWIN MISSIONS IN CHINA

The MPAA opened its Beijing office in 1994, marking the real beginning of Hollywood's return to China.[20] The twin priorities of the MPAA's China office were (i) ensure China's effective enforcement of IPR while (ii) pressing for greater market access for major Hollywood studios. By the mid-1990s, roughly 200 domestic films and 60 imports were released annually in China, with U.S. films limited to only 10 slots among the 60 foreign titles.[21] In the MPAA's view, piracy was driven by censorship, quota barriers, and time lag in China's importation of Hollywood films; it wanted China to import more Hollywood big productions so as to mitigate the problem of piracy. To effectively lobby for sanctions against China's IPR violations, the MPAA teamed up with the International Intellectual Property Association (IIPA), a private-sector coalition formed in 1984 to represent U.S. copyright-based industries in bilateral and multilateral efforts to improve international protection of copyrighted materials. The IIPA also acted to open up foreign markets closed by piracy and other market access barriers. Joint efforts by the MPAA and IIPA led the Clinton administration to apply the Special 301 designation to threaten China with imminent trade sanctions. In June 1994, acting USTR Mickey Kantor put China on the Special 301 Watch List by giving an ultimatum of six months for copyright enforcement.[22]

At the same time that the MPAA pushed for piracy crackdown, it also sought better distribution terms. Flat fee remained the rule of thumb in China for imports. China did, however, open a crack to the possibility of revenue-sharing imports, initially from relatively inexpensive Hong Kong. Early in 1994, China Film approached the veteran Hong Kong studio Golden Harvest Entertainment to explore distributing Golden Harvest films in the mainland on a revenue-sharing basis. Golden Harvest, together with Shaw Brothers, dominated Hong Kong box-office sales from the 1970s to 1980s with films featuring Bruce Lee, Jackie Chan, and Sammo Hung that made a name for Hong Kong martial arts pictures in the West. Martial arts films were also popular on the mainland, which Golden Harvest had long pursued by setting up a Shanghai office two years earlier to test the market. Golden Harvest and China Film signed a tentative agreement on revenue sharing in 1994.

Before any Golden Harvest single revenue-sharing film was actually distributed in China, Hollywood majors demanded the same distribution arrangement. Warner Bros. (WB) managed to reach a deal with the China Film Import and Export Corporation in September 1994 to distribute *The Fugitive* (Andrew Davis, 1993) on a revenue-sharing basis in six Chinese cities including Beijing, Shanghai, and Tianjing.[23] In return, WB agreed to help China gain "greater exposure for domestically produced Chinese films" and to advise and assist the China Film Import and Export Corporation in bringing back to China the most "current motion picture technology."[24] *The Fugitive* was chosen for its noncontroversial subject that bore no political risk.

But the Beijing Film Company had a last-minute change of heart in distributing the film in Beijing.[25] China Film instead approached the Haidian Film Company, a district film company in Beijing, to take over the film's Beijing distribution. The Beijing Film Company had the Beijing Cultural Bureau involved in trying to stop the screening. On November 11, 1994, the night before the film's premiere, ranking party members from the Beijing Film Bureau asked to see the film prints while trying to talk the manager of Haidian Film out of the screening. Han Maorui, the manager of Haidian, lied that he had yet to get hold of the

Chinese poster for *The Fugitive*.

film print. As recounted by Han in 2008, he retrieved the film prints from his company's storage the same night and drove around overnight in Beijing to ensure that the copies were out of the reach of the Beijing Film Bureau. Han phoned the managers at the thirteen theaters that had agreed to screen the film the next morning at 7 a.m. for them to safely retrieve the film copies from him. The film screened in Beijing on schedule without a hitch. It was a cold November day, but Beijingers lined up to buy tickets. A subsequent publicity poster sensationalized the suspense surrounding the film's Beijing debut: "Reform Era, Fierce Debate, Film Market, Risk Showing."[26]

The Fugitive opened in fifty-seven movie theaters in six key Chinese cities, drawing huge attendance despite the higher than usual ticket price.[27] Though the film screened for only seven days in Beijing, it grossed roughly US$820,000 in the first ten days, with an eventual total gross of about RMB 25.8 million (US$3.15 million).[28] Golden Harvest distributed

Drunken Master II (Jackie Chan, Lau Kar-leung, 1994) later in November, making the Jackie Chan film the first revenue-sharing Hong Kong film distributed in China.[29] Other Hollywood majors including Disney, Sony, and Twentieth Century Fox soon reached their own respective agreements to export films to China via revenue sharing.[30]

The newly recognized revenue-sharing formula officially ended "the 40-year-old tradition of buying outdated and low-grade but cheap foreign movies."[31] But unlike the equitable revenue-sharing formula commonly practiced elsewhere, the Chinese-style formula compelled Hollywood majors to bear heavy taxes and tariffs as well as the costs of marketing and print, while the CFIEC took in up to 46 percent of the total box office, with the provincial distributors and theaters taking an additional 8–10 percent.[32] In the end, China opened up its market for revenue-sharing films not to please Hollywood but to build up its domestic market on its own terms and according to its own timeline and rules that Hollywood was forced to adapt.

As Hollywood wrapped up its triumphant revenue-sharing debuts in China, the Clinton administration warned China's leaders in the last days of 1994 that unless strong measures were taken to severely penalize piracy and to allow greater market access in China for U.S. entertainment, publishing, and technology products, it would impose trade sanctions on over US$1 billion worth of Chinese imports starting from February 1995.[33] China's Ministry of Foreign Trade and Economic Cooperation (MFTEC) responded with a counterthreat to block, among other things, imports of U.S. films and entertainment products, ignoring that those were the very products that Washington accused China of pirating. China also threatened to suspend approvals of U.S. companies' applications to establish subsidiaries in China.[34] A trade war seemed likely, which would become the pattern of the Sino-U.S. trade talks in the ensuing decades, culminating in the most inflammatory rhetoric during the Trump administration.

WTO AND SINO-U.S. NEGOTIATIONS

The United States had a powerful weapon on hand in its battle against China: influence over World Trade Organization (WTO) membership. On January 1, 1995, the WTO officially launched, replacing the 1948

General Agreement on Tariffs and Trade (GATT) as the largest international economic organization in the world. China had been eager to join as one of the founding members of the WTO. But China's attempt was blocked by the United States, with the Clinton administration leading the opposition in an escalating effort to get China to crack down on piracy and open the market for U.S. companies, particularly the Hollywood majors. The United States demanded an immediate removal of quotas on U.S. film imports. Chinese officials scoffed at the Americans during the negotiation, asserting that some U.S. demands were in violation of China's sovereignty.[35] The negotiations continued up until the February deadline, with the final days spent on the issue of market access for U.S. film and music companies. Finally, on February 27, 1995, the two sides signed a twenty-two-page "Agreement on Enforcement of Intellectual Property Rights and Market Access," which was, as the *New York Times* reported, "the most comprehensive and detailed copyright enforcement agreement" that the United States had ever negotiated with any country.[36]

The immediate upshot of the agreement was an intense six-month crackdown on copyright violations in China, though the Chinese authorities had generally been inconsistent in enforcing copyright and trademark laws, as local authorities enjoyed wide latitude on how to punish or excuse offenders while having little incentive to prosecute businesses that provided local revenue. The United States side insisted upon due oversight and regular monitoring. To Hollywood's delight, the Chinese also agreed to allow the establishment of joint ventures for audio-visual production, initially only in large cities such as Shanghai and Guangzhou. The plan was to allow a total of thirteen cities to establish joint ventures by 2000.

In 1995, six new revenue-sharing Hollywood movies were imported, including *True Lies* (James Cameron, 1994), *Forrest Gump* (Robert Zemeckis, 1994), and *The Lion King* (Roger Allers and Rob Minkoff, 1994). These imports generated huge box-office revenues, totaling 70–80 percent of the total box office in 1995. The biggest hit was *True Lies*, which opened in April 1995 after being delayed for a month by talks between China and the United States in late February to avert a trade war.[37] The film went on to gross RMB 120 million nationwide, setting China's box-office record, "injecting vital capital to the failing industry, and guaranteeing jobs for nearly half a million workers in the Chinese film industry."[38] In the following years, star-studded, big-budget, high-tech Hollywood blockbusters such as *Natural Born Killers* (Oliver Stone, 1995), *Broken Arrow* (John Woo, 1995), *Twister* (Jan De Bont, 1997), *Toy Story* (John Lasseter, 1995), *Waterworld* (Kevin Reynolds, 1995), and *Jumanji* (Joe Johnston, 1995) all entered the Chinese market. Films from Hong Kong were another major source for revenue-sharing imports in China, second only to films from Hollywood.

The annual ten big imports revived Chinese audiences' cinema-going habit. "Going to the movies" once again became a popular entertainment and leisure choice. The imported blockbuster spurred domestic imitations, some with the label of "international co-productions," which at the time entailed token foreign input with major creative contributions from the domestic partners.[39] The MRFT, in its 1993 Document 3, had nudged domestic studios to explore and implement marketization policies including international co-productions, which by the end of the 1990s would yield Sino-Hollywood co-productions emulating Hollywood's blockbuster formula.

Domestic big pictures also imitated their foreign counterparts.[40] With budgets over RMB 10 million ($1.25 million) each, a big sum at the time, four films in 1995—*In the Heat of the Sun* (Jiang Wen), *The King of Lanling* (Hu Xuehua), *Red Cherry* (Ye Daying), and *Shanghai Triad* (Zhang Yimou)—set budget records for domestic pictures, with revenue for *Red Cherry* topping the big imports.[41] A film directed by Ye Ying (also known as Daying Ye), grandson of the well-known Ye Ting, a KMT general turned founding member of the CCP's People's Liberation Army who served five years in Chiang Kai-shek's jail, *Red Cherry* tells a survival story of two Chinese teenagers in a Moscow international boarding school during World War II. It was selected in the Panorama section of the Berlin International Film Festival in 1996 and became the Chinese entry for the Best Foreign Language Film at the sixty-eighth Academy Awards. The film went on to win the Audience Choice Award (Best Foreign Language Film) at the Palm Springs International Film Festival.

The domestic big pictures brought hope to China's domestic film industry. Chinese cinema made a quick recovery, with total 1995 box-office returns 15 percent higher than in 1994.[42] Total receipts from the Beijing market rose by 80 percent, and movie attendance in Beijing that summer increased by 70 percent over the previous year.[43] Chinese critics attributed Chinese cinema's renewed popularity to the film industry's belated "big picture consciousness," a perception that equated budget with quality.[44] Hollywood's high-cost production values quickly became the benchmark for quality for both Chinese audiences and film practitioners.

Protective Measures

Yet despite the success of a few domestic blockbusters, China's film industry as a whole remained in a slump. By 1996, Hollywood mega-productions were making up the entire list of ten imported revenue-sharing films. Chinese audiences were thoroughly charmed by Hollywood, just as earlier generations had been. Hollywood, rather than the Chinese domestic films, benefited most from the growing audiences. Film practitioners were increasingly fearful of Hollywood's swift and decisive return to China. When *True Lies* swept the Chinese box office in April 1995, China's eight major film studios issued a joint statement, demanding that the government take necessary measures to curb Hollywood's incursion on domestic revenues and screening time. They urged the government to limit the number of imports and the length of time that imports could be shown in cinemas, and to use part of import revenue to subsidize the domestic film industry.[45] The Ministry of Propaganda, which supervised the MRFT, and the Ministry of Culture hosted the Changsha Film Work Conference in March 1996 to launch the "9550 Project," which stipulated a target of 50 "leitmotif" movies that major state-run studios must produce during the ninth Five-Year Plan from 1996 to 2000.[46] Defined by then Chinese president Jiang Zemin, leitmotif movies were those that promoted patriotism, socialism, and collectivism as opposed to the money worship, hedonism, and excessive individualism glorified by Hollywood imports as well as domestic knock-offs of Hollywood films.[47] The goal was to make ten party-sanctioned propaganda films per year for the next five years. The fifty leitmotif films would receive significant financial support from the state as well as revenues from distributing Hollywood imports. The government mandated that two-thirds of screen time be reserved for domestic films and that all theaters contribute 5 percent of their annual box-office receipts to a film fund established exclusively for domestic film production. On major holidays, blackout periods would be imposed on foreign imports to make way for domestic movies.[48] The government also exempted value-added tax for film prints sold by domestic studios.[49]

To offer further incentive, the Film Bureau stipulated that for each quality leitmotif film, the domestic studio that produced it would be allowed to select one film from among ten approved foreign blockbusters to distribute and retain profits.[50] The quota was a one-to-one exchange: one big import for one quality domestic film. Studios that failed to fulfill production quotas would lose their eligibility for import distribution and suffer revocation of state compensation. In 1996, the veteran Beijing, Changchun, and Shanghai studios won distribution rights to imports on the strength of the domestic hits they produced the previous year. Changchun Studio was granted the rights to distribute *Waterworld*, while Beijing Studio obtained the rights to distribute *Jumanji*, and Shanghai Studio *Toy Story*. After sharing the box office with Hollywood and the participating theater chains, each of these films brought the studio about RMB 30 to 40 million (US$3.62–$4.83 million) in box-office receipts, a handsome sum for the cash-starved studios.[51]

This situation was not unique to China. While struggling to keep domestic production afloat under the onslaught of Hollywood imports, European countries had similar arrangements as early as in the 1920s. Germany, for one, tinkered with its quota law by trying (unsuccessfully) to impose a one-for-one contingent plan whereby one U.S. film would be allowed into Germany for each home-produced product.[52] By and large, none of the protective measures against Hollywood worked. Not in Europe. Nor in China.

The Persistence of Piracy

Meanwhile, the United States continued to complain about piracy, which had persisted, leading to USTR Mickey Kantor's renewed call in his annual report in February 1996 urging the U.S. government to push China to live up to the Enforcement Agreements.[53] Valenti worked closely with the U.S. government to force China to step up its offensive against piracy. While pressuring the U.S. government to act on behalf of the entertainment industry, the MPAA also acted unilaterally on its own behalf. Paid solely by Hollywood majors, the MPAA's antipiracy budget for China was not the biggest (nor the smallest either) among all Asian countries. It worked closely with Chinese customs while engaging law and intelligence analysis companies in Shanghai and Guangdong Provinces to track down and carry out raids on pirates. In a clever twist, the majors recruited former pirates as their well-connected licensees for local distribution in China. By converting sophisticated and efficient piracy networks into legitimate distribution channels, Hollywood majors managed to minimize their financial cost and losses.[54] Xianke, a pirated-copy distributor, was sued by the MPAA in the Chinese courts in 1994 and ordered to compensate the MPAA for damages, lawyers' fees, as well as court expenses. Warner Brothers turned around and appointed Xianke as an official distributor in 1996.

In May 1996, the USTR threatened to impose US$2 billion in tariffs on certain goods imported from China if China failed to take actions to fulfill its commitments in the copyright agreement by June 17. As usual, China threw a counterpunch with a list of U.S. automobiles and other products targeted for retaliatory trade barriers. The two sides were once again on the brink of a trade war. Valenti lent his support to the USTR's decision before the Special 301 Committee hearing on June 6, 1996. At the hearing, he nonetheless acknowledged that the Chinese government had made progress in improving antipiracy enforcement, especially at the retail and wholesale levels, and expressed his confidence that a breakthrough could be achieved in the next ten days to reverse the decision.[55] While waving its sticks, Hollywood also used carrots to entice and appease the Chinese government by sending studio representatives to Beijing Screen, an annual showcase of Chinese films organized by China Film, as well as the Film Market section of the Shanghai International Film Festival (SIFF), to select Chinese films for potential release in the United States. A last-minute accord was signed between the two sides on June 17, 1996.

We Want More Hollywood Films: The Lovefest

On June 19, 1996, two days after China consented to a new agreement to enforce antipiracy laws, Chinese premier Li Peng signed "State

Regulations on Administration of the Film Industry (Order No. 200 of China's State Council)," which officially included a provision that reserved at least two-thirds of screen time for domestic films. In practice, though, similar to the way theaters flouted the government's mandate to screen more Soviet films in 1950, a large percentage of cinema operators in China ignored the order to restrict imported-film screenings, particularly while handling popular blockbuster films. A case in point was *Titanic* (James Cameron, 1997), a film that broke box-office records in China.

A host of external factors played to *Titanic's* favor when the film was released in China in 1998. Saturation media coverage and promotion of the film began as early as January.[56] China's president Jiang Zemin, a self-declared Hollywood aficionado, was offered a sneak preview and raved about the film. Jiang called the Hollywood rendition of the real-life tragedy a masterpiece that captured the theme of class struggle by pitting the villainous rich against the heroic poor. Jiang urged China's Politburo to watch the Hollywood blockbuster, which, in the chairman's mind, articulated better the egalitarian spirit of socialism-communism than the domestic leitmotif films.[57] Jiang's endorsement paved the way for the film's timely release on April 1, shortly after it garnered eleven Academy Awards on March 23. The film received a blanket screening in over 1,000 cinemas across China, driving that year's movie attendance to over 30 million and total number of movie screenings to 390,000, a historic high in China.[58] Cinemas basically ignored screening mandates for domestic films during the period. Regulators failed to rein in the transgressions.

AVATAR AND THE AUDIENCE-THEATER ALLIANCE

Another example of friction between distributors and government policy, which highlights the tension between economic incentive and political obligation, was the case of *Avatar* (2009), again a James Cameron picture, eleven years later. Upon its release in China in late 2009, the sci-fi eco-fable quickly won the hearts of local audiences. Yet the release of *Avatar* clashed with the planned major rollout of a state-sanctioned leitmotif film, *Confucius* (2010), a biopic about the titular Chinese philosopher written and directed by the veteran Chinese female director Hu

Mei featuring the Hong Kong megastar Chow Yun-fat. Co-produced by Han Sanping, the head of China Film Group Corporation, an all-powerful state-run film conglomerate established in 1999, the film was scheduled for release in late 2009 in commemoration of the sixtieth anniversary of the founding of the PRC, as well as the 2,560th birthday of Confucius himself.

The plan was to pull *Avatar* from nearly 1,600 2-D screens across China to make way for *Confucius*. But Chinese audiences were not happy with the government's decision and eventually rose to Hollywood's defense by using social media to express anger and ridicule the decision when the government removed *Avatar* from 2-D theaters. Their action triggered a backlash against official maneuvering, which in turn implicated *Confucius*. As the Chinese state-run English newspaper *China Daily* reported, "Amidst the outpouring of anger and frustration toward movie industry manipulations are the voices that point to the thoughts of Confucius as a negative force in Chinese history." The sudden surge of anti-Confucius sentiment challenged the state's massive promotion of Confucius's thoughts as a quintessential Chinese alternative to Western culture. Confucius became collateral damage amidst the outcry against government policy. As an article in *China Daily* commented facetiously, "What serious scholars could never [succeed] in demystifying, and whom former chairman Mao Zedong, Lu Xun and all the revolutionaries failed to topple from the pedestal, the film authorities did with one simple stroke—by throwing a boomerang at Pandora . . . and instead hitting the man they had crowned with a halo."[59]

Western news reports cheerfully chimed in, speculating that the state removed *Avatar* because it felt threatened by the film's enormous popularity and by its purported theme of antirepression. In fact, it was unusual for a Hollywood blockbuster to get a release window so close to the Chinese New Year holiday, a time slot mandated for major domestic releases, so ending *Avatar*'s 2-D run about a week ahead of the holiday's start was the normal practice. *Avatar* continued to screen in the fewer yet more popular 900 3-D screens throughout China, generating over 64 percent of the film's total ticket sales in China. But the demand for *Avatar* was so high that audiences were miffed at having to see the film only at limited 3-D theaters. Upset and moved to action, fans went online on social media sites in huge numbers to express their passion for the blue people of Pandora and against poor Confucius. Their reaction was quick, widespread, and intense, transforming passive association—audience membership—into active participation in a popular movement. Theaters joined the campaign—many simply ignored the government's order to remove *Avatar*, forcing the government to restore *Avatar* to more screens. Public's resentment toward *Confucius* and the continued high demand for *Avatar* eventually led the Chinese government to reverse its decision, allowing *Avatar* to remain on some 2-D screens while pushing the official release date of *Confucius* to January 2010.

Here, a catalyzing event turned an audience into something more like a public movement, and the government backed down through accommodating action. The public triumphed in its effort to keep *Avatar* on-screen partly due to the backing of Chinese theater chains that wished to maximize their profits from screening the Hollywood megahit. Media regulation in China during the post-Deng era, prior to Xi's reign, was a bargaining process in which the twin forces of state control and commercial imperatives negotiated with each other, sharing a common interest in cultivating a stable climate of favorable public opinion. Confucius was expendable when the financial well-being of cinema exhibitors and distributors was at stake.

Learning from and Adapting to Each Other

Chinese distributors and theaters wanted not only to screen more Hollywood films but also to emulate Hollywood's distribution mechanism, seen as more efficient and lucrative. Taking a page from Hollywood, China's film industry stepped up its effort to form theater chains in the second half of the 1990s to better consolidate. Attempts by distribution companies to break the control of local governments started in the mid-1990s. By 1996, Yongle and Dongfang had become two major theater chains in Shanghai, and Beijing Zijingcheng Company and the New Film Alliance Distribution Company had become the two earliest theater chains in Beijing. The Shanghai and Beijing experiments were the first stage of a pilot distribution reform initiative aimed at breaking local monopolies.[60] Next came the restructuring of film distribution companies and the creation of comparable and competitive theater chains in Sichuan, Jiangsu, Zhejiang, and Fujian.

To better understand Hollywood's business model, the Film Bureau organized a trip for a delegation of theater chain managers to tour the United States between September and October 1997.[61] The delegation visited Warner Brothers, Sony-Columbia, Disney, and Universal Studios, as well as five multipurpose theaters.[62] The Film Bureau also sponsored a number of lectures and seminars to educate film professionals about the theater chain system.[63]

While the Chinese were learning as much as they could from Hollywood, Hollywood was learning to adapt to the Chinese way of operating, particularly when it came to dealing with censorship in China. In this regard, Hollywood had a steep learning curve, judging by the debacle of three "problematic" films distributed in 1997, the year when Hong Kong was to be returned to China from the UK, a high time for hyper-patriotism. By coincidence, three Hollywood studios released three feature films that were deemed critical of China: *Kundun* (Martin Scorsese) by Disney, *Seven Years in Tibet* (Jean-Jacques Annaud) by Sony Pictures, and *Red Corner* (Jon Avnet) by MGM. The first two films lacerated China's Tibet policy while the third denounced China's judicial system. All three were considered politically offensive and culturally insulting to the Chinese. Media critics in China treated the isolated instances as a conspiracy, calling the three films "laughable gimmicks . . . elaborately cooked up for the sake of 'demonizing' China" and for promoting "the worldwide expansion of the mainstay U.S. industry under their political auspices."[64] In October 1997, the Chinese government issued a temporary ban on all business dealings with the three studios. In a memo issued by the Ministry of Radio, Film and Television, Chinese authorities said that the films "viciously attack China [and] hurt Chinese people's feelings."[65]

Valenti had to weigh in as the official MPAA spokesperson to appease the Chinese. In a December 1997 speech pompously titled "A Grand Confluence: The Intersection of Storytellers from East and West: A Reciting of the Fruitful Results of an Asian/American Cinema Collaboration," Valenti stressed that a few specific films would not "disrupt or collapse a culture richly fertilized by several thousand years of historical glory," and should not "interrupt the long-range beneficial interests" of both sides.[66] Sun Jiazheng, the Chinese minister of RFT, happened to be on a scheduled visit to the United States in November 1997. Valenti assured Sun at the MPAA's office in Los Angeles that these films would not exert a long-lasting impact on the collective U.S. imagination.[67] The disappointing box office of *Kundun* (grossing US$5.53 million with a budget of US$28 million) and *Seven Years in Tibet* (grossing US$37.9 million, low only relative to its budget of US$70 million) seemed to buttress Valenti's claim in financial terms, though the two films' actual impact in the United States might not be as negligible as he wanted the Chinese to believe. One U.S. journalist observed that, thanks largely to the two Hollywood films, "now, whenever the Dalai Lama visits, he's greeted by crowds befitting a rock star."[68] The fact that Buddhism, particularly Tibetan Buddhism, was a hot spiritual trend in the U.S. at the time raised the Dalai Lama fever.

Among the three films, *Seven Years in Tibet* had less severe repercussions than the other two films. Starring Brad Pitt, *Seven Years in Tibet* portrays the legendary Austrian mountaineer Heinrich Harrer during his time in Tibet between 1944 and 1951, when he met the young fourteenth Dalai Lama amidst China's civil war that led to the eventual conquest of Tibet by China. The Chinese denounced the film's negative depiction of Chinese military officers and its positive portrayal of the fourteenth Dalai Lama, whom Harrer tutored. Brad Pitt and the celebrated French director Jean-Jacques Annaud were both banned from China, but the bans were quietly lifted in the late 2000s. Annaud reportedly wrote a letter of apology in 2009 and was invited back to China in the early 2010s. The French director redeemed himself by directing a Sino-French co-production, *Wolf Totem* (2015), a film that tells the story of a sent-down Beijing student in Inner Mongolia who befriends packs of local wolves and contemplates the nature of nomadic culture during China's chaotic Cultural Revolution. An adaptation of a popular novel of ecological focus that mourns the erosion of the Mongolian nomadic culture, the film was a popular hit in China and was selected as the country's official submission for the Best Foreign Language Film Oscar. However, the academy deemed the film ineligible, citing that the production was not sufficiently Chinese, given that its main creative inputs came from the French or the Americans. Persona non grata no longer, Annaud came to China's defense by denouncing the decision made by the academy. As for Pitt, he easily charmed his way back to China with his beguiling grin initially as the spouse of Angelina Jolie in 2014, and later in 2016 as the star of *Allied*, a romance and spy thriller set during World War II.

Disney's *Kundun* encountered more resistance from the Chinese. A film about the life of the Dalai Lama, *Kundun* included a segment depicting the brutal repression by the PRC in Tibet. The studio had been warned by the Chinese government in late 1996 not to release the film. Disney proceeded with its distribution regardless, citing the filmmakers' right to free speech in the United States and the company's contractual obligation to distribute the film. Neither the cultural nor legal explanations meant much to the Chinese, and China banned the film as well as Disney in China at a time when the company was planning to build a theme park near Shanghai. The controversy led to the firing of Disney president Michael Ovitz and the hiring of Henry Kissinger as a consultant to assuage China's outrage over *Kundun*.[69] The case became the first major censorship lesson for Hollywood. Disney's new chief, Michael D. Eisner, apologized for the film during his meeting with China's premier Zhu Rongji in October 1998, calling it "a stupid mistake." Eisner went on to say that "this film was a form of insult to our friends, but other than journalists, very few people in the world ever saw it."[70] Indeed Disney simply buried the film, though people certainly heard or read about it, given the wide press coverage as the result of China's protest. To further patch things up with China, Disney bought two Chinese films a year later in 1999 and offered to sponsor an acrobatic troupe from Shandong Province in a performance tour of Europe.[71]

Disney also played up its Chinese legend–based animation project *Mulan* that had been in development since 1994 as a goodwill movie to help promote Chinese culture and tradition globally. *Mulan* was finally ready for debut in 1998, following six years of development and production. Yet to observe the blackout months that blocked Hollywood imports and kept the lucrative holiday market exclusively for domestic films, the Chinese held the Disney animation hostage for eight months and granted it only a limited release starting on February 23, 1999, the day after the end of Chinese New Year celebrations. By then all the children had gone back to school, and pirated copies were in wide circulation. *Mulan* took in just $30,000 at the box office after a three-week run in the Hunan Province. In Shanghai, apparently only 200,000 of the city's 14 million population went to see the film in theaters.[72] The titular character Mulan being too "foreign-looking" in her Disney incarnation was partially blamed for the film's lukewarm reception in China. As reported by the *South China Morning Post*, some Chinese audiences thought Disney's version had more in common with *Xena: Warrior Princess* than their beloved national heroine. The "foreign Mulan," the *Baltimore Sun* reported, did not "exhibit the same depth of filial piety as her literary predecessor" and appeared "too self-aggrandizing." Disney's Western retelling of Mulan going to war motivated by her desire to escape from a patriarchal society and an overbearing family—rather than preventing her elderly father from risking his life—was too much of a deviation from the traditional Chinese tale.

Fast-forward to March 2020 when Disney did yet another version of *Mulan* (Niki Caro), this time a live-action remake casting a Chinese American actress. But a different controversy erupted as Liu Yifei, the lead actress playing *Mulan*, tweeted her support of Hong Kong police during months of at times violent prodemocracy protest against the Hong Kong police and the Chinese central government. The scandal would soon be eclipsed by the COVID-19 pandemic, which delayed the film's release, leaving uncertain the fate of Disney's new China film. When the live-action *Mulan* finally came out in fall 2020, despite being conceived as a "love letter to China" by the New Zealand director Niki Caro of *Whale Rider* (2002) fame, the film bombed in China, suffering from bad reviews partly driven by heavy early piracy. As *Fortune* reports, the film appeared on illegal streaming sites worldwide within hours of becoming available on Disney's streaming platform Disney+ on September 4. Rampant illegal downloading meant that many viewers in China had watched *Mulan* days before it came out in Chinese cinemas on September 11. Disney+ is not available in mainland China, but users with a virtual private network (VPN) can bypass regional restrictions. On one popular site for pirated content, *Mulan* was downloaded in China more than 250,000 times in three days, the *South China Morning Post* reported. In the end, Chinese audiences simply were not impressed by the Westernized version of ancient China.[73]

In the case of MGM's *Red Corner*, the studio clashed with its star Richard Gere who played an American entertainment lawyer accused of murder on a business trip to China and who must fight the charge in China's abusive judicial system.[74] The film's release date on October 31 happened to coincide with the U.S. visit of Chinese president Jiang Zemin. Chinese officials visited MGM and questioned the timing of the release. To make the matter worse, Gere—a devout Buddhist—was an ardent follower of the Dalai Lama. Gere fanned the controversy by denouncing China's treatment of the Dalai Lama at the Academy Awards in 1993. While invited to present the award for best art direction, Gere went off script to protest China's occupation of Tibet and called attention to what he said was China's "horrendous, horrendous human rights situation."[75] Susan Sarandon and Tim Robbins, two other presenters, also went off script to speak on behalf of Haitian refugees. The show's producer, Gil Cates, a veteran of the Academy Awards telecast and the founding dean of the UCLA School of Theater, Film, and Television, did not take the unexpected political speech well, calling it a political stunt and vowed to ban all three from future Oscars broadcasts. Gere's offense at the Oscars was far less consequential than the trouble he caused for MGM by promoting *Red Corner* as a way of making a larger point about China and Tibet.

To minimize damage with the Chinese, MGM developed a marketing plan for *Red Corner* that emphasized suspense without positioning it in political terms. Gere, however, insisted that the film was a repudiation of China's judicial system and thus about Tibet as well. As if the matter could not get trickier for the studio, Gere hosted a highly publicized "stateless" dinner in Washington the same night as President Clinton's state dinner for President Jiang of China. Gere continued to speak his mind about Tibet and went so far as to call for a boycott of the Beijing Olympics in 2008. Gere paid a price for his activism. Once at the top of studio A-lists, he has since been blacklisted and banned for life from China, which meant that he became the third rail for major Hollywood studios that prized the Chinese market.

MGM managed to return to China's good side by sanitizing Chinese elements in its new productions. In 2012, a new MGM film, *Red Dawn*, featured Chinese soldiers invading an American town. The film's production coincided with MGM's reorganization after it had filed for bankruptcy. Upon receiving complaints from China, MGM's leadership had all the Chinese terrorists in the film digitally removed during postproduction and replaced with North Koreans. China's crackdown on China-unfriendly films and Hollywood's ready accommodation would set a pattern for future Sino-Hollywood negotiation.

The Building of Movie Theaters and of Hollywood's Field of Dreams

Grauman's Chinese Theater opened in Los Angeles in 1927. Later, it promoted the mystical notion that "if you build it, they will come." Hollywood majors were selective in acquiring cinemas, eyeing mainly elegant venues with large capacity in big urban centers where first-run films played and big money was made. Control of the exhibition segment was crucial to Hollywood majors' market dominance in the 1920s, both domestically and worldwide.[76] The greater the exhibition base, the greater the money that would flow back to the producers to support their escalating film budgets. Theater building and acquisition became the key to maintaining market dominance. As Hollywood positioned itself to develop the Chinese market as its own next "field of dreams," one big challenge was China's poor exhibition infrastructure, which remained vastly underdeveloped. By the late 1990s, Hollywood needed China to build modern multiplexes to accommodate Hollywood films, as multiplexes would enable either simultaneous screening of different films or the screening of one popular movie with staggered starting times for greater profits. More and better theaters would create further demand for Hollywood blockbusters as more movies would be needed to fill the increased seating capacity.

Hollywood realized as early as the 1920s that lack of theaters was an obstacle to its expansion into underdeveloped parts of the world. Writing in *Scientific American* in 1921, O.R. Geyer observed that most of the American film export business went to Western Europe and South America while the rest of the world remained largely untouched. "In order to attain the highest possible development in these countries," he wrote, "many thousands of theaters must be built."[77] Paramount, for instance, moved into chain ownership of cinemas in Canada in 1920 through Famous Players Canadian Corporation (FPCC). Within a few years, FPCC owned over 200 theaters in Canada. By 1925, at least

95 percent of all movies screened in Canada were American. In China, though, Hollywood did not make direct capital investment in movie theaters until 1946, when the first U.S.-owned cinema was established in Shanghai.[78]

State restrictions on foreign theater ownership during the PRC era made this particular Hollywood dream a remote fantasy. Nevertheless, United Artists Theatre Company quietly and successfully extended its brand in China in 1997 when its Hong Kong–based subsidiary United Artists Cinema Circuit (UACC), in which UA had 5 percent equity investment, built China's first multiplex of six screens in Wuhan, a city now synonymous with COVID-19. At the annual CineAsia Film Exhibitors Convention in Singapore in December 1997, Valenti expressed Hollywood's wish to join partners "throughout Asia, especially in China" to invest in the building of "modern cinema auditoriums" for an "epic viewing" experience for the growing number of Asian moviegoers.[79] By 1998, more theaters had been built and major theater chains had been established in several Chinese provinces, providing a road map for launching large-scale theater chains on a national scale.

WHAT DOES CHINA WANT?

While heeding the call to build more theaters, China wanted something in return. In early 1998, Tong Gang, the president of China Film Corporation, indicated to Hollywood that China would give preferential treatment to foreign companies that acquired Chinese films for distribution overseas. Hollywood majors reacted quickly and positively, lining up to distribute Chinese films in the United States with China Film and other major Chinese studios.[80]

Sino-Hollywood film trade had been one-way since the PRC opened its market to American films. The Chinese had requested a certain degree of reciprocity on a number of occasions but were invariably turned down by the MPAA on the grounds that Chinese films, like most other foreign films, simply would not sell in the United States, where audiences had no appetite for subtitled films. Hollywood did purchase a few Chinese titles here and there as a token effort. *Inkstone* (*Yanchuang*, Liu Bingjian, 1996), bought by Twentieth Century Fox as a goodwill gesture, was the first Chinese film ever purchased by a major U.S. studio.

Around the same time, Warner Brothers bought *Xiu Nu* (Feng Gao, 1996) and *Being My Wife's Employee*[81] (Xu Geng, 1998), UIP bought *Spicy Love Soup* (Zhang Yang, 1998), and Sony Pictures purchased *Shower* (Zhang Yang, 1999). Among the Chinese titles Hollywood bought in the late 1990s, only *Shower* could be identified in IMDb, an industry database, with a U.S. box-office gross of just US$1.15 million. Most of the films languished on the shelves of the studios while the luckiest few might be granted very limited releases at small art-house theaters.

The fate of Chinese exports to the United States was not dissimilar to that of exports from other countries. As early as the 1920s, Hollywood began the practice of buying but not releasing foreign titles. Often the majors would purchase foreign movies to satisfy a particular country's laws without intending and indeed never releasing them for screening in the United States. The imports were left on shelves to gather dust. The cost of purchasing foreign films was so minuscule that it simply counted as part of the budget for exporting U.S. films.[82] Not until the early 2000s did Chinese films receive attention in the U.S. mainstream commercial cinema chains, with titles such as *Hero* (Zhang Yimou, 2002) and *House of Flying Daggers* (Zhang Yimou, 2004) making an impact, though most of these films were international co-productions.

It turns out 1998 was an "off year" for the Chinese domestic film industry, with "nothing good to talk about, apart from *Titanic*,"[83] which grossed RMB 360.1 million (US$43.5 million), more than triple that of the second most successful film up until then, *True Lies*.[84] Not a single Chinese film made any splash in the market in 1998.[85] *Titanic* pretty much decimated Chinese domestic films. Total box-office receipts for Hollywood revenue-sharing films were almost RMB 600 million (US$72.46 million) in 1998, nearly twice the level of 1995 and 1997 and more than 45 percent higher than in 1996, with *Titanic* alone taking over half of that year's total import receipts.[86] A Chinese film market built mostly on the success of *Titanic* proved volatile. In the following year, 1999, the Chinese film market hit a historic low. As an industry report acknowledged, in the first half of 1999, the national film market was "facing its greatest difficulties since the founding of New China."[87] By the end of May 1999, box-office receipts nationwide had dropped by an average of 60 percent over the same period in 1998. Box-office receipts for the entire year dropped to RMB 840 million (US$101.45 million) from RMB 1.45 billion (US$175.12 million) in 1998. Box-office gross in major markets fell by an average of 50 percent over 1998, with the gross in Shanghai declining by around 38 percent, approaching the lowest possible limit that the market could sustain.

Nonetheless, so confident was UA in China's market potential that in 1999 it opened, via its Hong Kong–based subsidiary United Artists Cinema Circuit (UACC), a six-screen multiplex in Shanghai, China's largest film market.

ANXIETY ABOUT HOLLYWOOD

By the end of the 1990s, revenue-sharing American mega-productions had captured about 70 percent of China's film market, leaving approximately 100 domestically made films with only 30 percent market share.[88] During much of the 1990s, 70 percent of Chinese domestic films failed to recover their royalty and print costs, 15 percent broke even, and only 15 percent made a profit.[89] One survey suggested that total box-office receipts for domestic films in 1998 was RMB 1.44 billion (US$173.9 million), falling from RMB 2.4 billion (US$290.9 million) in 1991. This number dropped further to RMB 810 million (US$97.8 million) in 2000. From 1994 to 1999, box-office gross for domestic pictures fell by 65 percent, declining further by 2001.[90]

Hollywood's market share, not the physical number of Hollywood imports, gave rise to a growing apprehension—indeed a sense of crisis—throughout the Chinese film community as well as academic and media circles by the end of the 1990s. A debate raged questioning the policy of importing ten megapictures per year and its impact on domestic films. Some challenged the practice of importing only U.S. blockbuster films while barring small art movies from Europe and Asia.[91] Zheng Dongtian, a veteran fourth-generation Chinese filmmaker and professor at the Beijing Film Academy, used the line "To be, or not to be" to encapsulate the anxiety the Chinese film industry felt about Hollywood in China.[92] Zheng did the math to project a grim scenario for domestic films. According to Zheng, box-office receipts of *Titanic* in Beijing in 1998 (US$4.22 million) were about one-fourth of the market's total intake in 1997 (US$15.82 million). Taking this as a base and applying it to the existing film market the size of Beijing and its population's purchasing power, Zheng projected that there would be limited space for other film screenings. His conclusion was that it would take only four *Titanic*s each year to saturate the market. This would force over one-half of imported blockbusters to struggle to find an audience each year. Should this occur, Zheng reckoned that there would be no market space left for Chinese domestic films.[93] Zheng's math actually anticipated China's theater construction and expansion in the following decade to accommodate the growing appetite of China's cinema-going audiences, regardless of whether the demand is driven by Hollywood or domestic pictures.

Dai Jinhua, a prominent culture critic and professor of comparative literature at Beijing University, lamented the failure of China's domestic film industry in fending off Hollywood. She warned that "like *Titanic*, the Chinese film industry is sinking amidst tender feelings and joyfulness, with little measures of resistance."[94] Citing the decline of film industries around the world as the result of Hollywood's penetration as a cautionary tale, Dai faulted the profit-driven distributors and exhibitors for promoting Hollywood films at the expense of domestic pictures.[95] She warned that the onslaught of Hollywood films would intensify "the squeezing power of transnational capital over domestic pictures."[96]

The popularity of Hollywood films led to volume control in China, allowing only a small number of films among the 200 annual Hollywood titles to enter the country. The Chinese government mandated that more than two-thirds of the annual screen time in China be reserved for domestic films, and at least 50 percent of box-office revenue be earned by domestic films. But the demand for Hollywood films saw no signs of waning, while the Chinese government showed no desire to loosen import and screen quotas. Sino-U.S. co-productions became a viable way for Hollywood to potentially bypass quotas and restrictions and meet the popular demand, though at a potentially hazardous political price.

6

How Lucrative Is the Chinese Market: Politics Intervened

Rather than bend towards capitalism, the CCP maintained central authority with protectionist policies that maximized domestic profits and forced foreign players to abide by a complex system of regulations.

—Jeremy Geltzer , 2017[1]

Looper (Rian Johnson, 2012), the science fiction thriller starring Bruce Willis, Joseph Gordon-Levitt, and Emily Blunt, changed the story's location from Paris to Shanghai in an effort to secure a co-production status for better box-office access. The film became the first Hollywood film to cast China as the future of humanity. Shanghai built a futuristic city skyline for the film, and the appearance of Chinese actress Xu Qing in the scene was to be a source of pride for the Chinese. In the final cut, however, the American producer did not have much use for the Shanghai scene or the Chinese character. To ward off potential Chinese fuss about the limited exposure of China and Chinese, the studio cut two versions of the film, with the Chinese version extending the Chinese scene by several minutes to allow both Shanghai and the Chinese actress more screen time. Chinese authorities were not pleased with the global cut eliminating most of the China elements, which defeated the purpose of a co-production aiming at showcasing China to the world. The cuts also raised eyebrows in the United States, with critics charging the Hollywood studio with ingratiating itself to the Chinese censors.

In practice, though, making multiple prints to please censors is nothing new to Hollywood. Cutting alternate versions had been a standard practice since the 1920s, when Hollywood needed to appease a variety of censorship mandates, including from the U.S. itself. Mae West's *Belle of the Nineties* (Leo McCarey, 1934)—whose title was supposed to be *Ain't*

No Sin, the title of her original story until censors objected—was made in several versions after it failed to meet the Hays Code, the industry's decency standard. A film featuring a beauty queen of the nightclub world that was marked by arson, theft, and constant sexual innuendo proved to be too sensational for the cultural guardians, so different cuts were made to meet the censorship regulations of different states. Multiple versions were also used to appease foreign censors. For instance, a version was made to meet the British requirement of white supremacy, which demanded that the central themes of films conform to an imperialist outlook. Alternate cuts were so prevalent that Will Hays, the motion-picture industry leader for whom the code was named, banned the practice in 1934. Studios that screened different films abroad without approval from the Hays office would be fined $25,000. Multiple cuts of U.S. films nevertheless remained a frequent practice through the 1950s. In the 1959 crime drama *Cry Tough* (Paul Stanley), the bedroom scene between John Saxon and Linda Cristal saw Cristal wearing a slip in the U.S. version but panties in the foreign release "to get a little more mileage out of it in Europe."[2] Six decades later, there was *Looper*, for some extra mileage in China.

The Valenti Lobby

If 1998, the year *Titanic* topped box-office charts and Michael Eisner apologized to China for making *Kundun*, was an off year for Chinese cinema, 1999 turned out to be a tumultuous year for Hollywood. The year marked the thirteenth anniversary of China's initial bid for WTO status. The United States and Chinese governments were eager to reach an agreement to pave the way for China's WTO membership by year-end. Hollywood majors pushed for an increase in import quotas and abolishment of China Film's distribution monopoly. These two issues were in fact presented as the top two priorities by Disney in early 1999 in the studio's own negotiations with China's State Administration of Radio, Film, and Television (SARFT), a successor to the MRFT, for the plan for the coming two years. Disney tried to talk the Chinese government into allowing a total of seventeen imports from the Hollywood majors from June 1999 to June 2000, and a total of twenty-five films from June 2000 to June 2001. The suggestion was for the two sides to reconvene in June 2001 to reassess the market and devise a new plan for the subsequent two years.

In an attempt to dismantle the China Film Corporation's distribution monopoly, Disney tried to convince the Chinese that increasing the number of Chinese distributors of U.S. films would benefit the Chinese film industry by transferring knowledge and skills in film exhibition and marketing to the local industry. Hollywood majors were wary of China Film's monopoly over import decisions and distribution since 1995, a year after China agreed to revenue-sharing imports. China Film generated 60 percent of its US\$12 million revenue in 1995, earning US\$1.2 million in profits.[3] American studios believed that Hollywood films could be more efficiently distributed in China if China Film faced competition, and that the dismantling of China Film's monopoly would significantly increase the studios' profits by enabling local exhibitors to work directly with Hollywood studios. The 1999 negotiation illuminated the tension between Hollywood's market logic and China's state-run monopoly practice.

Valenti paid a visit to China in late March 1999 as part of a trade mission led by U.S. commerce secretary William Daley. Valenti met for the first time Ding Guangen, the head of China's Ministry of Propaganda, known as the conservative media and cultural czar of China. Valenti offered to host a Chinese film festival in the United States in October that year: "This festival is a demonstration of our commitment to the future of the global film community. . . . We firmly believe that sharing the work of China's finest filmmakers will unveil to new audiences the tremendous creative talents that reside in this great nation and, perhaps, encourage China to open its screens to more films from abroad. . . ."[4] The quid pro quo between promoting Chinese film abroad and opening the Chinese market for more Hollywood films was not subtle in Valenti's hyperbolic pitch. He stated further that "it is my hope that the new millennium will bring us closer to a time when each of our nations can freely share the many wondrous, magical stories we yearn to tell. . . . Perhaps the festival will one day be looked back upon as a significant step toward that most worthy goal."[5] At the meeting, Valenti also pleaded for the Chinese to allow U.S. companies to build movie theaters in China, which fell on Ding's deaf ears.

In April 1999, a month after Valenti's visit to Beijing, Chinese premier Zhu Rongji came to the United States for what turned out to be strenuous four-day trade talks. Hollywood moguls including Gerald M. Levin of Time Warner and Michael Eisner of Disney were among the handful with access to private meetings with Zhu during his state visits in New York and Los Angeles. Levin, chairman and CEO of Time Warner, had presented a plan of "comprehensive cooperation" with China in a letter to Premier Zhu Rongji a month before Zhu's United States visit, proposing to set up a joint venture with Chinese partners to develop and produce films based on Chinese stories and distribute them in China and abroad. The framework further called for the importation and distribution in China of Warner Brothers productions or films acquired by Warner Brothers from both China and elsewhere, and to develop other media products and explore other movie-related businesses such as movie theaters and theme parks in China.

To guarantee the long-term success of the joint venture, Time Warner made a special commitment to reinvesting profits in China during the initial stage of importing and distributing Warner Brothers films. Time Warner had started a short-term training program in 1998, accepting Chinese interns from Fudan, one of the leading Chinese universities based in Shanghai. It sponsored *Fortune* magazine's Global Forum with the theme "China: The Next 50 Years" in Shanghai in September 1999 to highlight China's increasing global prominence. Time Warner's long-term aspirations for the Chinese market across different media platforms and businesses were shared by other major Hollywood studios, as theatrical release was but one small part of their overall grand China ambitions.

Hollywood also pushed hard for the Chinese government to reduce its high taxation on U.S. films, an effort dating back to 1995, a year after the revenue-sharing agreement was reached. China finally agreed, during the bilateral WTO negotiation in 1999, to reduce tariffs on imported foreign (mostly U.S.) films from the previous level of 9 percent to 5 percent, and to drop tariffs on home videos from 15 percent to 10 percent.[6] At the end of the talk, China made major concessions, agreeing to open up the country's insurance and telecommunication sectors and to lift restrictions on U.S. agriculture imports.

But the concessions were not enough for Zhu to secure an official nod from Washington for China's WTO bid. Among the several major remaining obstacles was Hollywood's market access to China, which was a tricky issue in 1999, as the year marked the fiftieth anniversary of the founding of the PRC and also the upcoming return of Macao to China after more than four hundred years as a Portuguese colony. To celebrate both the fiftieth anniversary and Macao's return to the "motherland," China reserved its market for state-funded propaganda films, practically blocking all Hollywood imports. To ensure cinema attendance for the leitmotif films, the state issued circulars to government agencies, state employers, and public schools to push for organized group viewings of party-sanctioned films. The mood was celebratory in China, with ordinary folks taking advantage of free entertainment and extra holiday breaks. Then a tragic event happened.

On May 7, 1999, during the NATO bombing of Yugoslavia, five U.S. guided bombs hit the Chinese embassy in the Belgrade district of New Belgrade, killing three Chinese journalists. The Chinese government promptly issued a condemnation, calling the incident a "barbarian act." The next day, the China Film Distributors and Exhibitors Association issued a public statement denouncing the incident while declaring a temporary ban on the showing of U.S. films in China, effective immediately. Cinemas across China stopped screening Hollywood titles on May 9. Films already slated, such as *Enemy of the State* (Tony Scott, 1998), were postponed from their original release dates. Theaters instead scheduled reruns of long-ago domestic war movies such as *Heroic Sons and Daughters* (Wu Zhaodi, 1964), a film set during the Korean War, and imported war films such as *Walter Defends Sarajevo* (Hajrudin Šiba Krvavac, 1972), a Yugoslavian war film set in Sarajevo during World War II.

One of the most popular foreign films in China in the 1970s, *Walter Defends Sarajevo* features Walter, a Yugoslav National Liberation Army leader who tries to stop Nazi soldiers from entering Sarajevo.[7] The repeated viewing of *Walter Defends Sarajevo* for Chinese audiences during the early days had made the film "one of the most-watched war films of all time."[8] Chinese children and streets were named after characters from the film, and a beer brand called "Walter" was marketed with a picture of Velimir Živojinović, the Serbian actor who played Walter. One of the best-known actors in former Yugoslavia with more than 340 films and TV series under his belt, Živojinović was enormously popular

Chinese poster for *Walter Defends Sarajevo*.

in China in the 1970s. Older Chinese audiences remembered fondly the soundtrack and accompanying image of the cool uncle Walter walking down the street scouting his next shooting target. Reruns of old war movies delighted Chinese audiences, old and young.

Though President Bill Clinton apologized for the bombing, making it clear that it was an accident rather than a hostile action, the bombing of the Chinese embassy in Belgrade stirred up a huge anti-America wave in China, leading to heated discussions about the cultural, ideological, and financial implications of Hollywood's market dominance there. Remarkably, Hollywood was undeterred. In a statement made to the Ways and Means Subcommittee on Trade focusing on U.S.-China trade relations and the possible accession of China to the World Trade Organization in June 1999, Valenti argued that the success in China of the ten (annual) revenue-sharing imports meant that China's import barriers ought to be dismantled.[9] He attributed Hollywood's China success to the Agreement on Enforcement of Intellectual Property Rights and Market Access signed in February 1995, which he saw as "a thorough blueprint for action," and a major step toward "a positive and constructive partnership" between China and Hollywood.[10] While testifying before the Subcommittee on Trade, Valenti urged the U.S. government to secure China's commitment to improve Hollywood's access to its market as "part of any acceptable WTO accession package with China." Hollywood estimated that its unrealized annual gain limited by restrictions in the importation and distribution of Hollywood films as well as video piracy in the country stood at US$200 million. Valenti set a goal for the MPAA "to secure a gradual increase in the number of films" into China.[11]

The China Resistance and Hollywood's Long-Range Plan

Meanwhile in China, "Pulling the Veil off Hollywood" appeared in the July 1999 issue of the *Chinese Film Market*, China's premium film trade magazine, reminding everyone that Hollywood's intention was not only to take over the global film market but also to export U.S. values through sanitized U.S. images. Hollywood films, the author argued, cultivated the myth that the United States was the center of the universe and the messiah of humanity.[12] The same trade magazine published another article in August, warning against Hollywood's alleged ideological penetration of every aspect of Chinese social and cultural life.[13] Alluding to the ongoing bilateral trade negotiations on China's accession to the WTO, the author called out the United States' "bullying" tactic in trade talks and its relentless cultural expansion and invasion. It also discussed the merits of protectionist film policies in Europe and South Korea.

While the Chinese film community grew fearful of China's joining the WTO, Hollywood was feeling giddy about the anticipated import quota increase from ten to twenty. Under the revenue-sharing terms agreed upon by the two sides, Hollywood distributors and China Film would split each film's box-office revenues fifty-fifty. Yet after the exhibitors' cut, government taxes, import tariffs, and other fees, the final return for the Hollywood majors amounted to only around 13 percent, whereas Hollywood's take in box-office gross in other countries and regions typically ran to 40 to 50 percent.[14] *The Lion King*'s box-office return from China was comparable only to that of a small central European country.[15] Hollywood studios' revenues from China in 1998 were a meager US$18 million, the equivalent of what the studios earned in Peru.[16] Twentieth Century Fox, the film's international distributor, received only about US$5 million from the Chinese market.[17] U.S. government statistics from 1999 suggested that film revenues from China were among the smallest in Asia, less than those in Singapore, Malaysia, Thailand, and the Philippines.[18]

But Hollywood knew to put things in perspective. The studios were on the China wagon for the long haul. As Larry Kaplan, senior vice president of Buena Vista International (BVI), remarked on the company's Chinese business in early 1996, "There's a future, but there's not much of a present."[19] He was referring to the arduous sixteen-month negotiation to secure the release of *The Lion King*, the short notice given to prepare the marketing kit, and the limited number of theaters available for blanket exhibition. Yet the unprecedented sale of the film's soundtrack (over 700,000 copies sold, "the most successful Western soundtrack album in history") in China compensated for the ordeals of the theatrical release, dealing with the red tape, infrastructural deficiencies, and cultural barriers.

Lured by the promise of explosive market growth, Hollywood was in China to "seed the garden and harvest returns later" with great patience.[20] As early as 1952, Eric Johnston, who headed the MPAA from 1945 to 1963, noted that Hollywood should start to consider exploiting new export markets rather than relying on the existing European market, which was becoming increasingly static though providing a major revenue source. In particular, he recommended that the major studios look to such markets as Africa and the Far East, where the moviegoing habit was still in its infancy. He emphasized that, though they may initially be low-income areas, they would potentially become wealthy markets in the long run.[21] Johnston's vision proved to be prescient, especially when it came to the Chinese market. The MPAA under Valenti did not miss a beat in trying to build a Chinese market once it was allowed back to China. Regardless of the actual income, U.S. films have accounted for the majority of films imported on a revenue-sharing basis in China. Among the 65 revenue-sharing films imported from 1994 to 2000, 48 (74 percent) were from the United States, 3 from the UK, and 14 from Hong Kong. From 1995 to 2001, a total of 134 films were imported from the United States, 61 of which were big revenue-sharing films.

After much diplomatic effort on the U.S. side in 1998, China did allow the screening of *Enemy of the State* (Tony Scott, 1998) and three other U.S. films, including *Star Wars: Episode I—The Phantom Menace* (George Lucas, 1999), later in 1999. But with a much-shortened screening period of roughly five months, the total box-office receipts for the Hollywood imports in

1999 were less than RMB 150 million (US$18.12 million), considerably lower than in previous years. In particular, *Mulan* and *Tarzan* (Chris Buck and Kevin Lima, 1999) grossed only RMB 11.17 million (US$1.35 million) and RMB 13.38 million (US$1.78 million), respectively.[22]

In fall 1999, the MPAA hosted a bicoastal Chinese Film Festival in New York and Los Angeles that featured ten Chinese films. The event coincided with the fiftieth anniversary of the founding of the People's Republic of China and included a Chinese delegation headed by China's top film official, SARFT vice minister Zhao Shi. Twentieth Century Fox offered to be the primary host of the Los Angeles leg of the event, providing exhibition venues and setting up grand receptions. Disney and Sony Pictures provided no less hospitality and goodwill toward the delegation, from offering senior-level business meetings to specially arranged and guided tours to their theme parks and studio facilities. It was during one of the dinners hosted by Sony Pictures that the studio announced its plan to co-produce their first Chinese-language film, *Crouching Tiger, Hidden Dragon* (Ang Lee, 2000), which would turn out to be a smash hit in the United States and much of the world when it came out a year later.

China Signs WTO Agreement

The Sino-U.S. agreement on China's accession to the WTO was finally signed on November 15, 1999. The agreement, which covers an array of industry sectors, from industrial goods to agriculture and services (e.g., information technology, telecommunication, insurance, banking, the audiovisual industry, etc.), secured "broad-ranging, comprehensive, one-way trade concessions on China's part," to quote the testimony of Ambassador Charlene Barshefsky before the House Committee on Ways and Means on China's WTO accession and PNTR a year later.[23] U.S. delegates to the WTO negotiation pushed hard for Hollywood's market access, given that intellectual-property-based industry had become the United States' greatest export industry since 1996, of which Hollywood film was the greatest driver.[24] The Chinese government committed to doubling its annual import quotas of revenue-sharing films from ten to twenty; allowing foreign investment in joint ventures for video distribution; permitting foreign investors to own up to 49 percent in companies that build and operate cinemas; reducing tariffs on films (from 9 percent to 5 percent) and home videos (from 15 percent to 10 percent); and protecting intellectual property under the terms of the WTO Agreement on Trade-Related Aspects of Intellectual Property (TRIPS).[25] Valenti hailed the agreement as "heartening," and a long-awaited breakthrough. "We are joyful that our friends in China have recognized the worth of American films in their country. . . . We look forward to working with China Film so that the American films that enter China are given the widest distribution. . . . This bodes well for the future," Valenti glowed.[26]

In the end, though, China managed to safeguard its quotas (two-thirds of all screen time for domestic films) in accordance with the special provisions on film trade in Article IV of the legal text of GATT: "Screen quotas may require the exhibition of cinematograph films of national origin during a specified minimum proportion of the total screen time actually utilized, over a specified period of not less than one year, in the commercial exhibition of all films of whatever origin, and shall be computed on the basis of screen time per theatre per year or the equivalent thereof; screen quotas shall be subject to negotiation for their limitation, liberalization or elimination."[27] China's "State Regulations" further subjected every foreign film to prescreening prior to its import to China, providing another means by which the Chinese government could exert control over foreign films' market entry. Chinese "State Regulations on Administration of the Film Industry" for bilateral film relations gave the Chinese government continuing leverage to protect its film market and to shield itself from the looming dismantling of screen quotas, as China reserved the right to ban certain films on various alternative grounds.

Legend has it that by the end of one of the six days of grueling negotiations in 1999, the Chinese delegates retreated to China Film Corporation's office to watch a newly finished Chinese film, *My 1919* (Jianzhong Huang), which told a story about how the Chinese diplomats stood up for the first time in history to the Western powers at the Paris Peace Conference at the end of World War I, resolving in China's favor a dispute over Article 156 of the Treaty of Versailles in 1919 that dealt with the concession of the Shandong Peninsula in 1922. China's chief trade representative suggested after watching the movie that a sequel be filmed with the title *My 1999* and be about the WTO negotiation.[28]

China's Permanent Normal Trade Relations Status in the United States

By early 2000, China was on course to officially join the WTO, under whose terms member countries are required to extend preferential trading treatment to one another, or Permanent Normal Trade Relations (PNTR) in the United States. The bill granting PNTR status was not automatic and required a vote from the U.S. Congress. Prior to China PNTR, U.S. law required that China's normal trade relations (NTR) status, initially granted in 1980, be reviewed and renewed on an annual basis. The annual renewal of China's NTR status was largely noncontroversial and relatively unopposed by Congress until 1989 when the Tiananmen Square crackdown occurred. Many members of Congress subsequently sought to use the annual renewal as leverage to pressure China over a wide range of trade and nontrade-related issues including China's human rights record. In May 1994, the year that China let in the first batch of revenue-sharing Hollywood films, the Clinton administration decided to de-link human rights from trade concerns, thus separating human rights considerations from the annual review of China's NTR status.

During the bilateral negotiation over China's WTO accession, the Clinton administration had pledged that, in return for significant market-opening commitments on the part of China, it would press Congress to enact PNTR legislation, ending the annual congressional review of China's trade status.[29] The Clinton administration began to push for Congress to grant PNTR to China once the agreement on China's joining WTO was reached in November 1999. Clinton believed that bringing China into the international system would not only serve U.S. national security interests but also encourage ideological and cultural changes in China and bring China into the U.S.-led global orbit and framework. As President Clinton put it in July 1999 in his speech to Congress, "Expanding trade can help bring greater social change to China by spreading the tools, contacts and ideas that promote freedom."[30] The Clinton administration argued that a failure to pass such legislation would prevent the United States from enjoying the full benefits of the WTO agreement that the administration had negotiated, including broad market access, special import protections, and rights to enforce China's commitments through the WTO dispute resolution procedure.

When the bill came up for debate in Congress in 2000, U.S. business leaders stood nearly united in their support of the bill, arguing that the vote would serve mainly to open China's markets to U.S. exports. The business community made the case that the bill would benefit working men and women, countering labor unions' charge that the bill would harm workers and cost jobs. They were joined in that argument by George W. Bush, who by then had locked up his party's presidential nomination. The bill's foes, however, argued that the deal would sacrifice U.S. leverage in forcing human rights concessions from Beijing.

Though there had been voices from Hollywood opposed to broader trade rights for China, the MPAA joined the coalition of business groups in their weekly meeting to plot strategy promoting the China trade deal. In February 2000, Valenti orchestrated a high-profile China Trade Relations Committee to lobby Congress to approve PNTR status for China amid strong opposition from organized labor and human rights groups. The committee was composed of influential media tycoons—including Michael Eisner of Disney, Rupert Murdoch of News Corp, Sumner Redstone of Viacom Inc., and Gerald Levin of Time Warner. Valenti emphasized Hollywood's increasing reliance on foreign markets and the significance of the PNTR to the U.S. entertainment industry.[31] Hollywood studio heads and their Washington lobbyists pressed the issue with members of the House of Representatives. Drawing on its expertise, Time Warner helped the coalition write scripts and develop protrade ads.

Valenti testified in April 2000 that "trade is much more than goods and services. It's an exchange of ideas. Ideas go where armies cannot venture. The result of idea exchange as well as trade is always the collapse of barriers between nations."[32] In May 2000, Jack Valenti interrupted his four-day trip attending the Cannes Film Festival to call six wavering House members including House Speaker J. Dennis Hastert (R-Ill.) and urged them to support the bill.[33] Valenti and other entertainment industry officials diligently talked to twenty-eight key lawmakers, including several from California, to drum up support for the measure. Valenti warned the lawmakers that the small steps China had taken in the direction of greater market access—such as doubling the import quota with promises of more in the future, reducing tariffs on films, and increasing foreigners' rights to own and build movie theaters in China—would be in jeopardy if Congress voted against Permanent Normal Trade Relations. To the skeptical lawmakers, Valenti said that "I'm trying to keep our eye on the distant objective, not the one nearest," and that "China can be a huge market for us, but I don't expect it to be overnight."

The entertainment industry also argued that normal trade ties would make it easier to crack down on piracy of U.S. movies and music in China. Valenti's group even treated wavering lawmakers to a private screening of *Lover's Grief Over the Yellow River* (Feng Xiaoning, 1999), a friendly Chinese film depicting a U.S. Air Force pilot performing heroic acts alongside Chinese troops against the Japanese in World War II, which was China's official Best Foreign Language Film submission to the seventy-second Academy Awards. The Chinese reciprocated the goodwill of Hollywood by establishing a reward mechanism in January 2000 to seriously crack down on piracy and offering a reward of RMB 300,000 (US$36,232) for each seized illegal reproduction line, an extraordinary amount in view of the low average income in China at the time. China launched three major antipiracy campaigns throughout 2000.[34]

The China PNTR bill passed the House of Representatives in May 2000 by a vote of 237 to 197. The U.S. Senate ratified the China PNTR in September 2000. It was signed into law on October 10, 2000, ending twenty years of annual reviews of China's trade status and clearing the way for Hollywood's further expansion into the Chinese market, while also accelerating the process of media conglomeration in China. News of the endorsement by the U.S. Congress was met with mixed reaction among the Chinese film community. With the anticipated quota increase to twenty for foreign imports, a sense of crisis prevailed.[35] SARFT and the Ministry of Culture jointly circulated a flurry of new motion picture regulations between June 2000 and December 2001,[36] including Document 320, "Some Opinions About Carrying Out Further Reform in the Film Industry," which would later be augmented by SARFT Documents 41 and 1519[37] that together aimed to transform China's film industry into large-scale, vertically integrated, semi-privately held conglomerates that were analogous to the Hollywood studio system in the U.S. prior to the Paramount Decree of 1948.[38] The main objective of the new policies was to create major film conglomerates with state-owned studios as their cores.[39] The document also stipulated that party secretaries should sit on the board of directors or act as legal representatives, thus ensuring the CCP's firm grip over the conglomerates. Document 320 ushered China's film industry into the era of party-controlled conglomeration, paving the way for the monopoly of powerful state-owned film groups, the essence of a Chinese-style state capitalist system, or the China model. Production reform also deepened with the issue of Document 320, which opened the door for a comprehensive marketization of film productions.[40] Document 1519 sought to establish two or more theater chains within provinces as well as theater chains that operated across provinces. The document specified that regions that failed to establish theater chains by June 1, 2002, would be unable to obtain any revenue-sharing film imports. In addition, before October 1, 2002, the regions of Beijing, Shanghai, Jiangsu, Zhejiang, Hubei, Hunan, Guangdong, and Sichuan were ordered to take the lead in setting up at least two theater chains; otherwise, these regions would be denied any revenue-sharing film imports.

Hollywood as Leverage and the Trials and Tribulations of Foreign Investment

During multiple conferences held between January and March of 2001, the SARFT further encouraged the establishment of three major film groups in the north, east, and northeast of China, with Beijing Studio, Shanghai Studio, and Changchun Studio acting as respective bases for each region. Three additional film groups based in Guangdong, Sichuan, and Shanxi Provinces would follow, reaching central, southwest, and northwest China. In April 2001, China established the Northeast China Theater Chain, consolidating seventy distribution companies across three provinces. The Hebei Zhonglian Theater Chain Company Limited was also formed, connecting seven distribution companies, one film studio, and seventeen exhibition units in Hebei, Shanxi, and Inner Mongolia Provinces.[41]

The government implemented regulations requiring theaters to meet certain criteria in order to exhibit revenue-sharing titles. Competing for and accommodating the screening of popular revenue-sharing Hollywood films was a powerful incentive for distributors and theaters, and Chinese regulators leveraged the Hollywood imports to encourage the film industry to upgrade China's film distribution and exhibition infrastructure. The government stipulated that theaters be equipped with digital ticketing systems and be part of a larger theater chain in order to screen revenue-sharing films. The establishment of more and better movie theaters became imperative. At the beginning of the 1990s, there were 15,000 operating cinemas in China; by 2000, the number had dropped to fewer than 4,000.[42] The nationwide theater-chain system reform was gradually but forcefully carried out throughout 2001.

China's new revenue-sharing import quota of twenty films a year went into effect in 2001, allowing foreign investors a share of up to 49 percent in theater operation, and permitting foreign investment into joint video distribution ventures.[43] The expanded quota motivated Chinese filmmakers to produce films capable of competing with Hollywood. With more exposure to Hollywood big-budget films, Chinese audiences' appetite for fast-paced entertainment grew, propelling local Chinese filmmakers to produce more commercial entertainment films to meet the market demand. Aided by growing budget, the "Chinese New Year film," a homegrown genre emerging in the late 1990s, would become China's answer to Hollywood entertainment fares, putting China's own brand of grassroots popular filmmakers such as Feng Xiaogang and Xu Zheng on the map of Chinese cinema. The twenty-film quota would remain unchanged until 2011.[44]

China's accession to the WTO was officially approved on December 11, 2001. On December 27, 2001, President Bush issued a proclamation extending PNTR status to China, effective January 1, 2002. The Chinese weekly *Southern Weekend* ran an article in March 2002 titled "Starting with *The Fugitive*, Chinese cinema itself has become the fugitive."[45] Fugitive or not, since revenue-sharing films accounted for the bulk of the Chinese box office, Chinese theaters were motivated to join theater chains and upgrade screening infrastructure and technology in order to obtain rights to exhibit high-grossing revenue-sharing titles. The Chinese Film Bureau declared in 2002 that "no time can be wasted in implementing theater chain system as a breakthrough of market reform. We must fight bloodily for a path."[46] The year 2003 saw more investment in theater construction and theater chain formation, and the trend continued well into the late 2010s. The number of theater chains would increase from thirty-four in 2007 to forty-eight in 2017. The expansion of theater chains helped stimulate massive theater construction and expansion in China, and in turn provided more venues for Hollywood imports, allowing for a much denser movie theater network that guarantees better screening channels.

State-enforced establishment of the theater chain system in China was a complete repudiation of the multilayered distribution model pursued under the planned economic system. Yet heavy and direct government intervention meant that the formation of various Chinese-style theater chains did not emerge naturally out of real market competition, as the Hollywood studios and Hong Kong's Shaw Brothers did, but rather by state directives. Overall, the Chinese-style theater-chain system was driven less by the market than by the state, which led to new monopolies and an unequal distribution of resources between private companies and state-owned distribution companies.

In 2003, the first year that the theater chain system was mandatorily executed, only two chains had annual box-office receipts of more than RMB 100 million. The year 2003 saw the founding of Huaxia Film Distribution Company (Huaxia) as China's initial step toward dismantling the distribution monopoly of the state-run China Film Export and Import Corporation (CFEIC). Formed on August 8, 2003, Huaxia became a second state-owned film distribution company. In June 2003, two months before Huaxia's formation, Shanghai Film Group, Changchun Film Group, and Xiaoxiang Film Group were established, paving the way for a further dissolution of the monopoly of the China Film Group Corporation, though the CFGC's market dominance continued, and the company released or jointly released almost all the blockbuster martial arts spectacles from *Hero* in 2002 to *Curse of the Golden Flower* in 2006, both helmed by Zhang Yimou.

In 2003, China issued, on a trial basis, "Several Opinions on Foreign Investment in Culture Industry," allowing up to 75 percent foreign ownership of joint business ventures in seven major Chinese cities.[47] Foreign investors were further allowed to own up to a 75 percent stake in cinemas that would be built in underscreened Chinese cities. In an effort to maintain the state's commanding role, China forbade foreign investors from establishing solely owned studios or theaters or to form joint ventures in China with private companies. Only domestic private investors were allowed to establish solely owned studios and theaters or to enter into joint ventures with state firms. Foreign investors could establish joint ventures only with state-owned companies and hold no more than a 49 percent interest. Yet in major cities like Beijing, Shanghai, Guangzhou, Xi'an, Chengdu, Wuhan, and Nanjing, foreign firms' ownership was allowed to reach as high as 75 percent and they could enjoy a cooperative term of up to thirty years on a trial basis. The same regulations also applied to Hong Kong and Macao investors, whose share was also allowed to reach 75 percent.[48] SARFT promulgated Documents 18, 19, 20, 21, and other regulations throughout 2003, followed by another set of supplementary regulations in 2004 and 2005 that allowed foreign and private capital to participate in both film production and theater construction. Warner Brothers made the most aggressive inroads in theater ownership in China, taking a 51 percent stake in a cineplex in Nanjing while acquiring a majority share in both Chongqing and Guangzhou through different joint ventures.

The Persistence of Piracy and the Departure of Valenti

In August 2003, amidst China's distribution reform, three major Hollywood studios—Twentieth Century Fox, Disney, and Universal Studios— won a civil lawsuit in Shanghai against two local companies selling pirated DVDs of Hollywood films. A local court ordered the defendants to pay the plaintiffs compensation and also issue a public apology in the local newspaper. But the MPAA pressed the Chinese government to apply criminal law to piracy so as to more forcefully deter violations. Piracy-related lawsuits in China had been resolved primarily through civil actions while criminal sanctions were seldom used. This issue became a major topic when the U.S. assistant secretary of commerce William H. Lash and Song Jian, China's state councilor and director of the IPR Office under State Council, met in Beijing a year later, in August 2004, to revisit the issue of market access. Wu Yi, the Chinese vice premier and former head of the Ministry of Foreign Trade and Economic Cooperation, was directly involved in bilateral dialogue on the issue. Wu announced earlier in 2004 that China would try to lower the criminal threshold for piracy while also increasing the number of infringing acts that were subjected to criminal penalties. Valenti credited the success in antipiracy enforcement in 2004 with the steady expansion of Hollywood's China market. As he put it, "How can we expect to beat piracy if there is not an assured supply of legal, good quality videos?" He went on to say, "If Chinese audiences do not have the option of seeing a legitimate film in the cinemas, pirated home video products will fill in the demand. . . . Only the criminal elements behind piracy will benefit from this decision while legitimate businesses are deprived of success."[49]

After serving as president of the MPAA for thirty-eight years, Valenti announced his retirement in 2004. The same year China produced, for the first time in decades, over 200 movies, and total industry revenue increased 66 percent to almost $435 million. Feng Xiaogang's *A World Without Thieves* (2004), Zhang Yimou's *House of Flying Daggers* (2004), and Stephen Chow's *Kung Fu Hustle* (2004) all earned handsome profits. The year saw domestic film receipts exceed foreign film receipts for the first time since 1994, despite a doubling of the number of foreign movies allowed into China annually since 2001. The top ten Chinese movies outperformed imports for the first time in 2004.[50]

Valenti was replaced that September by former secretary of agriculture Dan Glickman, who continued to push for U.S. studios' access to international markets. Glickman pressured the Chinese government to step up its effort in 2006 to foil piracy by initiating a series of rigorous crackdowns in Beijing. In October, the government instituted a "zero-tolerance" policy in Beijing's Chaoyang district, which included most of the city's embassies, Sanlitun, Lido, and many other expat haunts. The so-called One Hundred Days Campaign in the summer of 2006 drove many pirated DVD sellers out of business and forced others underground. The battle would resume in 2007 amidst the Sino-U.S. WTO dispute. Meanwhile, China had its own agenda in not rocking the boat with Hollywood.

Promoting Chinese Soft Power Abroad and Supporting
Domestic Production via Co-Production

SARFT founded China Film Promotion International in 2006 to raise the visibility of Chinese films at international festivals. The Chinese government started to use the term "soft power" in 2007 to encourage Chinese film and media industries to promote China's cultural influence globally. Co-productions had been identified as the major force in promoting Chinese cinema globally. Though a buzzword now, international co-productions have existed from the early PRC era, but few co-productions actually took place between 1958 and the end of the Cultural Revolution, a time of political turmoil. China established China Film Co-production Corporation (CFCC), a government agency that oversaw production efforts with overseas producers, in 1979, the year China officially established its diplomatic relationship with the United States. The agency's goal was to aid the CCP's United Front[51] effort by projecting abroad a positive image of China and Chinese people, as the country emerged from decades of isolation. CFCC, Beijing Film Studio, and seven other state-run agencies became the first batch of domestic producers that were allowed to participate in the much-coveted international collaborations.[52] Early collaborations were mostly assisted productions, in which the Chinese studios lent production aid, including supplying equipment and coordinating location shooting.

Early co-productions were sporadic, with few official regulations. As interest in collaboration grew inside China and out, the Ministry of Radio, Film and Television issued an official document on September 25, 1985, pushing for the optimal management of project submission, review, and content selection.[53] In December, the Ministry of Culture gave more detail for co-production submissions. Three months later in 1986, the film ministry mandated that all co-produced films go through CFCC before being submitted to the Film Bureau for approval, making CFCC the gatekeeper for co-productions. The number and scale of co-productions increased during the second half of 1980s, with a total of fifty-nine titles made from 1986 to 1990. Among them was *The Last Emperor* (1987), a Sino-Italian-assisted production that brought nine Academy Awards, including Best Picture and Best Director.[54]

As co-productions flourished, the film ministry issued "Rules Governing Sino-Foreign Cooperation in Film Production" on July 5, 1991, and before long followed up with a series of legal documents detailing regulations.[55] The annual number of co-productions increased from fourteen in 1991 to forty-one in 1995. More domestic studios wanted to participate in co-productions, prompting the government in 1995 to grant provincial-level film studios and others the right to participate in international co-productions. Some small domestic studios with a quota to co-produce but no cash to invest simply sold their quota for $20,000–$50,000 (RMB 130,000–324,000) each, mostly to Hong Kong producers who had projects and investments but no access to the quota.

To manage the growing number of international co-productions, CFCC stopped its involvement in productions to focus exclusively on administering co-productions under the charge of SARFT, an arm of the Department of Propaganda. CFCC established film trade relations with several countries and regions and served as the exclusive agent for co-production and a censor for script approval and production application screening and commercial registration. The last production CFCC directly invested in as a co-producer was Ang Lee's *Crouching Tiger, Hidden Dragon*. Lee approached CFCC in 1998 with the idea of co-producing a martial arts film. Taking two years to produce, the final film absorbed creative input from outside China and direct investment from Chinese partners, so was arguably a commissioned production. The Chinese were entitled to only the domestic copyright and revenue. The film turned out to be a critical and popular hit, winning major international awards and earning more than $213.5 million at the box office worldwide with a budget of $17 million, though its Chinese box office was a meek $2.3 million.

In 1999, CFCC became part of the newly formed China Film Group Corporation, which was the biggest film conglomerate in China at the time. The Chinese state allocated more resources to strengthen CFGC over the years, making it the country's dominant film producer by 2004,[56] wielding unparalleled power in film production and distribution in China, until private and internet-based media firms began to challenge its monopoly in the mid-2000s. China Film Group was deemed instrumental in aiding the revival of domestic productions.

On September 28, 2003, SARFT issued Order 19, "Provisions on the Administration of Chinese-Foreign Cooperative Production of Films,"[57] to allow all domestic producers, including private companies with a proper film production permit, to enter co-production deals with foreign partners. The measure allowed overseas capital to create joint production companies with state-run film companies but required the Chinese parties to hold at least 51 percent of the enterprise. The regulations permitted a film to cast a foreign actor in a leading role if the ratio of foreign to domestic performers was under 3:1. The previous rule was an even split, the level that remained for production crews. The increase in the presence of foreign stars gave a major boost to co-productions. Revenues from co-produced Chinese films sold overseas would increase from 58.8 percent in 2006 to 99.9 percent in 2010. The significance of co-production in contributing to Chinese cinema's "going out" campaign led to further government encouragement for co-productions as well as more government oversight to ensure that co-productions were in the best interest of the Chinese state.

The WTO Dispute

Valenti passed away in 2007, but the struggle over market access and piracy continued. In April 2007, the U.S. trade representative allied with the MPAA and two other professional associations to launch two cases at the World Trade Organization, accusing Beijing of insufficient effort to punish illegal copiers of films and music and for its continued restrictions on entertainment imports that violated trade rules.[58] The American side argued that by imposing more restrictive conditions on foreign companies, China was engaging in discriminatory practices, and that China's state-owned enterprises and large joint ventures monopolized film importing and distribution. China denounced Washington's move but said that "we will proactively respond according to the related WTO rules and see it through to the end." Piracy continued to be blamed for a portion of the massive U.S. trade deficit with China. As the issue was raised again in 2007, DVDs supposedly containing the latest Hollywood blockbuster movie *Spider-Man 3* were spotted for sale on Beijing streets, almost two weeks before its official release in the United

States. To demonstrate its determination to stop commercial piracy, China released an intellectual property action plan in April 2007 to draft and implement fourteen laws on intellectual property rights and usage.

While China gave an inch on the piracy front, it took away Hollywood's China access elsewhere. The Chinese government suddenly imposed a three-month protection period in early December 2007 to ensure the dominance of Chinese domestic pictures during the year-end holiday season, shutting out imports from Disney, DreamWorks, Paramount, and Warner Brothers, which had already received release clearance. Domestic films such as Feng Xiaogang's *Assembly* (2007) and popular films from Hong Kong and Taiwan such as Peter Chan's *The Warlords* (2007), Stephen Chow's *CJ No. 7* (2008), and the Taiwan/Hong Kong co-production *Kung Fu Dunk* (Kevin Chu, 2008) benefited from the Hollywood blackout period. The three months from the Christmas season in December 2007 to the Chinese Lunar New Year holiday in February 2008 marked the longest hiatus China had imposed on foreign films since its entry to the WTO.

Meanwhile, China Film Group continued to dominate the market for domestic films, producing epic-scale films of both leitmotif propaganda and popular commercial fare. Under the leadership of the veteran filmmaker Han Shanping, the company practiced what Han in 2007 termed "blockbuster strategy" to produce, simultaneously, epic-scale propaganda films using lavish state funding and blockbuster commercial fare using private funding. Han made it clear that he was emulating Hollywood's strategy of big-investment large-scale productions with megastars as China Film Group's operation model.[59] CFGC's fast and early rise derived largely from state backing, which granted the company and Huaxia exclusive distribution rights to lucrative imported films. Theaters frequently gave China Film Group releases preferential treatment in exchange for sufficient copies of blockbuster imports.[60]

In 2009, SARFT implemented measures to reward domestic films that managed to be picked by foreign studios for export. Responding to the government's "going out" call, the 2010 Shanghai International Film Festival hosted a forum with producers, directors, and studio heads to discuss how to go abroad. At the forum, Yu Dong, CEO of Bona Film Group, considered distribution the key to Chinese cinema's visibility in the United States, while the director He Ping, who used to work for

Columbia Asia, emphasized quality content.[61] But Feng Xiaogang argued that Chinese cinema did not meet the global standard set by Hollywood and that learning skills and technological processes through collaboration with Hollywood was essential. It is interesting to note that this is the year that Feng completed his disaster film about the historical Tangshan earthquake, *Aftershock*—his cinematic tour de force utilizing foreign experts in producing special effects.[62] The veteran filmmaker and ex-president of the China Film Directors Association Huang Jianxin (*The Founding of a Party*, 2011) emphasized that production management in Hollywood was the most advanced and that the Chinese needed to manage its productions according to Hollywood standards. Huang recalled how the Chinese learned a great deal about the transparent budget and execution process while assisting the shooting of *Kill Bill* (Quentin Tarantino, 2003).[63] Ren Zongren, the head of Shanghai Film Group, marveled at Hollywood's sophisticated producer system and considered a good production team essential.[64]

The top guns in the Chinese film industry continued to be enamored with the Hollywood way, however grudgingly. The Chinese government too came along to see co-productions, particularly with Hollywood, as a way to enhance soft power through the transfer of skills and other know-how. For the Chinese as latecomers, it was indeed more effective to acquire or access international resources through co-productions with Hollywood, the global cinematic powerhouse. Chinese policy makers thus encouraged more Sino-U.S. co-productions; for both the Chinese government and Chinese filmmakers, gaining access to the partner's market was an important incentive, especially in high-profile Sino-U.S. joint productions. If there was an overseas market for China, it was mostly for co-productions with major Hollywood studios. China clearly needed Hollywood to open the global market.[65]

As the United States awaited a WTO decision in its market access case against China, Dan Glickman made his tenth trip to China in June 2009, this time to attend the Shanghai International Film Festival.[66] While praising the diverse titles showcased at the festival, Glickman lamented that most of the festival films wouldn't make it to China's growing number of multiplexes due to an annual cap of twenty imports per year. "The challenge for China is how fast they'll move out of this top-down, central control of entertainment product," he said. Little did

Glickman know that the top-down and centralized control would persist long past his MPAA tenure. "Sometimes the Chinese can be extremely tedious and obtuse in their trade discussions," he complained, noting further that the growth of film piracy was costing studios billions each year in potential revenue. With five straight years of roughly 25 percent growth at the box office in China, Glickman maintained that there ought to be plenty of room for both good domestic and imported films. In an interview given to the *Hollywood Reporter*, Glickman asserted that China's long review period of between forty-five and sixty days for home videos for import as compared to the Asian average of ten days offered an easy opportunity for pirates. Glickman lobbied China's domestic content providers for a common effort to remove pirated online content quickly.

On January 21, 2010, after nearly three years of hearings and appeals, the WTO ruled that China had violated international trade rules and needed to end the government's monopoly on the distribution of imported books, movies, and films by March 19. China responded that it disagreed with the ruling but was nevertheless willing to comply. The lawsuit was deemed a major victory by the U.S. side. By now, the MPAA had a new chief executive in the office, Christopher J. Dodd, the onetime presidential hopeful who served for twenty years as a U.S. senator from Connecticut. Dodd made the opening of China's market one of his top priorities and actively championed an increase of China's annual import quota.[67] The Chinese side again expressed concern about Hollywood's aggressive stance. Mao Yu, deputy director of the Film Administrative Bureau, said at the 2010 Beijing Film Work Conference that if the quota were increased, more Hollywood movies would flow into China, and Hollywood would net 60 to 70 percent of total Chinese film revenue, instead of the 13 to 15 percent under the prevailing revenue-sharing agreement. He warned about potentially substantial reduced returns for China's domestic film industry and its negative long-term impact.[68] Regardless of the pushbacks from China's domestic film industry, Hollywood would end up helping to build China into the world's second largest film market by 2012, which in turn created more appetite for the U.S. studios to seek co-production deals with the Chinese.

In November 2013, Zhang Xun, then president of CFCC, told a group of Hollywood royalty crowding the fourth annual U.S.-China

Film Summit in Los Angeles that "we have a huge market, and we want to share it with you." But she reminded them of China's conditions: "We want to see positive Chinese images," Zhang urged.[69] "China has been opening up for thirty years and I think both U.S. and Chinese screenwriters want to write positive images," Zhang added, while complaining that depictions of Chinese as drug dealers or criminals were still too common.[70] She made it clear that the gimmicks of adding a few Chinese scenes and providing an alternative cut for the Chinese market, all in the hope of gaining a co-production status, would not pass muster. And the co-productions would aim for an international market, not a domestic one.

Hollywood's Oriental Dream

In 2012, the then Chinese vice president Xi Jinping and his U.S. counterpart Vice President Joe Biden signed a memorandum of understanding during Xi's visit to Los Angeles, raising Hollywood's China exports to thirty-four films per year from the prior twenty-four for the following five years, and Hollywood's box-office ceiling to 25 percent compared to the prior 13–17 percent since 1994. The prices for flat-fee titles were also raised from less than $20,000 per title to over $10 million for a high-profile title.[71] The memorandum stipulated that fourteen among the thirty-four titles be presented in IMAX or 3-D. Since then, Hollywood studios have scrambled to expressly convert films into 3-D for the Chinese market. As the result of the quota raise, imported films reversed the market share trend in 2012 by taking up 52 percent of the box-office revenues. But Chinese domestic films consistently accounted for over half of the box office in subsequent years. China cemented its position as the second largest theatrical market in 2012.

During his visit to the United States in February 2012, Xi Jingping also unveiled in Los Angeles a joint venture between DreamWorks Animation and two Chinese state-owned media groups, Shanghai Media Group and China Media Capital, signaling growing ties between China and Hollywood by China's incoming president.[72] On February 17, 2012, DreamWorks Animation SKG announced the name of the joint venture in Shanghai: Oriental DreamWorks. The Chinese side was to hold up to

55 percent stock of the new company, and Ruigang Li, the well-connected chairman of China Media Capital (CMC), would serve as the chairman and first CEO of the new joint venture.[73] The partnership with DreamWorks Animation to build an RMB 20 billion theme park in Shanghai catapulted CMC into the international limelight. The Chinese changed the iconic logo of DreamWorks—a boy fishing on a crescent moon—into a panda fishing, with a strong Chinese ink style, and the moon painted red.

After the Biden-Xi agreement in 2012, box-office revenue for Hollywood films spiked, reducing domestic box office in the first half of the year to 35 percent of gross revenue. The government responded by imposing a long late-summer blackout to balance box-office scales and meet the government's goal of at least 50 percent of screenings being reserved for domestic films. During the summer period known as Domestic Film Protection Month and other blackout periods that can last from several weeks to several months, import screenings are forbidden in favor of domestic films. Although officials have never admitted that such a policy exists, no revenue-sharing films have been released in China during the protection months.

Another protective measure has been dubbed "double-dating"—scheduling two Hollywood blockbusters of similar nature so that they would compete against each other instead of eroding business for domestic films. Thus, in 2012, *The Amazing Spider-Man* (Marc Webb) and *The Dark Knight Rises* (Christopher Nolan) were both released on August 27. China Film Group Corporation, which controls the release dates and lengths of theatrical runs of foreign films, runs an opaque process, making it difficult for Hollywood to plan ahead.

The sure way to bypass these restrictions is to co-produce films with Chinese partners. The differences between a co-production and an imported quota film could translate to millions of dollars' loss or gain in revenue. Co-production has thus become a meal ticket for foreign studios wishing to have a bigger market share in China. In addition to having a guaranteed China release, co-productions can dramatically improve the percentage of box-office receipts the U.S. producers can collect—to about 40 percent. There are other incentives too for co-productions. Foreigners can access financial resources within China only through a Chinese partner, thus giving further incentive for co-production, particularly at a time when cash-rich Chinese bring easy production investment. Hollywood also needs local Chinese partners to navigate red tape and handle logistical hassles. Foreign producers are required to pay a 20 percent tax on revenue gained from the Chinese market, but the Chinese Tax Authority offers 10 percent rebate for joint productions. The complexity of Chinese taxes means that a foreign party needs to rely on its Chinese partners to collect the 10 percent refund. A Chinese partner can further handle the bureaucratic process of submission and carefully lead a project to its final approval.

The 2012 agreement was formalized into an official trade agreement during Xi's state visit to the U.S. in September 2015, this time as the president of China. During Xi's 2015 state visit, the MPAA and China Film Group reached two new film agreements to increase market access for foreign films in China. Two terms were added to address Hollywood's grievances. One promised that China's state distributors would pay U.S. studios within a "reasonable" amount of time and the other granted international parties the right to audit their box office. Although "timely payment" is vague, Hollywood studios hope it will prevent a repeat of an episode from 2013 when China Film Group withheld tens of millions of dollars in revenue payments because of a dispute over which side should cover a new tax on ticket sales. A few months before the agreement, CFG allegedly underreported the historic performance in China of Universal's *Furious 7* in summer 2015 by as much as $30 million. The need for outside oversight of China's state distributors was made apparent a month after the agreement, when China Film Group was caught rigging the box office in favor of a state propaganda movie, attributing revenue from Hollywood titles including Paramount's *Terminator: Genisys* to domestic propaganda titles.

The September 2015 deal further canceled the cap for film buyouts (flat-fee films) that had been in place since 2000, initially at twenty titles per year but gradually increased to thirty to forty titles per year.[74] The cancellation does not give flat-fee imports a free pass to enter China. The buyout films remain subject to censors who filter all scenarios, scenes, and conversations that do not align with the government's values.

Hollywood tentpoles such as *Furious 7* (James Wan, 2015, $391 million), *Jurassic World* (Colin Trevorrow, 2015, $229 million), and *Avengers: Age of Ultron* (Joss Whedon, 2015, $240 million) all scored big in China in

2015,[75] jolting the local market into a panic. As a result, the unofficial summer blackout period was extended by several weeks to allow local titles to catch up. Far fewer Hollywood films secured prized weekend screenings in 2015. The increase in the number of revenue-sharing and flat-fee imports clearly does not sufficiently address Hollywood's appetite for the Chinese market, and vice versa. Co-production has thus become the key to both the American and Chinese film industries in their common pursuit of profit and influence, and cultural influence is by far more significant to the Chinese state than profit incentives.

A New Trade Deal?

The 2012 U.S.-China film agreement came due for renegotiation in 2017. Despite China's massive consumer market and growing appetite for the cinema, U.S. studios reap a relatively small percentage of revenue. The thirty-two films imported into China reportedly generated a total of $6.5 billion in revenue worldwide—but they generated just $500 million in China, or less than 8 percent of the total.[76] As *Quartz* mused, "By and large, Hollywood films made less than 5% of their worldwide revenue from the Chinese market, indicating that for all the effort producers currently expend to integrate Chinese talent and story elements, and to bend their own material in ways to please Chinese censors, Hollywood's headlong push into China remains primarily about getting early access."[77]

Foreign studios must also pay administrative fees to China Film Group, which further chip away at the overall profit on a film. In 2017, *The Fate of Fast and Furious*, the highest-grossing Hollywood film in China, did not generate as much China revenue for Hollywood because of the China revenue-sharing cap set at 25 percent as opposed to the standard 50 percent cap in the United States and 40 percent in most other countries. Hollywood hoped to win China's consent to bring more titles into China's market while also extracting a greater share of ticket revenue from just 25 percent of sales in China closer to the international norm of 40 to 50 percent.

But 2017 came and went with no progress. The Sino-Hollywood agreement was set to be yet renegotiated in 2018, holding out the promise that American studio productions would gain greater access to China, with

(1) an increase in the quota of revenue-sharing U.S. films, (2) more access to key viewing windows such as summer, and (3) an increased share of box-office receipts from 25 percent. China agreed in January 2018 to discuss "policies and practices that may impede the U.S. film industry's access to China's market."[78] The proposed new trade agreement sought to officially eliminate the import quotas but kept intact China's ability to block imports deemed inappropriate by China's film censorship board, a provision that could turn out to be "unofficial quotas."

Valenti's ultimate goal for China to eliminate all quotas on film, video, and TV, and to revise duties and taxes imposed on Hollywood imports, was to be fulfilled in 2018, but the plan was derailed by the unexpected trade war launched by the Trump administration against China. As the United States and China continued their trade talks, Hollywood proceeds stopped flowing out of China, and new Chinese regulations were enacted against non-Chinese programming. In April 2018, Chinese negotiators offered to ease annual quotas on imported films as part of broader trade talks with the U.S. officials, but the dialed-up trade war complicated the negotiation. Increasingly unpredictable government actions on both sides left Hollywood and the Chinese film industry in limbo.[79] The U.S. studios are vulnerable to disruptions in U.S.-China relations as Hollywood's biggest films now make a substantial share of their revenue in China. Yet Hollywood has remained one of the few industries where the United States commands a sizable trade surplus over China.[80] The dependence has been mutual as China has relied on big-budget U.S. films to keep its cinemas filled year-round. Conventional wisdom holds that steep reduction, or outright suspension, of U.S. film imports would stem China's box-office growth and thus hurting local distributors and exhibitors. In the meantime, both sides have continued to follow the expired agreement.[81]

China's film market continued to grow at a rapid rate as the country's booming real estate market had led to the accelerated construction of new multiplexes. The total number of movie screens passed the 20,000 mark by 2014 and over 40,000 by 2018, surpassing the total screen count of North America. As the Sino-Hollywood negotiations continued, China quietly nurtured the growth of its commercial film industry, becoming capable of producing its own popular hits rivaling those of Hollywood. One type of film in particular, the Chinese New Year Celebration film, has taken the domestic market by storm since 1997, owing much to the box-office success of New Year comedies by the popular filmmaker Feng Xiaogang (*Only Cloud Knows*, 2019) from the late 1990s to the late 2000s, and by another homegrown newcomer, Xu Zheng (*Lost in Russia*, 2020).

7

What Do the Chinese Watch: Popular Chinese Films Throughout the 2010s

Aftershock (like a lot of other big-budget contemporary Chinese films) seems to feel a duty: to hold within itself, on a symbolic level, the horrors and triumphs of the last four decades of Chinese history, from Cultural Revolution to economic miracle.

—Mike Hale, *The New York Times*[1]

A quartet of entrepreneurial film aficionados with can-do spirit put their passion and skills to good use by creating fantasy worlds, on demand, for their wealthy clients. The assortment of eccentric characters ranges from a rich man burdened with fancy banquets who is keen to experience meager living in a poor countryside to a bookseller who wants to star in a war movie modeled after *Patton* (Franklin J. Schaffner, 1970); they also include a chef who wants to be the star of a popular Qing dynasty TV drama, a film star who fancies anonymous living, and a man who wants to test his will by enduring torture like that undergone by heroes from classical Chinese revolutionary films. In between is a heartwarming segment about a long-distance commuting couple finally enjoying a newly renovated apartment together, though the wife is gravely ill with only months to live. The slogan for this fantasy-making company—"For one day, your dream comes true"—is a reference to Good Dreams, a production company in the early 1990s founded by Feng Xiaogang, a Chinese television practitioner turned popular filmmaker specializing in making comedies for the Chinese New Year market. The scene described is from Feng's New Year film debut *The Dream Factory*, made in 1997, the year the British handed Hong Kong over to China.

A number of modestly budgeted domestic films about contemporary life emerged on the Chinese screen in the late 1990s. These films quickly morphed into a new market phenomenon, Lunar New Year comedies, or what the film industry called "Chinese New Year films." Leading the charge in establishing New Year film as a marketable genre was Feng Xiaogang, a filmmaker known for his brand of Beijing-flavored and gag-laden urban comedy combining irony, sentimentality, and self-reflexivity that achieved domestic blockbuster status without relying on an imported big-budget blockbuster formula. While Feng would return in 2013 to his familiar conceit of a wish-granting business that manufactures reality for clients in another New Year celebration film, *Personal Tailor*, he made a detour for a film of a different nature as the 2010s dawned.

Earthquakes in China

Feng Xiaogang entered 2010 with *Aftershock*, a movie dealing with the devastating 1976 earthquake that killed 2.4 million people in Tang-shan, an industrial city 140 kilometers from Beijing. The story opens on July 28, 1976, the day of the earthquake. The setting is ordinary: two young children playing on the street; mom and dad madly in love, enough to make out in the lorry. Then the devastation. In typical disaster-film fashion, buildings collapse and people die. At first this looks like another familiar CGI-driven epic, but the story turns to the attempt to rescue the children. The mom tries to rush into a falling building, the father goes instead, with fatal results. The children are trapped under the rubble and the mom must choose one of the two to live, recalling a similar moment in *Sophie's Choice* (Alan J. Pakula, 1982). The chosen one is the son, who loses his arm in the process. The daughter, presumed dead, is mourned and placed near her father. The mom's choice sets the rest of the story in motion and turns the disaster film into a family melodrama,[2] belying the publicity poster, which marketed the film as an epic disaster film.[3] The disaster in *Aftershock* only serves as a teaser, the background that sets the devastating postpartum trauma drama in motion, never mind that the state-of-the-art special effects of the opening earthquake scenes claimed two-thirds of the $25 million total production budget.[4] The film deviates from the genre convention and focuses instead on the psychological scars of the survivors of the Tangshan earthquake and the process of healing and coping with a traumatic past.

Poster for *Aftershock*.

Unbeknown to the mother, the daughter in this fictionalized world sur-
vives and is adopted by a kind couple in the People's Liberation Army. She
bonds with her newfound family while trying to suppress the memory of
her birth family and of the betrayal of her birth mother. Meanwhile, in
Tangshan, the mother lives alone in self-imposed isolation, unable to make
peace with the choice she made. The surviving son lives close by to keep an
eye on his mother. The rest of the plot follows the three members of the
family as they go on their respective life journeys while struggling with
their loss. The parallel lives of daughter, son, and mother are interspersed
with major historical events in China, from Mao's death to Deng's economic reform.

It takes another earthquake, the devastating Wenchuan earthquake in
Sichuan Province in 2008, for the affected parties in this fictionalized
story to finally reconcile. The Wenchuan earthquake thirty-two years
later brings the daughter—who by then has settled in Canada—back to

China. Now a grown-up with a daughter of her own, she travels to Sichuan to assist with the rescue effort. A contrived moment sees her witnessing the devastation of a mother who is confronted with a similar "Sophie's choice." The experience becomes a soul-searching moment for her, leading to her appraisal of the past. Daughter and son unexpectedly reunite at the rescue site. The daughter learns of her mother's pain and suffering, realizing how much she has been loved all along and how cruel she is to have avoided her all these years. In a measured buildup, the film leads to a cathartic finale that reunites all three at their old home. The themes of filial piety, national rejuvenation, and unity are evident in the moment of reunion and healing. In many ways this is the story of a generation of Chinese living through the traumatic past, though the director Feng Xiaogang steadfastly eschewed any hints of political commentary.

Dubbed a "tear gas canister," *Aftershock* has been compared to *Mama, Love Me One More Time* (Chu Huang Chen, 1988), a sappy Taiwanese melodrama that caused a sensation a decade earlier. In a true family saga of historical proportions, Feng manages—to paraphrase Mike Hale writing for the *New York Times*—to pack into the 135-minute film, one adoption, "two amputations, three emotional reunions, four abandonments and more than 30 years of exquisite suffering, guilt and resentment, ending with a redemptive finale" brought about by another earthquake.[5] Emotional effects aside, *Aftershock* is a film of conflicting thematic and stylistic impulses.[6] The promise of a spectacular generic disaster movie in the first fifteen minutes soon gives way to a family melodrama with moral undertones deeply rooted in Chinese cultural traditions. The melodrama then abruptly transforms into documentary-style newsreel footage of Wenchuan earthquake coverage in 2008, before it winds back to melodrama and ends with an uplifting moral closure.

NATIONAL REJUVENATION AND THE TRIUMPH OF TRADITIONAL VIRTUES

The three disjunctive parts in *Aftershock* seem to appeal to the film's twin masters: the market and the party. While the disaster framework infused with Chinese melodrama conventions satisfies the market's demand for a Chinese-style blockbuster, the story of the rebirth of Tangshan and rescue efforts during the Sichuan earthquake speaks to the party's nation-building and rejuvenation campaign. Both real and metaphoric, *Aftershock* captures a nation in transition. The task assigned to Feng was to produce a blockbuster, one that merged political mission with commercial ambition. The Tangshan Municipality had conceived an image branding campaign to promote the city as a world-class cargo port; the idea was for the government to sponsor a "leitmotif film" about the rebuilding of Tangshan.

Always on the lookout for commercially viable films that toe the party line, SARFT liked the idea and helped to bring onboard the private company Huayi Brothers and the state company China Film Group. Tangshan's government invested half of the RMB 120 million total production budget, with the other two partners making up the difference. China Film Group put in only RMB 6 million as a token investment to acknowledge SARFT's support and CFG's responsibility for facilitating exhibition and distribution. Although putting in half of the budget, the Tangshan government agreed to significantly reduced proceeds, with 85 percent of its investment treated as "sponsorship" funds. To the Tangshan government, the investment was in image control and long-term economic gains. Tangshan wanted a heartwarming and uplifting film to celebrate the city's rebirth.[7] Huayi Brothers was the only investor that really cared about the film's profit margin, and for that Huayi went directly to its marquee commercial director, Feng Xiaogang.[8] It was a political-business arrangement from the beginning, and Feng was to be a good "team player."[9]

The film was an adaptation of a novella by the Chinese Canadian writer Zhang Ling, whose original novel focused on the struggle of the daughter, Fang Deng, as she grapples with her traumatic past. In the novella, the adult Fang is trapped in a marriage with a philandering husband and is suicidal. Her relationship with her own daughter is strained. It is revealed that Fang Deng's foster father sexually molested her, and her college boyfriend left her when she was pregnant, leading her to drop out of college. Told from the daughter's point of view, the novella cast an overwhelmingly dark view of human nature and human relations. Instructed to write a heartwarming film that would "cure" the daughter of her hatred for her mother, Su Xiaowei, the screenwriter, a member of the Film Review Board under SARFT, the body that enforces China's censorship guidelines,[10] deftly shifted narrative focus from the daughter to the mother, and in the process transformed the morbid and bleak novella into a celebration of the kindness of strangers and of one family's resilience and triumph against all odds. The plot was broadened from one person's mental journey to three interwoven journeys of mother, daughter, and brother spanning three decades, all anchoring on the mother and Tangshan as home, or the motherland, which is traditionally linked to the party in the CCP narrative.

To add to the heartwarming theme, the movie recast the foster parents as responsible PLA officers, with the father as a loving and protective parent who adores his adoptive daughter. The veteran actor Chen Daoming played the benevolent father, taking the Best Actor award at the fourth annual Asia Pacific Screen Awards. Su Xiaowei justified the change by insisting that "in everyday life, the great majority of fathers would not molest their adopted daughter. We chose to represent good relations between the father and adopted daughter as in a normal life."[11] Su acknowledged that another reason for the alteration had to do with China's lack of a film rating system: "Our film is not rated—adults and children can view it—so we intentionally altered this part." It was speculated that the party's rank and file refused to allow the establishment of a rating system out of concern that such would serve as an excuse for the proliferation of unseemly images on-screen. The unnamed rank and file reportedly said "over my dead body" to the rating system.[12]

Su's adaptation further eliminates the sexual aggression, the infidelity, and the strained relationship between mother and daughter. In the novella, the mother was a vain and shallow character whose decision to save the son was very much a part of the legacy of Chinese patriarchy that values sons over daughters. The film, however, transformed her into a loving and caring maternal figure, the voice of conscience who spoke for all the earthquake survivors; as Su puts it, "the movie is much more heartwarming."[13] In the climactic scene at the family's old apartment where the mother has stayed on guard all these years, the long-lost daughter kneels to ask for her mother's forgiveness. Instead of licking the wounds of the daughter, the film celebrates the mother's moral virtue and spotlights enduring family ties and values. The mother's otherwise hurtful choice is given a feel-good wrap-up. Rather than a victim of traumatic abandonment, the daughter is depicted as an ungrateful perpetrator who has condemned the mother to years of pain and suffering. The return to maternal virtue and family value is a recurring trope in post-Mao Chinese literature and arts, seen as the response to the Cultural Revolution period during which families were torn apart, and indeed turned against each other.

THE RECEPTION OF *AFTERSHOCK*

The film was a huge success in China, opening on 3,500 screens, the widest release in China at the time, though it was eventually eclipsed by *Avatar* and had to settle for the number two spot on the annual box-office chart. The film was also the first Chinese-language film to be shown on IMAX nationwide. It opened in Tangshan on July 12, 2010, thirty-four years after the earthquake. Over 10,000 residents of Tangshan City were invited to a local sports stadium for the premiere of the "first made-in-China IMAX film."[14] Wearing orange and blue T-shirts emblazoned with the phrase "Tangshan moves the world," audiences wept as they watched the on-screen family being torn apart, struggling, and eventually overcoming their pain and loss. Souvenir handkerchiefs were dispensed to mark the event. During nationwide screenings, tissues were handed out to audiences, with one local theater in Dalian going further to make special custom face wipes for audiences. The film's success solidified the party-sanctioned popular narrative as a politically and commercially viable formula.[15]

But Feng's excessive emotion coupled with feel-good messages in *Aftershock* came off as too propagandistic for the Western audiences to savor, even as Huayi Brothers lobbied heavily for China to send the film as an official Oscar submission. Feng Xiaogang himself cast doubt on the film's international appeal. *Variety* reported that Feng scoffed at the idea of an Oscar win, as the film was meant to appeal to Chinese audiences only.[16] *Aftershock* was released in the United States in only twenty theaters in areas with large Asian populations. Feng was criticized for his avoidance of critical issues surrounding the earthquake, including official negligence and the government's refusal to receive donations, both of which unnecessarily impeded rescue efforts and exacerbated human suffering. Feng hinted in a 2010 interview that censorship was at play: "This nation has suffered all kinds of natural and human disasters. But I could only talk about natural disasters because it is not permitted to mention human ones. So, a natural disaster has to be the villain here!"[17]

Another film dealing with natural disaster was on the horizon for Feng, this time a story about a little-known famine in China's Henan Province in 1942 that led to the death of three million people. The film was called *Back to 1942*, and, given the historical distance, Feng was able to tackle the human causes of the disaster.

"We Are All Descendants of the Victims": Back to 1942 *(2012)*

A three-year drought compounded by locusts, earthquakes, epidemics, high grain taxes, and ineffectual government intervention created a perfect storm in Henan in 1942, leading to a famine that killed up to three million people and displaced a large number of surviving victims. The ongoing war with Japan depleted resources, which exacerbated the situation, making the natural disaster into a humanitarian crisis of epic scale. *Back to 1942* documents the horror and chaos of the escape as refugees embark on a treacherous journey in the hope of leaving Henan before the Japanese arrive. Along the way, Japanese bombers strafe refugee lines as Chinese soldiers steal food and money from the refugees. Desperate women trade sex for food and the destitute turn on the dead and the dying.

FAMINE AND REMEMBRANCE

The film is an adaptation of Liu Zhenyun's 2009 novel, *Remembering 1942*. As Liu wrote in an op-ed piece for the *New York Times* in 2012, he was inspired to write the novel because the little-remembered famine was emblematic of what he saw as "China's 'collective amnesia.'"[18] The Henan-born Liu knew nothing about the famine until 1990 when a friend, who was writing about the history of disasters in China, asked him to collaborate on a piece about the Henan famine. During the research, Liu discovered that he himself was a descendant of famine survivors who had relegated the memory of 1942 to the dustbin of history. When asked what she remembered about 1942, Liu's own grandmother gave him a blank stare: "What about 1942?" Reminded that many people died of starvation that year, his grandmother said simply, "People died of starvation all the time; what's so special about that year?"

Back to 1942 triggered discussions about the Great Famine of 1959–61 caused by Mao's disastrous Great Leap Forward campaign. Coincidentally, the influential independent documentary filmmaker Wu Wenguang started to develop a documentary project, "Folk Memory Project on China's Three-Year Famine" in 2010, which linked the Henan famine to the famine caused by the Great Leap Forward, during which 15 million (to quote official numbers) lost their lives. Liu mused rhetorically in his op-ed, "Why are we [Chinese] so forgetful?" He speculated that "there are innumerable instances of starvation and cannibalism throughout Chinese history, and when people are constantly confronted with death through starvation, how else can they deal with it other than by forgetting?"[19]

Liu wondered what the government was doing in 1942 while three million people starved in Henan. He discovered that when drought was ravaging Henan, the province was besieged by Japanese troops; meanwhile the KMT government lacked resources to provide disaster relief. A decision was made to simply leave the disaster for the Japanese to handle by letting them take over Henan. As the KMT government stealthily retreated from Henan, the Japanese saw through the plot and held their troops at Henan's border, leaving the province a no-man's-land and the people of Henan to perish. Nobody cared and nobody reported the events. A year later, Theodore White of *Time* magazine, who had a brief stint as an adviser to China's propaganda agency, traveled to Henan with a fellow journalist, Harrison Forman of *The Times* of London. On their journey, they witnessed the horror of famine. Upon returning to Chungking, China's wartime capital, White related what he saw to Chiang Kai-shek, and reported the calamity in an article for *Time*. International attention forced Chiang's government to provide relief to the victims. But corrupt officials at all levels embezzled the funds, and the number of deaths from starvation skyrocketed.[20]

CENSORSHIP INTERVENED

Liu first broached the subject in 1994 in a novella, which caught the attention of Feng, who expressed interest in adapting the story into a film.

Liu was noncommittal. Feng was still an unknown quantity, and it took time to better understand the complex historical events and to develop a good script. Feng turned to making winter holiday comedies instead, quickly establishing his reputation as a popular filmmaker. Liu then reached out to Feng in 2000 to work on the project together. Huayi Brothers put up the preproduction fund for Liu and Feng to start their research the same year, but the project dragged on, as concerns lingered regarding the marketability of a film on famine.

As the team worked on the script, Feng took a detour to make *Aftershock*, and in between he made two light comedies, *If You Are the One* and its sequel. The comedy sequel opened the same year as the earthquake tragedy, bringing in a combined total of RMB 1.1 billion in box-office revenue. Wang Shuo, the screenwriter who conjured up the quick sequel to *If You Are the One*, goaded Feng about the famine project, urging him to cash in on his recent box-office success for the likely costly project of famine, in terms of both budget and popularity. Wang promised to hustle up another comedy quickie to recover any potential loss.

Liu published the story as a full-blown novel in 2009. By then Huayi Brothers was ready to put serious money into the project. But the company wanted assurance that the project would have the blessing of the authorities. SARFT approved the script in 2010 with several caveats: the project must amplify the warmth and kindness among the villagers to balance out the inevitable show of barbarism and cannibalism; it must de-emphasize the role of the American journalist while adhering to the party's guidelines on portraying religion; it must minimize violence and bloody images; and, most important, the project must avoid the sensitive topic of class conflict and focus instead on the struggle between China and Japan. Feng and his team spent another year tweaking the script according to these guidelines.

Feng finally executed the famine project, and the resulting *Back to 1942* largely followed the spirit of the censors. The landlord in *Back to 1942* is benevolent, indeed compassionate, sharing precious grain with villagers in need. There is no trace of class conflict. The culpability of the Japanese in exacerbating the natural disaster is highlighted. In one scene, a KMT army general demands grain for his soldiers in the name of patriotism. As he rationalizes: "If a peasant is dead, China is still there, but if soldiers are starving to death, China will die." All hints of domestic class conflict and struggle pale in comparison to the conflict brought by the Japanese invasion.

The prohibition against showing class conflict was particularly interesting, given the legacy of Chinese cinema exalting the proletariats' struggle against the moneyed class during the Mao era and Feng's early abomination of the rich and the corrupted. But times had changed, and class conflict now gave way to social harmony, a slogan designed to mitigate rising labor tensions and other incidents of social unrest targeting the rich and privileged. It is interesting to note that one year after Feng's film free of class conflict came out, Thomas Piketty's book *Capital in the Twenty-First Century* (2012) became a big hit in China, with President Xi Jinping praising the French economist's criticism of inequality in the West.[21] Yet Piketty's audacious follow-up, *Capital and Ideology* (2019), encountered a frosty reception in China due to his widened critical scope to include inequality in major economies elsewhere such as India, Brazil, Russia, and China.

Piketty's 2019 book finds that the share of China's wealth held by the top 10 percent of China's population rose from 27 percent in the late 1970s to 41 percent by 2015, comparable to levels of inequality seen in the United States. The book also criticizes the lack of detailed data on Chinese income tax, making it impossible to ascertain how the country's wealth has been distributed over the years. He further points out that there is no inheritance tax in China and that "it is truly paradoxical that a country led by a communist party, which proclaims its adherence to 'socialism with Chinese characteristics,' could make such a choice." The irony was not lost when Piketty stated point-blank: "So we find ourselves in the early twenty-first century in a highly paradoxical situation: an Asian billionaire who would like to pass on his fortune without paying any inheritance tax should move to Communist China." Beijing did not appreciate the unwanted scrutiny. Piketty's Chinese publisher demanded that all sections related to inequality in China be cut. Piketty declined to have his book translated in a botched fashion and took to Twitter to express his disappointment that "Xi Jinping's 'socialism with Chinese characteristics' shrinks itself from open discussion." The topic of inequality has become all the more sensitive since 2020, as China recovers from COVID-19, which has disproportionately hit its poor migrant workers and likely widened the income gap between urban and rural populations. On November 11, 2021, upon the completion of the sixth plenary session of the 19th CCP Central Committee in Beijing, a communique of the plenum on the major achievements and historical experience of the party at its hundredth anniversary was released. Noticeably absent were the stock class-based terms such as "workers," "peasants/farmers," or "working-class."

DEPICTION OF THE KMT

Interestingly, while casting blame on the Japanese, *Back to 1942* depicted the KMT in a more flattering light than what standard PRC narrative would have allowed. The CCP had routinely suppressed detailed historical accounts of major anti-Japanese military campaigns for fear of drawing attention to the constructive role of the Nationalist armies, which some suggested bore the overwhelming brunt of fighting the Japanese. During President Hu Jintao's era, the call for a "harmonious society" meant that Chinese historical films from the late 2000s to the early 2010s were able to stray from the harsher treatment of the KMT during Mao's era. Relationships with Taiwan were also improving under Hu. War films such as *City of Life and Death* (Lu Chuan, 2009) and *The Flowers of War* (Zhang Yimou, 2011) paid tribute to the bravery of Kuomintang soldiers. Even the leitmotif film *The Founding of a Republic* (Huang Jianxin and Han Sanping, 2009) featured an admirable Chiang Kai-shek played by the talented actor Chen Daoming,[22] who would reprise the same role in *Back to 1942*. Chiang in *Back to 1942* was seen as a beleaguered commander who struggled with competing priorities of fighting the Japanese and saving the people in Henan. Owing to Chen's brilliant performance, Chiang in the film came across as intelligent and caring, though ultimately falling victim to external forces beyond his control. The blame again rested solely on the Japanese invaders. Scenes depicting Chiang's anguished deliberation on whether to bring relief to the famine victims or to fight the Japanese while condemning millions to death were arguably the most engaging in the film.

But sympathetic portrayals of the KMT became taboo after Xi Jinping came to power in 2012. Seven years after backing Feng's *Back to 1942*, Huayi Brothers suffered a temporary setback in financing *The Eight Hundred*, a war film that paid tribute to the KMT.[23] Touted as a Chinese *Dunkirk*, the film featured a KMT regiment defending Shanghai against the Japanese army. Costing Huayi US$80 million to make, *The Eight Hundred* was the first domestic film shot entirely with IMAX cameras.[24] It was set to be released in the summer of 2019, before the seventieth anniversary of the founding of the PRC. But the influential Chinese Red Culture Research Association, an organization led by leftist Maoists, voiced objections to the film on the grounds that it highlighted the valor of the KMT and was thus inappropriate for release during the run-up to the anniversary. The Shanghai International Film Festival, in summer 2019, yanked the film from its opening-night slot, and the film was shelved. As a result, Huayi Brothers suffered a loss of approximately $46 million for the first half of 2019. *The Eight Hundred* finally hit theaters a year later, on August 21, 2020, after the ban on cinema-going due to COVID-19 was lifted and the government sought to quickly resuscitate China's film industry. The film was released to positive critical and popular reception.[25]

ANOTHER OSCAR BID

Unlike *Aftershock*, which he aimed exclusively for domestic consumption, Feng hoped that *Back to 1942* would harness his international reputation as the Holocaust film *Schindler's List* did for Steven Spielberg. China's attempt to penetrate the international marketplace was a particularly hot topic among filmmakers in the early 2010s. Featuring two Oscar-winning Hollywood stars, with Tim Robbins playing the Catholic priest Thomas Megan, and Adrien Brody playing journalist and historian Theodore White, *Back to 1942* was submitted as China's official Oscar contender but failed to win a nomination. The West saw the film as another preachy lesson in Chinese history.[26] In a terse and dismissive tone bordering on hostility, the *Guardian* called the film bombastic and overtly sentimental.

From the perspective of good storytelling, *Back to 1942* was no *Schindler's List*. Feng's famine epic switches laboriously and somewhat repetitively among the escaping refugees, the KMT officials, and the American journalist's reporting efforts without real emotional anchoring or compelling central characters. As the critic Daniel Eagan put it, "The air raids, refugee camps and forced marches tend to blur together," failing to build toward an emotional crescendo.[27] Feng, however, attributed the lack of success of his films overseas partly to the fact that foreign audiences "are not willing to understand a Chinese story."[28] Feng and Liu Zhenyun both participated in the "Tell a Chinese Story to the World" industry forum at the Shanghai Film Festival, what Liu called "the whimper of a weak nation." At the forum, Feng was dismissive of the effort of pleasing Hollywood. He stated bitterly that "when Hollywood makes films, it's not their primary concern how the Chinese audience might receive their stories. They only care whether the American audience understands; if you don't, that's your own problem."[29] This of course is not the case for Hollywood films that are aiming for the Chinese market.

Back to 1942 did not fare well domestically either, a rarity among Feng's films. With a budget of $35 million, the film scored $59.1 million within a month, which was considered a flop when compared to Feng's previous record.[30] The topic was simply too bleak to compete with light comedies and or overtake *Titanic*. It was 2012, the year after the revised Sino-U.S. Memorandum of Understanding (MOU) was signed. Revenue from imports led by *Titanic* 3-D surpassed domestic revenue, even though domestic films were strongly protected by the government.[31] Several Chinese films made it to the top ten on the box-office chart but Feng's *Back to 1942* was not among them. Jackie Chan's action comedy *Chinese Zodiac* (aka *CZ 12*) and a Chinese fantasy action film, *Painted Skin: The Resurrection* (Wuershan, 2012), together with the usual Hollywood titles—*Mission Impossible: Ghost Protocol* (Brad Bird, 2011), *The Avengers* (Joss Whedon, 2012), *Men in Black 3* (Barry Sonnenfeld, 2012), *Ice Age: Continental Drift* (Mike Thurmeier and Steve Martino, 2012)—made it to the top ten.

The one surprising domestic "black horse" that beat *Titanic* 3-D to top the box-office chart was *Lost in Thailand*, a slapstick road movie about three men finding inner peace in a lush land of green trees and thick raindrops. The film was made by a TV comedian turned first-time director, Xu Zheng, who had previously appeared in a small Sino–Hong Kong co-production, *Lost on Journey*, which came out in 2010.

Lost on Journey pairs an arrogant businessman with a naïve migrant worker on an unlikely joint trip home for the Lunar New Year that ultimately transforms both. Subtle, smart, ironic, and character-driven, *Lost on Journey* is a social realist comedy that captures the struggle of an unlikely pair in finding their way "home," literally and figuratively, during the largest annual human migration in the world. The actor featured in the film as the businessman was Xu Zheng, a comedian who gained fame playing a dim-witted pig seeking to become human in a red-hot TV series *Sunny Piggy* (2000), a fantasy-cum–romantic comedy adapted from the sixteenth-century Chinese classical novel *Journey to the West*. The show made the virtually unknown Xu Zheng a household name overnight. Xu subsequently appeared in TV comedies before making his big screen acting debut in *Crazy Stone* (Ning Hao, 2006), an immensely popular black comedy that went on to earn RMB 23 million (US$3 million) in box office on a meager production budget of HKD 3 million, or US$400,000.

Xu's real breakthrough came in *Lost on Journey*, directed by veteran Hong Kong filmmaker Raymond Yip. The film recalls *Planes, Trains and Automobiles*, a 1987 buddy road trip comedy directed by John Hughes of *Home Alone* (1990) fame, and starring Steve Martin as Neal Page, a high-strung marketing executive, and John Candy as Del Griffith, a good-hearted but annoying shower-curtain ring salesman. They share a three-day odyssey of misadventures trying to get Neal home to Chicago for Thanksgiving with his family. *Lost on Journey* features a similarly stressed-out corporate type who is saddled with a pesky road companion, Niu Geng, played by Wang Baoqiang of *The World Without Thieves* fame. Two years later, Xu and Wang teamed up to make a sequel, *Lost in Thailand* (2012), which became Xu's directorial debut.

Enter Xu Zheng and Lost in Thailand

Lost in Thailand reprised the duo for their cross-country odd-couple shtick that eventually transforms an uptight corporate boss played by Xu while bringing unexpected fortune to a clueless tourist played by Wang. Xu Zheng played Xu Lang, an inventor turned corporate executive who must go to Thailand to find his boss at a meditation retreat for a new gadget he just invented.[32] Estranged from his wife and his young daughter due to his single-minded devotion to work, Xu has only two days in Thailand to find his boss before returning to China for his divorce proceedings. The deadline sets the chaos in motion. On the plane Xu meets a thickheaded tourist, Wang Bao, who carries a photo of his "wife," the Chinese superstar Fan Bingbing. As in *Lost on Journey*, the stooge manages to ruin Xu's journey every step of the way with his endless self-inflicted mishaps. To complicate things further, Xu's black-clad corporate rival Gao follows him to Thailand, trying to sell Xu's invention for a quick profit. The villainous Gao is played by another well-known comedian, Huang Bo, who co-starred with Xu in the 2006 sleeper *Crazy Stone*. Huang's presence adds dramatic tension and enhances madcap moments, some gratuitous. In one cartoonish scene, a Caucasian man has a threesome with two local prostitutes with Xu trapped under the bed. Played for laughs, the scene is unnecessarily long, particularly considering that there is no rating system for films in China. But the vulgarity apparently did not offend Chinese audiences. Released in December 2012, *Lost in Thailand* raked in US$250 million, breaking the record for the highest-grossing domestic film at the time.

The success of *Lost in Thailand* owed much to "international tourism fever" in China in the early 2010s that sent millions of Chinese people abroad on packaged tours. Among the first batch of target countries were Japan, South Korea, Singapore, and Thailand, with the "exotic" Thailand being the hottest destination.[33] The film in turn boosted Chinese tourism to Thailand, prompting the Thai prime minister Yingluck Shinawatra to grant Xu a private audience.

Lost in Thailand's success came as a surprise to Xu Zheng. As a first-time director, Xu had trouble getting the project off the ground, until Beijing Enlight Pictures came along and threw in a US$4 million production budget. The paltry investment turned out to be a big success, suggesting that domestic films rooted in Chinese reality and capturing contemporary lives could have an edge over Hollywood blockbusters and domestic megapics in popular appeal. As Xu Zheng puts it, "There is hunger from the audience for movies that talk about the real-life situation in China."

THE SURGE OF SMALL DOMESTIC PICTURES

The unexpected success of *Lost in Thailand* was part of a surge of popular domestic films in 2013, the year of Chinese cinema, with several modestly budgeted and youth-oriented Chinese films such as *So Young* (Zhao Wei,

2013), *Finding Mr. Right* (Xue Xiaolu, 2013), and *Tiny Times* (Guo Jing-ming, 2013) scoring surprising victories over Hollywood imports. Though the number one blockbuster in 2013 went to *Journey to the West: Conquering the Demons* (Stephen Chow and Derek Kwok), a domestic fantasy comedy based loosely on the Chinese classic *Journey to the West*, most domestic films succeeded by spotlighting contemporary Chinese life, which was missing in the explosion-filled Hollywood action genre and the overbearing historical sweep of Chinese epics.[34] Indeed, by the early to mid-2010s, there was a noticeable fatigue among Chinese moviegoers with both the formulaic Hollywood action flicks and Chinese historical epics. One could only stomach so many explosions, superheroes, supernaturals, and supertragedies.

Equally important, while no longer forbidden fruit, the ubiquity of American films rendered Hollywood less exotic, though *Iron Man 3* (Shane Black) and *Pacific Rim* (Guillermo del Toro) still managed to occupy the top ten box-office charts, with the former ranking number two and the latter number five. What we witnessed in 2013 was the maturation of a generation of Chinese cinephiles coming of age in the company of (mostly pirated) Hollywood films. They had outgrown their adolescent infatuation with action films and now yearned for more sophisticated films with nuance and subtlety. They were ready to leave the action nest and venture out to explore films of diverse style and scale.

The U.S. film industry produces more than big-budget and high-tech action adventures; it also produces A-class quality films that elicit real emotions and provoke real thinking. But these adult films are not usually deemed to be viable exports. As the cliché has it, dim-witted global audiences are not capable of fathoming spoken words or savoring subtle verbal cues, so action and explosion are the only viable transcultural cinematic weapons. In a nutshell, Hollywood has mostly confined its exports to the pantheon of action-adventure, much as China's U.S. pictures have managed to relegate themselves to the martial-arts ghetto.

While 2014 proved to be yet another winning year for Chinese domestic pics, neither Xu nor Feng had directorial output then. Xu did co-star with Huang Bo in yet another Ning Hao moderately budgeted comedy road film, *Breakup Buddies*, which grossed over US$195 million to become the highest-grossing domestic film of the year, which kept Xu in the headline. *Breakup Buddies'* box office ranked below only *Transformers: Age of Extinction* (Michael Bay, 2014), whose success owed much to the promotional efforts of China Movie Channel (CCTV6) and its online subsidiary M1905.com, with which Paramount teamed up as production and promotion partners. The Chinese partner helped Paramount secure an attractive release slot to ensure its box-office performance.[35]

Xu returned with another *Lost* film a year later.

Lost in Hong Kong *(2015) and Mistimed Homage to Cantopop*

Riding high on his newfound popular success, Xu directed his second feature film, *Lost in Hong Kong*, in 2015, which he again starred in, cowrote, and co-produced. The film features Xu Lai, an aspiring art student turned married brassiere designer who mourns his wasted artistic talent and sets out for Hong Kong to attend the art exhibition of his art college sweetheart who made a name for herself in Hong Kong. His wife and her overbearing extended family unexpectedly tag along, jeopardizing his secret plan to see his old flame, which provides much of the film's comic kick. Worse, Xu soon finds himself accidently caught up, together with his trouble-prone brother-in-law, in a murder investigation in Hong Kong.

The film pays homage to the golden age of filmmaking in Hong Kong, and Xu Lai's misbegotten trip serves as an occasion for the filmmaker to showcase his knowledge as well as his love of Canton Pop, including Hong Kong cinema, which was trendy and ubiquitous to Xu's generation coming of age in the PRC. Born and raised in Shanghai in the 1970s and 1980s, Xu attended the Shanghai Theater Academy, earning a degree in acting. Like many of his compatriots, Xu began consuming Hong Kong films on VHS and Cantopop songs on cassettes when he was a teenager, and John Woo's *A Better Tomorrow* (1986) was said to have made a huge impression on him.[36] Comedies by Karl Maka and the Hui Brothers, and martial arts TV series such as *The Legend of the Condor Heroes* and the gangster series *The Bund*, were among his favorites.

Lost in Hong Kong is packed with hat tips to Hong Kong action, comedy, and art-house classics of the 1980s and 1990s, from Jackie Chan's *Police Story* (1985) to Wong Kar-wai's *Chungking Express* (1994), *C'est la vie, mon chéri* (Derek Yee, 1994), *A Chinese Odyssey* (Jeffrey Lau, 1995), *Comrades: Almost a Love Story* (Peter Chan, 1996), *City of Glass* (Mabel Cheung, 1998), and the more recent films *2046* (Wong Kar-wai, 2004) and *Kung Fu Hustle* (Stephen Chow, 2004). The soundtrack of the film consists of almost entirely iconic Hong Kong movie theme songs from that era. To Xu's fellow Chinese, the film was a nostalgic trip down the memory lane of Hong Kong's cinematic history.

But Xu's homage to Hong Kong, shot on location during the Umbrella Movement in 2014, met indifference in that troubled city. The timing was bad for a mainland film paying tribute to Hong Kong cinema, particularly a film featuring two mainland tourists wreaking havoc in Hong Kong. Hong Kong saw a series of sit-in street protests from September to December 2014, demonstrating against the decision by Beijing to prescreen candidates for the choice of Hong Kong's chief executive. The prevalent anti-China sentiment in Hong Kong had bled into the island city's pop-culture ecosystem. It did not help that *Lost in Hong Kong* included a cameo of the prolific director Wong Jing, who was becoming a divisive figure for his repeated critical remarks about his prodemocracy peers. With the shrinking Hong Kong market and greater opportunity in the north, Wong, like many established Hong Kong filmmakers, was mostly making films on the mainland by then. Unwittingly wading into the political firestorm, Xu confessed that "when I wrote the script, I wasn't aware of Wong's political stance."[37]

Interviewed in the *South China Morning Post*, Xu slyly defended his choice of a cameo from Wong by saying that "for a place with true freedom, everyone should have the right to express his own opinions."[38] Xu mentioned that his most memorable experience during the shooting was his brush with the Umbrella Movement protest, though he did not directly engage with the protesters. Xu's homage to Hong Kong pop earned paltry box-office figures of US$42,958 in Hong Kong. *Lost in Thailand* also fell on deaf ears in the island city, earning less than US$85,479. The resistance of people in Hong Kong to any cultural influence from mainland China was palpable. Complicating the issue, the film led to a surge in tourists from the mainland, which average Hong Kongers did not appreciate. It was some consolation that Xu refrained from wringing cheap culture-clash laughs in the film, considering tensions between Hong Kongers and mainland tourists over manners and styles of public conduct as well as cultural and political frameworks and allegiances.

The reaction was far different over on the mainland. *Lost in Hong Kong* won an unprecedented 100,000 screenings in its first twenty-four hours when it opened in September, grossing $1.8 million from midnight showings and $32 million on its opening day—the biggest debut ever for a Chinese film, and the third-largest opening-day performance overall in China, behind only *Furious 7* (James Wan, 2015) and *Avengers: Age of Ultron* (Joss Whedon, 2015).[39] It snared an unprecedented 87 percent share of the day's box-office receipts. *Lost in Hong Kong* also took in a handy $559,000 in the United States, receiving mostly appreciative reviews. The film eventually took in $255 million, beating the $208 million take of *Lost in Thailand*, making Xu the only Chinese filmmaker to have two titles grossing more than RMB 1 billion each at the box office.

Chinese Holiday Movies from Feng Xiaogang to Xu Zheng

With two fast-paced and feel-good road movies under his belt, Xu quickly established himself as a formidable figure in China's crowded holiday film market, challenging Feng, whose deliberately paced comedy vignettes featuring his long-term leading man, the slow-going comedian Ge You, were beginning to look jaded, if not entirely outdated. Indeed, Ge You was so low in energy and slow in physical movement and line delivery that he had become a meme for *sang*, a Chinese word that means "hollowed out," which evokes idleness, apathy, and passivity. In Feng's date movie *If You Are the One* and its sequel, Ge You plays a dejected man who is indecisive, reluctant, and incapable, or not particularly eager, to "conquer" his love interest. One of the frequently used expressions of the *sang* culture is "I am almost a disabled person."[40] In the sequel to *If You Are the One*, Ge You's character literally spends part of the film sitting in a wheelchair, pretending to be a disabled person presumably to test his lover's devotion. A screenshot of Ge You appearing as a skinny, balding, middle-aged man slouching on a couch staring blankly into the ceiling has become an infamous internet meme called "Ge You Slouch." The image itself comes from a decade-old popular sitcom, *I Love My Family* (1994), in which Ge plays a homeless idler. *I Love My*

Family was China's first multicamera sitcom directed by Ying Da, the American-trained dramatist, with the popular Beijing writer Wang Shuo serving as one of the chief screenwriters—both of them Feng's long-term collaborators.

When Xu directed his second film in 2015, Feng starred in *Mr. Six*, a crime drama directed by his acolyte Guan Hu, a sixth-generation independent filmmaker turned mainstream blockbuster director. Befitting the era of *sang*, Feng plays Mr. Six, an aging gangster who is forced out of retirement when his teenage son gets entangled with a group of entitled rich-kid punks who threaten his well-being. While Mr. Six lives by Beijing's traditional code of honor, his opponents are Western-style gangsters with fancy sports cars and designer clothes bankrolled by their corrupt politician parents. The young have no regard for the traditional code of conduct. The back-and-forth negotiations between the old-style geriatric gangsters and the fancy new racers leads to an epic battle on a frozen lake. Mr. Six, the antihero in the movie, is very much Feng's alter ego, a channel for him to vent the frustrations of his generation, and perhaps of his own evaporating magic touch with the young generation of moviegoers and his status as the godfather of Chinese holiday movies. The theme of the clash of values failed to connect with audiences, and *Mr. Six* fell behind *Monkey King: Hero Is Back* (Tian Xiaopeng, 2015), a Chinese animation film released in the summer that knocked *Mr. Six* off the tenth spot on the box-office chart.[41]

The same year that Feng dabbled in acting, a 3-D action-packed film, *Wolf Warrior* (Wu Jing), featuring a special forces PLA soldier battling a group of foreign mercenaries, appeared on Chinese screens to little notice. But the sequel, *Wolf Warrior II* in 2017, would break the Chinese box-office record and usher in the term "wolf warrior" as a metaphor for China's new breed of assertive and aggressive foreign diplomacy.[42]

I Am Not Madame Bovary *(2016): Feng's Turn to Experimental Art Film*

Between *Lost in Hong Kong* in 2015 and *Wolf Warrior II* in 2017, an exquisitely quaint film came out from Feng Xiaogang—*I Am Not Madame Bovary*—which signaled a new turn for the longtime popular filmmaker.

I Am Not Madame Bovary tells the convoluted story of a small-town woman, Li Xuelian, who conspires with her husband to get a sham divorce in order to secure a second apartment (the government outlaws couples owning a second apartment to prevent real estate speculation) only to have him betray her, marry someone else, and then move to the apartment with his new wife. To add insult to injury, he calls her Pan Jinlian, the name of an infamous adulterer in Chinese folklore. The English title replaces "Pan Jinlian" with "Madame Bovary" for easy reference.

I Am Not Madame Bovary, though, is not a film about infidelity. It is a film about one woman's challenge to an inept bureaucratic system. Scorned, the enraged village woman, played by the otherwise glamorous megastar Fan Bingbing, against typecasting, embarks on a revenge petition to overturn her sham divorce so that she can re-divorce her cheating husband, this time properly and for real, and to redeem her reputation. Her grievances are clumsily handled by a succession of self-serving and buck-passing officials. Li's battle against China's legal system lasts for a decade, causing collateral damage to a slew of low-level party functionaries. The clever film is at once a lampoon of the incompetence and laziness of government officials and the absurdity of one woman's quest for justice that, by law, does not rest with her.

Unbeknown to her, what Li is really seeking is moral rectification, which she believes can be accomplished via petition, a relic of an imperial grievance system that took morality into consideration, but which is now governed through a modern legal procedure. Here Feng touches upon the thorny issue of petition, a unique phenomenon in China, and a headache for the Chinese government. Petitioning has been a long-standing official administrative system in China for hearing individual complaints and grievances. In ancient imperial times, petitioners would go to the county magistrate or other high officials to voice their grievances by beating a drum installed at the gate for the sole purpose of hearing such complaints. If no one at the local level was able to help, petitioners would travel to the capital city to seek the attention of higher officials. During the PRC era, the National Public Complaints and Proposals Administration and local petitioning bureaus have been the designated organizations that receive visits from individuals or groups. The officers then channel the issues to respective departments while monitoring the progress and providing feedback to the filing parties. The number of people using the petitioning system has increased since 1993, dramatically straining a system that was never known as an effective mechanism for handling complaints.

To avoid embarrassment and reprisals from the central government, local governments were known to have abducted petitioners and forced them to return from Beijing. The thuggish practice is known as "intercepting," which is shown comically in Feng's film as we see how Li is under constant surveillance by the local officers who are fearful of what she might say to the higher-ups in Beijing. Since the early 2010s, with the growing number of petitioners coming to Beijing and creating unseemly sights in the capital city, leading to complaints from Beijing residents, China has attempted to reform the informal petition system and to push for accountability through law.

I Am Not Madam Bovary carefully exposes the complexities of China's petition culture, which was a tricky issue when Du Yang, the film's executive producer, sought official approval for the script he purchased in 2012. Du was advised to treat the issue with great care and to support the government's push for law and order. Du revised the script accordingly, and the project was finally endorsed by the state four years later.[43]

In the film, Li's persistence in seeking nonexistent justice does not hold ground according to the letter of the law, though the spirit of the law is a different matter. The same moral ambiguity is present in *The Story of Qiu Ju* (Zhang Yimou, 1992), which tells the tale of a pregnant village woman on a quest to seek both monetary compensation and an apology for her husband, who has been kicked in the groin by the village head during a dispute. The village head later saves both the woman and her newborn baby when she unexpectedly goes into labor. At the end of the film, Qiu Ju learns with much anguish that the village chief is punished for breaking one of her husband's ribs during a different scuffle. Here, justice prevails, but not to Qiu Ju's relief.

Neither film is about law and order but rather about the boundaries between law and humanity. Here we see the limits of law as an ultimate arbiter of morality and human emotions. Maybe all Li needs is a pair of sympathetic ears for her emotional and moral indignation. But nobody bothers to listen to her. Li's ex-husband dies during the course of her crusade, leaving it impossible for her to seek retribution for his illicit affair and to clear her name. The existential crisis of her case is part of the black humor, though the satirical bite dissipates somewhat as the story drags on, until an emotional coda with the revelation of Li's miscarriage capping a powerful end to her journey of petition.

In an interview with the Chinese media, Feng said that the film was about bureaucrats shirking responsibilities, which he saw as the real corruption, a theme he trumpeted in *Personal Tailor*, which portrayed "clean" bureaucrats not getting work done as more menacing and harmful than officials who took bribes but got the job done.[44] The curious position that values corrupt officials who "get the job done" over the inept do-gooders actually heeds the party's call for steering clear of the theme of class conflict and social division in arts and literature so as to downplay the wealth gap and diffuse popular resentment against the rich and the privileged who have benefited the most from crony state capitalism. Perhaps Feng had a premonition of the coming tax evasion scandal in 2018 that would engulf the Chinese film industry, implicating him personally and taking down the big-name performer Fan Bingbing, who starred in *I Am Not Madam Bovary*.

Despite Fan's star power, the film struggled at the box office, which did not surprise Feng. As he remarked to *Variety* in Toronto in 2016, he saw no obvious mass appeal in this film; he also confessed that he enjoyed the trajectory of moving from popular to rarefied, as opposed to the conventional path of many filmmakers moving from independent to mainstream.[45] Feng followed up *I Am Not Madam Bovary* with another personal pet project, *Youth*, in 2017, the year a domestic action film, *Wolf Warrior II*, made headline news, announcing the arrival of the Chinese heavy industry film, e.g., leitmotif blockbuster films, which would come to completely overshadow Feng's brand of popular holiday films.

Wolf Warrior II *and* Operation Red Sea: *Heavy Industry Films*

A story about Len Feng, a retired Chinese special forces operative who returns to his duties in a nameless African country, *Wolf Warrior II* opens with a five-minute-long sequence simulating a single, extended shot displaying a certain cinematic swagger that would come to be equated with China's newly realized assertiveness on a global stage. The opening scene witnesses a panorama tracking shot skimming over a tranquil river under the glittering sun and into an ocean. The camera lands on a cargo ship, which is under attack by pirates buzzing alongside the ship in speed-boats. Unperturbed, our hero, played by Wu Jing, the movie's star and di-rector and a renowned martial arts performer, steps off the ship's deck, dives into the ocean, and throws the pirates off one of the boats. Pirates come after Wu with guns and machetes under the water. Wu fights off every single one of them before tying them all up with a rope without ever surfacing to take a breath. He then boards the boat, snatches a sniper rifle, and fires at the other pirate boat. The slow-motion CGI (computer-generated imagery) bullet hits a pirate as he gets ready to shoot off a rocket launcher. The rocket misfires into the air before coming down toward the audience. We then see the movie's logo appear on the screen. This well-crafted and perfectly choreographed sequence showcases the sheer physi-cal grace and abandon of the kung fu master turned leading man Wu Jing, who reportedly did most of the underwater fighting himself.

As the story develops, we learn that Len Feng is in Africa to search for his fiancée who has gone missing under mysterious circumstances. While in Africa, he bonds with local people and rescues children from random eruptions of violence. When civil war breaks out in his unnamed adopted country, Len volunteers for a one-man mission to save a group of Chinese nationals trapped behind enemy lines, and in turn comes into conflict with a crew of dangerous mercenaries led by Big Daddy, a cartoonish character who embodies Wu's version of American military excess.

Registering acute antagonism toward the United States, the film makes the Americans not only the bad guys but losers, and the Chinese the good guys and winners. Frank Grillo, the Hollywood action actor, steps into the role of Big Daddy with grit and intensity. In one battle scene, Len Feng deftly flips over Big Daddy's tank. As Big Daddy crawls out of the wreckage, he muses, "I guess the Chinese military ain't as lame as I thought!" A few minutes later during his final confrontation with Len, Big Daddy tells his Chinese counterpart that "people like me will always be better than people like you!" In response, Len turns the fight around and hisses in Chinese, "That's fucking history." In soundly defeating the Americans and rescuing the world, China becomes the absolute world leader and savior. China's leadership position is reaffirmed in the film when it sends its people to defend the war-torn African country just as every other country is pulling its people out. "You think the American marines are the best in the world?" Len Feng asks. "That may be true, but where are they now?"

Antagonism toward the United States aside, the film is a copycat of Hollywood's action genre, with energetic hurtling from big set pieces to bigger set pieces created by a team of Americans including renowned actors, a stunt coordinator, and even a composer whom Wu Jing hired to help make a film that denigrates the United States. The stunt coordinator Sam Hargrave, for instance, worked as a double for Chris Evans—portraying the American hero—in the *Avengers* and *Captain America* movies. Combining flag-waving with explosions, Wu delivers a populist action fantasia akin to American movies of the 1980s.

From overblown nationalism to giddy spectacle, *Wolf Warrior II* holds a Chinese mirror up to *Top Gun* and *Rambo: First Blood Part II*, albeit coming decades later. Although not a co-production, *Wolf Warrior II* applies skills provided by the U.S. creative team to showcase China's largess in Africa and its newly acquired international power. *Wolf Warrior II* signals the official entrance of China into the global action fray, with the goal of leveraging the all-American genre for the celebration of Chinese patriotism and supremacy.

The film grossed US$870 million in China, but globally *Wolf Warrior II* had little traction beyond Asia, where it earned almost all of its proceeds. Jingoism cloaked as Chinese patriotism and racist depictions of nameless and witless Africans did not comport well with contemporary Western sensibilities or critics. Apparently, the world is not thrilled to banish American saviors only to embrace the Chinese as rescuers.[46] The film failed to capture hearts and minds of audiences beyond China, grossing only US$2.3 million in the North American market; its China box office accounted for 98.1 percent of its total gross. The film nevertheless offers a peek into a future in which Hollywood might no longer be the center of the moviemaking and viewing universe.

Wolf Warrior II appeared around the time when the notion of "heavy industry," i.e., high-concept, high-tech, and big-budget films that were at once propagandistic and crowd-pleasing, emerged in China.[47] Zhang

Hongsen, the screenwriter turned deputy director of SARFT, first used the term "heavy industry" in October 2015 to describe Hollywood-style capital-intensive, high-tech, and action-oriented leitmotif block-buster films as opposed to the "light industry" of artisanal, low-budget, and personal films—the kind that Feng Xiaogang has now turned to in recent years. The film Zhang cited as a harbinger of "heavy industry" was *Monster Hunt* (Raman Hui), a blockbuster mainland/Hong Kong co-produced 3-D fantasy-cum–comedy action adventure. Chinese film crit-ics and academics echoed Zhang Hongsen's call and started to promote "heavy industry" films showcasing cinematic tours de force as the best form of cultural soft power.[48] Rao Shuguang, a prominent film critic and theorist, for instance, stated in an article titled "'Heavy Industry Film' and Its Aesthetics: Theory and Practice" that the arrival of heavy industry films encapsulated the long-term ambition of Chinese cinema to transform from the country of big film market[49] to powerful film producer. *Wolf Warrior II* is lumped into the category of "heavy indus-try" films. The concept of heavy industry was replaced in 2018 by a new term, "neo-leitmotif film," which better captured the populist propa-gandist nature of these films.[50]

A year after *Wolf Warrior II*, another jingoistic Chinese heavy industry film, *Operation Red Sea* (2018), debuted. This time, Dante Lam, the famed Hong Kong action director trained in the tradition of John Woo, took the helm. The film tells a fictional story about the evacuation of 225 foreign nationals and roughly 600 Chinese citizens from Yemen's south-ern port of Aden during the Yemeni civil war in 2015. Promoted as a gift for the ninetieth anniversary of the founding of the Chinese People's Liberation Army and the party's nineteenth National Congress, *Opera-tion Red Sea* grossed USD$579 million, making it the fourth highest-grossing film ever in China and highest grossing Chinese film in 2018. Hailed as "China's first modern naval film," it was selected as Hong Kong's entry for the Best Foreign Language Film award at the ninety-first Academy Awards but failed to secure a nomination. But it still won Lam the Hundred Flowers Award for Best Director in China and the award for Best Action Choreography at the thirty-eighth Hong Kong Film Awards.

Dying to Survive *(2018)*

Both Xu Zheng and Feng Xiaogang were absent from the director's chair in 2018, the year *Operation Red Sea* made waves. Feng was preparing for his next personal "light industry film," *Only Cloud Knows*, while Xu returned to his acting routine, starring in *Dying to Survive*, a dramedy loosely based on the real-life exploits of a cancer patient who was jailed for leading a *Dallas Buyers Club*–style group that illegally imported unproven but cheap drugs. Xu Zheng co-produced the film with Ning Hao, who directed him in the popular 2014 film *Breakup Buddies*, which came in second at the box office, below only *Transformers: The Age of Extinction*.

The film version of the story centers on a struggling Shanghai shopkeeper played by Xu who sells cheap Indian "love drugs" nobody wants but who becomes an unlikely hero when he turns a moneymaking scheme into a life-changing crusade to address the plight of cancer patients. *Variety* praised it "a classy crowd-pleaser" but marveled that "a Chinese film that shows public protests and casts officialdom in a frequently unflattering light" could still receive "the stamp of approval from state censors."[51] Here the obsession of Western media with Chinese censorship precluded a more nuanced understanding of Chinese society.

Advocating for public welfare and ridiculing officialdom have become routine pastimes in arts and entertainment in China. The party tolerates and indeed encourages films that tackle pressing social issues, so long as such probing does not encroach on sensitive issues of national security or lead to mass social unrest, and there is an affirmative or positive ending that highlights the responsiveness and resolve of the central government. The Chinese state has always been receptive to the so-called "people's livelihood issues," or bread and butter issues, given that social harmony and stability rest heavily on how the government deals with these issues. The prohibitive cost of drugs and hospital treatment has been a festering national sore. Spotlighting national anxieties about overpriced medicines and limited medical resources concentrated mostly in big city hospitals, *Dying to Survive* struck a chord with the Chinese public and the leadership. The film opened in July 2018 and reached number three on the annual box-office chart. Its massive success was credited with influencing changes in government policies regarding the affordable supply chain of leukemia-fighting drugs. Chinese premier Li Keqiang cited the film in an appeal to regulators to "speed up price cuts for cancer drugs" and "reduce the burden on families"[52]

The film received renewed attention at the twenty-third Shanghai International Film Festival (SIFF) in the summer of 2020, during the COVID-19 pandemic, when the festival sought to boost film attendance by promoting outdoor screenings.[53] The pandemic-induced six-month lockdown in China put immense pressure on China's film industry in the first half of 2020, leading to production cancellations and postponements. There was a shortage of space as well for new movies when China allowed cinemas to open with restrictive measures starting on July 20. To support the film industry's recovery, SIFF cleverly turned to outdoor screenings and reruns, showing restored old Chinese classics such as *Big Li, Young Li, and Old Li* (Xie Jing, 1962), and more recent hits such as *Detective Chinatown* (Sicheng Chen) and *Dying to Survive*. At the opening ceremony of an outdoor cinema screening of *Dying to Survive*, Xu Zheng thanked SIFF for "bringing movies back to us."

What Does Not Sell in China: The Case of Crazy Rich Asians *(2018)*

The summer when *Dying to Survive* was making waves in China, an American film, *Crazy Rich Asians* (Jon M. Chu, 2018), created a sensation in the United States but failed to garner enthusiasm in China. A crossover between *The Great Gatsby* (Baz Luhrmann, 2013) and the U.S. prime-time soap opera *Dynasty*, albeit casting Asians, *Crazy Rich Asians* is a trite tale of clashes between East and West, love and duty, as well as nouveau riche tackiness and aristocratic hauteur. In the United States, the film was celebrated as the first Hollywood movie since *The Joy Luck Club* (Wayne Wang, 1993) to focus on Asians (mostly of Chinese descent) and cast mostly Asians and Asian Americans. Though cementing Asia's place in the oligarchic narrative of the world, the Asian *Great Gatsby* was greeted with little fanfare in much of Asia.

In the Chinese market, which the film surely covets, the pride of Asians and Chinese Americans and the complex issue of diversity and representation meet indifference as such are too remote for the Chinese in China to relate to. Furthermore, ethnically Chinese-looking people drenched in wealth are not exotic enough to the Chinese in China, as the country has its own share of obscene wealth and debauched extravagance. *Crazy Rich Asians* was a big flop in China on its opening weekend in cinemas. The film barely made RMB 6 million (US$862,000) from Friday to Sunday, was rated 6.2 out of 10 on film rating site Douban, and failed to get a rating on another popular Chinese film rating site, Maoyan. Chinese viewers complained about how bland the plot is, how Cinderella-style stories are Chinese TV cliché, and how Michelle Yeoh's scheming matriarch character pales in comparison to the cloak-and-dagger, life-and-death intrigues of popular Chinese imperial palace dramas such as *Story of Yanxi Palace* (2018) on the Chinese streaming platform iQiyi.

The caricature of the nouveau riche as rude and tasteless might actually be an insult to the Chinese who have yet to have the time to accumulate wealth the old-fashioned way—by inheriting it. It would take generations for the crude and boorish new money to evolve into pompous and arrogant old money, however "dignified" such might be. Indeed "the newly minted rich" has become a euphemism in the West in recent years for people from mainland China who line up at luxury boutiques and spend large. Interestingly, the dynastic fortunes in Singapore are mostly made by the overseas Chinese—families that built incredible wealth through multiple generations. The disconnect between the overseas Chinese and the Chinese on the mainland is palpable. The reception for *Crazy Rich Asians* stood in stark contrast to the spectacular performance of Xu Zheng's gentle medical comedy-tragedy *Dying to Survive*, which finds instant connection with Chinese audiences.

Nezha, The Wandering Earth, *and the Rise of China's Young Tech Wizard*

The number one blockbuster of 2019 was *Nezha*, a 3-D computer animation fantasy adventure featuring the popular Chinese mythological character Nezha, from the Chinese classic *Investiture of the Gods*, a gods-and-demons novel written during the Ming dynasty (1368–1644).

Released in China exclusively in IMAX and China Film Giant Screen theaters in early 2019 and followed by wider releases in other theaters in late July, *Nezha* soon became the highest-grossing non-U.S. animated film and the second highest–grossing non-English-language film of all time worldwide, overtaking the popular Japanese animation *Spirited Away* (Hayao Miyazaki, 2001).[54] The film was selected as the Chinese entry for Best International Feature Film at the ninety-second Academy Awards but it was not nominated.

Nezha was made by unknown director Yang Yu, a college dropout and self-taught computer animator who had spent six years trying to get his pet project off the ground. Looking to enter the online animation games market, Beijing Enlight Media, the company behind *Lost in Thailand*, offered Yang funding and technical support in 2015, and the result was another dark-horse megahit. The film almost single-handedly turned around the company's financial fortune, which was plagued at the time by several underperforming releases, including the cult director Lou Ye's *The Shadow Play*.[55] Prior to *Nezha*'s release, Enlight announced that it expected its profit for the first half of 2019 to plunge 95 percent compared to the same period in 2018. *Nezha* rescued Enlight.

Nezha's success marks the rising trend in Chinese cinema of the ascendance of a new generation of filmmakers with technological expertise and unconventional career paths. *The Wandering Earth* provided another example of this trend. Directed by the little known post-1980s millennial-generation filmmaker Frant Gwo, the film was a loose adaptation of the popular 2000 sci-fi novella of the same title by China's renowned sci-fi writer Liu Cixin, the winner of the 2015 Hugo Award for *The Three-Body Problem*,[56] and the 2017 Locus Award for *Death's End* as well as a nominee for the Nebula Award.[57] *The Wandering Earth* features a group of astronauts and rescue workers who guide Earth away from an expanding sun as they attempt to prevent Earth's collision with Jupiter. The film reached number two on the domestic box-office chart for the year. Gwo's career path is equally unusual: after studying law in college, he spent much of his time creating comic books and graphic designs before entering Beijing Film Academy to study film management in 2009. He made two feature films before being offered the sci-fi project in 2016. It took Gwo and his team three years to make the film.

In the wake of the success of *The Wandering Earth*, China's National Film Administration and the China Association for Science and Technology, a professional organization, issued a document in August 2020 to boost science fiction film productions.[58] Titled "Several Opinions on Promoting the Development of Science Fiction Films," the document encouraged the development of pro-China sci-fi content of high-tech production value. It further highlighted how the sci-fi genre fit into the state's broader ideological and technological goals. The document stated that to "thoroughly study and implement Xi Jinping thought" was the number one priority for Chinese sci-fi filmmakers. Xi has urged the Chinese film industry to create films that "highlight Chinese values, inherit Chinese culture and aesthetics, cultivate contemporary Chinese innovation" as well as "disseminate scientific thought" and "raise the spirit of scientists."[59] Chinese sci-fi films were called upon to develop and apply China's own homegrown visual effects (VFX) and digital technologies in making sci-fi content. The development of VFX technology in the era of Western sanctions was now accorded strategic importance. The elevation of film technology as a development priority reflected China's escalating competition with the West on the technology front.

Though focusing on hardware, the document acknowledged the problem of a lack of innovative ideas and scripts for sci-fi films, calling for generating strong sci-fi scripts through talent incubation and prizes and seeking new and original content from sci-fi literature, animation, and games. In a typical social engineering fashion, it urged film festivals to set up sci-fi divisions to promote sci-fi films and requested that elementary and middle school students watch "excellent sci-fi movies." It further encouraged universities to "strengthen the training of sci-fi–related talent." To broaden sci-fi films' reach, the document recommended that China establish a national science fiction film screening alliance.

The Chinese film industry did not normally offer production insurance or completion bonds, which was a common professional practice in Hollywood. Consequently, investors typically looked to invest in projects with quick returns, which hindered the creation of expensive, complex sci-fi films that require lengthy development and production schedules. To address this problem, the document urged Chinese financial institutions to "explore credit products and loan models specific to the characteristics of sci-fi movies," and insurance entities to "innovate in the development of intellectual property rights infringement liability insurance for sci-fi movies, as well as group accident insurance and personal accident insurance for specific actors and staff." Firms should also be encouraged to develop the means of "providing financing guarantee services for science fiction movies in a variety of ways." This new attention to film financing demonstrated policy makers' more sophisticated understanding about filmmaking in the era of IP and more ambitious approach that adds another layer to the heavy industry film model seen as most effective at carrying the torch for Chinese cultural power.

A Dwindling Hollywood in China by the End of 2010s

The Chinese film market in 2019 was dominated by China's homegrown films, leaving little room for Hollywood franchise movies just as China's theatrical revenues rose to a new all-time high.[60] By the end of 2019, China had 69,787 cinema screens, up 9,708 from 2018, according to the *People's Daily*, which also noted that more than 1.7 billion tickets were sold.[61] China called this a "golden age" for the Chinese film industry. Box-office revenue rose 5.4 percent to a new record of $9.2 billion (RMB 64.3 billion) in 2019. But the new theater expansion mostly happened in tertiary cities and counties, with audiences more attuned to local rather than foreign content, posing a challenge to Hollywood's China expansion. *Nezha* and *The Wandering Earth, My People, My Country* (Ning Hao et al., 2019), and *The Captain* (Andrew Lau, 2019) were four of the year's top ten grossers. American titles making it into China's top ten grossers were *Avengers: Endgame* (Joe Russo and Anthony Russo, 2019), which came in third, and *Fast & Furious Presents: Hobbs & Shaw* (David Leitch, 2019), which came in tenth.

Hollywood's box office might have already reached its saturation point in China by the end of the 2010s.[62] As reported by *Variety*, Chinese films performed proportionally better in the last three years of the 2010s than foreign films, which accounted for a shrinking slice of the box office.[63] Chinese films accounted for 64 percent of the total box office in 2019, or $5.9 billion (RMB 41.2 billion) in ticket sales, up from 62 percent in 2018 and 54 percent in 2017. Imports took up 22 percent of 2019's total number of screened titles, a rate that was largely consistent in the previous several years, but recent installments of Hollywood franchises, such as *How to Train Your Dragon: The Hidden World* (Dean DeBlois), *Jumanji: The Next Level* (Jake Kasdan), *X-Men: Dark Phoenix* (Simon Kinberg), and *Star Wars: The Rise of Skywalker* (J.J. Abrams), didn't perform so well in China, although *Avengers: Endgame* (Joe and Anthony Russo) and *Frozen 2* (Jennifer Lee and Chris Buck) made it to the top ten blockbuster chart for 2019. Ten of the fifteen films that earned over RMB 1 billion ($144 million) in 2019 were Chinese, as were forty-seven out of the eighty-eight films that made more than RMB 100 million ($14.4 million). It was indeed the case that "local films are catching up to Hollywood on many indicators like IP, story, special effects, and genre, while Hollywood films are caught in a bottleneck period of self-repetition and a lack of originality," as quoted by *Variety* from the Chinese website Mirror Entertainment.[64]

The rising visibility in China of smaller A-class quality pictures from the United States, such as *Green Book* (Peter Farrelly, 2018), further addressed the lack of originality in action-oriented Hollywood exports, though the success of *Green Book* owed much to the marketing campaign of the film's Chinese co-financier, Alibaba.[65] Hardly a runaway success in China, as it ranked at only number thirty on China's blockbuster chart,[66] *Green Book* nonetheless received more press coverage and positive critical and popular reviews than any other film in recent memory. Alibaba Pictures, the film studio arm of China's e-commerce giant Alibaba, invested in the production of *Green Book* alongside Participant Media, DreamWorks Pictures, and Steven Spielberg's Amblin Partners (the latter also minority-owned by Alibaba).

Alibaba began trumpeting its involvement in the film in the Chinese media immediately after *Green Book*'s Oscar nod. The overjoyed executive chairman Jack Ma invited several of his Chinese celebrity friends to the post-Oscar screenings, claiming that he had seen the movie three times and that it made him see "hope and kindness" in the world. The enthusiasm was reminiscent of the media hype *Titanic* (James Cameron, 1997) received in 2017, after Jiang Zemin endorsed it and urged the Chinese to learn to make a film like *Titanic*; the key difference was that this time the Chinese could take some credit for an Oscar-winning film. The state-backed media promptly claimed *Green Book*'s achievements as

China's achievement, stating that "the 91st Academy Awards can be viewed as the starting point for a new period of growing influence for China in the international film industry."[67] Also, "All of China is celebrating *Green Book*'s Oscar win," explained a social media influencer, Entertainment Unicorn, in a post that circulated on WeChat, which further claimed that "Alibaba surpassed even Netflix and Amazon to become the first internet company to co-finance and co-produce an Oscar Best Picture winner. After a film with Chinese investment won this award, it feels like Chinese cinema and our national pride are not so far from the Oscars after all."[68] Muted in the Chinese reception were critical voices overseas that faulted *Green Book* for its simplistic depiction of the complicated legacy of racism in America.

By 2019, the four major holiday periods—Lunar New Year, summer, National Day, and the calendar New Year—accounted for nearly 50 percent of the total annual number of audience trips to the cinema, while the market share of big blockbusters grossing more than US$287 million in China increased from 18.5 percent of the total box office in 2017 to 29.9 percent in 2018 and 36.9 percent in 2019.[69] Yet the beginning of 2020 brought the entire country to a halt, including the Chinese film market, particularly the winter holiday market, which arrived amidst the outbreak of COVID-19. The solo film that premiered in China on January 25, 2020, the Lunar New Year date, was Xu Zheng's *Lost in Russia*, an affecting story about an accidental joint journey to Russia of an overbearing mother and her resistant and reluctant adult son.

Lost in Russia *(2020) as an Internet Megafilm*[70] *and the Nostalgia for Soviet Films*

Lost in Russia's Chinese title is "Jiong Ma," meaning "mother awkward." It is a film about a businessman, Ivan Xu (played by Xu Zheng), who grudgingly boards a Russia-bound train to accompany his aging mother Lu on a trip to Moscow to realize her previously foiled dream of performing with her choir at the Moscow Grand Theater. As the film opens, Xu is in the midst of divorce proceedings and plans to fly to New York to thwart his soon-to-be ex-wife's business deal in the lingering hope of reconciling with her. He realizes that he has accidentally left his passport with his mother who has boarded a Beijing to Moscow trans-Siberian train. Through a series of rather contrived comedic incidents, he winds up on the same train with his mother on a six-day journey to Moscow where she hopes to sing at a concert promoting seventy years of Sino-Russian relations. The journey gives Xu and Lu plenty of time to bicker and bond as he deals with his own disintegrating marriage. Following the same *Lost* formula, the unexpected mother-son adventure through Russia turns out to be a journey of self-discovery for both, though here a trans-Siberian train and snowy Russia replace the tropical scenery of Thailand and the claustrophobic urban jungle of Hong Kong. *Lost in Russia* is a milder and gentler version of the more uproarious two previous *Lost* movies.

If Hong Kong was a misfire five years earlier amidst the political tension, Russia was a nice respite in 2020 amidst the escalating Sino-U.S. tension. The film pays tribute to Russia, not as yet another exotic location for filming, though there is plenty of stereotypical Russian culture and caricature in the film, but for the nostalgic glow of music and songs of the Soviet era, which form part of Xu's upbringing and his mother's memory and imagination. Xu and Lu stumble through a Russian wedding, ride marshrutkas (a type of taxi) through icy forests, and enjoy a nighttime view of Moscow's grand cityscape, though these scenes and references offer little depth and nuance about Russia, and mother and son show little interest in any deeper understanding of Russia. The Russia in their imagination is the one they were exposed to during Mao's era, through Soviet films. The only Russian character (apparently Chinese speaking) is a sexually charged "honeypot" who serves to spice up the otherwise sterile train ride and propels Xu to reflect upon his relationship with his wife. The crass adolescent humor remains, which hews to the bottom line of previous "Lost" franchise films. Elsewhere, moments involving a bear chase, a hot-air balloon landing, and a train-top scramble border on the fantastical, lending the film a magical touch.

More than erotic and magical, the Russia backdrop captures the nostalgic link between Xu's childhood and his mother's past, which was saturated with Soviet music and films. Xu's name, Ivan, comes from the Soviet war film *Ivan's Childhood* (Andrei Tarkovsky, 1962), which Jean-Paul Sartre praised as one of the most beautiful films he had ever seen.[71] The film won the Golden Lion Award at the Venice Film Festival in

1962 and was one of several Soviet films, including *Cranes Are Flying*, produced during the Khrushchev Thaw. It made its way to China as one of the internal reference films for criticism during Mao's era. A confidential collection of essays criticizing the film was published in 1963 by the China Film Workers Association Press.[72] The film was said to have influenced the production of a popular Chinese children's film, *Little Soldier Zhang Ga* (Cui Wei, 1963), which featured a naughty boy trying to join the Eighth Route Army by fighting Japanese invaders in his own way.[73] Xu was named after Ivan because his father, a film projectionist, treated his mother to a special private screening of *Ivan's Childhood* when they were dating.

In the film's climax, the mother leads a performance of a widely circulated Russian song during the Soviet era, "Oh, the Kalina Flowers Are in Bloom," about a young girl's love for a boy. The song comes from *Cossacks of the Kuban* (Ivan Pyryev, 1950) and is a classic Soviet song that was performed in the original film by a group of female singers on stage. The song was extremely popular in China during Mao's era. *Lost in Russia* manages to also fit in references to new Russian pop culture with one montage sequence featuring the 2017 Russian pop song "Zaya," which went viral on TikTok after *Lost in Russia* had its online debut.

The film was slated for theatrical release on January 24, 2020, but was withdrawn due to the COVID-19 pandemic. It was released the following day, on Douyin, Toutiao, and Xigua for free streaming, a welcome respite for Chinese viewers in home confinement. The Spring Festival, with its focus on kinship, seemed an opportune time for a sentimental film about family bonding and overcoming the generation gap. Huanxi, Xu Zheng's production company, released the film simultaneously on its own Huanxi Premium streaming platform and on ByteDance's Douyin and Toutiao platforms. This unusual online distribution became the springboard for Xu's new business relationship with online giant Byte-Dance, owner of the wildly popular short video platform TikTok. The Huanxi and ByteDance platforms cross-promoted the film while sharing revenues. ByteDance paid Huanxi an initial $91 million (RMB 630 million) for streaming privileges and for being credited as co-producer. Xu's company Huanxi retained the theatrical rights and could release the film later in the year. The shift to online streaming boosted the stock price of

Huanxi by 43 percent on the day of the streaming. *Lost in Russia* was streamed more than 600 million times by January 27.

The Lost *Trilogy as a Formula and Motif for a China in Transformation*

The overriding motif in the *Lost* franchise is "self-discovery," which is achieved through characters embarking on journeys in pairs. Relationships evolve over time and eventually transform both characters. This belief in individuals' inherent benevolence, and the triumph of compassion and virtue over cruelty and inequality, gives the *Lost* films their warm touch. It is interesting to note that the journeys in Xu's films are consistently male-centric. The featured character is always a stressed-out businessman in a midlife crisis who tries to shake off his unlikely travel companion in a foreign land. Serving as Xu's alter ego, the male lead is forced to take stock of his own core values as he tries to balance the competing demands of money, career, and marriage or human connection, a familiar theme of greed vs. love/happiness that has been explored in numerous Hollywood films since the dawn of cinema. The main characters in the *Lost* trilogy are trapped in China's full-blown capitalist rat race where success is defined by money and power, which have left them with material abundance but spiritual deprivation. As the contemporary Chinese bon mot has it: "There was no money but hope in the past, but there is plenty of money but no hope now."

Xu's films capture well the existential crisis of Chinese elites whose wealth, mobility, and pseudointellectual superiority fall short of bringing happiness. The lifestyle of the rich and the privileged is nonetheless what the middle class aspires to and lives for vicariously through Xu's films. In *Lost on Journey*, Success Li (the character's Chinese name) runs a toy factory and uses money as the solution to every predicament in life. In the rest of the *Lost* trilogy, the male lead lives a life of impromptu mobility hopping on and off the road to exotic locations with endless cash at his disposal. But financial success is no guarantee for happiness, and the underprivileged always look much happier and better adjusted. Xu's *Lost* trilogy can therefore be seen as a metaphor for the loss as well as gain of China's astronomical economic growth in the past decade. But the rich are benevolent in the end and the poor benefit from the largess of their more abundant partners. The mutually beneficial pairing and the transformation of both in Xu's *Lost* trilogy brings comfort to audiences and harmony to society, which drives home the party's message of positive energy. Any hint of social critique is harmonized in the merry-go-round circle of journeys with friends. As a cinematic franchise, the *Lost* trilogy nicely rounds up the presence of China's modestly budgeted and reality-based homegrown holiday comedy that offers a slice of contemporary Chinese life alongside the more flamboyant Hollywood blockbusters.

At a time when China's domestic megapics looked to Hollywood as models for blockbuster hits in the mid-1990s, filmmakers endowed with only modest budgets turned to Hong Kong genre films for inspiration, creating a unique brand of comedy that catered to the Lunar New Year holiday market and stoked the fancy of Chinese audiences. The holiday market later expanded beyond winter to include other major holidays throughout the year. Feng Xiaogang's Beijing-centered winter holiday films dominated the domestic market until Xu Zheng came along in the early 2010s, transforming domestic holiday films into Shanghai-based urban comedies, with his *Lost* trilogy attracting broader holiday markets.

In contrast to Feng's biting and at times condescending political satire, Xu's brand of comedy featuring urbanites was gentler, warmer, and more bourgeois. The rich and the powerful are not as offensive in Xu's as in Feng's films. Xu's urban entrepreneurs are more down-to-earth and relatable than the condescending pseudointellectuals in Feng's recent satires. In the end, though, it is the financially resourceful elites who are capable of transforming the lives of the poor and the nobodies in both Feng and Xu's films. Feng's Dream Works team can dress up the poor for at least one day while Xu's resourceful businessmen are generous and always ready to lend their hands to their lesser partners. Though touching upon hot-button social issues in his earlier holiday films, Feng's recent comedies have retreated to films of manners.

Though different in their style and approach, both Xu Zheng and Feng Xiaogang have undergone similar transitions in their thematic preoccupations, from denouncing greed and the wealth gap to the acceptance of the status quo. While *Lost on Journey* equated materialism with immorality, by the time *Lost in Russia* came out, the theme of "money and inequalities are evil" was long gone. While Feng's *The Dream Factory* in 1997 sided with the masses and the disfranchised by condemning the moral degradation of the rich, his *Personal Tailor* in 2013 showered empathy on the rich by highlighting their hard work and celebrating their personal ambition and drive. *Personal Tailor* went so far as to encourage compassion for official corruption seen as an occupational hazard for visionary politicians with can-do spirits. The final vignette of the film featured a public park cleaner who was granted a birthday present to experience the life of a multibillionaire for a day. The takeaway for her as articulated by the leader of the dream-making team was that being a billionaire is a hardship, and the uber-rich deserved our compassion.

One vignette in the film revolved around a government-employed chauffeur who wanted to be tested for his moral integrity by fending off rent-seeking hometown villagers, bribe-brandishing entrepreneurs, and seductive underlings. He learned a lesson in the end about the traps and temptations laid for those in power. The blame thus lies with the masses who would stop at nothing to corrupt the elites. Seen in this fashion, official corruption is the fault of the masses who form the web of corruption and foster the culture of corruption, instead of the result of a political and legal system that does not allow for due checks and balances, or a media system that forbids watchdog functioning. The evolution of popular holiday comedies, from Feng's satires of social issues to Xu's relationship foibles, offers a glimpse into the transformation of Chinese society. The Chinese film industry has evolved along the way, from a tentative domestic player intimidated by Hollywood to an aspiring global player ready to take on Hollywood. As a result, domestic blockbusters of the "heavy industry" model of big budget and high tech that infuses party-sanctioned patriotism with popular narrative are overtaking the more congenial holiday comedies, projecting a more confident and assertive China on the global stage.

8

Journey Home or to the West: Chinese Cinema's Hollywood Dream and the Sino-Hollywood (De)Coupling

Black Widow was finally released, yet it did not escape from pirates in China.

—Tank, *DeepFocus*, July 2021[1]

In an online article titled "Do Chinese Films Hold Global Appeal?" the ChinaPower podcast noted that only less than 1 percent of the total revenue of the top-twenty grossing Chinese features since 2005 came from overseas.[2] In comparison, U.S. blockbusters earn roughly two-thirds of their revenue from foreign markets. Indeed, the top grossing Chinese film each year since 2016—*Ne Zha, The Wandering Earth, Operation Red Sea, Wolf Warrior II,* and *The Mermaid* (Stephen Chow, 2016)—all earned more than 95 percent of their revenue from domestic sales.[3] *Operation Red Sea* and *Wolf Warrior II* gained little traction outside China. In comparison, every number one North American feature since 2009 earned an average of 65 percent of its revenue abroad. The top grossing Indian pictures also generally make 20 to 30 percent of their box-office revenue overseas. The ChinaPower article observed that the dismal overseas performance of recent blockbusters exemplified the limited international appeal of Chinese cinema.

What accounts for the failure of films from the PRC to appeal to global audiences? Some argue that differences in political systems have engendered Western resistance, if not vilification, of China, making it difficult if not impossible for Chinese films with the government's stamp of approval to receive positive coverage in the West. Such films are routinely dismissed as Communist propaganda due to their submission to the party directives. Chinese films critical of China, on the other hand, have received enthusiastic endorsement in the West. Zhang Yimou's early films critical of China, for instance, were celebrated in the West with awards and accolades, but his later films devoid of overt political commentaries were chastised for kowtowing to the Chinese government, which Zhang countered, protesting the coerced political codification of his films. While attempting to rebrand himself by making a commercial film, *Shanghai Triad* (1995), Zhang's apolitical narrative in this crime film was rejected by the international community for its deviation from the stock characters and story lines of political indignation. In 1999, Zhang withdrew his two films, *Not One Less* and *The Road Home*, from the annual Cannes Film Festival, stating that he "can't accept that the West has for a long time politicized Chinese film. If they are not anti-government, they are just considered propaganda. I hope this bias can be slowly changed."[4]

The Politicization of Chinese Cinema

Writing in the late 1990s, the Chinese cultural critic Chen Xiaoming observed that politics has long been the anchoring for Chinese film in the international arena, never mind that Zhang Yimou disavowed or at least downplayed the political readings of his films by Western critics, who saw his *Judou* (1991) as a jeremiad against the gerontocracy and *Raise the Red Lantern* (1992) as a political struggle against patriarchy and by extension state oppression.[5] Political readings of Chinese films have become part of the ritual by Western critics. Chen notes that "without politics as the inexhaustible theme and primary cultural background, Fifth Generation films would have received little international attention" and that politics "has been the determining factor in the reconstruction of the image of 'China' in the West." Thus, "without the strategic employment of political codes, Chinese film would lose its cultural identity and consequently be denied international recognition." Another Australia-based media scholar, Yingchi Chu, takes the West to task for equating Chinese media products with propaganda "simply because they issue from a Communist regime."[6]

Yet it is hard to avoid politics in our routine encounters with Chinese cinema, given that the politicization of cinema has been part and parcel of Chinese culture and art. Film production in China has been subject to strict political control since Mao's era. China's current government under President Xi Jinping has tightened up the leash even further. On October 15, 2014, Xi presided over a symposium in Beijing, attended by some of China's most renowned authors, actors, and scriptwriters. Xi gave instructions at the symposium that Chinese cultural workers should produce works that serve the people and promote socialist core values.[7] The reaction to Xi's talk from the West was predictively dismissive. A headline article in the *South China Morning Post* read "Xi Jinping's call for political art evokes bad memories of Cultural Revolution: Some see [the] President's speech to artists as echoing forebear's cultural edict that helped trigger the excesses of the Cultural Revolution." Xi's speech did echo Mao's famous Yan'an talk on literature and art in 1942, which urged Chinese writers and artists to produce works that served the working class by reflecting upon their lives. When CCP leaders issue directives such as these, the typical reaction from the West is suspicion and ridicule.

Elsewhere during the talk, Xi promoted traditional Chinese culture as an important source of socialist core values as well as the lifeblood of China and "a foundation for China to compete in the world."[8] Given that the world has shown little interest in socialist core values, films heeding Xi's call have remained a hard sell overseas. Peng Weiying, an Australia-trained Chinese media scholar, argues from a different angle that "cultural models, ideas, language, and way of telling stories that are specific to China have prevented Chinese films [from] being appreciated globally." Language barriers have deterred non-Chinese-speaking viewers from warming up to Chinese films, particularly in countries such as the United States where audiences have traditionally been averse to subtitled films and where revenues for the top-five foreign-language movies declined by 61 percent from 2007 to 2014. Aside from the problem of language, China's "long rambling stories in oral tradition" do not work well with global audiences accustomed to tightly woven three-act Hollywood stories, as the veteran Chinese American film producer Janet Yang contends.[9]

Going Out via Economic Might Instead

Chinese cinema's failure to appeal to global audiences has served to propel Chinese film companies to go abroad as an investment strategy, particularly to the United States, by financing Hollywood productions or purchasing U.S. entertainment assets. These promised a safer bet for profits as well as portfolio diversification, and the best way to "tap into the overseas markets."[10] China's "going out" policy in the early 2010s encouraged state-run CCTV, Xinhua, and China Film to develop foreign ventures and enabled private commercial enterprises to expand overseas operations.[11] Although these outbound investments have remained vulnerable to China's turbulent political and economic climate, they have certainly raised Chinese companies' global profile by securing prime worldwide entertainment assets. In recent years they have also won critical recognition for Chinese-invested American films, with a number of them receiving Oscar nods.

Chinese investment in Hollywood had become so ubiquitous by 2014 that, as the *Hollywood Reporter* noted while writing about the trade show American Film Market, the annual event "might as well have taken place in China instead of Santa Monica for the high-profile presence of Chinese interests and dealmakers."[12] Alibaba's Jack Ma too came to Hollywood in 2014, the year Alibaba Group, China's largest e-commerce company, made its own leap into the entertainment business by acquiring ChinaVision Media, a Chinese media company, and renaming it Alibaba Films. Alibaba Films soon invested in *Mission Impossible: Rogue Nation* (Christopher McQuarrie, 2015), *Teenage Mutant Ninja Turtles: Out of the Shadows* (Dave Green, 2016), and *Star Trek Beyond* (Justin Lin, 2016). One of the company's most prestigious investments was Peter Farrelly's *Green Book* (2018), which won three academy awards: Best Picture, Best Original Screenplay, and Best Supporting Actor for Mahershala Ali. Alibaba Pictures co-financed another Oscar-winning film, *1917* (Sam Mendes, 2019), which became one of the first foreign films to be screened in China since the COVID-19 outbreak.

Another early Oscar nod came from *Spotlight*, a 2016 feature film recounting the child sex abuse scandal in the Boston area that won Best Film and Original Screenplay awards at the eighty-eighth Oscars.[13]

The film's distributor, Open Road Films, is a joint venture between Regal Entertainment Group, which operates the second-largest theater circuit in the United States, and AMC Entertainment Holdings, controlled at the time by Wanda Group, a Chinese company with a voracious appetite for overseas acquisitions that became the poster child for China's going out campaign.

The Trials and Tribulations of Dalian Wanda

The company on the biggest spending binge in Hollywood from the early 2010s until the Chinese government crackdown starting in the late 2010s had been Wanda Group, the owner of China's largest theater chain. In 2012, Wanda acquired the Kansas-headquartered American Multi-Cinema (AMC), the number two movie theater chain in the United States, for $2.6 billion. With almost five thousand screens, AMC operated six times as many theaters as Wanda's Chinese theater chain. AMC would later purchase more theater chains in the United States and Europe, making Wanda the world's largest exhibitor, and also Hollywood's top customer.[14]

Wanda Group is a real estate company founded in 1988 in Dalian, a coastal city close to the North Korean border,[15] which was transforming itself into an affluent city under then-mayor Bo Xilai, the now jailed political rival of China's current president. The founder, Wang Jianlin, a former military man whose father joined in the Long March with the Red Army, and who himself served in the army for sixteen years, won contracts by working closely with city officials to develop residential and commercial buildings. Wanda first made a name for itself by completing a major development project in eighteen months and then proceeded to build residential properties and shopping centers.[16] Recognizing the importance of entertainment to such developments, Wang Jianlin included multiplex movie theaters as part of the first Wanda Plaza, which opened in Dalian in 2000. As cinema multiplexes boomed in China, Wanda aggressively pivoted to the theater chain business, and by 2010 operated the highest-grossing cinema circuit in China, taking in $212 million from 72 cinemas and 600 screens.[17]

Wang established Wanda Media Group in 2011 to produce content for its massive array of movie theaters as well as for department stores, theme parks, and tourist sites. Similar to the pioneering Hollywood studios such as Fox and Universal that turned to filmmaking to offer a reliable flow of quality content for their theaters, Wanda turned to film production to feed its vast theater chains.[18] Ironically, Wanda's vertically integrated practice of combining production with distribution and theater chains had been outlawed in the United States since the Paramount Consent Decree in 1948, although the federal court terminated the Paramount Decree in August 2020 to address the changing media landscape during the era of online streaming.[19]

GLOBAL SHOPPING SPREE

After dominating China's domestic cinema market, Wang turned his attention toward large theater chains in the United States. Wanda's global expansion coincided with the Chinese government's call to promote Chinese culture abroad, which Wanda heeded, not without self-interest, by buying up prestige assets overseas with cheap Chinese bank loans. Wanda purchased the AMC chain in 2012, with help from Thomas Tull, the CEO and founder of the venerable Hollywood production company (Legendary Entertainment) behind the big-budget franchising blockbusters *The Dark Knight* (Christopher Nolan, 2008), *Jurassic World* (Colin Trevorrow, 2015), and *The Hangover* (Todd Phillips, 2009), and Peter Loehr, a fluent Chinese speaker and veteran producer who led Legendary East, a subsidiary of Legendary focusing on Asia. In 2013, a year after Wanda acquired the AMC chain, he donated $20 million to the American film academy's history museum, with the proviso that a part of the museum bear the name of Wanda.

At the time the Chinese government encouraged its media companies to spread Chinese cultural gospel abroad, it also called for stimulating domestic film production and consumption. Late in 2013, Wang Jianlin dashed back to China with Hollywood megastars Nicole Kidman, Ewan McGregor, Catherine Zeta-Jones, John Travolta, and Leonardo DiCaprio by his side, to unveil an $8.3-billion film studio complex in Qingdao, an eastern port city known for its beaches bordering the Yellow Sea and for its beer, a legacy of German occupation (1898–1914). Next, Wanda announced plans to build another multibillion-dollar entertainment complex, this one in Wuxi, a city close to Shanghai. The Wuxi Wanda City was to compete head-on with the forthcoming Shanghai Disneyland amusement park.

Wanda returned to Hollywood in 2014, purchasing an eight-acre land parcel in Beverly Hills for $420 million with the intention to develop it into a luxury residential building and boutique hotel. But feuds with a local union and contractors stalled progress in 2016. That same year, Wang's AMC purchased the venerable Carmike cinema chain for $1.1 billion, raising AMC's total number of U.S. screens to 8,380, making it the largest theater operator in the United States.[20] To win regulatory approval for the Carmike purchase, the merged company had to agree to divest theaters in fifteen markets in the United States, which it later sought to disavow when COVID-19 decimated the movie business in the United States. Wanda acquired the Odeon and UCI cinema circuits in Europe for $1.2 billion the same year and proceeded to buy the Nordic Cinema Group for $929 million the following year,[21] making it AMC Europe's largest film exhibition company, with 2,700 screens across fourteen countries. Combined with its U.S. holdings, AMC under Wanda had gained control of over 11,000 screens in the short time span and became the leader in the world's most lucrative film markets.

As Wang went on a global shopping spree, his domestic cinema chain, Wanda Cinema Line, continued to expand, reportedly owning more than 300 theaters with 3,500 screens by the end of 2016, making it China's biggest chain, operating some 18 percent of mainland screens, most of them in profitable locations.[22]

In October 2016, Wanda staged a star-studded gala event for Hollywood executives and talent in Los Angeles at which Wang Jianlin personally unveiled the Qingdao Studio as part of his grand scheme to bring Hollywood production to China. In addition to state-of-the-art facilities and a skilled workforce, the complex boasted a five-star hotel—making it an attractive location for visiting filmmakers, talents, and crew, Wang emphasized, always the real estate man. Wang also announced a $750 million development fund that would offer a 40 percent rebate on production costs, the highest in Asia. The promise of co-production status and partnership with a company that operated the largest cinema chain in the PRC attracted significant attention from Hollywood producers.[23]

In November 2016, a month after the Los Angeles gala, Wanda was ready to pay an inflated price of close to $1 billion for Dick Clark Productions, the TV production company that produced the Golden Globes. The company had previously changed hands in 2012 for a mere $370 million. China's National Development and Reform Commission declined to approve the deal, partly over concerns about the massive price hike. The deal collapsed in March 2017.[24]

THE DOWNSIZING

Events took a different turn by the spring and summer of 2017, when the Chinese government confronted a constellation of financial concerns, including capital outflows, that impacted the value of the renminbi in global currency markets. Concerns arose that many Chinese flagship companies had overpaid for overseas acquisitions and relied upon low-interest loans from Chinese banks to finance foreign ventures. The government began to curb massive capital flight or outflows. An intense crackdown occurred during the months leading up to the Communist Party Congress in March 2018 when Xi Jinping was expected to consolidate his political power.[25] Wanda was one of the five big conglomerates targeted by the crackdown.[26] Dalian Wanda and three other targeted companies—Anbang, HNA, and Fosun—accounted for nearly a fifth of China's overseas acquisitions. One specific concern for the regulators was that the overseas acquisitions had been financed through a number of potentially risky channels, so that, in the event of default, the companies might not have adequate assets to pay off domestic investors. This could potentially lead to social instability, as people who had lost money in high-yielding financial investments might take to the streets to protest, which had happened quite a few times over recent years.

On April 25, 2017, Xi told top party leaders that "financial security is an important part of national security and a key foundation for the stable and healthy development of the economy."[27] The Chinese government was souring on Wanda's practice of obtaining easy Chinese loans to acquire expensive trophy assets overseas.[28] Following pressure from Beijing to curtail overseas real estate investments, Chinese investors began to off-load U.S. trophy properties. Wanda suspended new foreign acquisitions and sold off more than $9 billion in theme park and hotel properties,[29] substantially contracting its overall asset size.[30] The company unloaded billions of dollars' worth of assets between 2017 and 2018.

Qingdao Movie Metropolis. Source: Wulengjing Xiansheng, https://dp.pconline .com.cn/photo/list_3216137.html.

Wanda officially inaugurated the Qingdao Movie Metropolis in April 2018, dubbing it "Chinawood."[31] Encompassing an area equivalent to two hundred soccer pitches, the Qingdao Movie Metropolis fancied itself as the global capital of filmmaking. Wang boasted at the project's official opening that the Qingdao Movie Metropolis "is the largest investment the global film and television industry has ever seen." With four hundred acres of land, thirty soundstages, a theater, a school, a hospital, luxury hotels, and a shopping center housing the largest cinema in Asia, the scale was indeed impressive.

As it focused inward to develop its Chinese properties, Wanda agreed to sell the glitzy development site next to the Beverly Hilton hotel for more than $420 million in November 2018.[32] Back in China in April 2019, Wanda broke ground on a theme park project in Yan'an, the Chinese Communist Party's base during the Second World War and a town steeped in CCP mythology. This "red-themed" project was to be a gift commemorating the one hundredth anniversary of the founding of the CCP in July 2021. Back in the United States, as COVID-19 ravaged the U.S. exhibition industry, lockdowns and other pandemic-induced restrictions led to a record loss for AMC in 2020, after theater attendance plummeted over 90 percent.[33] Wanda promptly cut its stake in AMC to 23.1 percent by the end of 2020. It officially gave up its majority stake to hold only a minority stake of 9.8 percent in March 2021. By May 2021, Wanda owned only 10,000 of AMC's Class A shares, or 0.002 percent of the total shares outstanding.[34]

The Regional and Global Ambitions of Chinese Cinema: Now and Then

As it attempts to extend its Hollywood reach, Chinese cinema has also made its presence known along the ancient Silk Road, in countries situated on China's periphery, with the unveiling in 2013 in Kazakhstan by Xi Jinping of the ambitious Belt and Road Initiative (BRI). BRI aimed to link China to Europe along the Silk Road through Central Asia and Russia and currently connects seventy-one countries along the way via newly constructed roads, both physical and virtual (broadband). The BRI scheme has created opportunities for the regional expansion of Chinese media including Chinese cinema. In November 2017, Huawei, the Chinese telecom giant at the center of U.S. government security scrutiny, sponsored the First Central Asian Innovation Day in Astana, Kazakhstan, announcing the theme "Explore the New Digital Silk Road." In 2018, as mentioned in media scholars Michael Keane and Haiqing Yu's research, "Alibaba sponsored an 11-day training program in Hangzhou for 37 young entrepreneurs from seven BRI countries (Malaysia, Thailand, Indonesia, Pakistan, Cambodia, the Philippines, and Vietnam) on e-commerce, technological, and business innovations."[35] The goal is to secure China's cultural influence by encouraging the use of communication platforms owned, controlled, serviced, and invested in by Chinese companies.

Xi Jinping called the BRI project the "construction" of a "community of shared destiny" in the region. As Ying Zhu and Michael Keane (2020) note, it remains to be seen whether imposing a secular Chinese model of social governance onto a region where religions and cultures have collided for centuries could succeed.[36] Ostensibly packaged as a form of cosmo-politanism for our age, the "community of shared destiny" is reflected in films such as *Wolf Warrior II*, where Chinese heroes rescue African brothers and sisters, and in TV dramas such as *Legends of the Silk Road* (2015), where Uighurs and Han Chinese interact peacefully. Chinese content such as this espouses Chinese values of standing up against im-perial powers and helping people in developed countries to live together harmoniously.

It is worth noting that the regional and global ambitions of Chinese cinema are not unique to the PRC. When the PRC shut its doors to the outside world during Mao's era, the Hong Kong and Southeast Asia–based veteran studio Shaw Brothers, which started its filmmaking busi-ness in Shanghai in the 1920s, aggressively expanded into other countries. Shaw operated a chain of 139 cinemas across Singapore, Malaysia, Thai-land, Indonesia, and Indochina by the end of the 1930s. By the late 1950s, Shaw developed its Singapore-based film business into a trans-Asian media empire encompassing film studios producing Chinese- and Malay-language films, a massive distribution network importing films from Hong Kong, India, Europe, and the United States, and a circuit of more than 130 theaters throughout Southeast Asia.

Shaw's global ambition came with a missionary zeal to promote Chi-nese cultural tradition and civilization. In Shaw's own words, the com-pany's transnational effort aimed "to introduce through celluloid images to people of different races and linguistic backgrounds the cultural and artistic traditions of China."[37] In interviews given frequently to both Chinese and Western media in the 1960s, Runrun Shaw repeatedly as-serted the studio's goals in cultural and nationalistic terms. Shaw was to "bring the East into the West" and to chaperone Chinese cinema out of the racial ghetto of Chinatowns and into the global market. Decades of importing Hollywood, European, and Indian films to Southeast Asia helped the company build business ties with major studios beyond the Pa-cific. At a press conference in Taiwan in the early 1960s, Shaw stated his determination to work with Western film studios on an "equal basis" as a way to "declare the entry of the Chinese cinema" into the global com-munity of national cinemas.

To meet Runrun's aspiration of proselytizing Chinese culture and tra-dition, Shaw shifted from making hugely profitable yet parochial and localized Cantonese films to making Mandarin-language films. Mandarin Chinese is a northern dialect that had by 1932 become China's official language. The designation was decreed by the National Languages Committee, aka the Mandarin Promotion Council or the National Languages Promotion Committee, which was established in 1928 by the KMT's Ministry of Education to standardize and popularize the usage of Mandarin in the Republic of China. As a result, Cantonese films were banned in China in the 1930s as the KMT government promoted Mandarin as the sole national language representing the collective sensibility of ethnic Chinese around the world. To make the transition to Mandarin film production, the filming facility Movie Town opened a film school, hiring twenty-one Mandarin-speaking teaching staff from Shanghai to train new acting talent. Mandarin classes were also offered to the studio's mostly Shanghainese and later Cantonese-speaking actors and actresses.

Shaw switched to quality Chinese folklore–based Mandarin productions exclusively by the early 1960s, helping to construct a Mandarin-based pan-Chinese film culture throughout the diaspora. To make sure Chinese around the world who spoke various dialects could appreciate its Mandarin production, the studio inserted Chinese (and sometimes also English or Spanish) subtitles into all its films. The posh Chinese mythology–based Mandarin productions left the low-budget Cantonese-language films (mostly in black and white) to languish while drawing audiences in Hong Kong away from Hollywood pictures. For the first time in Hong Kong's history, "Chinese [Mandarin] films became as popular as Hollywood imports."[38] The same trend was prominent in the Chinese diaspora across Asia-Pacific, Europe, and the Americas as theater owners in Chinatowns across the world reportedly screened Shaw films instead of Hollywood films.[39]

To better facilitate the distribution of Chinese-language film overseas, Shaw made English and French copies of some of its Mandarin films. Runrun stipulated that all films distributed by Shaw must have both English and Chinese subtitles, which some saw as contributing to Chinese-language learning, especially among regions in Southeast Asia where Chinese language was suppressed by non-Chinese-majority governments.

The dream of a global Mandarin film has lived on. Jackie Chan's remark in 2016 that the stunning profits China made from *Warcraft* (Duncan Jones, 2016) would elevate the Chinese language echoed Shaw's aspiration half a century ago.[40] But Chan was too bullish in his assessment of the viability of Mandarin as a global cinematic lingua franca. Only a year later, in responding to the criticism that *The Great Wall* (Zhang Yimou, 2016) featured a white hero who spoke English in an essentially China story, Zhang Yimou put it bluntly: "If we didn't have Matt Damon, if we didn't speak English in the film, then it would just be a purely Chinese film." Zhang's off-the-cuff remark makes it clear that when it comes to global cinema, Chinese language is more of a liability than advantage.

Runrun Shaw saw Hollywood's global hegemony as the real barrier to any alternative films gaining a foothold in the mainstream U.S. market. Shaw had a structural disadvantage: the rigid boundaries between the underdeveloped East and South (Global South) and the industrialized North and West (Global North) in the 1950s and 1960s meant that the Global South was denigrated by the West as a primitive sweatshop churning out cheap, shoddy goods that threatened to depress the global capitalist system. The Shaw brothers, even with their drive, financial resources, and business acumen, achieved only limited success in changing the perception and transcending cultural and political barriers. Though a film giant in Asia, Shaw remained a marginal player in an unequal global political and economic system. Its films, big or small, were restricted to a racially bounded market in the West throughout the 1960s.[41]

Things would not be much different by the 2010s, when Wanda marched into Hollywood. But Wanda's economic muscle, buttressed by the growing Chinese market and on the back of a more assertive China, enabled the Chinese company to become a major player in the global film market. Wanda's grand foray into the U.S. market still fell short of altering the global filmmaking hierarchy with Hollywood as the center of power, which only reaffirmed Shaw's verdict concerning the entrenched global hegemony of Hollywood. But contemporary Chinese film companies are finding new ways of entering Hollywood.

Direct Chinese Investment in Hollywood Productions

Owing to the combined accident of geography, history, and national temperament, Hollywood has long enjoyed its status as the unchallenged cinematic hegemon. The major U.S. film studios have dominated global film production and distribution, dispatching hundreds of films annually into all significant international markets. For a film to reach a broad international audience, it needs the backing of one of the Hollywood majors for distribution. The injection of Chinese capital and the growing importance of China-led global market expansion have not fundamentally changed the dominance of Hollywood studios, though the rise of non-studio streaming services, such as Netflix, Amazon, Disney Plus, and a few Chinese internet platforms, is challenging the reigning power of Hollywood's brick and mortar studio system.

Though the streaming service has yet to alter the DNA of Hollywood-style storytelling, the significance of the international—particularly the Chinese—film market has reduced the relative power of U.S. domestic audiences in dictating the type of stories that the U.S. media industry produces. In 1993, the global success of *Jurassic Park* pushed Hollywood's overseas revenues ahead of domestic revenues for the first time. Foreign markets have grown only more significant every year, which explains why films popular in the United States do not always merit sequels, but some domestic "flops," with their ability to command the box-office overseas, keep on churning out the next installment. As Tom Shone put it in his *Financial Times* report, "The American audience's power has never counted for less."[42]

Wanda's retreat from Hollywood asset acquisition in the late 2010s was a moment of schadenfreude for Western media and some Hollywood executives, though Hollywood continued to embrace Chinese investments. In 2017, when Paramount Pictures needed cash, instead of turning to its parent company, Viacom Inc., the studio talked with nine investors—five from China—before agreeing to a $1 billion deal with Shanghai Media Group Corporation and Huahua Media.[43] But the deal fell through amidst China's intense clampdown on foreign investments.[44] China's involvement in Hollywood has become more selective since the late 2010s, geared toward investing in specific film projects rather than buying up entertainment assets, which might turn out to be a blessing for Hollywood. After beating the retreat from buying trophy U.S. assets, the Chinese are now in the business of directly investing in Hollywood films that sell to the world, including China. Once upon a time, the financially strapped Chinese film industry lusted for foreign and private investment, which later shifted into co-productions that rely on Chinese investment now that China has ample disposable and cheap cash.

The latest trend is for the Chinese companies to directly finance Hollywood films. For Chinese speculative financiers, gaining access to the U.S. market and in turn the rest of the world market is a compelling incentive. The United States was the biggest market in the world until 2020 when the Chinese gained the leading spot amidst COVID-19 chaos in the United States. Chinese companies now actively seek a slice of the U.S. market while gaining further international access via Hollywood's global distribution system. Several private Chinese production companies have emerged to bankroll individual Hollywood productions. Among them, Huayi, Perfect World Pictures, and Alibaba have funded films that won Academy Awards.

Oscars and China's Project-Based Investments in Hollywood Films

Huayi Brothers made its name by producing Feng Xiaogang's New Year films, including an early co-production with Columbia Asia on Feng's *Big Shot's Funeral* (2001). In April 2015, Huayi signed an eighteen-film co-financing and distribution agreement with Bob Simonds, chairman and CEO of STX Entertainment, to produce modestly budgeted A-class films as opposed to big budget blockbuster films.[45] Under the partnership, Huayi would be involved in the entire process from production to marketing to distribution. In return, Huayi would collect a share of the global revenues of the entire slate of eighteen films. Huayi also won the first right to distribute most STX movies in China.[46] The collaboration led to *Molly's Game* (Aaron Sorkin, 2017), which was nominated for Best Adapted Screenplay at the Academy Awards. Alibaba Pictures Group was a minority stakeholder in Steven Spielberg's Amblin Partners, the co-producer of *Molly's Game*. The majority of the STX-Huayi slate turned out to be financial flops, however, and mostly went unnoticed.

Another Chinese company, Perfect World Pictures, is a subsidiary of Perfect World, an online video game developer and operator founded in

2004 by the internet entrepreneur Michael Chi Yufeng. Perfect World co-distributed *Phantom Thread* (Paul Thomas Anderson, 2017) with Universal Pictures, and the film won the 2018 Oscar for Best Costume Design. Chi established Perfect World Pictures in 2018 and has since been involved in co-producing *Mamma Mia! Here We Go Again* (Oliver Parker, 2018) and *Jurassic World: Fallen Kingdom* (J.A. Bayona, 2018), among others. Perfect World Pictures also produced *Darkest Hour* (Joe Wright, 2017), which won Oscars for Best Actor and Best Makeup and Hairstyling. Perfect World Pictures further co-produced with BBC Films and Cross Street Films *Victoria & Abdul* (Stephen Frears, 2017), which was nominated for both the Best Costume Design and Best Makeup and Hairstyling Oscar. Perfect World Pictures thus became the Chinese company with the most Academy Awards and nominations under its belt. The three Oscar-nodded films were part of a US$500 million slate forged in 2016 between Perfect World and Universal Pictures, which funded the production of fifty Universal films over five years. Perfect World kept a low-key profile despite the Oscar nods.[47] Though none of the Academy-nominated films were box-office winners, the company also co-produced blockbuster films, among which *Jurassic World: Fallen Kingdom* (2018) snatched $1,309,484,461 in worldwide revenue.

One earlier critical success of China's Hollywood investment was *The Revenant* (Alejandro Gonzalez Iñárritu, 2015), invested in by Alpha Group, a Chinese animation and toy company founded in 1993.[48] The features division of Alpha Group launched a partnership with New Regency Productions, a U.S. production company with titles to 2013's *12 Years a Slave* (Steve McQueen) and 2014's *Birdman* (Alejandro Gonzalez Iñárritu), committing to invest up to US$60 million in three New Regency movies, including *The Revenant*.[49] By summer 2016, the joint venture failed to produce real financial gains, despite the Oscar nod. Its slate of eighteen movies and television programs failed to perform at the box office. Alpha has since withdrawn from investing in feature films.

Meanwhile, Hunan TV, China's leading provincial broadcaster, scored a victory with *La La Land* (Damien Chazelle, 2016) at the eighty-ninth Academy Awards with multiple wins, despite losing the Best Picture award to *Moonlight* (Barry Jenkins, 2016). The film's lead producer, Summit Entertainment, a veteran U.S. production company founded in 1993, was purchased in 2012 by Lionsgate Entertainment, which signed a co-financing and co-production pact with China's Hunan TV in January 2015 to produce feature films.[50]

Bona is one of the more aggressive Chinese studios investing in foreign content. In June 2017, Bona and Creative Arts Agency jointly launched a $150 million content acquisition and investment fund, with a focus on English-language global movies and large-scale co-productions. The fund was one of the initial investors in *Midway* (Roland Emmerich, 2019), which granted Bona distribution rights across greater China. Bona also co-financed the Brad Pitt space adventure *Ad Astra* (2019).[51] The company further invested in *A Dog's Way Home* (Charles Martin Smith, 2019), following the Chinese box-office success of *A Dog's Purpose* (Lasse Hallström, 2017), which earned $88 million, exceeding its $64 million in North America, where it was distributed by Universal. Bona invested early on in several high-profile Hollywood titles, including *The Martian* (Ridley Scott, 2015), and was a co-financier of *Once Upon a Time in Hollywood* (Quentin Tarantino, 2019).[52]

In 2018, the Golden Globe and Oscar–winning *Green Book* performed well in China, owing to Alibaba's marketing campaign, which positioned itself as the niche leader in distributing and marketing "socially conscious" Hollywood films.[53] Alibaba Pictures also co-financed *The Wandering Earth*, which became number two on the 2019 domestic blockbuster chart and was purchased by Netflix for international streaming. *The Wandering Earth* was also a critical hit in China, bolstering Alibaba Pictures' brand of socially and culturally relevant films.

Chinese entertainment companies' penchant for the Oscars might yet prove to be hazardous as the 2020s have dawned.[54] In 2021, *Better Days* (Derek Tsang, 2019), a Mandarin-language film made by a Hong Kong director, was nominated for Best International Feature, while Chinese-born filmmaker Chloe Zhao became the front-runner for Best Director. But China was not in the mood to take a victory lap, as *Do Not Split* (Anders Hammer, 2020), a thirty-five-minute short film about the 2019 Hong Kong democracy protests, was nominated in the Documentary Short category. It did not help that Chloe Zhao, whose *Nomadland* was nominated for Best Picture and Best Director awards, once made comments critical of China. Beijing did not air the Academy Awards live. Nor did it celebrate Zhao's win. The tricky situation puts both Hollywood and the Chinese film industry in a bind, with the former desperately needing the PRC market and the latter seeking Hollywood's endorsement while wary of domestic criticism. Hollywood is caught between the activist filmmakers who speak out about human rights issues in China and the corporate suits who want to access the Chinese market.

Aside from investing in Hollywood film productions, Chinese companies have also invested in content and other intellectual property as they race to carve out market share in the global IP (intellectual property) industry, following the path of major Hollywood film studios, which built a sustainable business model using IP to create a range of revenue-generating activities from theme parks to video games, video streaming services, and licensed consumer merchandise. In all, private- and state-backed Chinese companies have invested tens of billions of dollars in U.S. film ventures over the past decade. Perpetually cash-strapped Hollywood welcomed the infusion of Chinese funds and considered it as business as usual in the age of global mergers and acquisitions, only with Chinese firms replacing Japanese firms, which were conspicuous in the late 1980s, and South Korean firms prominent in the late 1990s. U.S. lawmakers, however, were not as nonchalant.

The U.S. Reaction

U.S. legislators responded with alarm to the expansion of China's investment into the heart of U.S. pop culture and saw it not as an innocent matter of a new East Asian superpower replacing the old ones. One deal in particular drew the ire of U.S. lawmakers: in 2016, Wanda purchased, for $3.6 billion, a majority share of Legendary Entertainment, a company tied to major Hollywood franchise films such as *Batman*, *Godzilla*, and *Pacific Rim*, all of which performed exceptionally well with Chinese audiences. The purchase gave Wanda control of Legendary East, a Hong Kong–based subsidiary company that developed co-productions specifically for East Asian audiences. In 2016, members of Congress wrote to various agency chiefs to express their concern over Chinese firms' encroachment on U.S. media assets, specifically citing Dalian Wanda. In a letter to the Government Accounting Office, the lawmakers asked,

"Should the definition of national security be broadened to address concerns about propaganda and control of the media and 'soft power' institutions?"[55] The letter laid out "growing concerns about China's efforts to censor topics and exert propaganda controls on American media" and called for greater oversight of Chinese corporate purchases, including movie theaters and studios.[56] The Republican congressman Christopher H. Smith from New Jersey stated that "Beijing is increasingly confident that its version of state authoritarianism can be exported, though the Communist Party's efforts at 'soft power' outreach have little credibility or impact at this point."[57]

But Legendary's China-related projects did not fare well at the global box office. The company's projects *Warcraft* and *The Great Wall* flopped in the United States, leading to the departure of both Peter Loehr and Thomas Tull in January 2017. Despite the financial failure, the purchase drew scrutiny from U.S. regulators who were concerned that, granted access, Chinese censors and consumers could potentially influence nearly every aspect of American moviemaking, from scripts to casting to sequels, and that Hollywood would prioritize economic interest above all else. The Chinese government has always treated Hollywood's popularity in China foremost as a political and ideological rather than economic issue, with which the U.S. government is now catching up. To U.S. lawmakers and media critics, China now poses an existential threat to Western liberal democratic principles and values.

As if to make the case for the wary U.S. lawmakers, Xi Jingping tightened political and ideological control over film content. In March 2018, Xi shifted China's film division to the Communist Party's Ministry of Propaganda from the previous State Administration of Press, Publication, Radio, Film, and Television, which had overseen content regulation and scheduled theatrical releases. The longtime Propaganda Ministry bureaucrat Wang Xiaohui was named the new head of the China Film Bureau in May 2018. The reorganization was seen as an official reminder and reenforcement of film's function as a party organ. Key duties for film regulators—including reviewing movie content, supervising imported and exported movies, and guiding movie production, distribution, and screening—now fell into the hands of ideologically driven party apparatchiks. The change signaled more rigid censorship over foreign films and tighter regulatory control of the film sector, where foreign parties remained blocked from distribution and exhibition activities.

In May 2020, Republican senator Ted Cruz from Texas introduced a bill to restrict federal government assistance to studios that altered their movies to gain entry into the Chinese market.[58] Breaching the long-standing practice of the U.S. government aiding the global expansion of its movie industry, this legislation would prohibit the U.S. government from providing technical or other types of support across agencies to film projects from studios that modified movies to meet the Chinese censor's demands. A month later, in July 2020, the issue of Chinese influence caught the attention of William Barr, then U.S. attorney general.[59] In a well-prepared speech delivered at the Gerald R. Ford Presidential Museum, William Barr faulted Hollywood for regularly censoring its own movies to appease the Chinese Communist Party and that "this censorship infects not only versions of movies that are released in China, but also many that are shown in American theaters to American audiences."[60] Barr charged further that "Chinese government censors don't need to say a word, because Hollywood is doing their work for them. This is a massive propaganda coup for the Chinese Communist Party."[61]

Speaking more like a film professor than an attorney general, Barr cited that "in 2018, films with Chinese investors accounted for 20 percent of U.S. box-office ticket sales, compared to only 3 percent five years earlier." Whoever prepared the speech for him wrote astutely that "in the long run, as with other American industries, the PRC may be less interested in cooperating with Hollywood than in co-opting Hollywood—and eventually replacing it with its own homegrown productions. To accomplish this, the CCP has been following its usual modus operandi. By imposing a quota on American films, the CCP pressures Hollywood studios to form joint ventures with Chinese companies, who then gain U.S. technology and know-how." Barr went on to quote a Chinese film executive's claim that "everything we learned, we learned from Hollywood." Barr cited that "in 2019, eight of the ten top-grossing films in China were produced in China."[62]

It remains to be seen whether the concerns of the U.S. government would significantly reduce Chinese financing of Hollywood films. The same month that Barr expressed alarm about the influx of China money into Hollywood, Sunac, a Beijing-based real estate company that had bought a collection of Chinese theme parks and the Qingdao Movie Metropolis from Wanda in 2017, closed a deal to co-finance, with MGM, George Miller's *Three Thousand Years of Longing*, a follow-up to Miller's *Mad Max: Fury Road* (2015). Sunac Culture, Sunac's entertainment subsidiary, is to distribute the film in China and participate in the film's worldwide box-office revenue. MGM will distribute the film in North America. The Sunac deal was among the few recent cross-border film agreements between Hollywood and China amidst the COVID pandemic and deteriorating diplomatic relations between Washington and Beijing.

The Rebound of the Domestic Market and the Case of The Wandering Earth: *Going Out or Returning Home?*

In 2019, a Chinese sci-fi film, *The Wandering Earth*, became the Lunar New Year's biggest release. The film tells a postapocalyptic story about a China-led global effort in saving the Earth from an imminent crash into Jupiter. Soldiers from numerous countries—including Russia, Korea, Indonesia, and Japan—rushed to rally behind the Chinese team. Conspicuously absent from the team effort was the United States. This intentional omission was speculated to be a jab at the real-life failures of the United States under Donald Trump to cooperatively address environmental issues. In the lead-up to the U.S. withdrawal from the UN Paris climate agreement, Trump dismissed climate change as a Chinese "hoax." In response, Chinese president Xi Jinping issued what was considered a "direct challenge" to Trump, stating that "there is only one Earth in the universe and we mankind have only one homeland."[63]

Political tit for tat aside, the film was a special-effects extravaganza with furious pacing and spectacular visuals. It was hailed in China as a milestone in Chinese science fiction filmmaking and one of the best and most authentic China stories.[64] Back in late 2013, when the Chinese film industry feared that the onslaught of Hollywood films would decimate domestic pictures, American studios hoped and prayed for China to make its own successful blockbuster movies in order to alleviate China's anxiety about Hollywood's takeover. *The Wandering Earth* represents just such a homegrown blockbuster capable of outperforming Hollywood imports.

Indeed, domestic films have surpassed Hollywood imports in box-office revenue since 2015. The trend has to do partly with the changing audience demographics in China. The fastest audience growth in China is now in smaller cities where the recent boom in theater construction was most evident. Movie patrons in smaller cities have had less exposure to Western culture and are thus more likely to prefer domestic films over Hollywood blockbusters, particularly feel-good patriotic films amidst the Sino-U.S. tensions, which have propelled militant action movies such as *Wolf Warrior II* and *Operation Red Sea* to the top of the box-office chart, beating Hollywood at its own game. With the growing popularity of patriotic domestic films cloaked in Hollywood-style crowd-pleasing storytelling, Hollywood's share of China's $8 billion market has declined since the late 2010s,

The possibility of building a feature film juggernaut to challenge Hollywood's dominance, at least in China, has certainly boosted the confidence of the Chinese government and domestic film industry. The lesson that motion pictures act as the locomotives of American culture and lifestyle is not lost in China. American tentpole features were used as a cudgel by party leaders such as Jiang Zemin and Xi Jinping as they urged the Chinese film industry to come up with its own answers to global successes like *Titanic*, which Jiang adored, or *Saving Private Ryan*, which Xi loved.

A big fan of Hollywood war films, which he sees as promoting American patriotism, Xi has encouraged Chinese producers to make internationally appealing films that also adhere to the party's guidelines. In August 2013, at his first national meeting on propaganda and ideology as the Chinese president, Xi Jinping instructed China's cultural workers to "tell China's story well, and properly disseminate China's voice."[65] A year later, at a foreign affairs work meeting in October 2014, Xi emphasized that China "must raise our country's soft power" and cultural workers "must make patriotism into the main melody of literature and art creation."[66] Both *Wolf Warrior II* and *Operation Red Sea* exemplified the types of stories Xi wishes to convey. *The Wandering Earth*, by extolling the virtue, prowess, and uniqueness of Chinese culture, appears to be yet another "China story" that Xi has in mind.

But such China stories have encountered persistent resistance from the West due to their marked jingoism and what many see as toxic Chinese nationalism. To fend off potential hostile Western reviews, the film-maker and some Chinese reviewers kept their distance from the ultra-nationalistic rhetoric and insisted that *The Wandering Earth* promoted internationalism rather than China-centricity.

POLITICAL CONTROL AND RETURN TO DOMESTIC MARKET

China's tightening political and ideological control has shown no signs of loosening up. At a meeting of China's high-level Central Commission for Deepening Overall Reform led by Xi in May 2019, as *Variety* reported, "Chinese authorities have pledged to make the recent state of heightened censorship and ideological control over film and TV content the new normal." In the run-up to the seventieth anniversary of the People's Republic on October 1, 2019, China's television regulator mandated that all television channels air only patriotic shows, and no "overly entertaining" costume or pop idol dramas would be allowed. The amusingly archaic CCP turn-of-phrase is symptomatic of the sort of Chinese government interference that courts ridicule. The ban might have been short-lived, but it kept the news in the headlines and undercut any attempt the party might make to redeem itself via good storytelling. The regular intrusion of patriotic mandates into the telling of positive China stories has instead highlighted the vicissitude of political censorship. In the end, "the stories Chinese cinema tells are not going to gain traction beyond its borders if popular films, its most visible avatars, continue to 'wander' the earth carrying little thematic weight while evoking ethnocentric insistence on the superiority of Chinese civilization."[67]

On the other hand, the domestic success of *The Wandering Earth* might yet convince Chinese filmmakers and financiers that the Chinese domestic market is where the future lies, and instead of "going out" and searching for the stars, Chinese film practitioners should return home and be earthbound. Indeed, demand for domestic film consumption has led to growth for local productions. In 2017, only one domestic production topped the box-office chart. By 2018, the top four grossing features in China were all domestic productions.

The Chinese government has outlined aggressive growth targets for the industry. At a national symposium held in February 2019, Wang Xiaohui, the director of China's National Film Bureau, called on China to become a "strong film power" that would match the United States by 2035.[68] This call is reminiscent of the ethos under Mao during the Great Leap Forward campaign in 1957. In November 1957, at a gathering of leaders of communist countries in Moscow to celebrate the fortieth anniversary of the October Revolution, the Soviet Communist Party leader Nikita Khrushchev proposed to catch up with and exceed the United States in industrial output within the next fifteen years. Mao Zedong put forward China's own objective to catch up with and surpass the United Kingdom in fifteen years. Wang Xiaohui was more modest in his stated goal, estimating that China's annual film production would reach one hundred movies, with each title earning over $15 million in revenue.[47] Chinese pictures met the target by topping $15 million each in 2019.

THE VIRUS INTRUDES

Just as Sino-Hollywood negotiations paused during the trade war, COVID-19 hit in early 2020, putting everything into lockdown, including film screenings in both the United States and China. Theaters in the United States stayed mostly closed throughout 2020 as the number of COVID-19 cases skyrocketed and the death toll spiked. As the United States' COVID-19 infection rates remained high, much of the film industry's chatter turned to the question of whether damage to the domestic theatrical film model might become permanent. Escalating political turmoil between Washington and Beijing undercut Hollywood's long-term foothold in China, further cutting into major studios' theatrical revenue.

In China, cinemas in low-risk areas resumed operation in July 2020.[69] By late August 2020, China had become the first global market to make a "full box-office recovery,"[70] with more than 90 percent of Chinese cinemas opening up, though at mandatory half-capacity. Chinese domestic fare dominated the market, decisively outperforming Hollywood films.[71] While foreign films accounted for 38 percent of China's annual box office in 2018 and 35.9 percent in 2019, they made up just 16.3 percent of total ticket sales in 2020. As *Variety* reported, in 2020, foreign films accounted for only 16 percent of total China box office of $3.13 billion, a tally that actually represented a drop of 68.2 percent from the $9.2 billion box office in 2019 and a 66.5 percent decline from 2018.[72] The most popular domestic genres have been patriotic war dramas and feel-good comedy and romance. While COVID-19 might have impacted Hollywood's China releases, the sharp decline in revenues from imports in China could also indicate the diminishing appeal of foreign content to Chinese audiences.

As the film market and industry in China rebounded, the U.S. film industry continued to suffer under the wrath of COVID-19. The total North America box-office revenue in 2020 was $2.28 billion, a more than 80 percent decline from the $11.4 billion gross of 2019. As the U.S. market ground to a halt, China's box office officially surpassed North America's by the end of 2020, making China the biggest movie market in the world.[73] North America had been the global box office's center of gravity since the dawn of the motion picture business. There had been predictions in recent years that China would soon replace North America as the number one market in the world. It took a pandemic to accelerate this transition.

Christopher Nolan's *Tenet* (2020) had a lukewarm reception when it came out in the United States to limited theatrical distribution under COVID-19 regulations. It underperformed in the United States, failing to match *Mulan*'s domestic box office of $60.9 million, although *Mulan* (Niki Caro, 2020) was available only on demand.[74] But *Tenet* received wider distribution with better box-office receipts in China. Nolan subsequently suggested in an interview that, instead of whining about *Tenet*'s lackluster domestic draw, American studios should be focusing on Hollywood's overseas market, particularly the Chinese market, where *Tenet* performed well, though failing to unseat the resurrected *The Eight Hundred* on opening weekend in September. Nolan's statement came as a shock to some in the United States who wanted to see a healthy domestic exhibition sector partly to fend off foreign influence, particularly Chinese influence, in Hollywood.[75] Some argued that less reliance on the Chinese box office, which tends to prize spectacle over storytelling, could be a blessing to American audiences, as studios might turn to producing midbudget quality-A movies targeting the U.S. adult film market. So perhaps COVID-19 might actually create an opportunity for Hollywood to free itself from the China influence that has put U.S. policy makers and media on alert.

The China Influence?

In a 2019 podcast interview with Peter Mattis, a research fellow in China studies at the Victims of Communism Memorial Foundation, Brad Carson, a professor at the University of Virginia's Batten School of Leadership and Public Policy who served in the U.S. House of Representatives in 2001–2005 and was undersecretary of the army and acting undersecretary of defense for personnel and readiness in the Obama administration, hazarded a doubt on the notion of China influence: "What China wants is this: a return to the Westphalian system, basically. What happens in each country's borders is what happens to that country's borders, and stays there. . . . What goes on within your borders is determined by the nation's capital, and other people don't have the right to get involved in it."[76] Carson made it a point to distinguish between what China wants now from what the Soviets sought during the Cold War by suggesting that the Soviets in their heyday were evangelical in "preaching the gospel of communism." Carson further pointed out that "the United States itself with our liberal views often have an evangelical approach. We think this is the better way to organize your society, and we will encourage and sometimes compel you to do that. Do you see the Chinese as being evangelical for this unusual capitalist/communist mix that they've got working?"

Peter Mattis responded indirectly by suggesting that China's influence was about more than national sovereignty and that China's influence peddling is rooted in how the Chinese government defines national security management, which the CCP sees as the absence of threat to the party's ability to govern. Mattis advocated the decoupling of the U.S. economy from China in order to "stunt their growth over time" while protecting U.S. domestic industry. When asked if he "fundamentally see[s] China, the Chinese Communist Party, as an existential threat to the U.S.,"

Mattis made a point that, given a choice, he would prefer spending time in Taiwan and the United States instead of the PRC "because it's a different atmosphere. It's a different way to live your life. It's a different way to engage your fellow citizens. . . . The idea that your citizenship has obligations to your fellow citizens and not to another political authority is an important piece of living in a democratic system."

While Mattis's view is representative of the overall U.S. sentiment on China, not all voices from the United States are as hawkish. In a piece titled "Chinese Communism Is a Magic Mirror," which was posted online on July 23, 2020, an anonymous author lamented that the new China watchers "grow exceedingly confident in their own abilities to define not just communism, but the ambitions and functions of the [Chinese Communist] Party, and the 92 million people it comprises."[77] The author regretted that "a cacophony of sweeping claims and unfiltered aggression aimed at the CCP and anyone suspected of being affiliated with it" has drowned out more sensible voices. In terms of the charge that the Chinese film industry attempts influence peddling, a *Wall Street Journal* article reminds us that China is not doing anything that Hollywood has not done before: "China's ambition befits the big screen—to compete with the U.S. as a global storyteller and spread its perspective in the same fashion American filmmakers have for a century."[78]

THE LIMITED INFLUENCE OF CHINESE CINEMA

Regardless of Western response, China has increasingly asserted itself on the global stage in recent years. Under Xi Jinping, China's self-anointed storyteller, "cultural self-confidence" has become a key idea that has been featured heavily in reports published in the Chinese Academy of the Social Sciences' Blue Books. A 2017 Chinese Communist Party think-tank text, entitled "The Chinese Logic of the Construction of Cultural Power," noted how Xi Jinping "utilized a series of new values, new ideology, new judgments, to further respond to the question confronting the Chinese people at this point in history: why and how to construct a socialist strong cultural power."[79]

While party intellectuals churn out the rhetoric, the crucial task of making Chinese culture relevant to the world falls to screenwriters, directors, and the producers of narrative content. Is China succeeding in its public relations campaign? In examining the CCP's attempts to improve and promote China's image around the world under Xi Jinping, a new volume, *Soft Power with Chinese Characteristics: China's Campaign for Hearts and Minds* (Edney, Rosen, and Zhu, 2020), paints a picture of a Chinese leadership that often struggles to convert material resources into genuine international affection. Political censorship and China's tainted global reputation continue to hamper Chinese filmmakers' global outreach, as does Western resistance to China influence. Thus far, the stories Chinese films tell are mostly playing to domestic audiences and those already converted in the Chinese diaspora. The influence of contemporary Chinese cinema is more limited than that of Shaw Brothers productions decades ago.

As the larger political and economic climate turned hostile between the U.S. and China, the economic dynamic between Hollywood and the Chinese film industry had shifted by the latter part of the 2010s, specifically with a reversal in financial pooling between China and the United States, with Chinese money playing an increasingly important role in financing both co-productions and Hollywood productions. The popularity of Hollywood blockbuster films in China has long compelled Chinese filmmakers to swiftly adopt Hollywood's way of telling stories. Back in 2012, Doug Belgrad, president of Columbia Pictures, told *Bloomberg News* that "the Chinese are using their financial relationships to get teaching moments whenever they can."[80]

One way of learning from Hollywood was to directly fund and be involved in individual U.S. productions. Instead of throwing billions of dollars chasing trophy assets such as movie studios, Chinese companies have become smarter and nimbler, switching to project-based investment. Chinese capital went into the production of six Hollywood movies in 2018, twice the number in 2017. Box-office revenue from these releases rose to RMB 3.6 billion (US$536 million) on the mainland, 28.6 percent more compared to the previous year.

Yet new production companies funded by Chinese investors are frequently headed by former Hollywood studio executives, and the output with real international appeal are prototypes of Hollywood films, both blockbusters and Academy Award films. "Whether China can eclipse Hollywood in the production, rather than just consumption, of blockbusters is a question that leaves industry watchers curious," wrote Tom Shone in his *Financial Times* piece, "Hollywood transformed: How

China is changing the DNA of America's blockbuster movies," back in 2014.[81] Shone wondered whether there might "come a day when U.S. teenagers don 3-D glasses to watch Jet Li save the world from aliens in a Chinese-produced blockbuster?"

By 2019, *The Wandering Earth* offered an early taste of how China might come to the rescue. But the Chinese government might again spoil the party for the Chinese filmmakers. The film's huge box-office success gave the CCP an idea that sci-fi film could be one route toward national rejuvenation. An official document was issued, suggesting that the sci-fi genre can fit into the CCP's broader ideological and techno-logical mission if it can highlight "Chinese values, inherit Chinese cul-ture and aesthetics, cultivate contemporary Chinese innovation . . . disseminate scientific thought . . . and raise the spirit of scientists."[82] Chinese sci-fi films are to be on the forefront of depicting China "in a positive light as a technologically advanced nation."[83] It remains to be seen if science fiction as one of the most imaginative film genres can survive rigid politburo thinking.

Shone wrote further that "the flood of American movies into Europe after the Second World War led to the French New Wave, during which a generation of French filmmakers filtered back to Hollywood their own heavily accented, free-form takes on the detective flicks and pulp fiction they had soaked up in their youth." In Asia, the flood of Hollywood films entered South Korea, leading to the rise of South Korean blockbuster films that eventually put South Korean cinema on the international stage, leading to a Best Picture Oscar for Bong Joon-ho's *Parasite* in 2019. South Korean cinema in turn influenced Hollywood productions. Hong Kong cinema too went through a similar trajectory with its smart and stylish crime films with bodies and bullets flying, affecting Hollywood's action genre. But the Sino-Hollywood cinematic traffic remains a one-way street when it comes to cultural influence.

Back to an Uncertain Future

Hollywood has come a long way in China since the mid-1990s when the first revenue-sharing film was allowed into the PRC market. When the

U.S. government debated policies concerning Sino-U.S. trade in May 2000, Jack Valenti lobbied hard for a new trade deal with China. Hollywood's collaboration with China took off in leaps and bounds during the immediate aftermath of the passage of the China PNTR. A decade later, the 2012 and 2015 film agreements under then vice presidents Biden and Xi officially solidified the Sino-Hollywood bilateral relationship. These agreements were supposed to be revisited by the end of 2017, with Hollywood expecting better terms going forward. Yet with the 2016 election of Donald Trump to the U.S. presidency, a new U.S. policy toward China was afoot. Though Trump built his insurgent campaign in part in opposition to what he called a bad deal with China, Beijing was still caught off guard by Trump's actual tough stand on China less than one year into his presidency.

Hollywood too was caught unprepared by the Sino-U.S. trade war at a time when Hollywood was eager to negotiate new distribution agreements with its Chinese counterparts.[84] Talks that had started in February 2017 were dragging along without progress. In earlier negotiations, the U.S. delegation had proposed raising the U.S. share of theatrical grosses to at least 28 percent. Foreign studios receive only up to 25 percent of the revenue earned in China, which is significantly lower than the 50 percent foreign studios make in the United States and the 40 percent earned in most other countries around the globe. The U.S. side was still waiting for China to respond when the larger U.S.-China trade talks put everything on hold. By the end of 2017, Hollywood executives realized that Trump's harsh trade rhetoric might torpedo the Sino-Hollywood talks altogether. It is worth recalling that it was Will Hays, the inaugural head of Motion Picture Producers and Distributors of America, who requested in 1934 that the U.S. government include motion pictures in negotiations on tariff and trade matters, which at the time and for decades after, worked to Hollywood's benefit. But the Sino-U.S. trade crossfire might be casting doubts on the old wisdom.

As the year 2019 drew to its end, pessimism prevailed in Hollywood for the less certain future of a new Sino-Hollywood deal. Then the pandemic hit, upending all talks and grounding film industries in China and the United States. As the year 2020 creeped in, Hollywood continued to struggle. China started to bounce back halfway through 2020. By early 2021, with the pandemic under control and travel discouraged, the theatrical movie business in China was returning in vengeance. With COVID-19 decimating the U.S. film market, the Chinese film market has been propelled into the number one position in the world in size and box office. But Hollywood content has been largely absent from the newly rebounded Chinese market. *Bloomberg* reports that the share of foreign films, including those from Hollywood, slipped to 16 percent of Chinese ticket receipts in 2020 from 36 percent the year before.[85] "Chinese consumer sentiment toward anything American is at an all-time, modern day low,"[86] said Chris Fenton, the onetime Sino-Hollywood dealmaker. Others are more bullish. John Penotti, president of SK Global, treats the ebbs and flows as business as usual: "It's a continuum."[87]

China's box office hit a record monthly low in June 2021, with Hollywood tentpoles and local commercial productions making way for the party's propaganda films celebrating the centenary of the founding of the CCP. In July 2021, the U.S. film industry breathed a collective sigh of relief when *Black Widow* was poised to premiere in forty-six overseas markets, in addition to its North America premiere.[88] But China was not on the roster, prompting a prolific Chinese film blogger to lament that "*Black Widow* is finally out but is relegated to the fate of piracy in China."[89] Though approved for release in China in March 2021, the film was not offered a release date on the mainland until August, which unleashed scores of pirated videos and torrents on illegal Chinese file-sharing and streaming sites. A variety of Chinese subtitles could be downloaded to pair with different versions of the pirated film. *Mulan*, Disney's $200 million live-action feature, met the same fate, garnering a lackluster $23 million opening weekend due to piracy and delayed and restricted screening on cinemas. Hollywood is back to square one in fighting the same battle against piracy and market restrictions in China that was started decades ago by Jack Valenti.

Hollywood's new modes of online distribution could further exacerbate piracy in China, unless Hollywood sets its China release dates before that of other markets; for example, *Avengers: Endgame* was released in China two days ahead of the United States. Simultaneous theatrical and online debuts might also help ward off the financial impact of piracy. Both approaches, however, would give the Chinese regulators—not the American and Chinese audiences—the utmost power of dictating the terms of Hollywood's global distribution. It might not be a coincidence that Warner Brothers postponed its worldwide debut of *Dune* (Denis Villeneuv) to October 22, 2021, from its initial date of October 1, which would have clashed with China's National Day celebration. Move like this might continue to draw the ire of the U.S. regulators.

9

The Sino-Hollywood "Courtship": Film as Cultural Persuasion and Box-Office Revenue

The film is a silent salesman of great effectiveness. . . . Through American motion pictures, the ideals, culture, customs, and tradition of the United States are gradually undermining those of other countries.
— C.J. North, head of the Motion Picture Section under the United States Department of Commerce (1926)[1]

If I could control the medium of the American motion picture, I would need nothing else to convert the entire world to Communism.
— Joseph Stalin[2]

[We] must strengthen the building of our international transmission capacity, and enhance our international discourse power, telling China's story properly in a centralized manner.
— Xi Jinping's speech to the party's News and Public Opinion Work Conference on February 19, 2016[3]

The path, the theory, the system, and the culture of socialism with Chinese characteristics have kept developing, blazing a new trail for other developing countries to achieve modernization. It offers a new option for other countries and nations who want to speed up their development while preserving their independence.
— President Xi Jinping's statement at the nineteenth Party Congress in November 2017

Seduced, abandoned, and cash-strapped, Hollywood can see only one way to remain in China's good graces, and that is to transform itself into a cog in the world's biggest and most sophisticated propaganda machine.

—Martha Bayles, February 6, 2018[4]

One of the things we're trying to do is view the China threat as not just a whole-of-government threat, but a whole-of-society threat on their end.

—Christopher Wray, Director of the FBI on February 14, 2018[5]

We will ensure that U.S. companies do not sacrifice American values in doing business in China.[6]

—Biden administration's Interim National Security Strategic Guidance issued March 5, 2021

Auctioning Hollywood

The first auction for first-run rights of a Hollywood blockbuster during the PRC era was held in Shanghai on October 12, 1998.[7] The auction, staged by Shanghai Paradise Company Ltd. and the Shanghai Auction Company, was for the rights to premiere the Polygram film *The Game* (David Fincher, 1997). The Grand Theatre was the top bidder, offering RMB 360,000 ($43,426). In total, seven theaters paid RMB 1.72 million for the right to screen the movie for the first eight days of its run in Shanghai. What were considered high bidding prices in China at the time drove down the profit margin, and the RMB 1.72 million was barely matched by box-office receipts. Nonetheless, a Paradise distribution executive argued that the auction was beneficial for distributors and exhibitors because it encouraged competition, a mechanism the Chinese film industry was slow to embrace as it struggled to make the transition from state subsidy to market incentives. Cinema managers in China generally agreed with Paradise's view, hinting that they would participate in future auctions but would become more fiscally prudent.

China's film industry has come a long way since October 1998. So has Hollywood's second entry into the mainland Chinese market since 1994. Auctions for Hollywood imports were a costly proposition for introducing market mechanism and have long been replaced by co-financing and exclusive China rights for Hollywood films. From financial pooling to joint venture to direct financing and distribution, the previously budget-strapped Chinese film industry has grown by leaps and bounds, from seeking foreign and private investment to co-financing and co-producing, and now going solo in domestic production and market penetration. But a strong and growing Chinese film industry has not succeeded in allowing Chinese films to compete effectively with Hollywood films on a global scale. Few Chinese films have entered the North America–led global mainstream commercial market, and the few that did manage to get distributed in the United States have garnered little critical or popular enthusiasm. Hollywood films continued to dominate the world, though less so in China since the COVID-19 lockdown.

What is the secret to Hollywood's success that the Chinese film industry, with its vast market, financial reserve, and state backing, simply can't replicate? What does the future hold for Hollywood in China and Chinese cinema in the world? As history continues to unfold, this postscript here ventures no conclusive verdicts but does offer a few concluding observations that reveal ambition, tension, and confusion in both Hollywood and the Chinese film industry, as personalities and film events interact with larger domestic and global forces.

On the cultural front, as historian Victoria de Grazia commented, Joseph Nye's soft power framework put forth in 1990 was heavily influenced by U.S. hegemonic and security worries and closely bound up with the Revolution in Military Doctrine, the Global War on Terror, and the need for the United States to adapt its unilateralism to work within a multilateral world.[8] Now that U.S. hegemony is being challenged by an ascendant China, the power dynamic has changed. What's at stake is more than competition between the old hegemon and the emerging hegemon; it is about whose version of the future will win the world's approval. So far, most of the developed world has shunned the Chinese version.

But American values and interests have encountered persistent resistance throughout history and the United States too has been fighting an uphill battle against widespread anti-Americanism, particularly in the Middle East during "the war on terror." In the early 2000s, U.S. embassies made concerted efforts to win hearts and minds abroad.[9] A cultural diplomacy effort was launched in October 2001 with the appointment of

Charlotte Beers, an advertising CEO, as undersecretary for public diplomacy and public affairs at the State Department, along with an allocation of US$15 million of government funding.[10] Film screenings were considered a vital element of these "cultural diplomacy" measures. In favor were independent and less commercial U.S. films that aimed to refute misconceptions and negative stereotypes about the United States.[11] As revealed by the British film scholar Paul Moody in his analysis of U.S. film–related Wikileaks cables: "Universities were explicitly targeted as sites where anti-American views could be challenged."[12] But the results were more frustrating than satisfactory, leading to Beers's resignation in 2003. In her final testimony to the Senate Foreign Relations Committee, Beers argued that the "gap between who we are and how we wish to be seen, and how we are in fact seen, is frighteningly wide."[13]

The exact phrase can easily apply to China's faltering soft power effort. This book offers a close look at how cinema serves as a battlefield for competing political and cultural values, all under the rubric of "soft power," which started to gain traction within Chinese policy circles in the 1990s. It bore no real policy implications until 2008 when, during the Beijing Olympics, the Chinese realized the gap between how China saw itself and how the world saw China, which Charlotte Beers discovered about the state of U.S. soft power five years earlier.[14] The negative reports in the West criticizing China's Tibet policy and human rights record during the 2008 summer Olympics was a moment of rude awakening for China. The rhetorical question of how China could "get what it wants through appeal and attraction"[15] was soon transformed into foreign policy discourse and a strategic framework for the Chinese leadership to articulate in major speeches and concrete efforts to create a more amicable international environment for China's policies and actions.[16] A "going out" project was launched by the external propaganda department to "gradually change China's image in international society from negative to neutral to positive."[17] The goal was to reset the global narrative about China.

Over the past two decades the Chinese film industry has overcome historical delays and matched Hollywood in market size and investment capital. Its greatest hurdle, however, is that it is beholden to the central government's insistence that, above all else, it needs to project and amplify Chinese pride, in contrast to the confident "cosmopolitanism" and arguably cultural and cinematic sophistication Hollywood radiates with ease. Unlike the U.S. government, which has facilitated Hollywood's global expansion but avoided direct interference into most of the stories Hollywood exports, the Chinese government protects the domestic market while it actively dictates what can and cannot be made into a film for both domestic and global consumption. Owing to the aid of Hollywood imports, China built an enviably robust domestic film market, which made the film industry self-sufficient domestically. But when it comes to global expansion, proselytizing Chinese culture mandated by the party is hardly a successful formula.

Hollywood, on the other hand, is less distinctively American and more of a clearinghouse for international financial, organizational, promotional, and creative talent gathered under the corporate rubric of what might be called—borrowing from Daoism—the "Hollywood Way." China's party leaders have long sought to import this Hollywood Way into their own film industry and redeploy it "with Chinese characteristics" to defeat Hollywood. A more nuanced approach in the past decade reveals the Chinese film industry seeking to co-opt Hollywood into the service of advancing China's soft power by producing joint projects and using co-production as both a training ground for Chinese practitioners and a platform for Chinese cinema to raise its global profile and enhance its cultural appeal.

Unlike its largely negative reaction toward Chinese censors' demands during the Republican era, Hollywood during its second China entry since mid-1994 has generally responded positively, if not overtly enthusiastically, in opening its studios and operations to China. In November 2017, Warner Brothers announced its new "U.S.-China Exchange Program," an initiative aimed at facilitating "industry and cultural best practice sharing."[18] Run in partnership with the MPAA and the Chinese State Administration of Press, Publication, Radio, Film, and Television, the consolidated state agency replacing former SARFT, and supported by the Chinese consulate general in Los Angeles, the program was essentially a training camp for Chinese film practitioners to learn the art and craft of filmmaking in Hollywood. The launch edition taught eight Chinese film execs about U.S. casting practices, the latest technology, and exposed them to Hollywood executives, agents, and managers.

Years of absorbing the Hollywood Way has led to the Chinese formula of party-sanctioned China stories delivered via the Hollywood-perfected narrative structure of a classical continuity cinema and production and marketing pipelines, which has grown increasingly successful domestically in China. But the formula continues to have little traction beyond the Chinese border. Linguistic barriers and the loaded term of cosmopolitanism aside, what else is standing between Chinese cinema and its global appeal now that the industry has acquired Hollywood's cinematic know-how?

The Artless Disappearances: Censorship as Bad Publicity

In 2017, Disney's *Christopher Robin* (2017) failed to secure a theatrical release in China. The film came out at a time when the Chinese government was busy cracking down on the chubby Winnie the Pooh, who had apparently become an icon of resistance among the foes of Chinese leader Xi Jinping.[19] In the summer of 2017, authorities began blocking images of Pooh on social media as comparisons had been drawn between the pudgy bear and Xi. In June, Chinese authorities blocked HBO after *Last Week Tonight* host John Oliver mocked Xi's sensitivity over being compared to Winnie the Pooh. Regardless of whether China's decision not to import *Christopher Robin* could be directly attributed to the Pooh crackdown, the linkage itself speaks volume about our habitual spasm when it comes to deciphering film or other cultural events in China, for which the Chinese government provides ample fodder, provoking even more defensive reactions from China.

Some bans are less benign and ambiguous. The same year, *A Taxi Driver* (Jang Hoon), a South Korean film about a cabdriver in Seoul who reluctantly takes a German journalist to the city of Gwangju where they bear witness to what became the Gwangju Massacre of 1980, was the highest-grossing local film ever released in South Korea and the country's official entry for the foreign-film category at the Oscars. The film soon gained popularity in China via online streaming. But in October 2017, the Beijing Cyberspace Administration Oversight Center issued an order to "find and delete all introductions, online encyclopedia entries, film reviews, recommendations, and other articles related to the August 2017 South Korean film *A Taxi Driver*."[20] The film disappeared at once from the Chinese internet. The crackdown was not surprising, given that the film depicted the antigovernment student demonstration that led to martial law and the Gwangju uprising during which government troops beat, shot, and killed hundreds of unarmed young protesters.

Members sitting on China's film censorship committee come from a variety of organizations including universities and relevant government agencies such as propaganda and film bureaus, many of them ranking senior members of their respective organizations[21] There has been a decentralization drive in recent years to incorporate more local instead of central government input into the film censorship process, which actually adds more uncertainty and volatility into the process. The opaque nature of film censorship and the multilayered process encourage self-censorship, as production companies seek to preempt any potential objectionable elements. The result is the stifling of creativity and imagination. In 2008, when *Kung Fu Panda* became a big success in China, there was a lot of uncomfortable discussion over why Hollywood could make a popular film about China's most famous animal and sport, but not China. The American political scientist Stanley Rosen speculated that Chinese filmmakers wouldn't have dared to make a film about a fat and lazy panda that might risk censors' ire about leaving "an image to the world that China is fat and lazy."[22]

In 2016, the Marvel Studios production *Dr. Strange* (Scott Derrickson, 2016) changed the nationality of a monk known as the "Ancient One" in the comic book from Tibetan to Celtic. Robert Cargill, a screenwriter for the film, explained that "the Ancient One was a racist stereotype who comes from a region of the world that is in a very weird political place. He originates from Tibet, so if you acknowledge that Tibet is a place and that he's Tibetan, you risk alienating one billion people."[23] The answer is a double-edged sword in its acknowledgment of the racist origin of the Marvel Studio production while also conceding that part of the concern was China's reaction. Cargill said further that there was the risk of "the Chinese government going, 'Hey, you know one of the biggest film-watching countries in the world? We're not going to show your movie because you decided to get political.'" The incident made its way into the speech the U.S. attorney general William Barr gave in July 2020 about Hollywood's capitulation to Chinese censorship.

Such instances, from comical to outrageous, have become routine occurrences, sparking more ridicule than anger. To coin a phrase from film historian Thomas Elsaesser for a different occasion, "The failure to per-form is also a performance of failure,"[24] which in this context serves only to highlight the ineptitude of China's propaganda effort in its repeated performances of failure. Though Western prejudice might be partly to blame for China's perpetual image-lifting battle, the Chinese party-state remains the main barrier. China's habitual and ruthless suppression of any alternative narratives that challenge the ethno-nationalist definition of who and what represents China undermines its very global image campaign. But China under President Xi is doubling down on its eradi-cation of any China story that deviates from the party line.

Resetting the China Discourse, the President Xi Way

As the *SCMP* (*South China Morning Post*) op-ed contributor Alex Lo writes, China's intellectuals and policy makers often fret about what they call the lack of "huayuquan," which Lo translates as the power to shape or affect discourse.[25] The term became part of a comprehensive CCP foreign policy in 2013. At the National Propaganda and Ideology Work Conference in August 2013, Xi urged China's cultural workers to seize "huayuquan" to tell China's stories and spread China's voice. The Chinese film industry was tasked to "tell the Chinese story effectively and relay China's voice faithfully."[26] Putting its money where its mouth was, China's top-down soft power by design approach was supported by gen-erous state and government resources,[27] and President Xi emerged to be "the custodian of 'the China story.'"[28]

In June 2017, China released *Xi Jinping Tells Stories*,[29] a collection of stories and parables selected from Xi's public and private speeches to highlight Xi's gift for storytelling. By September 29, 2017, the Hong Kong–based media watchdog China Media Project released a report, crowning Xi with the title "Storyteller-in-Chief." The report quoted a review of Xi's new book by Yang Zhenwu, the publisher of the *People's Daily*: "Telling stories well has been a common characteristic of celebrated statesmen and thinkers in China and beyond since ancient times—and it is a clear characteristic of General Secretary Xi Jinping's leadership style. Whether in his conference addresses, in conversation during his inspection tours, in his speeches during his overseas visits, or in his printed articles, he proves to be adept in using stories to convey deeper meanings and to move people. Woven through these stories is the tao (way) of Chinese history and culture. . . . They are concrete and vivid, relatable and profound, opening a window on the study of the spirit of [Xi's] series of important speeches."[30] Xi was quoted in Bandurski as emphasizing that "telling stories is the best form of international dissemination." An official party publication in November 2018 further praised Xi as a gifted teller of China stories.[31]

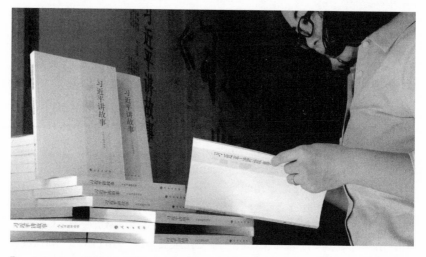

People buying *Xi Jinping Tells Stories*. Source: BBC, https://www.bbc.com/zhongwen/trad/chinese-news-41841836.

With marching orders to tell only party-sanctioned China stories, the race was on for the Chinese film industry to manufacture agitprop-filled blockbusters. Such China stories, authorized literally and figuratively by obtaining the dragon seal for film release issued only by the party's Propaganda Department since March 2018, have remained a tough sell globally. Yet the party remained relentless in getting the message out. In September 2020, at the gathering that marked the seventy-fifth anniversary of the victory of China's resistance against Japanese aggression and the World Anti-Fascist War, Xi made a speech, declaring that China would never allow "any individual or any force" to distort the history of the CCP or to smear the party's nature and mission; nor to distort and alter the path of socialism with Chinese characteristics, or to "deny and vilify China's great socialist achievements"; nor to separate the CCP from the Chinese people, or counterpose the party to the Chinese people; nor to "impose their will on China through bullying, change China's direction of progress," and so forth.[32] The third plenary session of the eighteenth Party Congress during the same month further called for the promotion of Chinese culture "throughout the world, and to build a system of discourse for the outside world."[33]

Two months later, the Fifth Plenum of the nineteenth Chinese Communist Party's Central Committee in Beijing in November reiterated the importance of transforming China into a cultural power by enhancing China's soft power, promoting Chinese cultural industry, and boosting Chinese people's confidence in Chinese culture.[34] The same month, Beijing hosted the first China International Audiovisual Conference (CIAC) from November 19–22, 2020, with the theme of "Telling China's Story Well to the World."[35] And to do it well, a spokesperson for the film bureau said that the "vast majority" of people working in film should "thoroughly study and implement the important guiding spirit of General Secretary Xi Jinping."

It appears that the party-state has convinced itself that jargon-filled defensive language could be a viable tool toward manufacturing international consent. Or could it? In analyzing the surprising overseas success of the non-state-orchestrated popular dating show on Chinese television, *If You Are the One*, a spinoff of Feng Xiaogang's same-title film, the Australian media scholar Sun Wanning contended that "China's attempt to promote soft power has little hope of yielding tangible results unless it ceases to be a top-down government initiative" and that "cultural products with genuine soft power potential can only come from creative enterprises that arise organically within the non-state sector."[36] Sun called the runaway success of such a non-state-supported popular entertainment program "accidental soft power," or "soft power by accident," and argued that "government action in any shape or form will smack of propaganda."[37]

China has long perceived the Sino-Hollywood competition through a political and ideological prism. The post-Mao Chinese state has managed the marketization of the Chinese film industry with two utmost goals in mind: making the industry competitive in the global markets while also ensuring that cinema remains an ideological instrument for political and cultural indoctrination. It has managed to straddle the boundary quite well, partly on the strength of China's market size and growing prominence in global geopolitics, and partly on the strength of engrained Chinese expectations about the nature and uses of cultural products such as film for enlightenment and nationalistic purposes. Under Xi, Chinese artists are urged to produce more work that "disseminate[s] contemporary Chinese values, embod[ies] Chinese traditional culture and reflect[s] Chinese people's aesthetic pursuit."[38] Xi emphasizes further that artworks should present patriotism as the main theme and foster correct viewpoints of history, nationality, and culture, as well as strengthen pride in being Chinese.[39]

The U.S. government is playing catch-up in treating Hollywood's China collaboration not simply as an issue of piracy and market access, which was the approach taken when Hollywood under Jack Valenti restarted its China expansion. The two new concerns are first that Hollywood has been co-opted to do China's global image-lifting campaign and second that Hollywood is bending its principles to appease China in its pursuit of China's domestic market. Though coveting the Chinese market, Hollywood makes blockbusters for the global market, and thus Hollywood's China-friendly films would indirectly support China's global influence. Despite a booming domestic market, the Chinese film industry has remained only a local power and "a prolific producer whose wares are mostly viewed within its borders, and among a vibrant diaspora around the world."[40] There is no direct promulgation of Chinese ideology to speak of, if the films China produces are not distributed and seen widely outside the country. Hollywood consequently becomes the only viable conduit for China to extend its cinematic influence.

Hollywood and the Chinese film industry have managed their delicate relationship well in the past two decades through their common pursuit of market and box office, despite the constant regulatory interference, mostly from China. But increasing pressure from the U.S. government and the changing public mood in the United States about China are putting Hollywood under intense scrutiny, casting a long shadow on the future Sino-Hollywood collaboration.

U.S. domestic scrutiny of Hollywood comes at a time when China turns increasingly inward, with a new generation of moviegoers reportedly less enamored with Hollywood-led U.S. pop culture. According to a January 2020 article in *Global Times*, an English-language daily under the auspices of the major CCP organ *People's Daily*, unlike the older-generation

Chinese who fancied big-name foreign brands, the young generation is turning to home brands.[41] Back in 2012, a report by the Pew Research Center saw 73 percent of Chinese respondents expressing admiration for U.S. technological and scientific advances and more than half the respondents favoring American ideas about democracy. Yet by 2020, a survey by the Eurasia Group Foundation revealed that 28 percent of Chinese respondents reported an unfavorable view of the United States, up from 17 percent a year earlier, while the number reporting a favorable view fell to 39 percent from 58 percent.[42] The *Global Times* article cites the growing recognition and love of traditional Chinese culture, patriotism, and better value for money as three major reasons for the shift, which partly explains why Chinese domestic films have outshined Hollywood imports in recent years.

A March 2021 article from the *SCMP* confirmed the waning appeal of U.S. products, including Hollywood film and TV, among the younger generation Chinese over the last few years.[43] Chinese millennials born between 1980 and 1995 and members of Generation Z, born between 1995 and 2010, are said to "have become increasingly apathetic or even negative about the political system in the United States and its democracy amid increased geopolitical competition between Beijing and Washington."[44] A young salesman in Shenzhen told the *SCMP* journalist that the attitude toward the United States among Chinese youth had changed so much that one would be pounced on if one dared to say America is more liberal and democratic.[45]

Generation Xi and China's Inward Turn

In an in-depth report for *The Economist* focusing on China's "post-1990s" youth, a shorthand term for those born between 1990 and 1999 that numbered 188 million, which is "more than the combined populations of Australia, Britain and Germany," Stephanie Studer notes the strong patriotic sentiment among the group, what she calls Generation Xi, who spent their late teens with Xi in power and received an education with more emphasis on patriotism than at any time since Mao.[46] An overhaul of the school curriculum after Tiananmen made mandatory courses on Marxism, nationalism, and the doctrines of Mao. Studer cites a finding in 2017 that there were already signs that students began to hold more favorable opinions of the party, and less favorable views of democracy and free markets. To secure the conversion, President Xi in 2019 instructed the party to "win over vast numbers of youth." The party responded by intensifying patriotism education at schools, cultivating new youth influencers online, and stepping up censorship. "Xi Jinping Thought" was added to the curriculum in 2020.

Years of political indoctrination primed Generation Xi toward fervent patriotism. Support for the party rose as youth embraced the narrative of an assertive China. Close to one in two tourism trips to CCP revolutionary sites are apparently made by Chinese under age thirty, and many young Chinese reportedly find such sites inspiring.[47] The result is a generation of youth eager to defend China by boycotting foreign brands, sports teams, and Hollywood films that are deemed insulting to China, leading to the overtaking of Hollywood imports by patriotic Chinese films such as *Wolf Warrior II*, *Operation Red Sea*, and *The Wandering Earth* in China's domestic market.[48] All three titles heeded Xi's call of taking pride in Chinese culture and China's accomplishments.

Tightened regulation over content, the shifting diplomatic and political environment, and lack of free and easy access to foreign content in recent years have together limited Chinese youth's exposure to foreign products. "Over time, they have gotten used to living in such an echo chamber," said one independent filmmaker interviewed by *SCMP*.[49] As youth are turning inward, gravitating more toward domestic pictures, China's total box-office revenues rose to RMB 61 billion (US$9.3 billion) in 2018, but box-office revenues for imported films, mostly Hollywood productions, fell by 10.5 percent. By 2020, the top three blockbusters were all patriotic domestic films.

The Mutual Apprehension

Anti-China rhetoric under the Trump administration served only to further alienate Chinese youth from the United States. As the *Economist* article put it: "Mr. Trump threatened to ban Huawei, a national champion; TikTok, a winning export; and WeChat, a lifeline to family back home for those overseas. A popular joke online is that Mr. Trump encouraged the Chinese to rally round the flag."[50] The botched U.S. response to COVID-19 as opposed to China's tough measures that led to faster recovery did not boost Chinese confidence in the United States. A survey in 2020 by researchers at the University of California, San Diego, found that university-educated Chinese youth displayed the largest jump in support for Xi Jinping's regime, as government competence and public order appeared increasingly attractive in a hazardous post-COVID world. As Feng Chucheng of Plenum, a think tank in Beijing, put it: "They are more confident that we do not have to follow the same path—in fact, that our path might be better."[51] In another survey of 20,000 Chinese run by Cary Wu of Toronto University in April 2019, four in five respondents under thirty said that they did not trust Americans.

The harsh anti-China rhetoric and attendant policies in the United States led to frequently unpleasant and at times hostile experiences for Chinese youth traveling and living abroad, which no doubt contributed to their antipathy toward the United States and liberal democratic values at large. As *The Economist* put it: "A new confluence of factors had already been turning well-educated Chinese away from the West, and America in particular." In 2018, the United States reduced the validity of visas issued to Chinese students in sensitive fields of study, including computer science, from five years to one. In September 2000, the United States revoked visas of 1,000 Chinese students and researchers whom it deemed security threats.[52] The feeling of distrust is mutual. In 2020, over half of American youths polled by the Pew Research Center in October expressed negative views of China.[53] Across the general population this number hit an all-time high of 73 percent. In the words of Christopher Wray, the FBI director, China was no longer just a "whole-of-government" threat, but a "whole-of-society" one. The hostility will no doubt add pressure on the future relationship between Hollywood and China.

Back in 2014, Jonathan Wolf, the American Film Market's (AFM) managing director, told the *New York Times* at the AFM's annual event that he had been watching what he called "a global shift away from U.S. product over the last 25 years."[54] The swing had been subtle and distant enough as global cinema production was still dominated by American studios, talent, and taste. Yet, as Wolf noted, by 2014, English-language film exporters had dropped to about 63 percent from 73 percent over a decade previous, while United States–based exporters accounted for roughly 47 percent of the American Film Market's pool, down from 53 percent a decade earlier. As a result, U.S. studios began to adopt the de-risking strategy, avoiding using their own capital and relying instead on money raised by others, often through foreign sales and direct investment, with China since playing a prominent role in financing Hollywood studio productions. It was in Hollywood's financial interest to keep on China's good side.

Not Yet Decoupling

The Chinese have always been ambivalent about Hollywood's China presence. They needed Hollywood to build up the Chinese market but were wary of Hollywood films' crushing impact on China's domestic productions. Yet despite the rising box-office share of domestic pictures, China's film market continues to rely on Hollywood imports to sustain its growth. In 2017, a year when China witnessed a downturn in box-office revenue, the Chinese market was largely sustained by *The Fate of the Furious* (F. Gary Gray, 2017) and *Pirates of the Caribbean: Dead Men Tell* (Joachim Rønning and Espen Sandberg, 2017). The growth of China's film market slowed further in 2018 as the Chinese authorities started to crack down on tax evasion by the entertainment industry amid a sluggish domestic economy and following the high-profile detention of A-list actress Fan Bingbing on charges of tax evasion.[55] The clampdown sent a chill through the industry, with the National Radio and Television Administration registering fewer films and TV productions. Annual growth in box-office revenues in China slowed to 9 percent in 2018, from 16 percent in 2017. Growth in attendance continued to decline in 2019, prompting the Chinese government to loosen restrictions on foreign investment, once again cracking the door open to foreign movie theater chains.[56]

China's National Development and Reform Commission (NDRC) issued a document on June 30, 2019, dropping the long-standing stipulation that "the construction and operation of cinemas must be controlled by a Chinese party."[57] The document did not make clear whether movie theaters in China could be directly controlled by foreigners, and if so under what ownership structures. Mathew Alderson, a partner at a consulting firm in Beijing, shared his view with the *Hollywood Reporter* that "flexibility in interpretation and implementation is a familiar strategy from Beijing" and that "we won't fully know what's possible until some international companies actually try to work through this system and we see how it is applied."[58] Alderson's comment captures well the ambiguities and intricacies of PRC policy. The *Hollywood Reporter* piece speculated that China's theater-building boom might be finally leveling off, though the size of China's market remained titillating to foreign investors.

Yet despite the slowdown, China's theatrical exhibition footprint attained a network totaling more than 64,900 screens by 2019, making it the largest and most state-of-the-art exhibition platform in the world. As the same *Hollywood Reporter* article reminded us, China may already have 50 percent more movie screens than North America, clocking in at 40,300. But, at 1.39 billion, China's population is more than four times that of the United States at 327 million. So there is still substantial room for growth.

What Difference Can One Virus Make: The Triumph of Chinese Cinema During the Era of COVID-19

COVID-19 turned out to be a blessing in disguise for the Chinese film industry, jolting the market by shutting it down during the first half of 2020 only to reboot it during the second part of 2020, and returning in force by China's Lunar New Year weekend in early February 2021, all the while shutting out Hollywood fare, making 2020 one of the worst years for Hollywood in China. This reinforced the inward trend of Chinese cinema-goers who had been gravitating toward patriotic films such as *My People, My Country* (2019) and *The Bravest* (Tony Chan, 2019), and leading to the blockbuster success of *The Eight Hundred* in summer 2020.

Entering 2021, China built more than 2,188 new screens in the first two months, bringing its nationwide tally up to 77,769, which contributed to Chinese cinema's spectacular market performance over the Lunar New Year holiday week, generating a record $1.2 billion in sales, with an assortment of domestic blockbusters dominating earnings.[59] The continued growth of China's exhibition sector came amid the news in March 2021 that Wanda gave up its majority stake in AMC Theatres in responding to both the booming Chinese market and the sluggish U.S. market, with Disney and Warner Brothers focusing more on online streaming.[60]

The Chinese film industry's rapid rebound benefited from a hefty rescue package the Chinese government provided, at a time when Hollywood was abandoned with little financial support from the U.S. government. Like Hollywood, China's film industry suffered a catastrophic blow, with up to 70,000 cinemas being forced to shut down by June 2020, and 6,600 films and TV productions coming to a halt.[61] During the shutdown, the Chinese government introduced preferential tax policies, fee waivers, consumption vouchers, and special funds to keep the cinema business afloat. Cinemas reopened at half capacity in China in May 2020. The same month, the Ministry of Finance and State Taxation Administration exempted taxpayers in the film industry from value-added tax (VAT) on income derived from the provision of film screening services. The exemption applied retroactively to January 1, 2020. Losses incurred by film companies were allowed to be carried forward over an extended period of eight years instead of the previous five years, and any taxes and fees already levied for 2020 could be deducted or refunded in the following months. Alongside tax breaks, the Ministry of Finance and China Film Administration exempted film-related business from paying the usual cultural construction fee collected by relevant tax authorities.

Local governments also rolled out their own support policies. In Beijing, the government issued a one-time publicity and distribution subsidy for Beijing filmmakers and special production subsidies for what the government deemed worthy projects. The Beijing Municipal Film Bureau also expedited the launch of the Beijing Propaganda and Culture Guidance Fund and the 2020 Municipal Film Special Fund to support selective projects. Further measures were introduced to support small and medium-sized movie theaters. Shanghai and Zhejiang in east China issued similar policies. Down south, the Guangdong Film Bureau allocated around RMB 50 million (US$14 million) in special film funds to over 1,000 theaters affected by the outbreak, with funds ranging from RMB 10,000 (US$1,414) to several hundreds of thousands of yuan.

The Chinese film industry itself took proactive measures to leverage online distribution platforms to capitalize on the millions of people stuck at home. The Chinese internet company ByteDance purchased rights to distribute Xu Zheng's *Lost in Russia* in January 2020. By the end of 2020, the Chinese film market scooped up a massive RMB 20.4 billion (US$3.16 billion) at the box office, with domestic movies claiming 83.7 percent of total box-office receipts.[62] A total of 650 Chinese movies were produced in 2020, and the number of screens across the country increased to 75,581. All of 2020's ten top-grossing movies were homegrown productions, among which *The Eight Hundred* reaped RMB 3.1 billion in ticket sales to become the world's highest-grossing film in 2020. Foreign productions took up only 16 percent of the total annual box-office revenue, with the best performing film *Tenet* ranked eleventh in box office. In February 2021, China broke the world's single-day record in box-office revenue during the Lunar New Year while Hollywood movies were largely absent from the Chinese market. All top five spots of all time on the box-office chart by Lunar New Year were Chinese domestic productions, which was a major milestone.[63]

Amidst the euphoria, Chen Sicheng, the director of the popular franchise film *Detective Chinatown*, remained cautious. At a film exchange event with audiences held on February 22, 2021, Chen tried to keep audience expectations in check and told them that "the position of our entire film industry does not match the position of China's entire cultural economy. It does not match China's overall national strength. Everyone knows that the film industry is one of America's seven pillar industries. But China's film industry is still too elementary, and it does not match our overall economic status." Chen pleaded for more audience support and pledged to make films to promote China: "We are a generation of filmmakers who take our responsibilities to heart. Please support and encourage us to do more in the future." Chen's concern was not unwarranted. Though his and a few other blockbusters made money in recent years, most domestic films were money losers, many languishing in obscurity without ever making their way to the big screen. China's total box-office revenue of US$3.06 billion in 2020, though well surpassing the U.S. total of US$2.1 billion, was still a far cry from Hollywood's record US$9.1 billion in 2019.[64]

Though 2020 was not a kind year for Hollywood in China, optimists looked to 2021 for Hollywood's return, with franchise tentpoles such as Marvel's *Black Widow* (Cate Shortland, 2021), Universal's *F9* (Justin

Lin, 2021), *A Quiet Place: Part II* (John Krasinski, 2021), MGM's *No Time to Die* (Cary Joji Fukunaga, 2021), and Legendary's *Godzilla vs. Kong* (Adam Wingard, 2021) ready to make their mark in China.[65] But the challenge of COVID-19 travel restrictions, the volatile political environment, foreign exchange controls, the desire to focus on recovery of the local film industry, and harsher public sentiment in both countries could complicate further Sino-U.S. collaboration. The year 2021 happens to be the year marking the 100th anniversary of the Chinese Communist Party, with nearly every major Chinese studio churning out patriotic blockbusters such as *The Battle at Lake Changjin* for release in 2021, making it challenging for Hollywood to secure screen space.[66] More worrisome were signs that Chinese consumers' allegiance to American popular culture was wavering. This came at a time when Hollywood was in a precarious position domestically, with production down and domestic box office virtually nonexistent due to COVID-19, rendering it all the more dependent on the global market, particularly the Chinese market. Unlike Hollywood, the Chinese box office is self-sufficient, with domestic films such as *Wolf Warrior II* and *Detective Chinatown 3* (Sicheng Chen, 2020) achieving global blockbuster numbers on the basis of their domestic box office alone and costing only a fraction of the budget of big Hollywood blockbusters.

Epilogue: What Can Two Decades Do to Sino-Hollywood Relations?

Almost a decade ago, the idea of writing a book on Sino-Hollywood relations came about at a conference, "The Intellectual Foundations of Global Commerce and Communications," at Harvard University in March 2013, a time when Dalian Wanda turned AMC's profit around less than a year after its acquisition of the U.S. theater chain in May 2012, which was the year Xi Jinping assumed power.[67] Wanda announced in May 2013 that the company would grow its global business, including expanding into the European market. By September 2013, Wanda's owner, Wang Jianlin, became China's richest person.[68] Also, 2013 was the year that China surpassed the United States as the country with the most billionaires, according to Shanghai-based research firm Hurun.[69]

The same month that Wang became China's richest man, Leonardo DiCaprio walked the red carpet as one of Wang's guests of honor at Wanda's ceremony announcing the $4.9 billion Qingdao Movie Metropolis.[70] Cheryl Boone Isaacs, the president of the Academy of Motion Picture Arts and Sciences, was also present at Wanda's ceremony. A week before, Wanda had donated $20 million to the U.S. Academy of Motion Picture Arts and Sciences for construction of its new film museum. Wang Jianlin predicted at the ceremony in 2013 that China's film market would become the world's biggest in five years. He was off by only two years. China officially overtook North America as the world's largest film market in 2020, and Wang had by then abandoned its global ambitions, returning to his home turf in China. By June 2021, Wanda had largely retreated from the film business, having sold most of its shares in AMC amidst the theater chain's steep revenue collapse due to the COVID lockdown.[71]

A decade ago in 2011, Ryan Kavanaugh, a Hollywood producer with China ambitions, predicted when unveiling his independent studio's joint venture in Beijing: "There's no reason we should have Chinese films and American films anymore. There should be global films." A decade later, Chinese and American films have grown far apart and become more distinct from each other, even as the two industries have become ever more entangled. The collusion in business continues but the government, media, and public scrutiny from both sides makes film collaboration a hazardous proposition. Some in the United States foresee a return to a business model where the U.S. studios make midbudget movies targeted at American adults rather than megabudget "monstrosities" aiming to please foreign markets.[72] As film critic Sonny Bunch put it, "A world in which Chinese filmmakers make films for Chinese audiences and in which American filmmakers make films for Western audiences isn't the worst thing that could happen."[73]

Despite cheery predictions, the Chinese market remains indispensable to the American film industry. In March 2021, *Avatar*, the 2009 James Cameron eco-fable, was re-released in China, garnering enough in ticket sales to push *Avatar* back to its top global gross position, a title the film held previously until *Avengers: Endgame* took the spot in 2019.[74] And for that, the film's producer Jon Landau issued a statement, thanking "our Chinese fans for their support."[75]

On March 26, *Godzilla vs. Kong* (Adam Wingard, 2021), a co-production between Warner Brothers and Legendary, which is owned by Dalian Wanda Group, a *Godzilla* franchise with its past two installments making more money in China than in North America, was released in China, five days ahead of its U.S. debut in theaters and on streaming platforms.[76] The film pulled in $21.5 million during its opening in China, breaking the box-office record debut in 2019.[77] It scored 9/10 on China's ticketing apps Maoyan and Taopiaopiao, and 7.1 on the Chinese reviews site Douban. It easily beat the holdover Chinese domestic New Year blockbuster *Hi, Mom* (Jia Ling, 2021) and the re-released *Avatar*. Yet the low-budget local drama *My Sister*, which cost just $4.6 million to produce and earned nearly $53 million in its debut, dethroned *Godzilla vs. Kong* at the Chinese box office by the third weekend.[78] *Godzilla vs. Kong* was nonetheless considered a success in China, bringing a collective relief to Hollywood, particularly after the flops of Warner Brothers' *Wonder Woman 1984* (Patty Jenkins, 2020) and Disney's *Mulan* (Niki Caro, 2020) and *Soul* (Pete Docter and Kemp Powersin, 2020) in China against Chinese domestic productions in 2020. Dalian Wanda Group was responsible for marketing and distributing *Godzilla vs. Kong* in China while Warner handled the rest of the world distribution.

Sino-Hollywood collaboration has continued whenever and wherever possible. Rance Pow, the head of an Asia film industry consulting firm, has remained hopeful that "Hollywood's brand of properties, stories and talent will remain compelling."[79]

What Has Happened to Soft Power?

In February 2019, at a national symposium held in Beijing, Wang Xiaohui, the newly anointed head of China's National Film Bureau, called on China to become a "strong film power" matching that of the United States, by 2035. Wang's call signaled that Chinese cinema was moving away from the gentle approach of soft power launched twenty years ago[80] and toward a more assertive approach that would project strong power.

Ten years ago in 2011, the Central Committee meeting of the Chinese Communist Party cautioned party members that "it is a pressing task to increase the state's cultural soft power" and to "build our country into a socialist cultural superpower."[81] That same year, to Beijing's delight, the Sino-U.S. co-production *Kung Fu Panda 2* (2011) managed to transform the animated panda from the small-time village fighter of the original *Kung Fu Panda* into a big-time hero fighting to save China. The chubby panda won the hearts and minds of audiences around the globe, softly projecting the glory of China's culture and natural abundance.

Things took a different turn in 2017, when a militant Chinese action film, *Wolf Warrior II*, stunned everyone with patriotic punches targeting the Americans. More stunning still was that the film's hard punch was matched by domestic box-office performance unbeatable by Hollywood imports. In September, one month after *Wolf Warrior II* proved the viability of the Chinese market for domestic films, NBCUniversal Pictures sold to Warner Bros. its interest in Oriental DreamWorks, the company that co-produced *Kung Fu Panda 2*. The parting was cited as a result of "disagreements over strategy."[82] Li Ruigang of China Media Capital, the joint venture's main Chinese partner, explained to the *Financial Times* that NBCUniversal wanted "to make films in China for the world," whereas China Media Capital is "focused more on China."[83]

Warner Brothers was no stranger to Li's China Media Capital. The two had formed a joint venture, Flagship Entertainment, together with the Shaw Brothers' TVB, in 2015. Flagship later co-produced *The Meg* (Jon Turteltaub, 2018), a rare crossover success in the U.S. commercial market of a Sino-U.S. joint production utilizing Hollywood resources, a feat Shaw Brothers would have been very pleased about.

By late November 2017, the restructured Oriental DreamWorks announced five new projects, all focusing on Chinese themes. The same year, the U.S. National Endowment for Democracy (NED) observed that China was turning decisively toward "sharp power," which "pierces, penetrates, or perforates the political and information environments in the targeted countries."[84] Translated into the world of filmmaking, cinematic sharp power cares little about wooing and changing hearts and minds; it rather competes and conquers. China's turn from soft to sharp and now strong power has done little to build trust and enhance relationships.

The United States too has resorted to a sharp-elbowed approach. So much so that in a piece provocatively titled "The Dangers of Groupthink on China" that came out on April 7, 2021,[85] Judah Grunstein calls for more reasoned assessment of China in the face of a gathering hawkish consensus in Washington. Grunstein warns about the herd mentality in Washington that has led to "the hardening of attitudes and the emergence of a sharper, more confrontational consensus to managing the challenge posed by China's rise as a peer competitor to the U.S."

At this moment in time, it is difficult to be sanguine about the Sino-Hollywood partnership. A decade ago, the term "courtship" could have been used to describe the fitful relationship that, however tentative and antagonistic at times, had brought two willing partners to the negotiating table in their common pursuit of prosperity and happiness, measured by box-office receipts and by the less tangible notion of soft power. While guilty of flooding the global market with its brand of entertainment at the expense of local industries, Hollywood has always pedaled softly, with plenty of charm and delight, though not always taste. The Sino-Hollywood relationship was initially more of an apprenticeship, as the two parties were by no means equals in finance, technology, and popular appeal. Though it continues to lag behind in popularity and recognition, a strong Chinese film industry now wants to be a competitor, one that smashes and conquers, all at the behest of the party. Prosperity no longer brings harmony when one partner starts to strong-arm the other.

The Departed *as a Metaphor?*

The Departed, Martin Scorsese's 2006 film that won the director his belated first Academy Award, was an adaptation of a 2002 Hong Kong crime film, *Infernal Affairs* (Andrew Lau and Alan Mak), which told a story about switching identities of mob informants and undercover cops and the infiltration of the triads into the elite police force. In the Hong Kong original, a young man is assigned by his crime boss to enter the police academy, and a young academy graduate is assigned to undercover work as a criminal. They both rise in the ranks and become invaluable assets as moles. The crime in question is drug dealing. In its Hollywood reincarnation, which moved the location from Hong Kong to Boston, the major crime that caught the attention of the police and the FBI was the illegal sale of missile-guidance microprocessors, which later turned out to be fake.

The seller is the crime boss Frank Costello, played by Jack Nicholson. The buyers are apparently Chinese government–associated gangsters, although they all speak Cantonese instead of Mandarin. While rendezvousing to do the trade, disagreements erupt, and the Chinese gang— except for the timid-looking government man—draw their weapons. Costello, the quintessential American mobster, makes a preemptive strike to stare down his Chinese counterpart by asking his middleman to inform the Chinese that "for his own good, tell Bruce Lee and the Karate Kids, none of us are carrying automatic weapons, because here, in this country, it don't add inches to your dick, but you get a life sentence for it!"

The scene captures well the contempt and displeasure the Boston crime boss has for the Chinese for violating the established mobster "trade norm" as defined by the American(s). Here in the film, China is simultaneously despised, repudiated, and feared. And the nuking of Taiwan is mentioned during the transaction, seeming to suggest what the microprocessor is for. Who would have thought that Scorsese was such a China expert who could foresee what has yet to come? If there were a sequel now, it would probably involve Huawei and 5G technology and the Chinese would be the seller rather than the buyer, or both, as they have both the cash to buy and the technology to sell! Incidentally, the film was banned in China for both violence and the plot twist that the Chinese were duped to buy fake microprocessors, which the Chinese censor found insulting. The scene serves as a metaphor for the perceived threat to the established institutional and cultural norms from an increasingly economically powerful China, with cinema as the image-making machine caught in the middle.

Despite the tensions, profit-minded cultural brokers continue to make co-productions and investment deals between the two film industries. The difference is that the deals are now made quietly and sometimes surreptitiously, unlike during the heyday when deals were announced loudly before any concrete steps were taken. Though challenged by China, the American film industry continues to serve as the global cinematic compass in terms of production operation and storytelling capability. Hollywood has been the world's master storyteller for over a century. What makes Hollywood the envy of the world, according to Martha Bayles, is "something unique and precious: creative freedom. This freedom has never been perfect. Throughout its history, the American Dream Factory has been subject to state censorship, self-censorship, and soul-killing commercial pressures. But it has never been enslaved. If it agrees to that now, the whole world will feel the loss."[86]

Meanwhile, tasked with the Sisyphean effort of spreading Chinese cultural gospel abroad, the Chinese film industry is retreating to its domestic turf by producing films popular only among the Chinese. Such films have evolved from the modestly budgeted satirical New Year films in the late 1990s to the big-budget patriotic macho blockbusters by the late 2010s, reflecting the changing political climate and cultural milieu in China. Most if not all of these films are directed by men. However, post-COVID Chinese cinema is witnessing the return of smaller pictures as well as pictures by female directors. The 2021 Lunar New Year saw a heartwarming comedy, *Hi, Mom*, about a woman who travels back in time to see her dead mother, which became the fourth highest grossing film in China and the highest ever for a female director.[87]

A nostalgic look at the period of economic reform in China in the 1980s, the film is a directorial debut by Jia Ling, a thirty-eight-year-old comedian who lost her mother to illness when she was nineteen. The film contemplates woman's identity and motherhood, which set off a national dialogue about womanhood and individual choices. It has surpassed *Wonder Woman* as the highest-grossing female-directed film. Another film by a little-known female director, Yin Ruoxin, titled *My Sister*, about Chinese society's preference for boys over girls, opened on April 2, 2021, soon becoming the number one blockbuster in China, beating *Godzilla vs. Kong* at the mainland box office. The movie also became the talk of the town, sparking a national conversation about China's patriarchal culture and the struggle between filial piety and individualism.

The rise of smaller-scale and more intimate personal films tackling a range of diverse social issues is a welcome sign, and perhaps the path forward toward a more robust Chinese domestic output of artistic quality and cultural influence. Much like the U.S. film industry, China's film industry is no longer monolithic, and a diverse range of commercial and art films now coexist alongside the leitmotif propaganda films. This turn of events suggests that the development of world cinema might benefit from a temporary decoupling of Sino-Hollywood—to allow for films of diverse style, politics, and cultural persuasions to flourish.

Acknowledgments

The idea of a project that charts the ups and downs of the Sino-Hollywood relationship germinated in March of 2013, when Richard John (from Columbia University) invited me to speak at a conference, "The Intellectual Foundations of Global Commerce and Communications," organized by the Harvard University History Department. A few individuals at the conference, among them Emma Rothschild and Heidi Tworek, shared their keen interest and encouraged me to further pursue

Poster for the Harvard conference in March 2013.

the project. I wish to thank them and Richard for nourishing a project that was in its very initial gestation.

Earlier that year, Richard and his Journalism School colleagues, including Michael Schudson and Vincent Ni, had put together an event for me at Columbia to discuss my then newly published book, *Two Billion Eyes: The Story of China Central Television*, also with The New Press. Anya Schiffrin, whose father co-founded The New Press and oversaw the publication of *Two Billion Eyes*, co-hosted the event. I later broached the idea of a possible book project on Sino-Hollywood with The New Press. Carl Bromley, the then editorial director at The New Press and a film buff himself, took special interest in the project and commissioned the book in 2015.

But the project was hardly turbocharged. Events—personal, professional, political, and pandemic—intervened. There were more than a few twists and turns, some predictable and some unexpected. As always, Marc Favreau, the director of editorial programs at The New Press, who had already tolerated my perpetual delays in bringing my last book to fruition, offered his steady support. Zoom calls with Marc earlier in 2021 helped me to pick up the pace. I am grateful for Marc's faith in me and for his editorial rigor that repeatedly sent me back to the editing table, which, despite my outbursts at the time, contributed to the final shape of this book. Together with Michael Keane, the China media scholar, Robert Kapp and Stephen Markscheid, both long-established China experts, lent their hands as I cut through various drafts. My daughter, Frances Hisgen, has been my most ardent proofreader, or "approver," never mind that she guards her own writings furiously, and never permits me to so much as alter one tiny punctuation.

Two PSC-CUNY research grants from the City University of New York in 2014–17 and a 2017 Fulbright Senior Fellowship made it possible for me to conduct initial research for the book. The book serves as a parting gift and a bittersweet bookend to my CUNY career spanning two decades. Among the various CUNY colleagues whose friendship and camaraderie have sustained me, my deepest gratitude goes to Mirella Affron, a mentor and dear friend whose wisdom and unwavering support have been instrumental to my professional and personal growth.

Early results of the research were presented at various academic and public events throughout the years, including a talk jointly organized by the Young China Watchers and the Hopkins Center in Shanghai in 2013; the "Soft Power in Action" Conference at Wilton Park in the UK jointly organized by the British Foreign and Commonwealth Office and the U.S. embassy in London; the "Cinema and Interdisciplinary Interpretation" Seminar at Columbia University with William Luhr and David Sterritt serving as co-hosts and Peter Biskind as respondent in 2014; an event at the Foreign Correspondent's Club of China (FCCC) in Shanghai organized by Lenora Chu and Rob Schmitz and another event at the FCCC in the Canadian embassy in Beijing organized by Peter Ford in 2015; the "Chinese Cinema: To and Beyond Hollywood" conference at Yale University co-hosted by Dudley Andrew and Ron Gregg; the "Theorizing Soft Power" Conference in Beijing organized by Victoria de Grazia at Columbia University's China Center; the symposium "Trade, War, and China in the 21st Century Beyond TPP—Does America Need a New Global Strategy?" organized by New America in Washington, DC, in 2016; the "Future of Asia Conference" organized by the Los Angeles World Affairs Council in Santa Monica in 2017; talks at a Young China Watchers' event in Hong Kong, the Mercator Institute for China Studies (MERICS) in Berlin, University of Texas at Austin (hosted by Thomas Schatz), CUNY's Graduate Center (hosted by Peter Hitchcock), Emerson University (hosted by Shujin Wang), Boston College (hosted by Martha Bayles), and the Fairbank Center at Harvard University (hosted by Ezra Vogel) in 2019; a talk in New York jointly organized by Columbia University's Weatherhead East Asia Institute and

Poster for the Yale University conference in April 2016, sponsored by Film and Media Studies and Films at the Whitney, Yale University.

School of the Arts with Richard Pena and Ying Qian co-hosting and a Town Hall meeting at the (U.S.) National Committee on Sino-US Relations in 2020; and, finally, a talk at the Seminar on Visual Culture in Modern and Contemporary China at the University of Oxford's China Center in Oxford in 2021 hosted by Margaret Hillenbrand. I wish to thank the wonderful individuals who created these opportunities for me to share my research in progress. Special thanks goes to Thomas Schatz, whose advice on my PhD dissertation decades ago piqued my initial interest in the entangled relationship between Hollywood and the Chinese film industry.

Parts of the research appeared in writing in publications including *The Atlantic*, *ChinaFile*, *Foreign Policy*, and *LA Times*; in interviews with NPR's *Market Place* and *Morning Edition*; and on a podcast on *Soft Power* produced by the Wilton Park Conference in the UK. A more complete snapshot of the research was published as a chapter in *Soft Power with Chinese Characteristics: China's Campaign for Hearts and Minds* (2019), a book I co-edited with Kingsley Edney and Stanley Rosen. I am indebted to Stan for noticing my early work on Sino-Hollywood in his review of my book *Chinese Cinema During the Era of Reform: The Ingenuity of the System* for *Foreign Policy* (January/February 2003) and for subsequently working with me on our two collaborative book projects.

The School of Communication and Film at the Hong Kong Baptist University offered further research grants for me to bring the book to its completion.

Together with proofreader Don Kennison, Emily Albarillo, associate managing editor, and Rachel Vega DeCesario, assistant editor, at The New Press chaperoned me through the final stages of the book's production.

I started my last New Press book in 2008, during the Beijing summer Olympics, a coming-out party for China that was graced by elite athletes and political dignities from around the world. As I wrap up this new New Press book, another Beijing Olympics has taken place, this time the 2022 winter Olympics, which was attended by the athletes but boycotted by diplomats from a number of countries including Australia, the UK, and of course the United States. This book bears witness to a moment in the Sino-Hollywood history marked by ups and downs, and to my personal life bracketed by departures and arrivals.

Notes

Introduction: From Paris Theater to Huaihai Cinema: As the Cinematic Universe Turns

1. Zhongguo tushu bianyi guan, ed., *Shanghai Chunqiu [Shanghai annals]* (Hong Kong: Nantian shuye gongsi, 1968), 2–88.

2. sites.google.com/view/russianshanghai/buildings/joffre-arcade.

3. Shi Zhecun, "At the Paris Theater," in *An Evening of Spring Rain* (Beijing: Panda/Chinese Literature Press, 1994), 38.

4. Shi Zhecun, "At the Paris Cinema," translated by Paul White, The Short Story Project, August 21, 2018, www.shortstoryproject.com/story/at-the-paris-cinema.

5. Lu Liu and Linqi Kong, "20 Shiji 20 Niandai de Kongque Dianying Gongsi Chutan [Peacock Film Company in the 1920s]," ed. Kong Lingqi, *Dangdai Dianying* [Contemporary Cinema], no. 9 (2019): 118–23.

6. S.J. Benjamin Cheng, "The Peacock Motion Picture Corporation," *Chinese Students Monthly* 18, no. 4 (1923): 34.

7. Lu Liu and Linqi Kong, "Peacock Film Company," 118–23.

8. Huanjiu Louzhu, "Naxie Nian, Shanghai de Dianyingyuan [Those Years, Cinemas in Shanghai]," 360doc, March 25, 2017.

9. "Gongxiang Dianying, Yuedu Shiguang: FILM Dianying Shiguang Shudian Liangxiang Shanghai [Sharing Films, Reading Times: The Debut of FILM Book Store]," *China News*, November 28, 2020, www.sh.chinanews.com/wenhua/2020-11-28/83153.shtml.

10. "Shanghai Wangshi Zhi Duoshao [How Much Do You Know About Shanghai's Past]," sh.wenming.cn, n.d., sh.wenming.cn/HPFQ/LNT/201104/t20110421_155228.htm.

1. Global Expansion and Local Protection: American and Chinese Film Industries from Inception Through the Early 1930s

1. Charles Higham, *Merchant of Dreams: Louis B. Mayer, MGM, and the Secret Hollywood* (New York: Dell Publishing, 1993); see also Raymond Moley, *The Hays Office* (Indianapolis: Bobbs-Merrill, 1964).

2. Matthew Johnson, "Regional Cultural Enterprises and Cultural Markets in Early Republican China: The Motion Picture as Case Study," *Cross-Currents: East Asian History and Culture Review* 4, no. 2 (2015): 658–693.

3. Yan Zhu, *Kepa de Shanghairen* [Tough Shanghairen] (Beijing: Zhongguo chang'an chubanshe, 2011).

4. Brodsky went on to co-found, with Hong Kong native Li Minwei, Hong Kong's first film studio, Huamei (Chinese American), in 1913, which made a single film, *Zhuangzi Tests His Wife*. That same year, Brodsky founded Variety Film Exchange Company and Variety Film Manufacturing Company in Hong Kong. In February 1914, Brodsky made his first film, *The Sport of Kings* (retitled *Hong Kong Races*), on the annual Hong Kong horse race. He made the critically acclaimed film *A Trip Through China* in 1917. The film earned him the reputation of the "King of Chinese Cinema."

5. Ramona Curry, "Pacific American Film Entrepreneur—Part One, Making a Trip thru China," *Journal of American–East Asian Relations* 18, no. 1 (2011): 58–94.

6. At other studios, the key marketing personnel came from sales, journalism, or press agencies.

7. It means "United China."

8. Means "Number One in the World."

9. Ying Zhu, *Chinese Cinema During the Era of Reform—The Ingenuity of the System* (Connecticut and London: Westport, 2003), 179.

10. Douglas Gomery, "Fashioning an Exhibition Empire: Promotion, Publicity, and the Rise of Public Theaters," in *Moviegoing in America: A Sourcebook in the History of Film Exhibition*, ed. Gregory A. Waller (Malden, MA: Blackwell Publishers, 2002), 124–137.

11. Richard Koszarski, "An Evening's Entertainment: The Age of the Silent Feature Picture 1915–1928," in *History of the American Cinema*, ed. Charles Harpole (New York: Charles Scribner & Sons, 1990), 84–85.

12. John Naughton and Adam Smith, *Movies: A Crash Course* (New York: Watson-Guptill Publishing, 1998), 30–31.

13. Ethan Mordden, *The Hollywood Studios: House Style in the Golden Age of the Movies* (New York: Alfred A. Knopf, 1988), 323–325.

14. Rudy Behlmer, ed., *Inside Warner Brothers (1935–1951)* (New York: Viking Penguin, 1985), 54–55; Naughton and Smith, *Movies*, 30–31.

15. The passage in 1890 of the Sherman Antitrust Act, a public relations gesture designed more to quiet critics than actually block cartel formation, would be applied to the film industry in 1913 and then again in the late 1940s, albeit leaving little long-lasting impact on Hollywood majors' domestic and international market control.

16. Kristin Thompson, *Exporting Entertainment: America in the World Film Market, 1907–1934* (London: BFI, 1985).

17. Founded in 1895 and active until 1916, Biograph was America's most prominent film studio and one of the most respected and influential studios worldwide during the height of the silent film era, rivaled only by Germany's UFA, Sweden's Svensk Filmindustri, and France's Pathé. The company was home to D.W. Griffith, Mary Pickford, Lillian Gish, and Lionel Barrymore.

18. Li Suyuan and Hu Jubin, *Zhongguo wusheng dianyhing shi* [History of Silent Film in China] (Beijing: China Film Press, 1996).

19. The first electric bus, what the Shanghainese called "little queue," appeared in Shanghai in 1914.

20. "Shanghai diyiliang dianche xingshi [The Operation of Shanghai's First Electric Bus]," movie.douban.com/subject/25810942.

21. Gerben Bakker, "The Economic History of the International Film Industry," EH.net (Economic History Association), February 10, 2008, eh.net/encyclopedia /the-economic-history-of-the-international-film-industry.

22. In 1912, D.W. Griffith shot *The New York Hat* on Washington Avenue in Coytesville and Main Street in Fort Lee. The film featured an all-star cast: Mary Pickford, Lionel Barrymore, Dorothy Gish, and Lillian Gish.

23. One on 1600 Broadway and the other on 730 Fifth Avenue; Universal later relocated its executive offices to 445 Park Avenue.

24. Twentieth Century Fox returned to Fort Lee thirty years later to shoot interiors for the now noir classic *Kiss of Death* (Henry Hathaway, 1947) at Holy Angels Academy, which was across the street from its 1917 studio. In 1919, the pioneer African American filmmaker Oscar Micheaux shot *Within Our Gates* in Fort Lee, presenting the black perspective to Griffith's *The Birth of a Nation* (1915). In 1931, *The Exile*, first all-"talkie" African American film by Oscar Micheaux, was shot at Metropolitan Studios in Fort Lee. The same studio produced the first "talking" version of *Alice in Wonderland* starring Ruth Gilbert in 1932. Micheaux shot his final film, *The Betrayal*, in Fort Lee in 1948.

25. Hye Seung Chung, *Hollywood Asian: Philip Ahn and the Politics of Cross-Ethnic Performance* (Philadelphia: Temple University Press, 2006), 100.

26. Zhen Jiang, "1920s–1930s: Hollywood Classic Horror Film in Shanghai," Master's diss. (Peking University, 2007).

27. *East Is West* (Universal Pictures, 1930).

28. David Putnam, *Movies and Money* (New York: Alfred A. Knopf, 1998); in his article "Birth of a Quotation: Woodrow Wilson and 'Like Writing History with Lightning,'" in *Journal of the Gilded Age and Progressive Era* (2010): 509–533, Mark E. Benbow disputed the quote attributed to Wilson.

29. Putnam, *Movies and Money*, 93.

30. Leslie Midkiff DeBauche, *Reel Patriotism: The Movies and World War I* (Madison: University of Wisconsin Press, 1997), 109.

31. Kerry Segrave, *American Films Abroad: Hollywood's Domination of the World's Movie Screens from the 1890s to the Present* (Jefferson, NC: McFarland Publishing, 1997), 15.

32. Segrave, *American Films Abroad*, 11.

33. Zhiwei Xiao, "American Films in China Prior to 1950," in *Art, Politics, and Commerce in Chinese Cinema*, eds. Ying Zhu and Stanley Rosen (Hong Kong: Hong Kong University Press, 2010), 55–70.

34. Zhiwei Xiao, "American Films in China," 55–70.

35. Beijing Municipal Archive (BMA), 1507-385-2. There is no date on Bi's proposal, but the emperor's comment on the proposal is dated February 23, 1906.

36. See Chung, *Hollywood Asian*.

37. Beijing Municipal Archive 1509-385 (7), "Guanli dianying ye xi guize shi yi tiao [Eleven Rules Governing the Showing of Motion Pictures in the Evenings]."

38. Jilin provincial archive, "Qingmo Jilinsheng dianying fangying shiliao [Historical Documents Concerning the History of Film Exhibition in Jilin During the Late Qing Period]"; Lishi dangan [Historical archives] 0 (/225), 56–58.

39. 有傷風化

40. The Beiyang government was the internationally recognized Chinese central government between 1912 and 1928. The name derives from the Beiyang Army, which took control of China when the Qing government was toppled. In China, though, the legitimacy of Beiyang was challenged by Sun Yat-sen's Guangzhou-based Kuomintang (KMT) government movement.

41. Beijing Municipal Archive, 1001 (2) 732-1, "Cheng wei shechang zhizao tongsu jiaoyu huodong yingpian qinglian you [The Case Concerning an Application to Set Up a Film Studio and Make Educational Films]," dated August 3–15, 1918.

42. No. 2 Historical Archive, "Selected Archival Documents," document 1057-553, from Zhiwei Xiao, "Policing Film in Twentieth-Century China, 1905–1923," in *The Oxford Handbook of Chinese Cinemas*, eds. Carlos Rojas and Eileen Chow (Oxford and New York: Oxford University Press, 2013), 468, footnote 17.

43. "Sheng jiaoyuhui shenyue Mingxing pian zhi pingyu [Comments on Star Motion Picture Company's Films by the Censors from the Provincial Government's Education Department]," *Shenbao*, July 5, 1923.

44. "Dianying shenyue weiyuanhui xiaoxi [News from the Film Censorship Committee]," *Mingxing tekan* [special issue, Star Motion Picture Company], no. 16, September 1926.

45. Li Shaobai and Hong Shi, "Pinwei he jiazhi [Taste and Values]," *Dangdai dianying* [Contemporary Cinema], no. 3 (1990): 58.

46. A letter grading system eventually replaced the code in the late 1960s.

47. Wanli Shan, *Zhongguo jilu dianying shi* [History of Chinese Documentary Cinema] (Beijing: Zhongguo dianying chubanshe [China Film Press]), translation in Matthew D. Johnson, "Regional Cultural Enterprises and Cultural Markets in Early Republican China: The Motion Picture as Case Study," *Cross-Currents, East Asian History and Culture Review*, no. 16 (2015).

48. Johnson, "Regional Cultural Enterprises," 117.

49. "Screen: People and Plays," *New York Times* (June 6, 1920), 65. See also Matthew D. Johnson, "Journey to the Seat of War: The International Exhibition of China in Early Cinema," *Journal of Chinese Cinemas* 3, no. 2 (2009): 109–122.

50. Johnson, "Regional Cultural Enterprises," 117.

51. Some argued that the company relocated to Shanghai in 1923. See Yin Fujun, and Sun, "Changcheng huapian gongsi 'kuahai' shijian kao [The Chronology of Changcheng Picture Company]," *Cinematic Literature*, no. 4 (2010): 21–22.

52. Chen Mo and Xiao Zhiwei, "kuahai de 'changcheng': cong jianli dao tanta—changcheng huapian gongsi lishi chutan ['Great Wall' from Establishment to Collapse—a Historical Research on Changcheng Picture Company]," *Contemporary Cinema*, no. 4 (2004): 36–44.

53. "Lai Man Wai," *Hong Kong Memory* (2012), www.hkmemory.hk/MHK/collections/ECExperience/pioneers/lai_man_wai/index.html.

54. Yaoqing Wei, "The Strategy of Promoting Domestic Film to Save the Country," Xinxin Studio Special Issue 1 (1925). According to Jubin Hu in *Projecting a Nation: Chinese National Cinema Before 1949* (Hong Kong: Hong Kong University Press, 2003), 198, "Since the article was published in a special issue of Xinxin Film Studio, it is a reasonable conclusion that the article was written by a publicity agent of Xinxin Studio."

55. Jianhua Chen, "D.W. Griffith and the Rise of Chinese Cinema in Early 1920s Shanghai," in *The Oxford Handbook of Chinese Cinemas*, eds. Carlos Rojas and Eileen Chow (New York: Oxford University Press, 2013), 23–38.

56. Jessica Ka Yee Chan, "Insulting Pictures: *The Thief of Bagdad* in Shanghai," *Modern Chinese Literature and Culture* 28, no. 1 (2016): 38–77.

57. Marie Cambon, "The Dream Palaces of Shanghai: American Films in China's Largest Metropolis Prior to 1949," *Asian Cinema* 7, no. 2 (1995): 40.

58. 沪光大戏院

59. "Weiyue sunshi liuwan yuan, Migaomei jiang dui Huguang xingsong [Breaking Contact with a Penalty of 60,000 Yuan, Huguang Face Litigation of MGM]," *Diangsheng* 8, no. 15 (1939): 682. Also cited in Zhiwei Xiao, "Hollywood in China,

1897–1950: A Preliminary Survey," *Chinese Historical Review* 12, no. 1 (2005): 71–96.

60. Zhang Zhongmin, "Jindai Shanghai gongren jieceng de gongzi yu shenghuo [Salary and Life of the Working Class in Modern Shanghai]." *Zhongguo jingjishi yanjiu* [Chinese economic studies], no. 2 (2011): 3–16.

61. For more detailed discussion, see Zhu, *Chinese Cinema During the Era of Reform*, chapter 6.

62. Ai Qing. "Mingxing yingpian gongsi kuarwenhua jiaowang hunzaxing tezhi [Intercultural Communication of Star Pictures]," *Contemporary Cinema*, no. 1 (2015): 183–186.

63. Howe would become one of the most sought-after cinematographers in Hollywood in the 1930s and 1940s and go on to win nomination for ten Academy Awards for cinematography, winning twice, for *The Rose Tattoo* (Daniel Mann, 1955) and *Hud* (Martin Ritt, 1963).

64. 四达通

65. 晨星

66. For the ban on *Ten Commandments*, see "Dianying shencha weiyuanhui gongbao [The News Bulletin of the Film Censorship Committee]" 1, no. 5 (1932): 30; for the ban on *Ben Hur*, see *China Weekly Review*, January 19, 1929, 347.

67. Zhiwei Xiao, "Prohibition, Politics, and Nation Building: A History of Film Censorship in China," in *Film Censorship Around the World*, eds. Daniel Biltereyst and Roel VandeWinkel (New York: Palgrave Macmillan, 2013), 118.

2. Into the 1930s and 1940s: Hollywood's Global Expansion and Chinese Cinema's Local Buildup

1. Ge Yinghong, "On National Style [Guanyu minzu xingshi]," *Literature Monthly* [Wenxue yuebao] 1, no. 2 (1940).

2. Tan Ye and Yun Zhu, *Historical Dictionary of Chinese Cinema* (Lanham, MD: Rowman & Littlefield, 2012); Gabrielle H. Cody and Evert Sprinchorn, *The Columbia Encyclopedia of Modern Drama* (New York: Columbia University Press, 2007).

3. Jessica Ka Yee Chan, "Insulting Pictures: *The Thief of Bagdad* in Shanghai," *Modern Chinese Literature and Culture* 28, no. 1 (2016): 60.

4. Hong Shen left Shanghai for Chongqing after the Japanese invasion in 1937 and staged plays to advocate resistance against Japan. He returned to teach at Fudan University after the end of the second Sino-Japanese War in 1945. He was forced out because of his pro-Communist political stand and went to teach briefly at Xiamen University in Fujian Province before leaving for the CCP-controlled Northeast China in 1948. After CCP took over China, Hong Shen was appointed

director of the Bureau of External Cultural Relations under the Ministry of Culture and vice president of the China Theatre Association.

5. Wang Yiman, "The Crisscrossed State: Propaganda and Protest in China's Not So Silent Era," in *Silent Cinema and the Politics of Space*, eds. Jennifer M. Bean, Anupama P. Kapse, and Laura Evelyn Horak (Bloomington, IN: Indiana University Press, 2014), 192.

6. Wang Yiman, "The Crisscrossed State," 192.

7. Wang Yiman, "The Crisscrossed State," 192.

8. For a detailed account of the case see Ying Zhu, "The Battle of Images: Cultural Diplomacy and Sino-Hollywood Negotiation," in *Soft Power with Chinese Characteristics: China's Campaign for Hearts and Minds*, eds. Kingsley Edney, Stanley Rosen, and Ying Zhu, 100–116.

9. Cheng Wan, "Chumu jingxin de xiaoxi [Shocking News]," *Yingxi shenghuo* [Movie life] 1, no. 6 (1931): 5–6.

10. Memorandum of conversation dated March 3, 1934, State Department files. Also quoted in Chung Hye Seung, *Hollywood Asian: Philip Ahn and the Politics of Cross-Ethnic Performance* (Philadelphia: Temple University Press, 2006).

11. Xiao Zhiwen, "Nationalism, Orientalism, and an Unequal Treatise of Ethnography: The Making of *The Good Earth*," in *The Chinese in America: A History from Gold Mountain to the New Millennium*, ed. Susie Lan Cassel (Lanham, MD: AltaMira Press, 2000), 281.

12. Chung Hye Seung, *Hollywood Asian: Philip Ahn and the Politics of Cross-Ethnic Performance*, 95; Frederick L. Herron, "Letter to Willys Peck," State Department files on China, 893.4061 Motion Pictures, NARA, November 9, 1936.

13. Marie Cambon, "The Dream Palaces of Shanghai: American Films in China's Largest Metropolis Prior to 1949," *Asian Cinema* 7, no. 2 (1995): 40.

14. Benshi, meaning a voice actor who translated the title cards and provided some form of dialogue or explanation to the story on-screen, had difficulty in keeping up with the translations when sound arrived. Studios like United Artists simply stopped exporting films to Japan while Paramount applied subtitles in films and the benshi became obsolete.

15. It cost studios roughly $800 in customs duties for an average-length feature export to China and $200 to $300 for censorship charges in Shanghai in the mid-1930s.

16. Wilbur Burton, "Chinese Filmers Inspire Trick Law That May Force U.S. Out of Market," *Variety* 111, no. 19 (July 25, 1933): 594; "China's Gov't Film Commissioner Scans Industry in U.S. and Europe," *Variety* 127, no. 16 (June 16, 1937).

17. Wilbur Burton, "Chinese Reactions to the Cinema," *Asia* 34 (October 1934): 594; "78% Pix Shown in China from the U.S.," *Variety* 118 (April 3, 1935): 114.

18. Wang Chaoguang, "Minguo nianjian Meiguo dianying zai hua shichang yanjiu [The Marketing Research of American Cinema in Republican China]," *Dianying Yishu* [Film Art], no. 258 (January 1998): 57–64.

19. Zhou Jianyun, "Guanshui yu zhongguo dianying [The Right to Taxation and Chinese Cinema]," *Dianying yuebao* 5 (1928): 116; Ying Dou, "Zhipian gongsi ying jinji zhuyi zhege wenti [Production Company Should Urge to Pay Attention to this Issue], ed. China Film Archive, (Beijing: China Film Press, 1996), 118–119, first published in *Yingxing* 16, 18, (1928); see also Chaoguang Wang, "Minguo Nianjian Meiguo Dianying Zai Hua Shichang Yanjiu [The Marketing Research of American Cinema in Republican China]," *Dianying Yishu* [Film Art], no. 1 (1998): 57–65.

20. China produced sixty-seven films in 1933, with only fourteen in sound.

21. See "Lianhua xuanyan" (The Opening Statement of the United Film Exchange) published in the special edition of *Shenzhou gongshi Shanghai zhiye* [The Evening of Shanghai] 4 (1926): 39.

22. Luo's father was a comprador for a foreign bank.

23. Zhu Shilin is also romanized as Chu Shek Lin.

24. Poshek Fu, "Rewriting Lo Ming-yau: Between China and Hong Kong," in *The Hong Kong–Guangdong Film Connection*, ed. Hong Kong Film Archive (Hong Kong: Hong Kong University Press, 2005).

25. Li Fanding, *The Lianhua Film Company: Business and Movies* (Jinan Up, 2013), 7.

26. Paul G. Pickowicz, "The Theme of Spiritual Pollution in Chinese Films of the 1930s," *Modern China* 17, no. 1 (January 1991): 49, doi:10.1177/0097700491017 00102.

27. Sun Yu, *Yin Hai Fan Zhou: Hui Yi Wo de Yi Sheng* [Afloat on the Silver Sea: recalling my life] (Shanghai: Shang Hai Wen Yi Chu Ban She, 1987).

28. Er Feng, "The Responsibility Our Film Audience Should Shoulder in Regards to the Chinese Film Revival Movement [Wo guo dianying guanzhong duiyu guopian fuxing yundong ying fu de zeren]," *Shadow Play Journal* 1, no. 9 (1930): 32–33. Feng Er is obviously a pen name. Since *Shadow Play Journal* was run by Lianhua Film Studio, this article in fact represented the stand of Lianhua Studio.

29. Luo, Mingyou, " Wei guopian fuxing wenti jinggao tongyi shu [A Letter to People in the Film Trade for Reviving the Chinese Film]," *Shadow Play Journal* 1, no. 9 (1930): 44.

30. Yu Muyun, *Xianggang dianying shihua* [Hong Kong Film History], vol. 2 (Hong Kong Subculture Ltd., 1992), 12. See also in Feng Qun, "Luo Mingyou yu lianhua yingpian gongsi [Luo Mingyou and Lianhua Productions]," *Lv Fengjing: Qiaoxiang Dianyingren yu dangdai zuojia* [Green Scenery: Oversea Republic Chinese Filmmakers and Contemporary Writers] (Xinhua chubanshe, 2014), 51–52.

31. Matthew D. Johnson, "Regional Cultural Enterprises and Cultural Markets in Early Republican China: The Motion Picture as Case Study," *Cross-Currents: East Asian History and Culture Review*, no. 16: 122; Lu Hongshi, *Zhongguo dianying: Miaoshu yu chanshi* [Chinese Cinema: Description and Explanation] (Beijing: Zhongguo dianying chubanshe, 2002), 25–42; see also Fang Fang, *Zhongguo jilupian fazhan shi* [History of the Development of Chinese Documentary Film] (Beijing: Beijing xiju chubanshe), 25.

32. Lily Kong, "Shaw Cinema Enterprise and Understanding Cultural Industries," in *China Forever: The Shaw Brothers and Diasporic Cinema*, ed. Fu Poshek (Urbana: University of Illinois Press, 2008), 35.

33. Lily Kong, "Shaw Cinema Enterprise," 40.

34. Zhu Chunting and Zhu Minjuan, "Shaoshi xiongdi buji fuye cheng fuyuan [Shaw Brothers: Not Inheriting the Family Business]," in *Shao yifu zhuan* [Shaw Empire] (Hubei renmin chubanshe, 2008), 49.

35. Law Kar, "Shaw's Cantonese Productions and Their Interactions with Contemporary Local and Hollywood Cinema," in *China Forever: The Shaw Brothers and Diasporic Cinema*, ed. Fu Poshek (Urbana: University of Illinois Press, 2008), 59.

36. "Yuandong zuida de yule gongying ku: Shaoshi [The Shaw Brothers Studio: The Largest Supplier of Entertainment in Asia]," *Nanguo dianying* 59 (January 1961): 30–33.

37. Xinhua Dianying Gongsi 新华影业公司

38. Hu Xu and Gu Quan, *Manying—Guoce dianying mianmian guan* [Man'ei: Perspectives on National Policy Films] (Shanghai: Zhonghua shuju, 1990).

39. Zhang Yingjin, *Chinese National Cinema* (New York and London: Routledge, 2004), 84.

40. Hu Jubin, "Colonial and Anti-Colonial Nationalism," *Projecting a Nation: Chinese National Cinema Before 1949* (Hong Kong: Hong Kong University Press, 2003), 116.

41. 中央电影摄影场

42. 中国电影制片厂

43. Pan Jienong, "Interpreting American Style: The So-Called 'Techniques' in Commercial Films in Capitalist Countries [Shi meiguo zuofeng: zibenzhuyi guo jia de shangye dianying de suowei "shoufa" yu "jiqiao"]," *National Daily*, September 3, 1941.

44. Pan Jienong, "Interpreting American Style."

45. On Chongqing film audience composition, see Yang Cunren's "About Filmmaking for the Peasants [Nongcun yingpian de zhizuo wenti]," *China Film* 1, no. 1 (1941); and Wang Pingling's "The Production and Exhibition of Wartime Education Film [Zhan shi jiaoyu dianying de bianzhi yu fangying]," *Times* 3, no. 4 (1941): 3.

46. Zheng Boqi, "The Soviet Cinema's Influence on Chinese Cinema [Sulian dianying geiyu Zhongguo dianying de yingxiang]," *Sino-Russian Culture* 7, no. 4 (1940).

47. Hu Jubin, "Colonial and Anti-Colonial Nationalism," 144; also cited in Xia Yan, *Lan Xun Jiumeng Lu* [Old Memories] (Beijing: Joint Publishing, 2000), 255–256.

48. Hu Jubin, *Projecting a Nation: Chinese National Cinema Before 1949* (Hong Kong University Press, 2003), 121; see also Shi Dongshan, "Chinese Cinema Since the War of Resistance Against Japanese Aggression [Kangzhan yilai de Zhongguo dianying]," *Sino-Russian Cultures (Zhongsu wenhua)* 9, 1 (1941).

49. See "Fang Zhang Shankun (An Interview with Zhang Shankun)," *China Film* [Zhongguo dianying] 1, no. 1 (1937).

50. Cai Chusheng, "Kangzhan hou de minying dianying, dangqian jue da de weiji [The Privately Owned Film Industry and Its Great Crisis Since the War]," *Sadangbao*, December 18, 1938.

51. Zhang Shankun, "Yiye huanghou daoyan zhe yan [On Directing *Empress for One Night*]," *Qingqing Movie* 4, no. 27 (1939). *Empress for One Night* is a love story about an emperor and a lower-class woman (see *General Catalogue of Chinese Cinema*, 546). Zhang Shankun cites this film as an example of a film that had no "national consciousness" because the filmmakers had no choice.

52. Zhang Yingjin, *Chinese National Cinema*, 88; see also Zuo Guifang and Yao Liqun, eds, *Tong Yuejuan* [Actress Tong Yuejuan] (Taipei: Wenjianhui: 2001), 66–67.

53. 崑崙影片公司

54. Shimizu Akira, *Shanghai soka eiga watakushi-shi* [History of Shanghai Zujie Films] (Tokyo: Shinchosha, 1995), 301–304. See also Zhang Yingjin, *Chinese National Cinema*, 88.

55. Fu Poshek, "The Ambiguity of Entertainment: Chinese Cinema in Japanese-occupied Shanghai, 1942 to 1945," *Cinema Journal* 37, no. 1 (1997), 66–84, 72–77. See also Zhang Yingjin, *Chinese National Cinema*.

56. Twenty-four in 1943, thirty-two in 1944, and twenty-four in 1945. See Du Yunzhi, *Zhongguo de dianying* [Chinese Cinema] (Taipei: Huangguan, 1978); Du Yunzhi, *Zhonghua minguo dianying shi* [A History of Cinema in the Republic of China] (Taipei: Wenjianhui, 1988).

57. Keyin Zhao, "The Fate of Da Guangming Cinema's Owner Hu Zhifan and His Wife Jin Suwen," *Cuhk.edu.hk*, 2015, mjlsh.usc.cuhk.edu.hk/Book.aspx?cid=4&tid=5940.

58. Thomas Schatz, *The Genius of the System* (New York: Pantheon Books, 1988).

59. When the Communist army took control of the city.

60. Chen Jihua, Li Shaobai, and Xing Zuwen, eds., *History of the Development of Chinese Cinema* (Beijing: ZDC, 1981), 161–162.

61. See Cai Chunfang, "Zhanhou shanghai shichang dianshi shichang shang de zhongwai duikang (1947–1949)—yingpian gongsi jian de shoulun yingyuan zhengduozhan [Postwar Shanghai Film Market's China-West Rivalries (1947–1949)—First Battle Between Theaters]," *Wenhua yishu yanjiu* [Cultural and Art Studies] 8, no. 2 (2015): 95.

62. *Code Name Heaven No. 1* [Tianzi diyihao], 1946, directed by Tu Guangqi; *Long Live the Mistress!* [Taitai wansui], 1947, directed by Sang Hu; *Phony Phoenixes* [Jiafeng xuhuang], 1947, directed by Huang Zuolin.

63. Xia Yan, "A Modern Chinese Film: The Tears of Yangtze," *China Digest* 3, no. 6 (February 9, 1948): 18–19.

64. Wang Zhaoguang, "Zhanhou Shanghai guochan dianhingye de qishi [Lessons from the Postwar Shanghai Film Market]," *Dianying yishu* 5 (2000): 26–32.

65. Yingjin Zhang, *Chinese National Cinema*, 95.

66. "Shisi jia yingpian gongsi xiang Li Weiguo tichu liangdian yaoqiu: Xiyuan duo ying guopian zhengqv guoji shichang [Fourteen Production Companies Made Two Requests to Li Weiguo: Theaters Show More Domestic Films and Aim for International Markets]," *Tiebao* 4 (January 11, 1948).

67. Wang Zhaoguang, "Mingguo nianjian duanying zai hua shichang yanjiu [A Market Analysis of Hollywood Films in China During the Republican Era]" *Danying yishu* 1 (1998): 57–65.

3. From Hollywood to Soviet Model: Building a Socialist Cinema

1. "Suqing Yingmei Youdu Yingpian, Shanghai Gejie Fenfen Tichu Jianju, Yaoqiu Zhengfu Yange Jiancha Qudi [The Purge of the American and British Poisonous Films; Shanghai People Demanding Governmental Censorship]," *People's Daily* (September 21, 1949).

2. 上海大戲院

3. Xuelei Huang, "The Heroic and the Banal: Consuming Soviet Movies in Pre-Socialist China, 1920s–1940s," *Twentieth-Century China* 39, no. 2 (2014): 93–117.

4. See *Dongnan Daily* (December 24, 1948). Cited in Suzanne Pepper, *Civil War in China: The Political Struggle, 1945–1949* (Lanham, MD: Rowman & Littlefield, 1999), 90; Hu Jubin, *Projecting a Nation: Chinese National Cinema Before 1949*, 162.

5. Robert Farley, "China and America Have Already Gone to War (It Was Called the Korean War)," *National Interest* (October 16, 2019), nationalinterest.org/blog /buzz/china-and-america-have-already-went-war-it-was-called-korean-war-88236 ?page=0%2C1.

6. See Dishan Liu, "'Shiqinian' Shiqi Waiguo Dianying Jinying Wenti [Censorship on Foreign Films During Seventeen Years]," *Wenyi Yanjiu* [Literary Research], no. 10 (2012): 95–105.

7. Rong Wang, "Shanghai Guanzhong wei Jinbu Dianying er Huanhu [Shanghai Audiences Cheer for Progressive Films]," *People's Daily* (March 19, 1951).

8. Liu, "Shiqinian." See also Wang, "Shanghai Guanzhong."

9. See "Dianying Lifaye Tongyegonghui guanyhu Tiaozheng Dianying Lifa Jiage de Laihan ji Youguan Wenjian [Letters from the Film Barber Trade Union on the Adjustment of Film Barber Prices and Related Documents]," Beijing, 1950.

10. See "Beijingshi Dianyingyuan Shangye Tongye Gonghuihan [Letter from Beijing Cinemas Business Association]," September 7, 1950.

11. Liu, "Shiqinian," 97.

12. One source cited 169 large-scale organized complaining meetings and numerous small sessions spread across 134 cities by December 1953. See Kuisong Yang, "Xinzhongguo Chengli Chuqi Qingchu Meiguo Wenhua Yingxiang de Jingguo [The Process of Removing American Cultural Influence in the Early Years of New China]," History of the Chinese Communist Party, June 3, 2011, cpc .people.com.cn/BIG5/218984/218997/219022/14818487.html.

13. David Emil Mungello, "Reinterpreting the History of Christianity in China," *Historical Journal* 55, no. 2 (June 2012): 533–552; see also Pepper, *Civil War in China*; check also Garnett Lee White, "Southern Baptist Missions in China, 1945–1951," master's thesis (University of Richmond, 1967).

14. Huang, "The Heroic and the Banal," 93–117.

15. Tina Mai Chen, "Internationalism and Cultural Experience: Soviet Films and Popular Chinese Understanding of the Future in the 1950s," *Cultural Critique* 58 (Autumn 2004): 82–114. On Mao Zedong's distrust of Stalin, see Sergei Goncharov, John W. Lewis, and Litai Xue, *Uncertain Partners: Stalin, Mao and the Korean War* (Stanford: Stanford University Press, 1993).

16. Shuguang Rao and Qi Shao, "Xinzhongguo Dianying de Diyige Yundong: Qingchu Haolaiwu Dianying [The First Movement of Films in Communist China: Purge of Hollywood Films]," *Aisixiang*, August 2, 2010, m.aisixiang.com/data/35176 -2.html. *In the Heat of the Sun* includes a sequence in which an outdoor screening of the model performance ballet film *The Red Detachment of Women* (Hongse niangzijun) suddenly stops due to a film break. The projectionist hastily puts on a reel from one of the Lenin films. As it starts, several wags on stools in the front rows recite the dialogue just before it is heard on-screen, to the general hilarity of their companions.

17. Jia Hua, "Kanle 'Gongke Bailin' yihou geng jiandingle wo canjia junshi ganxiao de xinxin [After Watching *The Fall of Berlin* I Was Even More Confident in My Decision to Attend Military Cadre School]," *Dazhong Dianying* 7 (1950): 2.

18. Chen, "Internationalism and Cultural Experience."

19. Roy Appleman, *Escaping the Trap: The US Army X Corps in Northeast Korea, 1950,* 14, College Station, Texas: Texas A&M University Military History Series, 1990.

20. Xue, Yan, Li, Jian et al. (2000), 朝鲜战争—— 长津湖之战四 [Korean War—Battle of Changjin Lake, Part Four] (in Chinese), Beijing: Chinese Academy of Social Sciences.

21. Patrick C. Roe, *The Dragon Strikes: China and the Korean War, June–December 1950,* Novato, California: Presidio, 2000.

22. Steven Lee Myers and Amy Chang Chien, "Chinese Journalist Detained After Criticizing Government-Sponsored Blockbuster," *New York Times,* October 8, 2021.

23. See Ying Zhu, "From Hollywood to Soviet Model: Building a Socialist Chinese Cinema," in *The Odyssey of Communism: Visual Narratives, Memory and Culture,* eds. Michaela Preisler and Oana-Celia Gheorghiu (Newcastle upon Tyne, UK: Cambridge Scholars Publishing, 2021), 149.

24. See Table 25.1 in Laikwan Pang, "Between Will and Negotiation: Film Policy in the First Three Years of the People's Republic of China," in *The Oxford Handbook of Chinese Cinemas,* eds. Carlos Rojas and Eileen Chow (Oxford and New York: Oxford University Press, 2013), 477.

25. Publicity Department of Shanghai Working Committee Youth League, "Muqian Shanghai Xuesheng Qunzhong Sixiang Diaocha [A Survey on Current Thought of Students and Citizens in Shanghai]," October 23, 1951.

26. Yang, "Xinzhongguo."

27. See Tina Chen, "Internationalism and Cultural Experience," 109, which refers to Jay Leyda's 1972 book, *Dianying, Electric Shadows: An Account of Films and the Film Audience in China.*

28. See Chen, "Internationalism and Cultural Experience," 110.

29. Chen, "Internationalism and Cultural Experience."

30. Chen, "Internationalism and Cultural Experience," 82–114.

31. Cf. Zhang Zicheng, ed., *Waiguo yishu yingpian ziliao huibian, 1949–1992* [Collected Materials on Imported Foreign Films] (Beijing: Zhongguo dianying chubanshe, 1993); Paul Clark, *Chinese Cinema: Culture and Politics since 1949* (Cambridge, MA and New York: Cambridge University Press, 1987), 185.

32. The film would be featured in the sixty-second Venice International Film Festival in August 2005, together with Tsui Hark's *Seven Swords,* as part of the retrospective *The Secret History of Asian Cinema.* Chen advocated in 1950 the establishment of a school that trained CPC's film management cadres. The Film Art Cadre School became the predecessor of Beijing Film Academy.

33. "Yuan Muzhi," Baidu Baike, baike.baidu.com/item/%E8%A2%81%E7%89%
A7%E4%B9%8B. See also "Yuan Muzhi," m.zwbk.org/lemma/112849.

34. "Changchun Film Studio [Changchun Dianying Zhipianchang]," in *Zhong-guo Dakaike Quanshu Zongbianji Weiyuanhui "Dianying" Bianji Weiyuanhui*, ed. China Encyclopedia: Film [Zhongguo Dabaike Quanshu: Dianying] (Beijing: China Encyclopedia Press, 1998), 46.

35. Shuguang Rao, "A Sketch of One Hundred Years of Chinese Market [Bai-nian Zhongguo shichang saomiao]," in *Zhongguo Dianying Bianjibu*, ed. China Film Yearbook Centennial Special Volume [Zhongguo Dianying Nianjian Zhong-guo Dianying Bainian Tekan] (Beijing: China Yearbook Press, 2006), 500.

36. "Beijing Film Studio [Beijing Dianying Zhipianchang]," in *Zhongguo Da-kaike Quanshu Zongbianji Weiyuanhui "Dianying" Bianji Weiyuanhui*, ed. China En-cyclopedia: Film [Zhongguo Dabaike Quanshu: Dianying] (Beijing: China Encyclopedia Press, 1998), 30–31.

37. Николай Алексеевич Лебедев, *Dang Lun Dianying* [Party's View on Cin-ema], trans. Guming Xu et al. (Beijing: Shidai Chubanshe [Time Publication], 1951).

38. Kristin Thompson, "Government Policies and Practical Necessities in the So-viet Cinema of the 1920s," in *The Red Screen: Politics, Art in Soviet Cinema*, ed. Anna Lawton (New York: Routledge, 1992), 23.

39. Zhixiu Xie, "Yuan Muzhi Yu 'Dianying Cun' [Yuan Muzhi and 'Film Vil-lage']," *Ninbo University Journal*, no. 1 (2005): 41–43.

40. In a sign of tightened political control, the Film Bureau was recently moved back to be under the care of the Propaganda Ministry. To March 2018, the Film Bureau was under the State Administration of Press, Publication, Radio, Film, and Television, whose job was to regulate content, including censoring films and sched-uling theatrical releases.

41. Pang, "Between Will and Negotiation."

42. Clark, *Chinese Cinema*, 35.

43. Zhongguo dianying faxing fangying gongsi.

44. See *Literature and Art Gazette* [Wenyi Bao] (February 1952): 37. Paul Clark also mentioned the incident. See Clark, *Chinese Cinema*, 36.

45. Ji Yu, "Guojia Yizhi Yu Shaoshuminzu Dianying: Zhou Enlai Chuli Ying-pian 'Neimeng Chunguang' Shijian Yanjiu [National Will and Ethnic Minority Films: A Study of Zhou Enlai's Handling of the Film *Springtime in Inner Mongo-lia*]," *Dianying Yishu* [Film Art], no. 4 (July 5, 2013): 131–142.

46. He was simultaneously appointed as a vice premier from 1956 to 1966 as a showcase of the CCP's friendly ethnic minority policy.

47. Ji Yu, "Guojia Yizhi Yu Shaoshuminzu Dianying.

48. "Film banned by Mao becomes a modern hit," *South China Morning Post* (April 1, 2012), www.scmp.com/article/997130/film-banned-mao-becomes-modern -hit.

49. Zedong Mao, "Yinggai Zhongshi Dianying 'Wuxun Zhuan' de Taolun [The Discussion of the Film *Wuxun Zhuan* Should Be Taken Seriously]," *People's Daily* (May 20, 1951).

50. Zedong Mao, "Yinggai Zongshi Dianying 'Wuxun Zhuan.'"

51. Enlai Zhou, "The fruitful experience of studying Soviet Film makes (us) even better able to serve the people," 1950. Cited in Chen, *Internationalism and Cultural Experience*, 111.

52. Pang, "Between Will and Negotiation," 474.

53. "Shanghai Film Studio [Shanghai Dianying Zhipianchang)]," in *Zhongguo Dakaike Quanshu Zongbianji Weiyuanhui "Dianying" Bianji Weiyuanhui*, ed. China Encyclopedia: Film [Zhongguo Dabaike Quanshu: Dianying] (Beijing: China Encyclopedia Press, 1998), 46.

54. "Shanghai Film Studio," 46.

55. For a more detailed account of the specialties of various studios, see George Semsel's "China," in *The Asian Film Industry*, ed. John A. Lent (London: Christopher Helm, 1990), 11–33.

56. George Semsel, "China."

57. Lida Oukaderova, *Cinema of Soviet Thaw: Space, Materiality, and Movement* (Bloomington: Indiana University Press, 2017).

58. By Josephine Woll, a scholar on Russian film. See Chris Fujiwara, "The Cranes Are Flying: A Free Camera," *Criterion Collection* (March 27, 2020), www .criterion.com/current/posts/200-the-cranes-are-flying-a-free-camera.

59. Letterboxd, "The Cranes Are Flying," Letterboxd.com, n.d., letterboxd.com /film/the-cranes-are-flying.

60. Wenhua Li, *Wangshi Liuying: Li Wenhua de Dianying Rensheng* [The Past with Trace-Li Culture's Film Life] (Beijing: Huawen Press, 2011), 115.

61. Chris Fujiwara, "The Cranes Are Flying: A Free Camera," March 27, 2020, https://www.criterion.com/current/posts/200-the-cranes-are-flying-a-free-camera.

62. Fujiwara, "The Cranes Are Flying."

63. Li, *Wangshi Liuying*, 99–100.

64. Li, *Wangshi Liuying*, 112.

65. Fujiwara, "The Cranes Are Flying."

66. Martina Petkova, "'Hundred Flowers' Campaign: Communist China's Deadly Flirtation with Free Speech," *History of Yesterday* (July 30, 2020), history ofyesterday.com/hundred-flowers-campaign-communist-chinas-deadly-flirtation -with-free-speech-5873317184df.

67. Sovexportfilm was a Soviet corporation that handled the international circulation of Soviet films.

68. Guangxi Dai, "Dai Guangxi Fangtanlu [Interview with Dai Guangxi]," in *Yinhaifujie: Xuren Juan* [Floating on the Silver Sea: Volume on Scholars] (Minzu Press, 2011), 27–32.

69. Zhouyi Wang, *Revolutionary Cycles in Chinese Cinema, 1951–1979* (New York: Palgrave Macmillan, 2014).

70. Mia Yinxing Liu, *Literati Lenses: Wenren Landscape in Chinese Cinema of the Mao Era* (Honolulu: University of Hawai'i Press, 2019).

71. Liu, *Literati Lenses*, 111.

72. (Xinzhongguo ershier da mingxing.)

73. Li, *Wangshi Liuying*, 142–143.

74. Liu, *Literati Lenses*, 39.

75. The film would be rehabilitated in 1978 and sent to represent China at the Cannes Film Festival in 1979.

76. Sina Culture, "Jiyi de Shenhua: 80 Niandai Yizhipian Yu Huaijiu [The Myth of Memory: Dubbed Films and Nostalgia in 1980s]," cul.sina.cn, October 21, 2015, cul.sina.cn/wh/2015-10-21/culzl-ifxizetf7775970.d.html?vt=4&cid=97157&node_id=97157.

77. The veteran filmmaker Xie Tieli directed the movie.

78. "家住安源"

79. *China Daily*, "Cultural Comeback of Modern Peking Opera," China.org.cn (June 18, 2005), www.china.org.cn/english/2005/Jun/132400.htm.

80. Tiedong Zhou, "Xinzhongguo dianying duiwai jiaoliu [Foreign Exchanges of Chinese Cinema in New China]," *Dianying Yishu* [Film Art], no. 1 (2002): 113–118.

81. The quotation is originally from the *Hollywood Reporter*, quoted in Matthew Roe, "Anarchic Cinema: Salt of the Earth," *Film Inquiry* (February 12, 2019), www.filminquiry.com/anarchic-cinema-salt-of-the-earth.

82. Bosley Crowther, "*Salt of the Earth* Opens at Grande—Filming Marked by Violence," *New York Times* (March 15, 1954).

83. "Salt of the Earth (1954 film)," *Wikipedia*, https://en.wikipedia.org/wiki/Salt_of_the_Earth_(1954_film)#cite_note-22.

84. Zhou, "Xinzhongguo dianying,"113–118.

4. Internal Reference Films and the Never Vanishing Hollywood Presence in China

1. Shuying Zhou and Liuen Zhao, "Baojian hushi tan Jiang Qing (xu) [Health Nurses Talking About Jiang Qing (Continued)]," interview by Changgui Yan and Yufeng Li, *Yanhuang Chunqiu*, no. 5 (2014): 45.

2. Shuo Wang, *Dong Wu Xiong Meng* [Wild Beasts] (Beijing: Zhong Guo Dian Ying Chu Ban She, 2004).

3. The movie apparently failed to aid Lin in his coup, and the private plane carrying him and his entourage crashed in Mongolia on September 13, 1971, as the group tried to escape. Xiu Su, *Wo de Peiyin Shengya* [My Life of Dubbing] (Shanghai: Wen Hui Chu Ban She, 2005), 14–17.

4. Zhou and Zhao, "Health Nurses," 41–46.

5. Zhou and Zhao, "Health Nurses," 41–46.

6. Yunyou Kan Tianxia, "Peng Li Peng Wai: Yibu Shaghai Yizhichang de Linglei Lishi [In and Out of the Studio: Different History of Shanghai Dubbing Studio]," 360doc, July 16, 2017, www.360doc.com/content/17/0706/19/30458787_669398646 .shtml.

7. Yunyou Kan Tianxia, "Peng Li Peng Wai."

8. "China Focus: Kept in Translation: A Company's 60 Years in Bringing Foreign Films to China—Xinhua | English.news.cn," Xinhua (March 31, 2017), www.xinhuanet.com//english/2017-03/31/c_136174478.htm.

9. Dong Ding, "Huiwang Neicanpian [Looking Back at Reference Films]," blog.sina, 2014, blog.sina.com.cn/s/blog_5faa5a2a0100zcfi.html.

10. Hongxing Fu, "Zhongguo Dianying Ziliaoguan Guanzhong Qunluo de Yanbian Ji Qi Jiaoyucelue [The Changes of the Audience of Chinese Film Database and Its Education Strategy]," *Dangdai Dianying* [Contemporary Cinema], no. 4 (2009): 37. See also Wenhua Li, *Wangshi Liuying: Li Wenhua de Dianying Rensheng* [The Past with Trace-Li Culture's Film Life] (Huawen Press, 2011), 113.

11. Chusheng Cai, *Cai Chusheng Wenji* [Cai Chusheng Collection], vol. 3 (Beijing: Zhongguo Guangbo Dianshi Chubanshe [Chinese Broadcasting and Television Publication], 2006), 161–341.

12. Guangxi Dai, "Yike Xiangwang Zhen, Shan, Mei de Xin: Yi Huangmei Tongzhi [A Heart for Truth, Goodness, and Beauty: My Memories on Comrade Huangmei]," *Dangdai Dianying* [Contemporary Film], no. 1 (2004).

13. Other titles include *The Day the Earth Caught Fire* (Val Guest, 1961), *The Naked Island* (Kaneto Shindo, 1960), *Twin Sisters of Kyoto* (Noboru Nakamura, 1963), *Miss Julie* (Alf Sjöberg, 1951), *08/15* (Paul May, 1954), *Marty* (Delbert Mann, 1955), *The Secret Code* (Lucian Bratu, 1960), *First Year* (Witold Lesiewicz, 1960), *Shadow* (Jerzy Kawalerowicz, 1956), *Night Train* (Jerzy Kawalerowicz, 1959), *Higher Principle* (Jiří Krejčík, 1960), and *Tamango* (John Berry, 1958); see Chusheng Cai, *Cai Chusheng Wenji* [Cai Chusheng Collection], vol. 3 (Beijing: Zhongguo Guangbo Dianshi Chubanshe [Chinese Broadcasting and Television Publication], 2006), 161–341.

14. Xiu Su, *Wo de Peiyin Shengya* [My Life of Dubbing] (Shanghai: Wen Hui Chu Ban She, 2005), 14–17.

15. "沪内一至八号"

16. Shuying Zhou and Liuen Zhao, Baojian hushi tan Jiang Qing (xu) [Health Nurses Talking About Jiang Qing (Continued)], interview by Changgui Yan and Yufeng Li, *Yanhuang Chunqiu*, 2014.

17. Guangxi Dai, "Dai Guangxi Fangtanlu [Interview with Dai Guangxi]," in *Yinhaifujie: Xuren Juan* [Floating on the Silver Sea: Volume on Scholars] (Minzu Press, 2011), 27–32.

18. Zhen Li, *An Oral History of Film Culture in China* (Beijing: Minzu Chuban-she [Ethnic Press], 2011).

19. See Koukou, "Fanchuashoumen Bikan de Dianying, Jiang Qiang de Neican-pian [A Must-See Film for Sailors, Jiang Qing's Reference Film]," *Douban* (February 15, 2016), movie.douban.com/review/7774720.

20. *Economic Observer*, "Hong Wuxie de Youhuo [The Seduction of *The Red Dancing Shoes*]," finance.sina.com.cn (June 21, 2013), finance.sina.com.cn/roll/20130621/235315877951.shtml.

21. Adrienne L. McLean, "The Red Shoes Revisited," *Dance Chronicle* 11, no. 1 (January 1987): 31–83, doi.org/10.1080/01472528708568965.

22. "Liu Qingtang," baike.baidu.com, n.d., baike.baidu.com/item/%E5%88%98%E5%BA%86%E6%A3%A0#1.

23. Danhuangliu, "Jiangqing de Liangren Mishu: Gaosuniyige Zhenshi de Ji-angqing [Jiang Qing's Two Secretaries: To Tell You a Real Jiang Qing]," bbs.wenxuecity.com, February 23, 2015, bbs.wenxuecity.com/jiangqing/692442.html.

24. Yu Zhang, "Fangwen Zheli de Liming Jingqiaoqiao de Zuozhe [Interview with the Author of *The Dawns Here Are Quiet*]," *Shijie Wenxue [World Literature]*, no. 5 (1984): 280–93.

25. Baochang Zhang, Zhongnanhai neibu dianying [Zhongnanhai Internal Film], interview by Shixian Zhang, *Chuancheng*, no. 7 (2010): 41.

26. Zhou and Zhao, "Health Nurses," 41–46.

27. Wenhua Li, *Wangshi Liuying: Li Wenhua de Dianying Rensheng*, 99–100.

28. Jingxian Xu, *Shinian Yimeng—Qian Shanghai Shiwei Shuji Xu Jingxian Wenge Huiyilu* [Ten Years a Dream—Memoirs of Former Shanghai Municipal Party Secretary Xu Jingxian of the Cultural Revolution] (Hong Kong: Time Publishing, 2006), 339.

29. "文艺特档库"

30. "十三号库" Shanshan Ding, "'Neicanpian' de Fangying Jiqi Dui Xinzhongguo Dianying de Yingxiang [The Screening of 'Reference Film' and Its Influence on Chinese Cinema]," *Wenyi Yanjiu* [Literary and Artistic Studies], no. 8 (2016): 103–114.

31. China Film Publishing, *"Si Ren Bang" Shi Dianying Shiye de Sidi* [The "Gang of Four" Is the Mortal Enemy of the Film Industry] (Beijing: Zhongguo Dianying chubanshe [China Film Publishing], 1978), 194–197.

32. "Jiang Zemin Yiyu Ling Ziaoli Wei Zhongguo Yingmi Suo Shuzhi [Jiang Zemin's Words Made Xiao Li Well Known to Chinese Cinephiles]," info.vanpeople .com (March 2, 2016), info.vanpeople.com/524416.html.

33. Ronglai Zheng, "Kan Neibu Dianying [Watching Internal Films]," *Qunyan*, no. 8 (2011): 41.

34. Xiaoou Sun, "Wo de Neibu Dianying Qingjie [My Complex on Internal Films]," *Beijing Jishi*, no. 10 (2009): 82.

35. "Some of the meetings convened by the central ministries and commissions in Beijing also asked people to watch the internal reference films, and some watched the poisonous films without criticism, and the scope is wide." Ding, "Neicanpian," 108.

36. J. Hoberman, "Forgotten Masterpiece: Antonioni's Travelogue from China," *New York Times* (December 28, 2017), www.nytimes.com/2017/12/28/movies/chung -kuo-cina-antonioni-moma-forgotten-masterpiece-a-china-travelogue.html.

37. Shuyun, "Jiemi Wenge Qijian Xifang Daoyan Laihua Pai Jilupian Guocheng [Western Directors Came to China to Make Documentaries During the Cultural Revolution]," news.sina.com.cn (August 14, 2007), news.sina.com.cn/c/2007-08-14 /203713662595.shtml.

38. Ross Terrill, *The New Chinese Empire: And What It Means for the United States* (New York: Cornelia And Michael Bessie, 2004), 294.

39. Elaine Yau, "Revisiting Chung Kuo, Antonioni's 1972 Film Shot in Communist China," *South China Morning Post* (March 18, 2019), www.scmp.com/lifestyle /arts-culture/article/3002134/chung-kuo-revisited-how-antonionis-1972 -documentary.

40. John Watkins, "Jizhe Laihong: Gongchandang Paide Naxie 'Yangbanxi' Zenmeban [Journalist Lai Hong: What About Those 'Model Films' Made by the Communist Party?]," *BBC News* (March 1, 2018), www.bbc.com/zhongwen/simp/fooc -43155512.

41. See Clarence Tsui, "Why Albanian Films Are Big in China: Cultural Revolution Nostalgia," *Exit News* (April 1, 2017), exit.al/en/2017/04/01/why-albanian-film s-are-big-in-china-cultural-revolution-nostalgia.

42. Tsui, "Why Albanian Films Are Big in China."

43. See Paul Clark, *Youth Culture in China: From Red Guards to Netizens* (Cambridge: Cambridge University Press, 2012).

44. Yubao Gu, "Tuji Yizhi Maihua Guniang [Blitz Dubbing of *The Flower Girl*]," *Tianjing Daily* (October 7, 2008).

45. Jingqin Tian, *Beijing dianying ye shiji, 1949–1990* [Achievements of the Beijing Film Industry] (Beijing: Zhongguo dianying chubanshe, 1999).

46. Paul Fischer, *A Kim Jong-Il Production: Kidnap, Torture, Murder . . . Making Movies North Korean–Style* (London: Penguin Books, 2016).

47. Gu, "Blitz Dubbing of *The Flower Girl*."

48. "Jin Richeng Yuanchuang '*Maihua Guniang*' Wuyue Shanghai Changxiang 'Maihuage' [Kim Il-Sung Original Opera *The Flower Girl* Was Shown in Shanghai in May]," Sohu Yule (March 26, 2008), yule.sohu.com/20080326/n255919204 .shtml.

49. "Maihua Gunian" [The Flower Girl], ent.sina.com.cn (February 19, 2008), ent .sina.com.cn/x/2008-02-19/01431915365.shtml.

50. "Das Blumenmädchen (the Flowergirl)," nordkorea-info.de, n.d., www.nordkorea -info.de/das-blumenmaedchen--the-flowergirl-.html.

51. "Dianying Yinyue Zhisheng Peiyin Yihanpoduo [Regrets in the Dubbing of *The Sound of Music*]," ent.sina.com.cn (March 12, 2008), ent.sina.com.cn/m/f/2008-03-12/03441944977.shtml.

52. Fu, "Zhongguo dianying ziliaoguan," 38.

53. Andor Genesis, "Yexu Nide Fumu Bi Ni Haizao Jiu Kanguo Xibu Shijie He Weilai Shijie Le [Maybe Your Parents Have Seen Westworld and Futureworld Earlier Than You]," web.archive.org (September 10, 2017).

54. "Wenge Hou Shoubu Denglu Zhognguo de Waiguo Dianying Xi Gaocang Jian Zhuyan [The First Foreign Film to Land in China After the Cultural Revolution Starred Ken Takakura]," news.sohu.com (November 18, 2014), news.sohu.com/ 20141118/n406138676.shtml.

55. "Manhunt (1976)," Letterboxd, letterboxd.com/film/manhunt-1976.

56. China Film was responsible for translating dialogue before passing film prints to be re-voiced by one of the dubbing studios.

57. There have been increasing demands in recent years from the Chinese audiences in major cities to have imported foreign films subtitled instead of dubbed.

58. "Golden Dubbing Age Falls on Deaf Ears," *China Daily* (December 19, 2003), www.chinadaily.com.cn/en/doc/2003-12/19/content_291801.htm.

59. Tom Shales, "*Man from Atlantis* Fitting for Saturday Morning Slot," *Washington Post* (September 23, 1977).

60. "Zai Mao Zhuxi Geming Luxian Zhiyin Xia [Under the Guidance of Chairman Mao's Revolutionary Line]," *People's Daily* (December 22, 1968): 1.

61. In the late 1970s, the scar literature movement, the first public exploration of the cost of the Cultural Revolution, included writings that described the experiences of the sent-down youth.

62. "Jialisen Gansidui [Garrison's Gorillas]," Wikipedia, zh.wikipedia.org/wiki.

63. Mengduo, "Meiju Shenme Shihou Chuanru Zhongguo [When Did American Shows Come to China]," daily.zhihu.com (June 29, 2014), daily.zhihu.com/story/3998163.

64. Shiding Tang, *Zhongyang Dianshitai de Diyi Yu Bianqian* [CCTV's Initials and Changes] (Beijing: Dongfang Chubanshe [Orient Publishing], 2003).

65. "Jialisen Gansidui Tingbo Muhou [Behind the Shutdown of Garrison's Gorillas]," news.ifeng (December 8, 2012), news.ifeng.com/history/1/midang/200803/0321_2664_452162.shtml.

66. Julian Baum, "Rambo Busts Through China's 'Open Door,'" *Christian Science Monitor* (October 15, 1985), www.csmonitor.com/1985/1015/oram.html.

67. Personal interview with an anonymous viewer.

68. Personal interview with an anonymous viewer.

69. Personal interview with an anonymous viewer.

70. Lishikong, "Cong Huihuang Dao Shiluo: Shanghai Dianying Yizhichang de 60nian [From Flourishment to Decline: The 60 Years of Shanghai Dubbing Studio]," *Jiemian* (June 6, 2017), m.jiemian.com/article/1303181.html.

71. Ying Zhu and Seio Nakajima, "The Evolution of Chinese Film as an Industry," in *Art, Politics, and Commerce in Chinese Cinema*, ed. Ying Zhu and Stanley Rosen (Hong Kong: Hong Kong University Press, 2010).

72. For a detailed account of the evolution of China Film, see Emilie Yueh-yu Yeh and Darrell William Davis, "Re-Nationalizing China's Film Industry: Case Study on the China Film Group and Film Marketization," *Journal of Chinese Cinemas* 2, no. 1 (January 2008): 37–51.

73. Zhen Ni, ed., *Reform and Chinese Cinema* [Gaige Yu Zhongguo Dianying] (Beijing: China Film Press, 1994), 45–46.

5. Wolves at the Doorstep: Hollywood Reenters China

1. Douglas Gomery, "The House That Jack Built: How Valenti Brought Hollywood to the World," *The Nation* (April 3, 2000): 41.

2. David M. Halbfinger, "Jack Valenti, 85, Confidant of a President and Stars, Dies," *New York Times* (April 27, 2007), www.nytimes.com/2007/04/27/movies/27valenti.html.

3. Ting Wang, "Hollywood's Crusade in China Prior to China's WTO Accession," *Jump Cut: A Review of Contemporary Media* 49, no. 1 (2007).

4. "Culture Joins Cash Resistance to U.S. Films in Red China," *Variety* 295, no. 2 (June 27, 1979).

5. "Open Door Policy," BBC News, news.bbc.co.uk/2/shared/spl/hi/asia_pac/02/china_party_congress/china_ruling_party/key_people_events/html/open_door_policy.stm.

6. Tiedong Zhou, "Xinzhongguo Dianying Duiwai Jiaoliu [Foreign exchanges of Chinese cinema in New China]," *Dianying Yishu* [Film Art] 1 (2002): 113–118.

7. Tiedong Zhou, "Xinzhongguo Dianyig Duiwai Jiaoliu."

8. Gwynn Guilford, "The Expatriate Presence in Urban Centers that has Boomed Since the Late 1990s Adds Demand. Illegal Online Streaming Since the 2000s," *Asia Times* (April 1, 2007), www.atimes.com/atimes/China_Business/IA04Cb01.html.

9. Wang, "Hollywood's Crusade."

10. See IIPA website (www.iipa.com), under "Copyright and Trade Issues."

11. Shujen Wang, *Framing Piracy: Globalization and Film Distribution in Greater China* (Lanham, MD: Rowman & Littlefield), 77–79.

12. Shujen Wang, *Framing Piracy*.

13. Zhen Ni, *Gaige Yu Zhongguo Dianying* [Reform and Chinese Cinema] (Beijing: Zhongguo Dianying Chubanshe [China Film Press], 1994), 50.

14. Nicholas D. Kristof, "China Applauds as Its Officials Plunge into Profit," *New York Times* (April 6, 1993): 6.

15. Nicholas D. Kristof, "China Applauds."

16. For a more detailed account of the crisis and reform in the Chinese film sector, see Ying Zhu, "Chinese Cinema's Economic Reform from the mid-1980s to the mid-1990s," *Journal of Communication* 52, no. 4 (2002): 905–921; and Ying Zhu, *Chinese Cinema During the Era of Reform—The Ingenuity of the System* (Connecticut and London: Westport, 2003).

17. Fang Cheng, "Dianying de yongtan [Film Speaks]," *China Film Market* no. 8 (1997).

18. Congming Tian (former minister of SARFT), "Zhazhu jiyu, shenhua gaige, fanrong dianying shiye-zai quanguo guangbo yingshi xuanchuan gongzuo huiyi shang de jianghua [Seize Opportunities, Deepen Reforms, and Revitalize Chinese Cinema]," speech at the national film and television working conference, *Zhongguo dianying bao* [China Film News] (March, 1, 1994): 3.

19. "Wu Mengchen Tan Zhongying De Gaige Silu [Wu Mengchen on the Reform of China Film]," *Zhongguo Dianying Bao* [China Film News] (March 3, 1994): 1.

20. Wang, "Hollywood's Crusade."

21. T.L. Stanley, "Hollywood Heads East: China's Two-Legged Sword Is Opportunity Tinged with Risk and Procedural Headaches," *Brandweek* (January 28, 1996): 37–38.

22. Stanley Rosen. "The Wolf at the Door: Hollywood and the Film Market in China," in *Southern California and the World*, eds. Eric J. Heikkila and Rafael Pizarro (Westport, CT, and London: Praeger, 2002), 49–77.

23. Zhou, *Xinzhongguo Dianying*, 118.

24. Don Groves, "WB Inks China Deal," *Variety* (September 13, 1994).

25. Yang Lin, "Shouyingri Haibao Xieshang Fengxian Shangying [Risky Release Written on the Premiere's Poster]," *Sina News* (December 19, 2008), .news .sina.com.cn/c/2008-12-19/091616880301.shtml.

26. Yang Lin, "Shouyingri Haibao."

27. "Wangmingtianya daigei zhongguo dianying de qishi [What Chinese Commercial Films Can Learn from *The Fugitive*]," *Zhongguo dianying bao* [China Film News] (December 22, 1994): 2.

28. Don Groves, "'Fugitive' Off and Running at Chinese B.O.," *Daily Variety* (November 28–December 4, 1994): 48.

29. Don Groves, "Golden Harvest Sets Chinese Distrib Deals," *Daily Variety* (November 29, 1994): 4. Zhou, *Xinzhongguo Dianying*, 118.

30. Zhou, *Xinzhongguo Dianying*, 118.

31. Rosen, *The Wolf at the Door*, 49–77.

32. G. Song. "Sketches of Chinese Film of 1994," *Drama and Film News* (February 10, 1995) (in Chinese).

33. Peter Behr, "U.S. Threatens Chinese Over Pirated Movies, CDs; Trade Sanctions Could Exceed $1 Billion." *Washington Post* (January 1, 1995): A27.

34. Andrew Bilski and Alison Nankivell, "Trade War," *MacLean's* (February 20, 1995): 18.

35. Seth Faison, "U.S. and China Sign Accord to End Piracy of Software, Music Recordings and Film," *New York Times* (February 27, 1995): A1.

36. Seth Faison, "U.S. and China Sign Accord."

37. Reuters, "'True Lies' a Hit in Chinese Debut," *SFGate* (April 24, 1995), www .sfgate.com/entertainment/article/True-Lies-a-Hit-in-Chinese-Debut-3035799.php.

38. Emilie Yueh-yu Yeh and Darrell William Davis, "Renationalizing China's Film Industry: Case Study on China Film Group and Film Marketization," *Journal of Chinese Cinemas*, no. 1 (2008): 40.

39. See Berry's article in Stringer regarding *dapian*: Chris Berry, "What's Big About the Big Film? 'De-Westernizing' the Blockbuster in Korea and China," in *Movie Blockbusters*, ed. Julian Stringer (Oxford and New York: Routledge, 2003), 217–229.

40. A detailed comparative analysis of the process of "de-Westernization" of blockbusters in China and South Korea is available in Berry, "What's Big About the Big Film?"

41. Tongdao Zhang, "Kuayue Xuanhua: 1995 Nian Zhongguo Dianying Huigu [A Retrospective of Chinese Cinema in 1995]," *Dianying Yishu* [Film Art] 3 (1996): 23.

42. Lao Mei, "Guochan Dianying: Shuguang He Yinyang [Domestic Films: Dawn and Shadow]," *Dianying Yishu* [Film Art], 2 (1996): 44.

43. Cheng, *Dianying De Yongtan* [Film Speaks], 10. Anthony Kuhn, "Raising the Red Curtain," *Los Angeles Times* (October 17, 1995): D1, 7.

44. The term "big picture consciousness" is taken from Zhang, "Kuayue xuanhua," 23.

45. Thomas Real, "Chinese Directors Back U.S. Films," *United Press International* (April 16, 1995).

46. Guanghui Cao, "Duochu jingpin, zaichuang huihuang [Produce More High-Quality Works and Create Glories Again]," *Liaowang* [Outlook] 16 (1996): 31–33.

47. Zemin Jiang, "A Speech on the Sixth National Conference of the China Federation of Literary and Art Circles and the Fifth National Conference of the Chinese Writers Association," in *China Film Yearbook 1997* (Beijing: Zhongguo Dianying Chubanshe, 1997), x, 1–3.

48. Tong Gang, "Grab the Opportunity; Make Good Plans Together; Promote a Prosperous Film Industry in China," in *China Film Yearbook 1997* (Beijing: Zhongguo Dianying Chubanshe, 1997), 38–42.

49. Guangen Ding, "Produce More Outstanding Works; Prosper Chinese Film Industry," in *China Film Yearbook 1997* (Beijing: Zhongguo Dianying Chubanshe, 1997), 7–10.

50. Zhiqiang Wang, "A Summary on 1995 Imports," in *China Film Yearbook 1996* (Beijing: Zhongguo Dianying Chubanshe, 1996), 203–205.

51. Jianghua Fan, Mao Yu, and Yang Yuan, "96 Zhongguo dianying shichang zongshu [A Comprehensive Report of the 1996 Chinese Film Market]," *Zhongguo Dianying Shichang* [Chinese Film Market], no. 1, 5.

52. Kerry Segrave, *American Films Abroad: Hollywood's Domination of the World's Movie Screens from the 1890s to the Present* (Jefferson, NC: McFarland Publishing, 1997), chapter 2.

53. Dennis Wharton, "Showbiz Org Lobbies for China Piracy Crackdown," *Daily Variety* (February 8, 1996): 21.

54. Wang, *Framing Piracy*.

55. Statement of Jack Valenti, Chairman and CEO, MPA, before the Special 301 Committee, 1996. MPAA Press Release, June 6, 1996.

56. Weng Li, "Tainannikehao shichang xianxiang de qishi [Inspirations from the Market Phenomenon of *Titanic*]," *Zhongguo Dianying Shichang* [Chinese Film Market] 6 (1998): 5–6.

57. Emily Parker, "'Titanic' Takes China by Storm Following Jiang's Endorsement," *Wall Street Journal* (April 14, 1998), www.wsj.com/articles/SB8924953 19302117000.

58. Qiang Mao, "1998 nian meiguo fenzhangpian quanguo shichang fenxi [Analysis of the 1998 Nationwide Market for American Revenue-Sharing Films]," *Zhongguo*

Dianying Shichang [Chinese Film Market] 41 (1999): 6–7. Lin Xi, "Qishi yu sikao [Revelations and Reflections]," *Zhongguo Dianying Shichang* [Chinese Film Market] 12, 7.

59. Raymond Zhou, "Confucius Loses His Way," *China Daily* (January 1, 2020), www.chinadaily.com.cn/life/2010-01/29/content_9396402.htm.

60. Shi Zhao, "Accelerate the Promotion of the Reformation and Development of the Film Industry," *China Film Yearbook 2003* (Beijing: China Film Yearbook Press, 2003), 25–32.

61. A trip was also organized to Singapore.

62. "Heshi caiyou zhongguodianying de hangkongmujian? [Impressions of Managers of China's Urban Theaters on Visiting the U.S.]," *China Film Yearbook 1998/1999* (Beijing, China Film Yearbook Press, 1999), 435–436.

63. Ji Yang, "Zhongguo dianying faxing fangying xiehuiÄzhongguo chengshi yingyuan fazhan xiehui lianhe juban dianying yuanxian zuotanhui [A Seminar on the Theater Chain System]," *China Film Yearbook 2003* (Beijing, China Film Yearbook Press, 2003), 254.

64. "A Renewed Understanding of American Blockbuster Films," *Chinese Education and Society* 36, no. 1 (2003): 48–54.

65. Sharon Waxman, "China Bans Work with Film Studios," *Washington Post* (November 1, 1997), www.washingtonpost.com/archive/lifestyle/1997/11/01/china-bans-work-with-film-studios/9f3a23e3-4d83-4749-898c-bd1fef276f03.

66. Jack Valenti, *A Grand Confluence: The Intersection of Storytellers from East and West: A Reciting of the Fruitful Results of an Asian/American Cinema Collaboration* (speech at CineAsia, Singapore), MPAA Press Release (December 3, 1997).

67. Christopher Stern, "China, Hollywood Hug and Thaw Out," *Variety* (November 4, 1997): 17–23.

68. Susan Hogan, "In and Of the Moment," *Dallas Morning News* (September 11, 2004), www.dallasnews.com/sharedcontent/dws/dn/religion/stories/091104dnrel mindfulness.9f417.html.

69. Bernard Weinraub, "At the Movies: Disney Hires Kissinger," *New York Times* (October 10, 1997): E1: 7.

70. John Bleasdale, "Kundun: Scorsese's Buried Masterpiece," Film School Rejects (March 15, 2018), filmschoolrejects.com/kundun-scorseses-buried-masterpiece.

71. James Bates and Maggie Farley, "Hollywood, China in a Chilly Embrace," *Los Angeles Times* (June 13,1999): A1, A30.

72. Lisa Wehrstedt, "Disney's Classic 'Mulan' Flopped in China Because Audiences Didn't Think the Heroine Looked Chinese Enough," *Insider* (June 26, 2020), www.insider.com/disney-classic-mulan-flopped-china-audiences-didnt-think-she-looked-chinese-enough-2020-6.

73. Naomi Xu Elegant, "Disney Tailored 'Mulan' for China. It Still 'Never Had a Chance' at the Mainland Box Office," *Fortune* (September 20, 2020), fortune .com/2020/09/20/disney-mulan-2020-china-box-office-flop.

74. Bruce Orwall, "MGM Clashes with Richard Gere over Politics of 'Red Corner' Film," *Wall Street Journal* (November 3, 1997).

75. Tatiana Siegel, "Richard Gere's Studio Exile: Why His Hollywood Career Took an Indie Turn," *Hollywood Reporter* (April 18, 2017), www.hollywoodreporter .com/features/richard-geres-studio-exile-why-his-hollywood-career-took-an-indie -turn-992258.

76. Segrave, *American Films Abroad*, chapter 2.

77. O.R. Geyer, "Winning Foreign Film Markets," *Scientific American* 125, no. 8 (1921): 132.

78. Ying Zhu, "Commercialism and Nationalism: Chinese Cinema's First Wave of Entertainment Films," *CineAction* 47, summer (1998): 58.

79. Valenti, *A Grand Confluence*.

80. Xuan Ying, "Jiaqi guochan yingpian zouxiang haiwai de qiaoliang—'Beijing fangying' huodong jishi [Setting Up the Bridge Leading Domestic Films to Overseas Markets—Coverage of 'Beijing Screen']," *Zhongguo dianying shichang* [Chinese Film Market] 6, (1998): 1.

81. Gei taitai dagong.

82. Segrave, *American Films Abroad*.

83. Ying Xing, "Huimou 1998 zhongguo dianying shichang [Looking Back at the 1998 Chinese Film Market]," *Shichang bao* [Market Daily] (January 13, 1999): 3.

84. The record would later be surpassed by *Titanic* 3-D in 2012, which grossed RMB 946 million.

85. Xing, *Huimou 1998*, 3.

86. Mao, *1998 nian meiguo*, 6.

87. Du Gao, "Wending junxin, gongdu nanguan-jiujiu shangbannian dianying shichang ganyan [Stabilizing Morale, Surmounting Difficulties Together—Reflections on the Film Market in the First Half of 1999]," *Zhongguo dianying shichang* [Chinese Film Market] 7 (1999): 6.

88. Dongtian Zheng, "'To Be, or Not to Be?'—Jinru WTO yihou de zhongguo Dianying shengcun Fenxi [An Analysis on the Survival of the Chinese Film Industry After Entering into WTO]," *Film Art*, no. 2 (2000): 4–8.

89. Yongzhi Wang and Ren Yi, "The Embarrassment Caused by Importing Mega Films," *Chinese Sociology and Anthropology* 32, no. 1 (1999): 9.

90. Kehong Chen, "WTO yu xinshengdai [WTO and the New Generation of Filmmakers]," *Zhongguo dianying shichang* [Chinese Film Market], no. 1 (2002): 14–15.

91. Wang and Yi, "The Embarrassment," 9.

92. Dongtian Zheng, "Taitannike mantou [Titanic Steamed Bread]," *Zhongguo dianying shichang* [Chinese Film Market], no. 6 (1998): 7.

93. Dongtian Zheng, "Taitannike mantou."

94. Jinhua Dai, "Zhongguo dianying: zai kuaile zhong chenmo . . . [Chinese Film: Sinking in Happiness . . .]," *Xiandai chuanbo* [Modern Communications], no. 1 (1999): 22.

95. Jinhua Dai, "Zhongguo dianying," 21–22.

96. Jinhua Dai, "Zhongguo dianying," 21.

6. How Lucrative Is the Chinese Market: Politics Intervened

1. Jeremy Geltzer, "Censoring the Silk Screen: China's Precarious Balance Between State Regulation and a Global Film Market," *Journal of International Media & Entertainment Law* 6, no. 2, 2017.

2. "Hollywood: Sexports," *Time*, September 19, 1960.

3. Anthony Kuhn, "Raising the Red Curtain," *Los Angeles Times* (October 17, 1995): D1, 7.

4. Brooks Boliek, "China Film Fest Part of Détente," *Hollywood Reporter* (April 1, 1999).

5. Brooks Boliek, "China Film Fest."

6. Written testimony of Bonnie J.K. Richardson, vice president, Trade and Federal Affairs, MPAA, before the U.S.-China Commission public hearings on WTO compliance and sectoral issues, 2002. U.S. Department of State, January 18, 2002.

7. Goran Gocić, *Notes from the Underground: The Cinema of Emir Kusturica* (New York: Wallflower Press, 2001), 16.

8. Pavle Levi, *Disintegration in Frames: Aesthetics and Ideology in the Yugoslav and Post-Yugoslav Cinema* (Palo Alto, CA: Stanford University Press, 2007).

9. Statement of Jack Valenti, chairman and chief executive officer, Motion Picture Association of America, before the Committee on Ways and Means Subcommittee on Trade, regarding U.S.-China trade relations and the possible accession of China to the World Trade Organization, 1999. MPAA Press Release, June 8, 1999.

10. Statement of Jack Valenti, regarding U.S.-China trade relations.

11. "Valenti Supports Normal Trade Relations for China and WTO Accession Conditional on Market Access," MPAA Press Release, June 8, 1999.

12. Yabo Zeng, "Jiekai Haolaiwu de miansha [Pulling the Veil off Hollywood]," *Zhongguo dianying shichang* [Chinese Film Market], no. 7 (1999): 10.

13. Xin Yu, "Daodan xiji yu wenhua kuozhang [Missile Attack and Cultural Expansion]," *Zhongguo dianying shichang* [Chinese Film Market], no. 8 (1999): 8.

14. Don Groves, "Trade Push May Crack Great Wall for U.S. Pix," *Variety* (May 15–21, 2000): 75.

15. "Disney's 'Lion King' Comes Out Roaring in Theaters in China," *Wall Street Journal* (October 30, 1995).

16. James Bates and Maggie Farley, "Hollywood, China in a Chilly Embrace," *Los Angeles Times* (June 13, 1999): A1.

17. Bates and Farley, "Hollywood, China in a Chilly Embrace," A1, A30.

18. Jonathan Peterson, "Cultural Issues Color Movie Export Picture; Asia: Foreign Access to China's Film Industry Is One of Several Issues That Remain in Limbo as Trade Talks with the Country Have Hit Snags. Hollywood Seeks Much Greater Access to Its Market, but Chinese Leaders Are Wary of the Influence of Foreign Values," *Los Angeles Times* (October 31, 1999): 1.

19. T.L. Stanley, "Hollywood Heads East," *Brandweek* 37, no. 5: 37–38.

20. *Wall Street Journal*, "Disney's 'Lion King.'"

21. Thomas H. Guback, *The International Film Industry: Western Europe and America Since 1945* (Bloomington: Indiana University Press, 1969), 98.

22. Ying Zhang, "1998 nian jinkou yingpian shichang zongshu [A Comprehensive Report on the 1998 Market for Imported Films]," *China Film Yearbook* (Beijing: Zhongguo Dianying Chubanshe, 1998), 229–231.

23. Testimony of Ambassador Charlene Barshefsky before the House Committee on Ways and Means on China's WTO Accession and PNTR, 2000. American Embassy in China Press Release, May 3, 2000. In "Hollywood's Pre-WTO Crusade in China," Ting Wang covered aspects of the Sino-Hollywood WTO negotiations. See her article in *Jump Cut: A Review of Contemporary Media* 49 (spring 2007).

24. Dongtian Zheng, "'To Be, or Not to Be?'—Jinru WTO yihou de zhongguo Dianying shengcun Fenxi [An Analysis on the Survival of Chinese Film Industry After Entering into WTO]," *Film Art*, no. 2 (2000): 4–8.

25. Testimony of Ambassador Charlene Barshefsky.

26. Brooks Boliek, "China to Allow More U.S. Films," *Hollywood Reporter* (November 16, 1999).

27. World Trade Organization, *Legal Texts: GATT, 1947 (General Agreements on Tariff and Trade* (Geneva: World Trade Organization, 1947), www.wto.org/english /docs_e/legal_e/gatt47_01_e.htm.

28. Zeng, "Jiekai Haolaiwu de miansha," 10.

29. Wayne M. Morrison, "Issue Brief for Congress: China-U.S. Trade Issues," CRS (Congressional Research Service), March 14, 2002, fpc.state.gov/documents /organization/9061.pdf.

30. President Bill Clinton's Statement on House Action on Proposed Legislation to Extend Normal Trade Relations with China, July 27, 1999, www.govinfo.gov /content/pkg/PPP-1999-book2/html/PPP-1999-book2-doc-pg1337-2.htm.

31. Carl Bromley, "The House that Jack Built: How Valenti Brought Hollywood to the World," *The Nation* (April 3, 2000): 39–41.

32. Valenti urged the Senate to grant PNTR to China. See MPAA Press Release, April 11, 2000. This, of course, has remained a pipe dream.

33. Janet Hook, "Film Industry Lobbies for China Trade," *Times* (May 23, 2000).

34. Shujen Wang, *Framing Piracy: Globalization and Film Distribution in Greater China* (Lanham, MD: Rowman & Littlefield), 87.

35. Jingfu Li, "Daole zui weixian de shihou lema? [Are Domestic Films in Most Critical Situation?]," *Popular Cinema*, no. 15 (2004): 63.

36. SARFT and Ministry of Culture, "Some Opinions," 1–3; SARFT and Ministry of Culture, "The Detailed Regulations," 15–16.

37. SARFT and Ministry of Culture, "The Detailed Regulations to Implement Structural Reform of the Mechanism of Film Distribution and Exhibition, in *China Film Yearbook*," *China Film Yearbook 2002* (Beijing: Zhongguo Dianying Chubanshe, 2002), 15–16; SARFT and Ministry of Culture, "Some Opinions About Carrying Out Further the Reformation in the Film Industry," in *China Film Yearbook 2001* (Beijing: Zhongguo Dianying Chubanshe, 2001), 1–3.

38. Jeremy Geltzer. "Censoring the Silk Screen: China's Precarious Balance Between State Regulation and a Global Film Market," *Journal of International Media and Law*, no. 6.

39. SARFT and Ministry of Culture, "Some Opinions," 1–3.

40. SARFT and Ministry of Culture, "Some Opinions," 1.

41. Shi Zhao, "Accelerate the Promotion of the Reformation and Development of the Film Industry," *China Film Yearbook 2003* (Beijing: China Film Yearbook Press, 2003), 25–32.

42. *China Film Yearbook 2002* (Beijing: Zhongguo Dianying Chubanshe, 2002), 175.

43. Jianzhong Liu, "Dianying de rushi tanpan yu wo'men de chengnuo [WTO Negotiation with Regard to Film and Our Commitment]," *in WTO yu zhongguo dianying* [WTO and Chinese Cinema], eds. Zhenxin Zhang and Yuanying Yang (Beijing: Zhongguo dianying chubanshe, 2002), 3–8.

44. Tracy Liang, "History of China Import Film Quota and Revenue-Sharing Remittance," *GHJ Advisors* (April 20, 2017), www.greenhassonjanks.com/blog /history-of-china-import-film-quota-and-revenue-sharing-remittance.

45. "Zongshu: Huishou jinkou dapian banian fengyu licheng [A Comprehensive Retrospection on Eight Years' Vicissitudes of Imported Blockbusters in China],"

Nanfang Zhoumo [Southern Weekend] (March 2, 2002), yindw.com.cn/wintonews /200203/0302/news13011072.html.

46. Shi Zhao, "Creatively Fulfill the Target and Task of the New Era—a Talk on the National Film Work Forum," in *China Film Yearbook 2002* (Beijing: Zhongguo Dianying Chubanshe, 2002), 27.

47. Patrick Frater, "WB Bails on China Plexes," *Variety* (November 8, 2006), variety.com/2006/film/news/wb-bails-on-china-plexes-1117953593/?jwsource=cl.

48. This document was jointly issued by the SARFT, the Ministry of Culture, and the Ministry of Commerce; "Provisional Regulations of the Foreign Investment in Film Theaters," in *China Film Yearbook* (Beijing: Zhongguo Dianying Chubanshe, 2004), 18–19.

49. "Valenti testifies that China and Russia are top copyright violators, links piracy to organized crime and terrorism," MPAA Press Release, June 9, 2004.

50. Yin and Wang, "The Industry Year," 24. Sheila Melvin," From Operas to Blockbusters: China's 100 Years On-screen," *New York Times* (January 26, 2006), www.nytimes.com/2006/01/26/arts/from-operas-to-blockbusters-chinas-100 -years-on-screen.html.

51. Officially called "the Multiparty Cooperation and Political Consultation Under the Leadership of the Communist Party of China," the United Front is a political strategy of the CCP in building strong relationships with influential non-CCP groups and individuals to advance the party's interests in and outside China. Managed primarily by the United Front Work Department, the United Front effort has expanded its targets of influence under Xi Jinping. The department itself encompasses multiple subservient front organizations and affiliates within China and abroad.

52. F. Wang, "Zhongwai Hepaipian Yu Zhongguo Dianying Quanqiuhua Zhanlue [On Coproduction and the Strategy of China Film Globalization]," *Contemporary Cinema* (2012), 11.

53. Y. Weng, "Zhongmei Hepai Sanshi Nian [China-U.S. Co-Production for 30 Years]," *Movie*, no. 7 (2012): 60.

54. Wang, "Zhongwai Hepaipian Yu Zhongguo Dianying Quanqiuhua Zhanlue."

55. Weng, "Zhongmei Hepai," 64.

56. H. Yin and X. Wang, "The Industry Year of Chinese film," *Contemporary Cinema*, no. 2 (2005): 18–26 (in Chinese).

57. 《中外合作摄制电影片管理规定》

58. Ben Blanchard, "China Warns U.S. Piracy Case Will Harm Trade Tries," *Reuters* (April 24, 2007), www.reuters.com/article/us-china-piracy/china-warns -u-s-piracy-case-will-harm-trade-tries-idUSPEK10366920070424.

59. Nan Yu, "Sanping Baye: Zhongying Longduan Zhongguo Shichang [Sanping's Dominance: CMPC Monopolizes Chinese Film Market]," *Nanfang Renwu Zhoukan* [Southern People Weekly] (August 29, 2011), magazine.sina.com/gb/southernpeopleweekly/266/20110830/1841113416.html.

60. Li Li, "Han Sanping de Zuihou Shiming: Zhongying Shangshi [Han Sanping's Last Mission: CMPC Gets Listed]," *Sina Finance* (January 15, 2011), finance.sina.com.cn/stock/newstock/zxdt/20110115/00089257347.shtml.

61. L. Tang, *Women xuyao zenyang de dianying* [What Kinds of Film We Need] (Beijing: World Publishing Corp., 2012), 58–59.

62. L. Tang, *Women xuyao*, 54–55.

63. Huang, cited in Tang, *Women xuyao*, 61, 65.

64. Ren, cited in Tang, *Women xuyao*, 64.

65. Wang, *Zhongmei Hepai*, 38–53.

66. Jonathan Landreth, "Dan Glickman Prods China in Shanghai," *Hollywood Reporter* (June 14, 2009), www.hollywoodreporter.com/news/dan-glickman-prods-china-shanghai-85360.

67. Richard Verrier, "A Boost for U.S. Films in China?" *Los Angeles Times* (May 12, 2011): B4.

68. Yang Xiao, "Haolaiwu quanqiu gongchengluedi, zhongguodianying jinru beizhan zhuangtai [China Film Industry Prepares for Hollywood's Global Expansion]," *Beijing Youth Daily* (April 15, 2010), ent.ifeng.com/movie/news/mainland/detail_2010_04/15/526755_0.shtml.

69. Dominic Patten, "China Wants to See More 'Positive Chinese Images' from Hollywood, Government Coproduction Chief Tells Confab," *Deadline* (November 5, 2013), deadline.com/2013/11/china-film-us-china-film-summit-iron-man-3-627911.

70. Dominic Patten, "China Wants to See More."

71. Tracy Liang, "History of China Import Film Quota."

72. "China's Vice President Xi to Unveil Landmark Hollywood Deal," *China Times* (February 15, 2012), www.thechinatimes.com/online/2012/02/2275.html.

73. Daniel Ren, "Li Ruigang: Shanghai's Rising Media Star Set to Rejuvenate TVB," *South China Morning Post* (April 23, 2015), www.scmp.com/news/hong-kong/education-community/article/1774742/li-ruigang-shanghais-rising-media-star-set.

74. www.ghjadvisors.com/blog/history-of-china-import-film-quota-and-revenue-sharing-remittance.

75. Dave McNary, "'Jurassic World: Fallen Kingdom' Stomps to $34.4 Million Opening Day in China," *Variety* (July 15, 2018), variety.com/2018/film/news/jurassic-world-fallen-kingdom-china-box-office-opening-1202848103.

76. Josh Horowitz, "The 'Fast & Furious' Franchise Is Huge in China, but Probably Isn't Making Much Money There," *Quartz* (May 12, 2017), qz.com/981277/the-fast-furious-franchise-is-huge-in-china-but-probably-isnt-making-much-money-there.

77. Horowitz, "The 'Fast & Furious' Franchise."

78. Ying Zhu, "Here's How the Trade War Is Affecting Hollywood," *ChinaFile* (March 8, 2019), www.chinafile.com/reporting-opinion/viewpoint/heres-how-trade-war-affecting-hollywood.

79. Claire Atkinson, "Hollywood Spent Years Courting China. Now Trump's Tariffs Could Demolish Those Deals," NBC News (July 25, 2018), www.nbcnews.com/business/business-news/hollywood-spent-years-courting-china-now-trump-s-tariffs-could-n894051.

80. Patrick Brzeski, "Will Hollywood Get Caught in Trump's China Trade War Crossfire?" *Hollywood Reporter* (July 13, 2018), www.hollywoodreporter.com/news/will-hollywood-get-caught-trumps-china-trade-war-crossfire-1126182.

81. Brent Lang and Patrick Frater, "China Film Quota Talks Could Be a Casualty in Trump's Trade War," *Variety* (March 29, 2018), variety.com/2018/film/news/china-film-quota-hollywood-trump-trade-war-1202739283.

7. What Do the Chinese Watch: Popular Chinese Films Throughout the 2010s

1. Mike Hale, "Earthquakes and Seismic Suffering," *New York Times* (October 31, 2010), www.nytimes.com/2010/11/01/movies/01after.html.

2. It is a choice laden with the burden of Chinese culture that traditionally favors the son. The choice the fictional mother makes, predictable and inevitable to ordinary Chinese, traumatized my eleven-year-old American daughter who watched the film with me in Shanghai. My daughter has since developed a wariness if not apprehension of most PRC films except for comedies.

3. Maggie Lee, "Aftershock—Film Review," *Hollywood Reporter* (October 14, 2010), www.hollywoodreporter.com/news/aftershock-film-review-29834.

4. Wendy Su, *China's Encounter with Global Hollywood* (Lexington: University of Kentucky Press, 2016), 103.

5. Hale, "Earthquakes and Seismic Suffering."

6. Shuyu Kong, *Popular Media, Social Emotion and Public Discourse in Contemporary China* (London: Routledge, 2014).

7. Wei Li, "Tangshan da dizhen, yici zhuliu jiazhiguan de zhuti cehua [Aftershock: Producing a Film with Mainstream Values]," *Sanlian shenghuo zhoukan* [Sanlian Life Weekly], no. 29: 47.

8. Wei Li, "Tangshan da dizhen."

9. Rongrong Ma, "Yike jiao Feng Xiaogang de shu [A Growing Tree Called Feng Xiaogang]," *Sanlian shenghuo zhoukan* [Sanlian Life Weekly], no. 29 (2010): 62–65; Rongrong Ma, "Interview with Feng Xiaogang: I Believe That Kindness Is Strength," *Sanlian shenghuo zhoukan* [Sanlian Life Weekly], no. 29 (2010): 52–56.

10. Bruce Humes, "Zhang Ling's 'Aftershock': The Movie, the Screenwriter and the Part-Time Censor," Bruce Humes blog, July 28, 2010, bruce-humes.com/2010/07/28/zhang-lings-aftershock-the-movie-the-scriptwriter-and-the-part-time-censor.

11. Bruce Humes, "Zhang Ling's 'Aftershock.'"

12. Revealed to me during a private conversation I had with a censorship board member.

13. Bruce Humes, "Zhang Ling's 'Aftershock.'"

14. Kong, "Popular Media," 20.

15. Gary Rawnsley and Ming-Yeh T. Rawnsley, eds., *Global Chinese Cinema: The Culture and Politics of "Hero"* (London: Routledge, 2010).

16. Clifford Coonan, "China Sends 'Aftershock' to Oscars," *Variety* (September 27, 2010), variety.com/2010/biz/markets-festivals/china-sends-aftershock-to-oscars-1118024680.

17. Ma, Yike jiao Feng Xiaogang [Interview with Feng Xiaogang], 52–65.

18. Zhenyun Liu, "Memory Loss," *New York Times* (November 30, 2012), www.nytimes.com/2012/11/30/opinion/global/why-wont-the-chinese-acknowledge-the-1942-famine.html.

19. Liu, "Memory Loss."

20. White recounted the horrific famine in his 1946 book *Thunder Out of China* and in his 1978 autobiography *In Search of History: A Personal Adventure*. Theodore White and Annalee Jacoby, *Thunder Out of China* (New York: Da Capo Press, 1946); Theodore White, *In Search of History: A Personal Adventure* (New York: Warner Books, 1978).

21. "Xi Jinping: Zai Zhexue Shehui Kexu Zongzuo Zuotanhui Shang de Jianghua [Xi Jinping's Talk in the Forum on Philosophical and Social Science]," www.moe.gov.cn, May 19, 2016, www.moe.gov.cn/jyb_xwfb/moe_176/201605/t20160519_245223.html.

22. Chen was married to Du Xian, a popular CCTV prime-time news reader who was sacked in 1989 after expressing emotions in her reporting of the Tiananmen Square crackdown.

23. Ying Zhu, "The Same Old 'China Story' Keeps Chinese Sci-Fi Earthbound," *ChinaFile* (September 30, 2019), www.chinafile.com/reporting-opinion/culture/same-old-china-story-keeps-chinese-sci-fi-earthbound.

24. Ye Yuan, "Delayed Chinese War Drama 'The Eight Hundred' Cleared for Release," *Sixth Tone: Fresh Voices from Today's China* (August 3, 2020), www.sixthtone

.com/news/1006012/delayed-chinese-war-drama-the-eight-hundred-cleared-for
-release.

25. "Zhexie Dianying Zhide Yikan Ma? Dianying: Babai [Are These Films Worth Watching? Film: The Eight Hundred]," hznews.hangzhou.com.cn, August 22, 2020, hznews.hangzhou.com.cn/wenti/content/2020-08/22/content_7797730.htm.

26. Xan Brooks, "Back to 1942 Review," *The Guardian* (November 11, 2012), www.theguardian.com/film/2012/nov/11/back-to-1942-review.

27. "Film Review: Back to 1942," *Film Journal* (November 30, 2012), fj.webedia .us/content/film-review-back-1942.

28. Karen Chu, "Feng Xiaogang Unveils Epic 'Remembering 1942' at the Shanghai Film Festival," *Hollywood Reporter* (June 16, 2012), www.hollywoodreporter.com /news/feng-xiaogang-remembering-1942-shanghai-338567.

29. Karen Chu, "Feng Xiaogang Unveils Epic."

30. Patrick Frater, "China Sends 'Back to 1942' on Oscar Trail," *Variety* (October 6, 2013), variety.com/2013/film/news/china-sends-back-to-1942-on-oscar-trail -1200701403.

31. Weiying Peng, "China, Film Co-Production and Soft Power Competition," PhD diss. (Queensland University of Technology, 2015).

32. Omer M. Mozaffar, "Planes, Thailand and Automobiles," Roger Ebert review, February 6, 2013, www.rogerebert.com/reviews/lost-in-thailand-2012.

33. Xincheng Huang, "The Development of Comedy Films in Mainland China Since the New Century from Jiong Series," dissertation (Shanghai Normal University, 2020).

34. "2013 Nian Neidi Dianying Piaofang Zongpaihangbang [Top Box Office Chinese Movies in 2013]," 58921.com/alltime/2013.

35. Erich Schwartzel and Laurie Burkitt, "Lights! Camera! China! 'Transformers' Knows Its Audience," *Wall Street Journal* (June 26, 2014), www.wsj.com/articles /for-transformers-audience-action-is-in-china-1403805965.

36. Xiaolin Yingshi, "Gangjiong: Xu Zheng Zhijin Fage Yingxiongbense de Jingdian Pianduan [A Clip of *Lost in Hong Kong*: Xu Zheng's Tribute to a Better Tomorrow]," 163 Video, 3g.163.com/v/video/VNMC3U028.html.

37. Edmund Lee, "Will Local Audiences Warm to Chinese Filmmaker Xu Zheng's 'Lost in Hong Kong'?" *South China Morning Post* (November 17, 2015), www .scmp.com/lifestyle/film-tv/article/1879532/will-local-audiences-warm-chinese -filmmaker-xu-zhengs-lost-hong.

38. Edmund Lee, "Will Local Audiences Warm to Chinese Filmmaker."

39. Patrick Brzeski, "'Lost in Hong Kong': 5 Things to Know About China's Latest Blockbuster," *Hollywood Reporter* (September 28, 2015), www.hollywoodreporter .com/news/china-blockbuster-lost-hong-kong-827532.

40. (我差不多是个废人了)

41. For a detailed discussion of the animation, see my piece on the film in *ChinaFile*.

42. Jamie Dettmer, "China's 'Wolf Warrior' Diplomacy Prompts International Backlash," *Voice of America* (May 6, 2020), www.voanews.com/covid-19-pandemic /chinas-wolf-warrior-diplomacy-prompts-international-backlash.

43. Hongmo, "Dujia Zhongbang! Guanyu Fengxiaogang Wo Bu Shi Pan Jinlian de Bage Yiwen [Exclusive News! Eight Questions About Feng's *I Am Not (Madame Bovary)*]," kknews (October 18, 2016), kknews.cc/zh-hk/entertainment/llaeb2.html.

44. "Renmin Ribao Zhuanfang Feng Xiaogang: Guanyuan Budandang Jiushi Fubai [*People's Daily*'s Interview on Feng Xiaogang: Officials' Irresponsibility Is Corruption]," web.archive.org, November 24, 2016, web.archive.org/web/20161124155651 /http:/ent.163.com/16/1124/08/C6KFC531000380BQ.html.

45. Patrick Frater, "Feng Xiaogang's 'Madame Bovary' Release Delayed," *Variety* (September 21, 2016), variety.com/2016/film/asia/mystery-distribution-delay-for -feng-xiaogangs-madame-bovary-1201866753.

46. Ying Zhu, "Here's How the Trade War Is Affecting Hollywood," *ChinaFile* (March 8, 2019), www.chinafile.com/reporting-opinion/viewpoint/heres-how-trade -war-affecting-hollywood.

47. Zheng Wang, "Liulang Diqiu Daoyan Guo Fan de 'Lizhi Yu Qinggan' [The Reason and Emotion of the Director of the Wandering Earth]," *thepaper* (February 6, 2019), www.thepaper.cn/newsDetail_forward_2959580.

48. Shuguang Rao and Guochong Li, "'Zhonggongye Dianying' Jiqi Meixue ['Heavy Industrial Film' and Its Aesthetics: Theory and Practice," *Dangdai Dianying* [Contemporary Film], no. 4 (2018): 102–108.

49. Rao and Li, "'Zhonggongye Dianying.'"

50. "Xinzhuliu Dianying de Jueqi Ji Qi Qishiyiyi [New Mainstream Blockbuster's Rise and Significance]," gd.ifeng.com (April 16, 2018), gd.ifeng.com/a/20180416/ 6504404_0.shtml.

51. Richard Kuipers, "Film Review: 'Dying to Survive,'" *Variety* (August 16, 2019), variety.com/2019/film/reviews/dying-to-survive-review-1203303457.

52. Chinese premier Li Keqiang cited the film in an appeal to regulators to "speed up price cuts for cancer drugs" and "reduce the burden on families."

53. Caixin Global, "Shanghai Film Festival Rekindles Childhood Memories with Outdoor Screenings," *China Film Insider* (July 31, 2020).

54. Alex Dudok De Wit, "'Nezha' Smashes $460 Million Box-Office, Set to Overtake 'Avengers: Endgame' in China," *Cartoon Brew* (August 9, 2019), www .cartoonbrew.com/box-office-report/nezha-smashes-460-million-set-to-overtake -avengers-endgame-in-china-177974.html.

55. Patrick Brzeski, "How Chinese Animation Film 'Ne Zha' Became a Surprise $400M-Plus Hit," *Hollywood Reporter* (August 8, 2019), www.hollywoodreporter .com/news/how-chinese-animation-film-ne-zha-became-a-surprise-400m-hit -1230167.

56. Alexandra Alter, "How Chinese Sci-Fi Conquered America," *New York Times* (December 3, 2019), www.nytimes.com/2019/12/03/magazine/ken-liu-three-body -problem-chinese-science-fiction.html.

57. Netflix recently optioned the *Three-Body Problem* trilogy to adapt for a serial drama on its streaming site. *Game of Thrones*' showrunners David Benioff and Dan Weiss signed on to the project.

58. Rebecca Davis, "China Issues Guidelines on Developing a Sci-Fi Film Sector," *Variety* (August 17, 2020), variety.com/2020/film/news/china-guidelines -science-fiction-1234737913.

59. Rebecca Davis, "China Issues Guidelines."

60. Rebecca Davis, "China's Box-Office Hit New Heights in 2019, as Hollywood's Share Shrank," *Variety* (January 2, 2020), variety.com/2020/film/news/china-box -office-2019-review-ne-zha-wandering-earth-avengers-1203455038.

61. Rebecca Davis, "China's Box-Office Hit New Heights."

62. Patrick Frater, "China's Box Office Went Its Own Way in 2019, to Hollywood's Detriment," *Variety* (December 24, 2019), variety.com/2019/film/asia/hollywood-2019 -setback-china-box-office-1203451505.

63. Rebecca Davis, "China's Box-Office."

64. Rebecca Davis, "China's Box-Office."

65. Patrick Brzeski, "Why China Has Embraced 'Green Book' Like a Blockbuster," *Hollywood Reporter* (March 6, 2019), www.hollywoodreporter.com/news /why-china-has-embraced-green-book-like-a-blockbuster-1192597.

66. "Chinese Films Box Office Ranking," Maoyan, piaofang.maoyan.com/rankings /year.

67. Lang Qin and Jingjing Tan, "Commentary: Oscar Recognition Shows China's Growing Presence in Global Entertainment Industry," Xinhua (February 26, 2019), www.xinhuanet.com/english/2019-02/26/c_137850151.htm.

68. Brzeski, "Why China Has Embraced."

69. During the same period, market share of mid-level films grossing RMB 10 million to RMB 2 billion fell over the same period from 80.5 percent to 62.3 percent.

70. 网大电影 in Chinese.

71. Jean-Paul Sartre, "Discussion on the Criticism of Ivan's Childhood," *Nostalghia*, n.d., nostalghia.com/TheTopics/Sartre.html.

72. China Film Worker's Association, Special Collection on *Cranes Are Flying* (China Film Worker's Association Press, 1963).

73. Chunru Xing, ed., *Zhongguo Yishu Shihua: Dianying Yishu (Shang)* [Chinese Art History: Film (Part I)] (Liaohai Press, 2007).

8. Journey Home or to the West: Chinese Cinema's Hollywood Dream and the Sino-Hollywood (De)Coupling

1. Tank, "Hei Guafu Zhongyu Shangying, Zai Zhongguo que Zhineng shi 'Dao-ban de Ming' [Black Widow Was Finally Released, yet It Did Not Escape from Pirates in China]," Deep Focus (July 8, 2021), www.163.com/dy/article/GECMITP M0517DBIK.html.

2. ChinaPower, "Do Chinese Films Hold Global Appeal?" *ChinaPower* (2019), chinapower.csis.org/chinese-films.

3. The films all earned over $500 million each.

4. Dana Harris, "Zhang Pulls 2 Cannes Films, Blames West," *Hollywood Reporter* (April 21, 1999).

5. Chen Xiaoming, Liu Kang, and Anbin Shi, "The Mysterious Other: Postpolitics in Chinese Film," *boundary 2* 24, no. 3 (1997); Author(s): www.jstor.org /stable/303709.

6. Yingchi Chu, "The Politics of Reception: 'Made in China' and Western Critique," *International Journal of Cultural Studies* 17, no. 2 (2014): 160.

7. Press Trust of India, "Artists Should Use Their Talent to Promote Socialism; Xi," *Business Standard* (October 16 2014), www.business-standard.com/article/pti-stories /artists-should-use-their-talent-to-promote-socialism-xi-114101601057_1.html.

8. Xinhua News Agency, "Art Must Present Socialist Values: Xi," *Global Times* (October 15, 2014), www.globaltimes.cn/content/886477.shtml.

9. Steven Zeitchik and David Pierson, "Reel China: It's Rough Out West for Chinese Films," *Los Angeles Times* (July 3, 2011), www.latimes.com/entertainment /la-ca-china-blockbuster-20110703-story.html.

10. Yingzhi Yang and Jane Li, "Chinese Gaming Company Perfect World Just Picked Up a Few Oscars," *South China Morning Post* (March 5, 2018), www.scmp .com/tech/enterprises/article/2135820/chinese-gaming-company-perfect-world-just -picked-few-oscars.

11. Zhengrong Hu and Deqiang Ji, "Ambiguities in Communicating with the World: The 'Going-Out' Policy of China's Media and Its Multilayered Contexts," *Chinese Journal of Communication* 5, no. 1 (March 1, 2012): 32–37.

12. Michael Wolff, "Michael Wolff on Hollywood's Disappearing Chinese Money," *Hollywood Reporter* (February 20, 2015).

13. Huayu, "Cong Huangye Lieren Dao Lvpishu, Zhongguo Ziben zai Aosika de Jinjizhilu [From 'The Revenant' to 'Green Book,' Chinese Capital's Advance at the Oscars]," *Jiemian* (January 28, 2019), www.jiemian.com/article/2830265.html.

14. Jeremy Kay, "Dalian Wanda Group Completes AMC Acquisition for $2.6bn." *Screen Daily* (September 4, 2012), www.screendaily.com/dalian-wanda-group-completes-amc-acquisition-for-26bn/5046096.article.

15. This portrayal of Wang's personal history and Wanda's corporate history has been derived from personal interviews as well as mainstream and industry press. Most important, see Patrick Brzeski, "Wanda Chairman Reveals Ambitious Plan to Invest Billions in 'All Six' Hollywood Studios," *Hollywood Reporter* (November 2, 2016), www.hollywoodreporter.com/features/wanda-chairman-wang-jianlin-plans-invest-billions-hollywood-942854; Michael Forsythe, "Wang Jianlin, a Billionaire at the Intersection of Business and Power in China," *New York Times* (April 28, 2015), www.nytimes.com/2015/04/29/world/asia/wang-jianlin-abillionaire-at-the-intersection-of-business-and-power-in-china.html.

16. Patrick Brzeski, "Wanda Chairman Reveals."

17. "China's Wanda Cinema Line Ready for IPO," *Screen Daily* (March 4, 2011), www.screendaily.com/chinas-wanda-cinema-line-ready-for-ipo/5024552.article.

18. Douglas Gomery, *The Hollywood Studio System: A History* (London: British Film Institute, 2005); Ross Melnick, *American Showman: Samuel "Roxy" Rothafel and the Birth of the Entertainment Industry, 1908–1935* (New York: Columbia University Press, 2014).

19. The United States Department of Justice Office of Public Affairs, "Federal Court Terminates Paramount Consent Decrees," *United States Department of Justice—Justice News* (August 7. 2020), www.justice.gov/opa/pr/federal-court-terminates-paramount-consent-decrees#:~:text=A%20federal%20court%20in%20the,distribute%20films%20to%20movie%20theatres.

20. Kay, "Dalian Wanda Group."

21. Michael Rosser, "China-Controlled AMC to Buy Odeon and UCI Cinemas for $1.2bn," *Screen Daily* (July 12, 2016), www.screendaily.com/news/china-controlled-amc-to-buy-odeon-and-uci-cinemas-for-12bn/5106685.article; Patrick Frater, "Wanda Expands Global Theater Reach as AMC Pays $929 Million for Nordic Cinema," *Variety* (January 23, 2017), variety.com/2017/film/finance/wanda-expands-global-theater-reach-as-amc-pays-929-million-for-nordic-cinema-1201966877.

22. Nancy Tartaglione, "China Will Overtake U.S. in Number of Movie Screens This Week: Analyst," *Deadline Hollywood* (November 15, 2016), deadline.com/2016/11/china-cinema-screens-overtake-us-box-office-2019-1201852359.

23. Patrick Brzeski, "Wanda's Big Qingdao Studio Pitch: Will Hollywood Take the Bait?" *Hollywood Reporter* (October 19, 2016), www.hollywoodreporter.com/news/wandas-qingdao-studio-pitch-hollywood-939629.

24. Patrick Brzeski, "China Blocks Banks from Financing Dalian Wanda's Foreign Acquisitions (Report)," *Hollywood Reporter* (July 16, 2017), www.hollywoodreporter

.com/news/china-blocks-banks-financing-dalian-wandas-foreign-acquisitions
-1021641.

25. Xi abolished presidential term limits in 2018, which allows him to rule indefinitely.

26. Keith Bradsher and Sui-Lee Wee, "In China, Herd of 'Gray Rhinos' Threatens Economy," *New York Times* (July 23, 2017), www.nytimes.com/2017/07/23/business/china-economy-gray-rhinos.html; Ryan Faughnder, Jonathan Kaiman, and David Pierson, "This Chinese Billionaire Rode into Town Late Last Year Looking Like a Hollywood Conqueror. What Happened?" *Los Angeles Times* (July 6, 2017), www.latimes.com/business/hollywood/la-fi-ct-wanda-hollywood-struggles -20170706-story.html.

27. Lucy Hornby, "Chinese Crackdown on Dealmakers Reflects Xi Power Play," *Financial Times* (September 8, 2017), www.ft.com/content/ed900da6-769b-11e7 -90c0-90a9d1bc9691.

28. Patrick Brzeski, "China's Wanda Film Co. Hit by Massive Investor Sell-Off," *Hollywood Reporter* (June 21, 2017), www.hollywoodreporter.com/news/general -news/shares-chinas-wanda-film-suspended-trading-sudden-crash-1015898.

29. Jianlin Wang, "Wanda Group 2018 Work Report," *Wanda Group* (January 15, 2019), www.wanda-group.com/mobile/2019/Latest_0115/4563.html.

30. Keith Bradsher, "Debt-Ridden Chinese Giant Now a Shadow of Its Former Size," *New York Times* (August 1, 2017), www.nytimes.com/2017/08/01/business /dalian-wanda-group-china-debt.html.

31. Guillaume Guguen, "'Chinawood' Hopes to Challenge Hollywood for Cinematic Dominance," *France24* (April 30, 2018), www.france24.com/en/20180430 -chinawood-challenge-hollywood-cinema-qingdao-oriental-movie-metropolis.

32. Esther Fung, "Chinese Exodus from U.S. Real Estate Accelerates with Sale of L.A. Site," *Wall Street Journal* (November 15, 2018), www.wsj.com/articles/chinese -exodus-from-u-s-real-estate-accelerates-with-sale-of-l-a-site-1542301496.

33. Shirley Zhao, "AMC's Chinese Owner Gives up Control Over World's Largest Cinema Chain," *Bloomberg* (March 15, 2021), www.bloomberg.com/news/articles /2021-03-15/amc-s-chinese-owner-gives-up-control-over-largest-cinema-chain.

34. Kimberly Chin, "AMC's Largest Shareholder Wanda Group Pares Down Stake," *Wall Street Journal* (May 21, 2021), www.wsj.com/articles/amcs-largest-share holder-wanda-group-pares-down-stake-11621644038.

35. Michael Keane and Haiqing Yu, "A Digital Empire in the Making: China's Outbound Digital Platforms," *International Journal of Communication* 13 (2019): 4634.

36. Ying Zhu and Michael Keane, "China's Cultural Power Reconnects with the World," in *BRICS and Shifting Paradigms of Global Communication*, eds. Daya Thussu and Kaarle Nordenstreng (New York: Routledge, 2020), 212.

37. "Yuandong zuida de yule gongying ku: Shaoshi [The Shaw Brothers Studio: The Largest Supplier of Entertainments in Asia]," *Nanguo dianying*, no. 59 (January 1961): 30–33.a.

38. *Xianggang nianjian* [Hong Kong Report], vol. 20 (Hong Kong: Huaqiao ribao she, 1967), 119–120.

39. Law Kar, "Xianggang dianying de haiwai jingyan [The Overseas Experience of Hong Kong Cinema]," in *Overseas Chinese Figures in Cinema*, ed. Law Kar (Hong Kong: Urban Council, 1992), 16; see also discussions in introduction to Fu Poshek, "Introduction: The Shaw Brothers Diasporic Cinema," in *China Forever: The Shaw Brothers and Diasporic Cinema*, ed. Fu Poshek (Champaign, IL: University of Illinois Press, 2008), 15.

40. For detailed remarks from Chan, see Ying Zhu, "Here's How the Trade War Is Affecting Hollywood," *ChinaFile* (March 8, 2019), www.chinafile.com/reporting -opinion/viewpoint/heres-how-trade-war-affecting-hollywood.

41. The popularity of Mandarin films began to wane in the 1970s as a new generation growing up in Hong Kong with little tie to the imaginary mainland developed a taste for local dialect-based pop culture. Shaw Brothers failed to register the growing local consciousness of Hong Kong audiences. The quality and market shares of Shaw Brothers products declined steadily throughout the 1980s and Shaw Brothers Studio largely ceased producing films by the end of the 1980s.

42. Tom Shone, "Hollywood Transformed How China Is Changing the DNA of America's Blockbuster Movies," *Financial Times* (July 25, 2014), www.ft.com /content/60338b6c-1263-11e4-93a5-00144feabdc0.

43. Erich Schwartzel, "Paramount Pictures Gets a $1 Billion Infusion from China," *Wall Street Journal* (January 19, 2017), www.wsj.com/articles/paramount -pictures-gets-a-1-billion-infusion-from-china-1484868302.

44. Meg James and Ryan Faughnder, "Paramount Pictures Loses Huahua Media Slate Film Financing Deal," *Los Angeles Times* (November 7, 2017), www.latimes .com/business/hollywood/la-fi-ct-paramount-huahua-film-financing-20171107 -story.html.

45. Clifford Coonan, "STX's Bob Simonds: Huayi Brothers Deal Will 'Supercharge' Film Financing Facilities," *Hollywood Reporter* (April 1, 2015), www .hollywoodreporter.com/news/general-news/stxs-bob-simonds-huayi-brothers -785781.

46. James Rainey, "STX Entertainment Gets Investment from China's Tencent and PCCW," *Variety* (August 11, 2016), variety.com/2016/film/asia/stx-tencent -pccw-investment-1201835710.

47. Yang and Li, "Chinese Gaming Company."

48. Anita Busch, "Alex Schwartz Joins China-Funded Alpha Animation as Production Head," *Deadline* (October 19, 2016), deadline.com/2016/10/alex-schwartz-alpha-animation-china-production-head-1201839140.

49. Xinhua News Agency, "China's Growing Presence in Hollywood Film Market," *China Daily* (March 1, 2016), www.chinadaily.com.cn/culture/2016-03/01/content_23692715_2.htm.

50. Patrick Frater, "Lionsgate Seals $1.5 Billion Deal with China's Hunan TV," *Variety* (March 17, 2015), variety.com/2015/biz/asia/lionsgate-seals-co-finance-co-production-pact-with-chinas-hunan-tv-1201454954.

51. Patrick Frater, "China's Bona Film Boards Brad Pitt's 'Ad Astra,' 'A Dog's Way Home' (EXCLUSIVE)," *Variety* (December 12, 2018), variety.com/2018/film/asia/brad-pitt-china-bona-film-ad-astra-dogs-way-home-1203087749.

52. Rebecca Davis, "China's Bona Film Boards Quentin Tarantino's 'Once Upon a Time in Hollywood,'" *Variety* (January 27, 2019), variety.com/2019/film/news/quentin-tarantino-bona-film-once-upon-a-time-in-hollywood-1203120215.

53. Melody Yuan, "'Green Book,' a Tale of Friendship Thriving on China's Big Screens," *East West Bank* (March 20, 2019), www.eastwestbank.com/ReachFurther/en/News/Article/Green-Book-a-Tale-of-Friendship-Thriving-on-Chinas-Big-Screens.

54. Steven Zeitchik, "Fearful of Political Criticism, China Won't Show the Oscars Live; Beijing's Decision Adds a New Wrinkle to the Hollywood-China Relationship," *Washington Post* (April 3, 2021), www.washingtonpost.com/business/2021/04/03/oscars-china-broadcast-hong-kong-zhao.

55. Edward Wong, "Chinese Purchases of U.S. Companies Have Some in Congress Raising Eyebrows," *New York Times* (September 30, 2016), www.nytimes.com/2016/10/01/world/asia/china-us-foreign-acquisition-dalian-wanda.html.

56. Nancy Tartaglione, "Hollywood & China: U.S. Gov't Agency Agrees to Review Foreign Investment Panel," *Deadline Hollywood* (October 4, 2016), deadline.com/2016/10/china-hollywood-congress-wanda-foreign-ownership-gao-1201830426.

57. Edward Wong, "Chinese Purchases of U.S. Companies."

58. Ted Johnson, "Ted Cruz Introduces Bill to Restrict U.S. Government Help for Studios If They Alter Movies to Gain Entry into Chinese Market," *Deadline* (May 21, 2020), deadline.com/2020/05/ted-cruz-china-hollywood-1202941024.

59. Ted Johnson, "Attorney General William Barr Blasts Hollywood for Censoring Movies 'To Appease the Chinese Communist Party,'" *Deadline* (July 16, 2020), deadline.com/2020/07/william-barr-china-hollywood-studios-1202987361.

60. Ted Johnson, "Attorney General William Barr."

61. Ted Johnson, "Attorney General William Barr."

62. United States Department of Justice Office of Public Affairs, "Attorney General William P. Barr Delivers Remarks on China Policy at the Gerald R. Ford Presidential Museum," *United States Department of Justice—Justice News* (July 16, 2020), https://www.justice.gov/opa/speech/transcript-attorney-general-barr-s-remarks -china-policy-gerald-r-ford-presidential-museum

63. Tom Phillips, "China's Xi Jinping Says Paris Climate Deal Must Not Be Allowed to Fail," *The Guardian* (January 19, 2017), www.theguardian.com/world/2017 /jan/19/chinas-xi-jinping-says-world-must-implement-paris-climate-deal.

64. Ying Zhu, "The Same Old 'China Story' Keeps Chinese Sci-Fi Earthbound," *ChinaFile* (September 30, 2019), www.chinafile.com/reporting-opinion/culture/same -old-china-story-keeps-chinese-sci-fi-earthbound.

65. "The Fable of Master Storyteller," *China Media Project* (September 29, 2017), chinamediaproject.org/2017/09/29/the-fable-of-the-master-storyteller.

66. "Xi Jinping: Wenyi Buneng Zai Shichangjingji Dachao Zhong Mishi Fangxiang [Xi Jinping: Literary and Artistic Works Cannot Lose Their Way in the Tide of the Market Economy]," Xinhuanet, October 15, 2014, www.xinhuanet.com /politics/2014-10/15/c_1112840544.htm.

67. Zhu, "The Same Old."

68. ChinaPower, "Do Chinese Films Hold Global Appeal?"

69. Xinhua News Agency, "China Focus: Beijing Film Festival Sheds Light on Post-Epidemic Cinema Development," Xinhua News Agency (August 27, 2020), www.xinhuanet.com/english/2020-08/27/c_139321825.htm.

70. Rebecca Davis, "China Is World's First Market to Achieve Full Box Office Recovery, Says Analytics Firm," *Variety* (August 27, 2020), variety.com/2020/film /news/china-first-box-office-recovery-1234751777.

71. Sun Jiashan, "Films Likely to Feature More Original Stories," *China Daily* (November 3, 2020), global.chinadaily.com.cn/a/202011/03/WS5fa095eba31024 ad0ba82a4a.html.

72. Rebecca Davis, "Foreign Films Account for Just 16% of Total China Box Office, Worth $3 Billion in 2020," *Variety* (January 4, 2021), variety.com/2021/film /news/china-box-office-2020-annual-total-maoyan-1234878626.

73. Patrick Brzeski, "It's Official: China Overtakes North America as World's Biggest Box Office in 2020," *Hollywood Reporter* (October 18, 2020), www.hollywoodreporter .com/news/its-official-china-overtakes-north-america-as-worlds-biggest-box-office -in-2020#:~:text=China%20is%20officially%20home%20to,to%20data%20 from%20Artisan%20Gateway.

74. Brandon Katz, "Warner Bros. Will Reportedly Lose Up to $100 Million on 'Tenet,'" *Observer* (November 4, 2020), observer.com/2020/11/tenet-box-office-christopher -nolan-film-100-million-loss-warner-bros.

75. Sonny Bunch, "What Might a Biden Admin Look Like for Showbiz?" *Bulwark+* (November 7, 2020), screentime.thebulwark.com/p/what-might-a-biden-admin-look-like.

76. Peter Mattis and Brad Carson, "Jaw-Jaw: Peter Mattis on the Intentions of the Chinese Communist Party," *War on the Rocks* (May 28, 2019), warontherocks.com/2019/05/jaw-jaw-peter-mattis-on-the-intentions-of-the-chinese-communist-party.

77. China Opinion, "Chinese Communism Is a Magic Mirror," *China Opinion* (July 23, 2020), medium.com/@anotherchinaopinion/chinese-communism-is-a-magic-mirror-52fec4a71bd6.

78. Erich Schwartzel, "Hollywood's New Script: You Can't Make Movies Without China," *Wall Street Journal* (April 18, 2017), www.wsj.com/articles/hollywoods-new-script-you-cant-make-movies-without-china-1492525636.

79. Zhuanghai Shen, *The Chinese Logic of the Construction of Cultural Power* [wenhuaqiangguojianshe de Zhongguoluoji] (Beijing: People's Publishing House, 2017).

80. Bao Chang, "China's Investment in Silver Screen," *China Daily* (December 6, 2010), www.chinadailyasia.com/business/2010-12/06/content_56405.html.

81. Tom Shone, "Hollywood Transformed How China Is Changing the DNA of America's Blockbuster Movies," *Financial Times* (July 25, 2014), www.ft.com/content/60338b6c-1263-11e4-93a5-00144feabdc0.

82. Ben Child, "To Ideology and Beyond: Will China's Sci-fi Movies Plot Their Own Course?" *The Guardian* (August 21, 2020), www.theguardian.com/film/2020/aug/21/to-ideology-and-beyond-will-chinas-new-sci-fi-directors-plot-their-own-course?utm_term=546b50b83a958759d7a78c6586b46ced&utm_campaign=FilmToday&utm_source=esp&utm_medium=Email&CMP=filmtoday_email.

83. Rebecca Davis, "China Issues Guidelines on Developing a Sci-Fi Film Sector," *Variety* (August 17, 2020), variety.com/2020/film/news/china-guidelines-science-fiction-1234737913.

84. Erich Schwartzel and Wayne Ma, "Beijing's New Superpowers Over Movie Industry Frustrate Hollywood Studios," *Wall Street Journal* (May 27, 2018), www.wsj.com/articles/hollywood-studios-hit-plot-twist-in-talks-with-china-1527418803.

85. Shirley Zhao, "Hollywood Struggles for Fans in China's Growing Film Market," *Bloomberg* (February 16, 2021), www.bloomberg.com/news/articles/2021-02-15/hollywood-struggles-for-fans-in-china-s-growing-film-market.

86. Shirley Zhao, "Hollywood Struggles for Fans."

87. Xinhua News Agency, "Spotlight: Hollywood Insiders Weigh In on Future of U.S.-China Co-Productions," *Line Today* (July 26, 2020), today.line.me/hk/v2/article/Spotlight+Hollywood+insiders+weigh+in+on+future+of+U+S+China+co+productions-9qErDR.

88. Rebecca Davis, "*Black Widow*'s China Delay Rings Alarm Bells for Hollywood," *Variety* (July 9, 2021), variety.com/2021/film/news/black-widow-china-box-office-troubles-1235016323.

89. Rebecca Davis, "*Black Widow*'s China Delay."

9. The Sino-Hollywood "Courtship": Film as Cultural Persuasion and Box-Office Revenue

1. C.J. North, "Our Silent Ambassadors," *Independent* (June 12, 1926): 699; also quoted in Kristin Thompson, *Exporting Entertainment: America in the World Film Market, 1907–34* (London: British Film Institute, 1985), 122.

2. Quoted in Neal Rosendorf, "Comments on the Congressional Symposium on American Film and Public Diplomacy 11/14/2007," USC Center for Public Diplomacy Blog, uscpublicdiplomacy.org/blog/comments-congressional-symposium-american-film-and-public-diplomacy-11142007.

3. Quoted in "How Xi Jinping Views the News," China Media Project, March 3, 2016, chinamediaproject.org/2016/03/03/39672.

4. Martha Bayles, "Dream Factory, or Propaganda Machine?" Hudson Institute, February 6, 2018, www.hudson.org/research/14188-dream-factory-or-propaganda-machine.

5. Michal Kranz, "The Director of the FBI Says the Whole of Chinese Society Is a Threat to the U.S.—and That Americans Must Step Up to Defend Themselves," *Business Insider* (February 14, 2018), www.businessinsider.com/china-threat-to-america-fbi-director-warns-2018-2.

6. President Joseph R. Biden Jr. Interim National Security Strategic Guidance, March 2021, 21, www.whitehouse.gov/wp-content/uploads/2021/03/NSC-1v2.pdf.

7. Ying Zhu, *Chinese Cinema During the Era of Reform* (Westport, CT: Praeger, 2003), 144.

8. Victoria De Grazia, "Soft-Power United States versus Normative Power Europe: Competing Ideals of Hegemony in the Post–Cold War West, 1990–2015," in *Soft-Power Internationalism: Competing for Cultural Influence in the 21st-Century Global Order*, ed. Burcu Baykurt and Victoria De Grazia (New York: Columbia University Press, 2021).

9. Paul Moody, "Embassy Cinema: What WikiLeaks Reveals About U.S. State Support for Hollywood," *Media, Culture & Society* 39, no. 7 (2017): 1063–1077.

10. Victoria de Grazia, *Irresistible Empire: America's Advance Through Twentieth-Century Europe* (Cambridge, MA: Belknap Press, 2005), 474.

11. A cable from Linda Jewell, the U.S. ambassador in Quito, Ecuador, WikiLeaks (December 22, 2005): 05QUITO2920.

12. Paul Moody's relevant passage and his conclusion. See Moody, "Embassy Cinema."

13. Victoria De Grazia, *Irresistible Empire*, 475.

14. Wanning Sun, "Soft Power by Accident or by Design: *If You Are the One* and Chinese Television," in *Screening China's Soft Power*, edited by Paola Voci and Luo Hui (New York and London: Routledge, 2017), 196–211.

15. Joseph Nye's definition of soft power in *Bound to Lead: The Changing Nature of American Power* (New York: Basic Books, 1990).

16. Craig Hayden, *The Rhetoric of Soft Power: Public Diplomacy in Global Contexts* (Lanham, MD: Lexington Books, 2011).

17. Yiwei Wang. "Public Diplomacy and the Rise of Chinese Soft Power," *Annals of the American Academy of Political and Social Science* 616, no. 1 (2008): 269, doi .org/ 10.1177/0002716207312757.

18. Warner Brothers Press Release, "Warner Bros. Kicks Off U.S.-China Exchange Program with a Two-Day Talent Management and Casting Workshop in Burbank, CA," November 14, 2017, www.warnerbros.com/news/press-releases/warner-bros-kicks-us -china-exchange-program-two-day-talent-management-and-casting.

19. Tatiana Siegel, "Disney's 'Christopher Robin' Won't Get China Release Amid Pooh Crackdown," *Hollywood Reporter* (August 3, 2018), www.hollywoodreporter .com/heat-vision/christopher-robin-refused-china-release-winnie-pooh-crackdown -1131907.

20. Samuel Wade, "Minitruth 2017: 'A Taxi Driver' and 1989 Echoes," *China Digital Times* (December 27, 2017), chinadigitaltimes.net/2017/12/minitruth -2017-october-taxi-driver-echoes-tiananmen.

21. "Zhongguo Didanying Shencha Weiyuanhui [China's Film Censorship Committee]," Baidu Baike, baike.baidu.com/item/.

22. "Film and the Chinese Government," Facts and Details, n.d., factsanddetails .com/china/cat7/sub42/item1833.html.

23. Edward Wong, "'Doctor Strange' Writer Explains Casting of Tilda Swinton as Tibetan," *New York Times* (April 26, 2016), www.nytimes.com/2016/04/27/world /asia/china-doctor-strange-tibet.html.

24. Quoted in Victor Fan, "Poetics of Failure: Performing Humanism in the Chinese Blockbuster," in *Screening China's Soft Power*, eds. Paola Voci and Luo Hui (New York and London: Routledge, 2017), 57.

25. Alex Lo, "Why China Lacks 'Discourse Power,'" *South China Morning Post* (September 15, 2020), https://www.scmp.com/comment/opinion/article/3101656 /why-china-lacks-discourse-power.

26. Cai, Mingzhao, "Jiang hao zhongguo gushi chuanbo zhongguo hao shengyin [To Tell the China Story Effectively and Transmit China's Voice Faithfully]," *People's*

Daily (October 10, 2013), www.politics.people.com.cn/n/2013/1010/c1001–23144775
.html. Cited in Wanning Sun, "Soft Power by Accident or by Design," 196.

27. Young Nam Cho and Yong Ho Jeong, "China's Soft Power: Discussions, Resources and Prospects," *Asian Survey* 48, no. 3 (2008): 453–472.

28. David Bandurski, "The Fable of the Master Storyteller," China Media Project, September 29, 2017, chinamediaproject.org/2017/09/29/the-fable-of-the-master-storyteller.

29. *People's Daily* Opinion Department (2017), *Xi Jinping Jiang Gushi* (*Xi Jinping Tells Stories*). Beijing: *People's Daily* Press.

30. Translation from Bandurski, "The Fable."

31. Hui Ouyang, "Xi Jinping Xiang Shijie Jianghao Zhongguo Gushi de Sixiang [Xi Jinping's Thoughts on Telling China's Story Well to the World]," *CPC News* (February 22, 2019), theory.people.com.cn/n1/2019/0222/c40531-30897581.html.

32. "Xi Jinping Says Will Never Allow Smears Against Communist Party," *The Standard* (September 4, 2020), www.thestandard.com.hk/breaking-news/section/3/154705/Xi-Jinping-says-will-never-allow-smears-against-Communist-Party; see also "Xi Focus: Xi stresses carrying forward great spirit of resisting aggression," Xinhua News Agency, September 4, 2020, www.xinhuanet.com/english/2020-09/04/c_139340869.htm.

33. Alex Lo, "Why China Lacks."

34. Jiashan Sun, "Films Likely to Feature More Original Stories," *China Daily* (November 3, 2020), global.chinadaily.com.cn/a/202011/03/WS5fa095eba31024ad0ba82a4a.html.

35. Propeller TV, "Beijing TV and Film International Screening: Telling China's Story Well to the World," *PR Newswire* (November 26, 2020), www.prnewswire.com/news-releases/beijing-tv-and-film-international-screening-telling-chinas-story-well-to-the-world-301180767.html.

36. Wanning Sun, "Soft Power by Accident or by Design," 197.

37. Wanning Sun, "Soft Power by Accident or by Design," 209.

38. Leo Lewis, "Work for Morality, Not Money, Chinese President Tells Artists," *The Times* (October 18, 2014), www.thetimes.co.uk/article/work-for-morality-not-money-chinese-president-tells-artists-8srhmwqhk7c.

39. Xinhua News Agency, "Art Must Present Socialist Values: Xi," *China Daily* (October 15, 2014), www.chinadaily.com.cn/china/2014-10/15/content_18744900.htm.

40. Michael Cieply, "Hollywood Works to Maintain Its World Dominance: 'Dawn of the Planet of the Apes' Made More Than 70% of Its Money from the Foreign Box Office," *New York Times* (November 3, 2014), www.nytimes.com/2014/11/04/business/media/hollywood-works-to-maintain-its-world-dominance.html.

41. Lanlan Huang, "Chinese Gen Z Prefers Domestic Products to Foreign Ones," *Global Times* (January 22, 2020), www.globaltimes.cn/content/1177712.shtml.

42. Ankit Panda, "Survey: Chinese Report Less Favorable Views of U.S. Democracy," thediplomat.com, April 9, 2020, thediplomat.com/2020/04/survey-chinese-report-less-favorable-views-of-us-democracy.

43. Huifeng He, "China's Millennials, Generation Z Leading Nation Away from Hollywood Films, American Culture, U.S. Brands," *South China Morning Post* (March 20, 2021), www.scmp.com/economy/china-economy/article/3126180/chinas-millennials-generation-z-leading-nation-away-hollywood.

44. Huifeng He, "China's Millennials."

45. Huifeng He, "China's Millennials."

46. *The Economist*, January 23, 2021.

47. Stephanie Studer, "How Nationalism Is Shaping China's Young," *The Economist* (January 23, 2021), www.economist.com/special-report/2021/01/21/how-nationalism-is-shaping-chinas-young.

48. Alicia Liu, "China's Top Four Grossing Movies of All Time: Hollywood's Influence on the Chinese Film Market Recedes," *US-China Today* (December 17, 2020), uschinatoday.org/features/2020/12/17/chinas-top-four-grossing-movies-of-all-time.

49. Quoted in Huifeng He, "China's Millennials."

50. *The Economist*, "As Attitudes to the West Sour, China's Students Turn Home," *The Economist* (January 21, 2021), www.economist.com/special-report/2021/01/21/as-attitudes-to-the-west-sour-chinas-students-turn-home,

51. *The Economist*, "As Attitudes to the West Sour."

52. BBC, "U.S. Revokes Visas for 1,000 Chinese Students Deemed Security Risk," BBC (September 10, 2020), www.bbc.com/news/world-us-canada-54097437.

53. Laura Silver, Kat Devlin, and Christine Huang, "Unfavorable Views of China Reach Historic Highs in Many Countries," Pew Research Center, October 6, 2020, www.pewresearch.org/global/2020/10/06/unfavorable-views-of-china-reach-historic-highs-in-many-countries.

54. Michael Cieply, "Hollywood Works."

55. Caixin Global, "Entertainment Slowdown Hits Filmmakers' Bottom Lines," *China Film Insider* (April 11, 2019), chinafilminsider.com/entertainment-slowdown-hits-filmmakers-bottom-lines.

56. Patrick Brzeski, "China Opens Door for Foreign Movie Theater Chains, But Will They Enter?" *Hollywood Reporter* (July 9, 2019), www.hollywoodreporter.com/news/china-opens-door-foreign-movie-theater-chains-but-will-they-enter-1223076.

57. Quoted in Patrick Brzeski, "China Opens Door."

58. Patrick Brzeski, "China Opens Door."

59. Rebecca Davis, "China Built More Than 2,000 New Screens in the First Two Months of 2021," *Variety* (March 12, 2021), variety.com/2021/film/news/china -movie-theaters-reopen-build-more-1234929177; *Hi, Mom* grossed $750 million and counting, followed by *Detective Chinatown 3* with $670 million and *A Writer's Odyssey* at $140 million. During the same period, the biggest film in North America was Warner Brothers' *Tom & Jerry*, with an opening of just $13.7 million. See also Patrick Brzeski, "Why China's Huge Theatrical Recovery Doesn't Mean Big Business in Berlin," *Hollywood Reporter* (March 2, 2021), www.hollywoodreporter .com/news/why-chinas-huge-theatrical-recovery-doesnt-mean-big-business-in -berlin.

60. Georg Szalai and Patrick Brzeski, "China's Wanda Gives Up AMC Theaters Majority Stake," *Hollywood Reporter* (March 12, 2021), www.hollywoodreporter .com/news/chinas-wanda-gives-up-amc-theatres-majority-stake.

61. Dorcas Wong, "China's Film Industry to Benefit from New Support Policies, Tax Breaks," *China Briefing* (June 17, 2020), www.china-briefing.com/news/chinas -film-industry-benefit-new-support-policies-tax-breaks.

62. Xu Wei, "China Film Market a Marked Global Triumph," *Shine* (January 22, 2021), https://www.shine.cn/feature/entertainment/2101223605.

63. Rui Zhang, "Booming Chinese Film Market Is Still Vulnerable," China.org .cn, March 2, 2021, china.org.cn/arts/2021-03/02/content_77262930.htm.

64. Kevin McSpadden, "China's 2021 Box Office Numbers Reach US$3 Billion in a Few Months, Significantly More Than the U.S. Made for All of 2020," *South China Morning Post* (April 22, 2021), www.scmp.com/news/people-culture/article /3130477/chinas-2021-box-office-numbers-reach-us3-billion-few-months.

65. Patrick Brzeski, "Will Hollywood Films Bounce Back in China in 2021?" *Hollywood Reporter* (January 6, 2021), www.hollywoodreporter.com/news/will-hollywood -films-bounce-back-in-china-in-2021.

66. Louise Tutt, Liz Shackleton, and Jeremy Kay, "The Talking Points for the Global Film Industry in 2021," *Screen Daily* (January 7, 2021), www.screendaily .com/features/the-talking-points-for-the-global-film-industry-in-2021/5155936 .article.

67. "AMC Returns to Profit After Acquisition by Wanda," Dalian Wanda Commercial Management Group Co., Ltd., May 14, 2013, www.wandaplazas.com/en /2013/lastest_0514/17.html.

68. Michael Cole, "Wanda Owner Wang Jianlin Is Now China's Richest Person— and More of Today's China Real Estate Links," *Mingtiandi* (September 10, 2013), www.mingtiandi.com/real-estate/cre-digest/todays-china-real-estate-links -september-10-2013.

69. *Jing Daily*, "China's Billionaire Growth 'Defies Gravity' in 2013," *Jing Daily* (September 13, 2013), jingdaily.com/chinas-billionaire-growth-defies-gravity-in-2013.

70. Noe Gold, "Dalian Wanda CEO: China to Be 'Center of the Global Film Industry,'" *Jing Daily* (September 24, 2013), jingdaily.com/dalian-wanda-ceo -china-to-be-center-of-the-global-film-industry.

71. Etan Vlessing and Georg Szalai, "AMC Theatres Posts $4.58 Billion Full-Year 2020 Loss Amid Pandemic," *Hollywood Reporter* (March 19, 2021), www .hollywoodreporter.com/business/business-news/amc-theatres-posts-946-million -quarterly-loss-amid-pandemic-4137583.

72. Sonny Bunch, "Let a Thousand Film Markets Bloom," *Bulwark+*, March 13, 2021, screentime.thebulwark.com/p/let-a-thousand-film-markets-bloom.

73. Sonny Bunch, "Let a Thousand Film Markets Bloom."

74. Christopher Palmeri, "'Avatar' to Retake Top-Grossing Film Title After China Rerelease," Bloomberg | Quint, March 13, 2021, www.bloombergquint.com /pursuits/-avatar-to-retake-top-grossing-film-title-after-china-rerelease.

75. Tony Osoweje, "'Avatar' Reclaims Top Spot as Highest-Grossing Film After China Re-release," CNN, March 15, 2021, edition.cnn.com/2021/03/15/media /avatar-reclaims-highest-grossing-film-title-intl-scli/index.html.

76. Rebecca Davis, "'Godzilla vs. Kong' Sets China Release Date Ahead of U.S. Debut," *Variety* (March 1, 2021), variety.com/2021/film/news/godzilla-vs-kong -china-release-date-1234918409/#:~:text=Picture-,Warner%20Bros.,in%20the- aters%20and%20on%20streaming.

77. Patrick Brzeski, "China Box Office: 'Godzilla vs. Kong' Roars with $21.5M Friday," *Hollywood Reporter* (March 26, 2021), www.hollywoodreporter.com/news /china-box-office-godzilla-vs-kong-roars-with-20m-friday.

78. Travis Clark, "China's Box-Office Dominance Was Accelerated by the Pandemic and It Has Big Implications for Hollywood's Future," *Business Insider* (April 9, 2021), www.businessinsider.com.au/what-chinas-box-office-dominance-means-for -hollywood-2021-4

79. Travis Clark, "China's Box-Office Dominance."

80. See Kingsley Edney, Stanley Rosen, and Ying Zhu, "Introduction," in *Soft Power with Chinese Characteristics: China's Campaign for Hearts and Minds* eds. Kingsley Edney, Stanley Rosen, and Ying Zhu (New York and London: Routledge, 2020), 2–3.

81. *The Economist*, "The Red Carpet: Inside China's Film Industry," *Business Insider* (December 25, 2013), www.businessinsider.com/the-red-carpet-inside-chinas-film -industry-2013-12.

82. Jennifer Wolfe, "NBCUniversal Shedding Oriental DreamWorks Stake," *Animation World Network* (September 5, 2017), awn.com/news/nbcuniversal -shedding-oriental-dreamworks-stake.

83. uk.movies.yahoo.com/warner-bros-launches-china-exchange-173221280 .html.

84. Christopher Walker and Jessica Ludwig, "The Meaning of Sharp Power: How Authoritarian States Project Influence," *Foreign Affairs* (November 16, 2017), www.foreignaffairs.com/articles/china/2017-11-16/meaning-sharp-power.

85. Judah Grunstein, "Dangers of Groupthink on China," *World Politics Review* (April 7, 2021), www.worldpoliticsreview.com/articles/29551/avoiding-groupthink -to-manage-the-us-china-relationship.

86. Martha Bayles, "Dream Factory."

87. Helen Davidson, "Mum's the Word: Hit Chinese Film 'Hi, Mom' Sparks Debate About Motherhood," *The Guardian* (February 26, 2021), www.theguardian .com/world/2021/feb/26/hi-mom-comedy-about-death-and-parenthood-becomes -one-of-chinas-biggest-film-hits.

Index

About the Author

Ying Zhu is professor emeritus at the City University of New York and director of the Center for Film and Moving Image Research in the Academy of Film, Hong Kong Baptist University. The recipient of a fellowship from the National Endowment for the Humanities, she is the author of three other books including *Two Billion Eyes: The Story of China Central Television* (The New Press) and co-editor of six books including *Soft Power with Chinese Characteristics: China's Campaign for Hearts and Minds*. She is the founder and chief editor of the peer-reviewed journal *Global Storytelling: Journal of Digital and Moving Images*. She resides in New York and Hong Kong.

Publishing in the Public Interest

Thank you for reading this book published by The New Press. The New Press is a nonprofit, public interest publisher. New Press books and authors play a crucial role in sparking conversations about the key political and social issues of our day.

We hope you enjoyed this book and that you will stay in touch with The New Press. Here are a few ways to stay up to date with our books, events, and the issues we cover:

- Sign up at www.thenewpress.com/subscribe to receive updates on New Press authors and issues and to be notified about local events
- www.facebook.com/newpressbooks
- www.twitter.com/thenewpress
- www.instagram.com/thenewpress

Please consider buying New Press books for yourself; for friends and family; or to donate to schools, libraries, community centers, prison libraries, and other organizations involved with the issues our authors write about.

The New Press is a 501(c)(3) nonprofit organization. You can also support our work with a tax-deductible gift by visiting www .thenewpress.com/donate.